LGBTQ People and Social Work

LGBTQ People and Social Work
Intersectional Perspectives

EDITED BY BRIAN J. O'NEILL, TRACY A. SWAN,
AND NICK J. MULÉ

Canadian Scholars' Press
Toronto

LGBTQ People and Social Work: Intersectional Perspectives

Edited by Brian J. O'Neill, Tracy A. Swan, and Nick J. Mulé

First published in 2015 by
Canadian Scholars' Press Inc.
425 Adelaide Street West, Suite 200
Toronto, Ontario
M5V 3C1

www.cspi.org

Copyright © 2015 Brian J. O'Neill, Tracy A. Swan, Nick J. Mulé, the contributing authors, and Canadian Scholars' Press Inc. All rights reserved. No part of this publication may be photocopied, reproduced, stored in a retrieval system, or transmitted, in any form or by any means, electronic, mechanical, or otherwise, without the written permission of Canadian Scholars' Press Inc., except for brief passages quoted for review purposes. In the case of photocopying, a licence may be obtained from Access Copyright: One Yonge Street, Suite 1900, Toronto, Ontario, M5E 1E5, (416) 868-1620, fax (416) 868-1621, toll-free 1-800-893-5777, www.accesscopyright.ca.

Every reasonable effort has been made to identify copyright holders. CSPI would be pleased to have any errors or omissions brought to its attention.

Library and Archives Canada Cataloguing in Publication

LGBTQ people and social work : intersectional perspectives / edited by Brian J. O'Neill, Tracy A. Swan, and Nick J. Mulé.

Includes bibliographical references and index.
Issued in print and electronic formats.
ISBN 978-1-55130-726-8 (pbk.).—ISBN 978-1-55130-727-5 (pdf).
—ISBN 978-1-55130-728-2 (epub)

    1. Social work with sexual minorities—Canada. 2. Social service—Canada. I. O'Neill, Brian, 1947-, editor II. Swan, Tracy A., 1946-, editor III. Mulé, Nick J., 1963-, editor

HV1449.L43 2015   362.89'6   C2015-901343-7   C2015-901344-5

Text design by Integra
Cover design by Em Dash Design

Printed and bound in Canada by Webcom

Canadä

Contents

Intersecting LGBTQ People and Social Work: An Introduction   1
Tracy A. Swan, Brian J. O'Neill, and Nick J. Mulé

PART I: Critical Reflections and Internal Tensions   15

CHAPTER 1: The Politicized Queer, the Informed Social Worker: Dis/Re-Ordering the Social Order   17
Nick J. Mulé

CHAPTER 2: "We Are Expected to Work As If We Are Not Who We Are": Reflections on Working with Queer Black Youth   37
Marie-Jolie Rwigema, Onyinyechukwu Udegbe, and David Lewis-Peart

CHAPTER 3: Queer Disability and the Reality of Homo-Ableism   53
Lawrence Shapiro

CHAPTER 4: The Invisibility Paradox: Oppression and Resilience in the Context of LGBT Aging   67
Louise Stern

CHAPTER 5: Cross-Dancing as Culturally Restorative Practice   87
Jeffrey McNeil-Seymour

CHAPTER 6: The Silent *B*: The Erasure of Bisexuality   107
Ron Goodine

PART II: Fields of Service, Practice, and Organizational Change   127

CHAPTER 7: Transfeminist Theory and Action: Trans Women and the Contested Terrain of Women's Services   129
Jake Pyne

CHAPTER 8: Beyond Stress and Burden: Exploring the
Intersectionality of Gay Caregiving   151

Hossein Kia

CHAPTER 9: Child Welfare Practice with Sexual Minority
and Gender-Diverse Youth: A Social Justice Perspective   173

D. Margo Nelson

CHAPTER 10: Collaboration and Affirmation: Supporting Younger
Lesbian and Bisexual Women and Transgender Youth in
Small Cities and Rural Communities   193

Wendy Hulko

CHAPTER 11: Collective Trauma as a Personal/Social Concern
for LGBTTTSQ Persons   213

Susan McGrath, Bill Lee, Ken Moffatt, Mirna Carranza,
and Andrea Lagios

CHAPTER 12: Roadblocks and Pathways to Settlement: Experiences
and Needs of Lesbian, Gay, and Bisexual Newcomers   233

Brian J. O'Neill and Hossein Kia

CHAPTER 13: Resisting the Binary: The Role of the Social Worker in
Affirmative Trans Health Care   255

X. Sly Sarkisova

PART III: Social Work Education and Pedagogy   **275**

CHAPTER 14: Christian Fundamentalism and Anti-Oppressive
Practice Social Work Pedagogy: Rethinking the Inclusion of
Fundamentalist Beliefs within the Queer-Positive Classroom   277

Sarah Todd and Diana Coholic

CHAPTER 15: Somewhere over the Rainbow: Reflections on
Teaching a LGBT-S Bachelor of Social Work Course   297

Norma Jean Profitt

CHAPTER 16: Qualitative Arts-Based Inquiry into Transgender
Subjectivities in Social Work Education　　　　317

Arkell Wiley

CHAPTER 17: Transformative Engagement in LGBTQ
Student/Field Instructor Relationships　　　　339

Tracy A. Swan and Sheri M. McConnell

CHAPTER 18: Shaking the Foundations: Moving Gender and
Sexual Diversity Education to the Centre of the Child and
Youth Development Classroom　　　　361

Andrea Ridgely, Marilyn McLean, Mandy Bonisteel,
and Soni Dasmohapatra

Contributor Biographies　　　　383

Index　　　　393

Intersecting LGBTQ People and Social Work: An Introduction

Tracy A. Swan, Brian J. O'Neill, and Nick J. Mulé

Purpose and Objectives

This book evolved over many years and represents the thoughtful contributions of many people. It reflects the unique perspectives and experiences of diverse lesbian, gay, bisexual, transgender, transsexual, Two-Spirit, queer, and questioning (LGBTQ[1]) community members. Given the prohibition of discrimination on the basis of sexual orientation flowing from the Canadian Charter of Rights and Freedoms and provincial and territorial human rights codes, and recent attempts to extend this protection to issues of gender identity, and in some cases gender expression, we believed Canadian social workers and educators had knowledge and experience to share that could be relevant here at home and in countries other than our own. We also wanted to produce a book that contributed to organizational and social change, while honouring those who paved the way that we might do so.

A unique feature of this anthology is an explicit focus on intersectionality and its application to social work practice, organizational change, pedagogy, and the pursuit of social justice. We chose not to provide a specific definition of intersectionality, fearing it could compromise how the authors might employ it. Understanding the focus of their writing, authors were also free to choose the terminology they preferred to describe various identities and community members. Having the freedom to apply their own understanding of intersectionality and identities/subjectivities has resulted in a collection of unique chapters.

The authors include LGBTQ and straight social work academics, diverse social work students, practising social service workers and managers, as well as social activists. Collectively, the chapters reflect current ideological and theoretical perspectives that capture the most relevant and complex issues impacting LGBTQ communities and individuals. The authors also bring into focus the significance of understanding multiple intersecting identities, and gender and sexual diversity in a variety of contexts from varied standpoints. The chapters embody the authors' commitment to social change and their desire to eliminate oppression impacting the lives of LGBTQ people, whether racialized, from diverse cultures, younger or older, physically and/or intellectually challenged, colonized, and/or living in remote geographical locations. Additionally, the anthology captures the breadth and depth of critical thinking on current agency policies and practices with LGBTQ individuals possessing intersecting identities and subjectivities, in various fields of service. Various authors also challenge all members of the queer community to recognize their culpability in the oppression of others who are marginalized within the more dominant LG communities across Canada and in other countries.

While the chapters reflect a variety of identities and perspectives, it is beyond the scope of one book to address the nuances of all the permutations of intersecting identities and subjectivities. One very important topic that is missing is that of language-based identities and the ongoing tensions between francophone and anglophone Canadians. Despite this omission, we believe readers will find the anthology contains a variety of challenging and thought-provoking chapters.

As a collection, the chapters can be used in teaching a wide range of courses in BSW and MSW programs, and provide a valuable research resource for doctoral students. The book can be employed in related fields, such as community medicine, counselling psychology, nursing, and occupational therapy. It also contributes to interdisciplinary programs such as

Equity Studies, as well as Gender and Women's Studies, and is a helpful source for college courses that prepare students for delivering social services. In addition to being a resource for academics, students, frontline workers, and social service providers from a variety of fields, the book is a source of information for agency policy makers, and queer and allied social activists and community workers.

Structure and Organization of the Book

The book contains 18 chapters and is divided into three sections. Recognizing the importance of considering how members of the queer community individually and collectively contribute to the oppression of others, we cast our view inward and begin at home. Part I, "Critical Reflections and Internal Tensions," addresses current social and political tensions that exist within and among LGBTQ communities in Canada. These six chapters deepen insight into the diversity of identities within LGBTQ communities and highlight the political and personal implications of social work's continued focus on the essentialized identities of mainstream LG groups. Each chapter critically considers and cogently demonstrates how the more privileged and powerful members of the LG community perpetuate oppression socially, culturally, and politically. The authors demonstrate how this focus reproduces neoliberal, heteronormative, and cisgendered[2] notions that shape the current social order. Each chapter reflects the unique perspectives and observations of the authors, many drawing on their own experiences to highlight political, social, and personal implications of their continued oppression and marginalization.

Part II contains seven chapters that focus on "Fields of Service, Practice, and Organizational Change." The authors critically consider and apply various theoretical perspectives to address oppressive agency policies and social work practices impacting diverse LGBTQ populations in specific fields of service. The chapters provide examples demonstrating the discriminatory impacts of agency policies and practices that arise in the provision of services for diverse LGBTQ people and communities. While not all fields of service are addressed, the authors provide a variety of important analyses and recommendations that can contribute to changes in policy and practice in other fields of service that work with the same populations. Similarly, recommendations that pertain to one population with specific intersecting identities can provide guidance for development of inclusive policies and practices for other LGBTQ individuals and communities in the same field of service.

The final part, "Social Work Education and Pedagogy," includes five chapters that critically address a variety of complex issues that arise in the classroom and various academic and field education settings. Writing from their unique standpoints, the authors employ diverse theoretical and pedagogical perspectives and reflect on their personal experiences in these different contexts. The authors highlight the complexity of the challenges they have encountered and bring into focus competing *tensions* that arose for themselves and LGBTQ students with different intersecting identities and subjective positions. Each chapter demonstrates the limitations of current theoretical and pedagogical perspectives, and systematically demonstrates the value of adopting alternative theories and approaches for navigating the many challenges identified.

Part I: Critical Reflections and Internal Tensions

Writing as a politicized queer, Nick Mulé challenges readers to critically consider the implications of social work's continued focus on mainstream members of LGBTQ communities. Within the context of his critique, Nick demonstrates how both the profession and LGBTQ members perpetuate neoliberal, heteronormative, and cisgendered notions and continue to marginalize progressive politicized queers. More specifically, he systematically highlights how mainstream LGBTQ members seek approval and respect from more powerful heteronormative members of society to such an extent that some will emulate heterosexual social structures to achieve acceptance. Nick also addresses how social workers in the non-profit sector contribute to conventional conceptions of the social order through policies, funding, programs, and services that, for the most part, fail to address the needs of many LGBTQ populations. He indicates social workers inadvertently become actors in the non-profit industrial complex that contributes to a narrowed social construction of LGBTQ communities. Employing queer liberation and critical social work perspectives to deconstruct these concerns, Nick highlights the importance of social workers becoming aware of the contributions politicized queers can make to dismantling the current social order and to creating a more inclusive and diversified one.

In the second chapter, Marie-Jolie Rwigema, Onyinyechukwu Udegbe, and David Lewis-Peart reflect on their conversations as three queer Black social work practitioners and graduate students with experience working primarily with queer youth of colour in Toronto, Canada. Through their reflexive discussion the authors articulate how the intersection of racism and heterosexism is manifested in their work with these populations. The interlocking systems of oppression at play are mutually constitutive, involving both the authors as practitioners and the youth they work with. The challenge identified is how to engage in effective and meaningful practice, whether with queer Black youth or beyond, in the context of predominantly white social services and a culture centred on whiteness.

In the third chapter, Lawrence Shapiro, who self-identifies as "a bad ass, fat ass Jew bi amputee," provides a non–social work personal narrative. Subsequent to outlining the ongoing failure to adequately accommodate people with disabilities in mainstream society, Lawrence illustrates how both the disability and lesbian and gay communities have also failed to address such issues. Delving into the intersection of his many identities, he highlights the difficulties he has experienced accessing and being understood in disability communities based on his sexuality, and in LGBTQ communities based on both his disability and his sexuality. Limitations are critically exposed, providing personal insight into long-standing prejudices and oppression perpetuated by the two communities, insights that have implications for social work in addressing such challenges.

The next chapter, by Louise Stern, explores how an intersectional lens can assist social workers in exploring alternative storylines that challenge mainstream assumptions about the experiences of non-heterosexual aging. Noting that aging is a universally experienced process, Louise posits that many LGBTQ adults experience aging very differently from their non-LGBTQ counterparts because of their position as a marginalized, stigmatized, and invisible population both in mainstream society and in the LGBTQ community. She demonstrates that each older LGBT adult encounters unique consequences as they negotiate aging, consequences that are dependent on the intersection of other identity positions, making the aging process unique for each older LGBT person. Through this analysis, Louise brings into focus how the challenges faced by queer seniors also foster increased resilience, strength, and coping skills that other individuals may not have. She recommends that all interactions and interventions with older LGBT adults reflect the uniqueness of each person's lived experiences while embedding them within a socio-historical and cultural context that acknowledges the influence of wider social processes.

Jeffrey McNeil-Seymour's chapter draws upon a study in which he explored how Aboriginal people who identify as lesbian, gay, bisexual, transgender, and/or Two-Spirit understand the construction of multiple identities, privileges, and oppressions. Through the social constructions of gender and sexual identity that are rooted in Western society, there has been a successful incorporation of colonial "isms" and "phobias" within Aboriginal communities and, as Jeffrey suggests, an imposition of identity. He argues that social work has arrived at a critical intersection that requires an Indigenous lead and expansion of spaces for conversations about gender, sexuality, and identity to take place. He holds that otherwise, social work ultimately risks silencing those who fall outside the confines of the LGBTQTS acronym. Throughout the chapter

Jeffrey explores discursive departures and arrivals with social justice, the social construction of Two-Spiritedness, and implications for culturally restorative social work practice.

The final chapter of this section is a personal reflection by Ron Goodine on his experiences as a bisexual man that captures shifting identities within an LGBTQ context. His discussion is informed by his perspective as a middle-class helping professional in his 50s. Interweaving theories, examples, and his personal experiences, Ron demonstrates how cultural assumptions that only heterosexual and homosexual identities are valid contribute to the erasure of bisexuality in mainstream heterosexual society and in gay/lesbian communities. He provides insights into the diversity of those who identify as bisexual, demonstrates how the erasure of bisexuality is perpetuated, and highlights the unique challenges those who identify as bisexual may encounter. Using an intersectional framework to deconstruct the assumptions of normative sex and gender identities, Ron then presents an anti-categorical approach that privileges a queer perspective and makes normative categories problematic.

Part II: Fields of Service, Practice, and Organizational Change

In the initial chapter of Part II, Jake Pyne, who practised in women-only services before transitioning, deconstructs the history of conflict between some feminist rape crisis and shelter service providers and trans women. He argues a feminist ideological framework does not adequately capture the complexity of this conflict. Jake contends feminist ideology becomes a means by which trans women are excluded from the important services they require. Jake also demonstrates how this exclusion is supported by other forms of social violence, such as racism. Employing transfeminist ideology, he presents responses to feminist positions that contribute to the exclusion of trans women and disputes analysis that neglects experiences of trans women with intersecting marginalized identities. Systematically demonstrating how transfeminism offers approaches to conceiving of and creating inclusive services, Jake contributes an important resource for social work.

In his chapter, Hossein Kia revisits findings of a study he conducted with five gay men who provided informal care within same-sex relationships. Building on stress and burden theory, and feminist and constuctivist perspectives on informal caregiving, Hossein demonstrates how an intersectional framework provides important new insights into the unique realities of gay caregivers. Previously hidden individual experiences and unexamined aspects of participants' identities related to sexual orientation, race, culture, age, geographic location, and ability/disability become visible. Hossein concludes with a comprehensive discussion of ways an intersectional perspective can inform social policy and social work practice in relation to caregiving.

Margo Nelson's chapter considers the relevance of human rights and social justice, and critically discusses the experiences of young LGBTQ people with intersecting identities who are associated with child welfare. Based on her analysis of current human rights legislation and child welfare policies, she concludes that a human rights focus does not adequately address the unique challenges of LGBTQ youth in care. Margo proposes that a framework based on a feminist ethic of care could be more useful in child welfare, as it challenges inequities resulting from reliance on liberal Western jurisprudence and legislation. Employing ethical principles, current research, and child welfare program examples, Margo demonstrates how child welfare agencies can help mitigate the oppression of LGBTQ youth and concludes with recommendations relevant to creating inclusive policies, programs, and practices.

In the next chapter, Wendy Hulko presents selected research findings that explore experiences of younger lesbian, bisexual, and transgender women who reside in small cities, some of whom come from rural communities. She demonstrates how geographic location impacts the lived experiences of the participants and focuses on how a sense of invisibility and isolation are created when geographic location intersects with age, sexual orientation, and gender identity. Drawing on findings of the study, Wendy highlights the importance of developing supportive communities to help alleviate young people's experiences of homophobia, heterosexism, gender oppression, and geographic isolation. She demonstrates the relevance of collaborative social work community practice that contributes to *community building* for younger lesbian, bisexual, and transgender women in smaller cities. Wendy concludes with concrete recommendations that emphasize social work community practice, research, and policy that address young LBTQ women's invisibility and need for accessible, safe collective meeting spaces.

In the fifth chapter of this section Susan McGrath, Bill Lee, Ken Moffatt, Mirna Carranza, and Andrea Lagios focus on interviews with LGBTQ community leaders and activists, one of the three marginalized community groups involved in a study that explored the meaning of collective trauma as a shared injurious experience. All the LGBTQ participants also had other social identities. Subsequent to discussing the nature of trauma and participants' experiences of marginalization, the authors highlight a significant finding: discrimination experienced by individual members of the community had a traumatic effect on other members who had not experienced the event directly. They conclude *marginalization* does not adequately capture the emotional responses that influence the nature of community relations and community practice. The authors propose *communities of affinity* as a new conceptual tool to inform social work practice, bringing into focus those dimensions that bind diverse queer communities across space and time, while not minimizing differences due to race, gender, ethnicity, and class.

The next chapter, by Brian O'Neill and Hossein Kia, is based on a study regarding the needs of LGB immigrants and refugees, and their experiences with settlement services and LGB community organizations. Based on interviews with LGB newcomers, settlement service workers, and members of LGB community organizations, the authors found newcomers encountered racism within general LGB communities, and heterosexism and homophobia within both their cultural and dominant-group communities. In addition, the authors found LGB newcomers were reluctant to approach either settlement services or LGB community organizations for help in mitigating their isolation, particularly in smaller centres. Brian and Hossein provide recommendations for settlement services and LGB community organizations to make them more responsive to the needs of LGB newcomers.

Part II concludes with a chapter by X. Sly Sarkisova, who focuses on trans-identified people and examines the ways in which social work practitioners can resist the normative conceptualizations of gender endemic to health care systems. While gains have been made by trans and gender variant activists in achieving greater access to medical technologies of transition, many trans-identified people still face significant barriers to appropriate health care. X. Sly cautions that social workers may play a role in facilitating or impeding trans-related care and may participate in the delegitimization of trans experiences. The role of reflexive practice in addressing a lack of knowledge of trans-related issues and resources, cisnormative thinking with regard to the gender binary, unwillingness to advocate on behalf of trans individuals, and the uncritical acceptance of current health care services are all explored. X. Sly calls on practitioners to develop critical awareness and strategies for challenging systemic barriers that may impact trans individuals.

Part III: Social Work Education and Pedagogy

In the initial chapter in the final section, Sarah Todd and Diana Coholic reflect on a 2007 article they wrote on negotiating pedagogical space that could be affirming for LGBTQ students and at the same time respectful of Christian fundamentalist students. They revisit the theoretical context of their pedagogy and what new insights the consideration of intersectionality, queer theory, and meanings of classroom silence might contribute to addressing conflicting dynamics sometimes played out among the students. Sarah and Diana acknowledge that no tidy solutions emerged from their reflection, but contend that these theoretical lenses provide a nuanced understanding of the complex pedagogical challenges they highlight.

In her chapter, Norma Jean Profitt provides a personal narrative in which she explores the complexities of gender and sexual diversity and, drawing on critical and queer theories, identifies pedagogical, systemic, and personal issues encountered in the classroom and academy when teaching in a BSW program. Throughout, Norma Jean highlights the richness of experiences based on intersecting identities and meanings. She proposes that professional education on gender and sexual diversity that incorporates intersecting identities should be contextualized within a framework of ethics and social justice. Norma Jean demonstrates the value of the proposed framework and provides the reader with policy and pedagogical recommendations that challenge dominant neoliberal discourses and promote social justice.

Writing from a student's perspective, Arkell Wiley considers the erasure of trans-identified individuals within the academy and the social work profession. The author presents arts-based graduate research that employed queer research methodologies to investigate the experiences of five trans social work students. Drawn to this inquiry by personal experience as a trans student, Arkell demonstrates how dominant discourses on gender and sexuality contribute to the invisibility of transgender issues. Arkell employs an intersectional framework and conceptualizations of transgender identities to highlight the diversity of positions held by trans people, and to analyze meanings that emerged from his own reflexive work and that of the participants. The author shows how misinformation and the invisibility of trans content in the curriculum contributed to feelings of isolation and perpetuated transphobia. Arkell proposes strategies to enhance the quality of trans-focused social work practice and education, changes that help mitigate the erasure of trans issues and the many implications that impact trans people.

Moving out of the classroom, Tracy Swan and Sheri McConnell focus on a critical component of social work field education for LGBTQ students, the field instructor–student relationship. They identify limitations in some current approaches to field instruction that fail to capture the influence of intersecting identities and subjective positions of both the field instructor and student. Tracy and Sheri systematically demonstrate the value of an intersectional framework that incorporates critical reflexive practices for field instruction with LGBTQ students. Informed by post-modern feminist approaches to social work supervision and anti-oppressive practice, they highlight many of the complex issues that can impact the student–field instructor relationship and compromise the quality of LGBTQ students' learning. Employing an exemplar that emphasizes a dialogical approach, the authors demonstrate concrete strategies for navigating the complexities they identify. Through this process, Tracy and Sheri present a model of field instruction that is informed by intersectionality and characterized by power sharing and critical empathy, a model that validates the students' diverse identities and contributes to learning and consolidation of a positive professional identity grounded in respect for differences.

In the final chapter, Andrea Ridgely, Marilyn McLean, Mandy Bonisteel, and Soni Dasmohapatra explore challenges involved in addressing gender and sexual diversity in modernist child and youth development courses. They discuss how educators can provide professional education that challenges conventional teaching about identity development, while recognizing that all learners and educators are products of the very systems they seek to challenge. The authors also consider the complexity of enabling an exploration of gender and sexual diversity while confronting rigid binary thinking. Building on their insightful analysis, the authors present concrete and creative teaching strategies we believe will prove very helpful for people teaching in a range of human services.

Concluding Comments

The authors have helped us produce a unique anthology that is both relevant and current. An explicit focus on intersectionality is a particular strength of this comprehensive collection. The chapters address issues impacting the well-being of LGBTQ individuals with diverse intersecting identities from a variety of perspectives. Various authors demonstrate the relevance of employing an intersectional framework, and still others have given voice to previously silenced members of the LGBTQ community. They have also formulated many thoughtful recommendations to inform future social work pedagogy, agency policy, and different forms of practice in diverse contexts and fields of service. We hope you share our perception that the contributing authors have provided informative, progressive, thought-provoking works that reflect the many unique contributions highlighted throughout the introduction.

Notes

1. Throughout the introduction, we have chosen to employ *LGBTQ* to capture diverse gender and sexual identities and expressions outside of heterosexuality and/or cisgenderism. Therefore, LGBTQ should be understood to convey lesbian, gay, bisexual, transgender, transsexual, Two-Spirit, queer, and questioning persons and communities. Authors have used their own versions based on the content of their respective chapters, and this is also reflected in the brief descriptions of these chapters in this introduction.
2. *Cisgender* refers to those whose biologically assigned sex at birth aligns with their perception of gender. For example, someone whose biological sex at birth is deemed female and who grows up to identify with the female gender is cisgender.

PART I
Critical Reflections and Internal Tensions

CHAPTER 1
The Politicized Queer, the Informed Social Worker: Dis/Re-Ordering the Social Order

Nick J. Mulé

What attention social work gives to LGBTQ populations tends to be directed at mainstream segments of these communities that seek acceptance and respect from mainstream society via assimilation (Ruiz, 2008; Sycamore, 2004). Although LGBTQ communities are multidimensional, high-profile mainstream segments often emulate heterosexual social structures to seek approval. This can include same-sex marriage, having or adopting children after marrying, or transitioning from one gender to another within the confines of a traditional binary. These equality-based sites premised on heteronormative conditions tend to resonate with mainstream straight society. The neoliberal, heteronormative, and cisgendered notions that dominate our current social order serve to further marginalize politicized queers among LGBTQ movements. Social workers, who figure prominently in the non-profit sector—which tends to cater to conventional conceptions of the social order via policies, funding, programs, and services—for the most part fail to address the needs of LGBTQ populations. In doing so, they inadvertently become actors in the non-profit industrial complex (NPIC). The NPIC, in turn, contributes to a narrowed social construction of LGBTQ communities. This chapter exposes the trappings of the NPIC, its implications for the intersectional diversity of LGBTQs, and the importance of social workers undertaking critical practice that is open to progressive ideas that can affect change from within. These issues are deconstructed, employing queer liberation and critical social work perspectives to highlight the importance of social workers becoming informed of the existence of politicized queers, and of how these queers contribute to the disordering and re-ordering of the current social order to be more inclusive and diversified.

For the purposes of this chapter, queers, such as myself, are LGBT people who have deliberately reclaimed a label that was once considered pejorative, are disinterested in being part of the mainstream, celebrate our differences, believe in a distinct queer culture, are politicized, and are non-assimilationists (Brown, 2007). As with most, if not all, minoritized and/or marginalized groups, LGBTQ populations consist of multiplicities and variations rendering us non-monolithic. Often what emerges from these multiplicities is a higher profile contingent that is referred to here as the LGBT segment, because of its tendency toward mainstreaming. What may be less apparent to social workers and other helping professionals is the diversity within minority populations, such as LGBTQs, in which some groups are pushed to the margins by dominant groups, such as mainstream LGBTs. Queers are one such marginalized group. Although not fully agreed upon within queer communities, *queer* is defined here as inclusive of non-normative sexual orientations and gender identities and expressions. Regarding the latter, sometimes *genderqueer* is used to signify a departure from restrictive biomedical definitions of sex and binary notions of gender (Queer Ontario, 2013).

Queer discourse has been historically influenced by the activism of the gay liberation movement of 40 years ago and various forms of resistance, such as those that emerged during the AIDS crisis, and radical social reform movements, such as Queer Nation (Warner, 2002). In the past 20 years or so, queer theory has also had an influence in academe, particularly given the influx of queer-identified scholars (Jagose, 1996; Turner, 2000). Yet there is a tensioned relationship, if one at all, between the gay liberationist perspective, which has since evolved into queer liberation (see Queer Ontario, 2010), and queer theory (Crosby et al., 2012;

Jagose, 2000). The former is based on modernist notions of self-defined sexual orientation, gender identity, and expressions whose differences from the norm are celebrated. Liberationists seek civil rights as a means to an end, but not an end in and of themselves, and engage in identity politics for collective purposes. Ultimately, liberationists advocate living their lives as they choose, not defined by heteronormative society. Queer liberationist perspectives also work toward the liberating of all of society from imposed social constraints on sexual experiences and gender identity and expression (Altman, 1971; Smith, 1999; Warner, 2002).

In contrast to the queer liberationist perspective, queer theory is post-modernist and generally eschews identity politics and sexual and gender labels, emphasizing the fluidity of sexuality and gender, challenging fixed notions of both. Ultimately, queer theory seeks a society free of such labels, allowing people to engage with a variety of sexualities and genders (Jagose, 1996; Sullivan, 2003). The tension between the two perspectives is that queer liberation is collectivist, grassroots, and movement-based, with applied goals of effecting change through activism. In contrast, queer theory is academically based and individualized, and as such does not offer applications for societal change beyond the hope of influencing discourse.

Part of the multiplicity of LGBTQ people is our varying social locations and positions. These can include race, ethnicity, religion, class, age, (dis)ability, marital status, sex, and gender. Focusing on two—race and class—in particular, and how they intersect with gender and sexual diversity, can have profound implications both within and outside the LGBTQ communities. In the West the dominance of Caucasians has become infused, producing a culture of whiteness that is very difficult to penetrate, despite the influx of racialized immigrants since the 1960s. This is further complicated by prejudice and discrimination in the form of racism and classism played out in LGBT communities, and homophobia, biphobia, transphobia, heterosexism, and cisgenderism in racialized communities (James, 1975; see O'Neill & Kia, this volume; Rwigema, Udegbe, & Lewis-Peart, this volume). The LGBT community is often touted as becoming established by means of its development as a consumer market. Yet such commercialization calls for the purchase and consumption of alcohol, club tickets, bar cover charges, items in specialty shops, entrance costs at bathhouses, travel, and services at spas and beauty clinics, to name a few. This commercialization promotes a media-created popular culture classist lifestyle that requires disposable income unavailable for many (Jeppesen, 2010). Although this business/media invention is not necessarily embraced by all, it nonetheless can have an alienating and isolating effect on those who are poor. Such negative implications can doubly affect racialized, poor LGBTs.

Hence, many racialized and/or poor people, including those who are LGBT, will inevitably turn to non-profit organizations for some level of support. Yet the proliferation of non-profits and the downloading of state support for them, further linked with neoliberalism, have created an industry producing band-aid solutions focusing on the individual. The NPIC has become a revolving door that rarely allows racialized and/or poor individuals to break free (INCITE!, 2007). By contrast, critical social work theorizes that many social problems are socially constructed and that systemic structures play a paradoxical role in both helping and oppressing (Fook, 2012; Mullaly, 2007). Implicated in this is the social worker who may be either a social change or social control agent. The former would be aligned with critical social work challenging the NPIC often from within, the latter comfortably and quietly employed by the NPIC unquestioningly. This places the social worker in a professional dilemma, particularly in our neoliberalized world, of having to navigate between a commitment to social work principles of social change through social justice work (CASW, 2005) or attaining and maintaining employment in the NPIC that makes no commitment to social reform.

The purpose of this chapter is to urge social workers to not see LGBTQ communities as monolithic and, more importantly, to become informed by some of the most marginalized voices therein. Progressive, radical, critical queer voices expose the insidiousness of the NPIC and how social workers, particularly the non-politicized, are implicated. Does social work contribute to sustaining the current social order or to re-ordering it? This chapter sheds light on a queer liberationist perspective that can easily be linked to critical social work, yet challenges social workers to act on such a perspective. It also focuses on how the NPIC marginalizes queers, especially based on class and race and how this negative intersectionality—multiple vulnerable and disadvantaged social locations that contribute to compounded oppression—converge to curtail advocacy toward challenging the existing social order. A discussion follows in two parts, with the first deconstructing the social order with a subversive process of diagnosing it as disordered, and the latter proposing re-ordering the social order toward the demarginalization of politicized queers. This discussion is written in the first person in order to share my theoretical/conceptual framework as I position myself as a politicized queer activist, academic, and social worker. Noteworthy is that although this chapter focuses on politicized queers within LGBTQ movements, the analysis and principles articulated can apply to other politicized populations who are similarly situated.

Non-Profit Industrial Complex (NPIC), Negative Intersectionality, and Implications for Advocacy

The concept of the NPIC involves systemic relationships among the state (all levels of government), the owning (privileged) classes, foundations (funders), non-profit/NGO social services, and social justice organizations (INCITE!, 2004). Rodriguez (2007) states,

> The NPIC is the set of symbiotic relationships that link together political and financial technologies of state and owning class proctorship and surveillance over public political intercourse including and especially emergent progressive and leftist social movements, since about the mid-1970s. (pp. 21–22)

Further, non-profit organizations, as well as the sector as a whole, are transitioning from industrial to post-industrial society and from national state to transnational policy regimes. As a result, non-profits are increasingly ensconced in new public management and a mixed welfare economy. They are central to "civil society–social capital" approaches, hence the nexus between social capital/social cohesion and participation in voluntary associations. Non-profits are also under higher social accountability expectations, requiring greater transparency and improved public institutional governance (Anheier, 2009). This, combined with governments' reduced funding of the sector, has resulted in claims of over-professionalization and bureaucratization of the non-profit sector in both Canada (Evans, Richmond, & Shields, 2005) and the US (Salamon, 1999), in which the "business model" impedes on the "community-based model" (Helmig, Jegars, & Lapsley, 2004).

The NPIC has also contributed to the feminization of the social work profession and social services (Baines, 2004; Barnoff & Coleman, 2007). Thus, traditional notions of the nurturing, caring woman as symbolic of social work foreground other social locations such as race and class. For example, the feminization of the discipline is inextricably linked with class as one of the lower paying of the human service/caring professions. With regard to race, the dominance of the white race in the West continues, regardless of the immigration of diverse ethno-racial populations, due to cultural capital, class structures, and power imbalances that continue to advantage and privilege whites (Croatoan, 2012). Whether Black Americans (Allen, 2007), Native populations (Thunder Hawk, 2007), or South Africans (Sachdev, 2012), the NPIC's focus on problematizing the individual without attention to socially constructed structures positions racialized populations as disenfranchised and a drain on society, further marginalizing them. Associated with such positioning is class status as determined by people's socio-economic conditions (INCITE!, 2007). The NPIC positions itself as the caretaker of the working and poor classes, sustaining its own existence on its "benevolent" service provision, yet making no contribution to deconstructing class apparatuses and addressing racialization and othering. Individuals who are socially located on a number of these sites are often constructed as the weak and vulnerable—a form of negative intersectionality—on which the NPIC thrives.

Sexual orientation, gender identity, and gender expression are also social locations occupied by individuals independently or in relationships, communities, and social movements. Premised on an oppressive historical context that continues for many based on mainstream society's difficulty embracing these populations, LGBTQ people have long been recipients of services within the NPIC. The trajectory of LGBTQs being subjects of the NPIC may appear progressive. Once the subjects of psychiatric diagnosis (homosexuality) that systemically labelled us as "mentally ill" or "sick" (Duberman, 1991; Queerupture, 2010), today LGBTQ specialized services or programs in mainstream services address issues such as coming out, support, substance use/addictions, suicide prevention, and general counselling as uniquely experienced in these communities (CRHC, 2013). The real question is, is this "progress" focused on creating coping mechanisms to live in a heterosexist and homophobic world, is it to effect systemic change, or is it an attempt to do both? For trans populations, "progress" continues to be systematically psychiatrized with the diagnosis of "gender dysphoria" (APA, 2013). This has systemic implications, as such a diagnosis is required in order to access medical interventions such as hormonal drugs and sex reassignment surgery via health insurance plans (Daley & Mulé, 2014). Ultimately, if services provided by the NPIC cater to the maintenance of the status quo, upholding traditional notions of the social order in the process, where does that leave politicized queers committed to social change and social justice?

Politicized queers are less interested in upholding the social order than in questioning it. Our worldview utilizes a critical lens with which to question norms, hegemonic perspectives, and socially constructed discourses. If such critical analyses result in recognition of social injustice for ourselves and others, we are inclined to take action in the form of advocacy in attempts to effect social change. Yet advocacy itself has become increasingly compromised in the NPIC. As charities and non-profits (without charitable status) continue to be scrutinized for their spending of public funds, they become ever more professionalized in order to compete for funding. Governments and funders (often one and the same) set neoliberalized mainstreaming agendas that non-profits are expected to abide by in order to maintain funding received (Robert & Kelly, 2011; Samimi, 2010). The neoliberal agenda legitimizes services for the "problem" individual and/or the individual's family, yet problematizes non-profits that attempt to address broader systemic and structural social problems and their constructions, at the expense of advocating for and implementing equitable redistribution of resources (Evans, Richmond, & Shields, 2005). Hence a social order is constructed in which classism, racism, sexism, heterosexism, ableism, ageism, and cisgenderism are sustained and perpetuated. The social justice aspects of charities and non-profit missions are questioned as "political" and drift as a result (Kivel, 2007; Mulé, 2011).

The result of this incursion on the part of government and funders is a socially constructed fine line between social service and social justice–direct service provision, and social advocacy (Kivel, 2007). The former is legitimized as "good works" and the latter delegitimized as "political" by funders. The consequences of being labelled "political" can be severe, in the form of loss of funding and revoking of charitable status (Robert & Kelly, 2011). The neoliberal governance structures being imposed on non-profits and charities in particular[1] come with professionalized bureaucratic procedures, which have a constraining effect on already under-resourced non-profits, straining their limited capacity and compromising their autonomy and advocacy abilities in the process (Evans, Richmond, & Shields, 2005). Therefore, we see how the NPIC, coupled with neoliberalism, within which social work looms large, sustains the status quo at the expense of advocacy. Furthermore, when applied at the intersection of anti-racism, anti-poverty, and anti-homophobia work among others, Rodriguez (2007) points out how the power of the NPIC manifests in neocolonial ways:

The NPIC is not wholly unlike the institutional apparatus of neo-colonialism, in which former and potential anticolonial revolutionaries are "professionalized" and granted opportunities within a labyrinthine state-proctored bureaucracy that ultimately reproduces the essential coherence of the neocolonial relation of power itself. (p. 39)

These perspectives are well known by, and contribute to, the critical worldview of politicized queers who recognize the NPIC's co-optation of the very social justice issues the LGBTQ movement, NGOs, and activists work on, while the NPIC contributes to the erosion of advocacy in the process (Croatoan, 2012; Mananzala & Spade, 2008; Mulé, 2011; Sachdev, 2012). What also needs to be acknowledged is the elevated level of strength required to be part of a politicized queer contingent, as it calls for the ability to resist heteronormative values in mainstream society and assimilationist values in the mainstream LGBT movement, thus the ability to stand up against being marginalized by both. This commitment to contesting the current social order provides valuable information to social workers in understanding the experience of politicized queers and, further, to work with us in resistance. The following discussion looks at the current social order as disordered and ways and means of re-ordering it.

Discussion

Disordering the Social Order

In an economically driven society in which the globalization process has been dominated by large corporations that self-assign more and more power over nation states, a capitalist, consumerist social order is constructed in which providing returns to corporate shareholders supersedes addressing those in need. An underlying socio-political perspective that serves to manifest such globalization is neoliberalism, which conveniently lays responsibility for social oppressions on the individual, effectively releasing corporations and governments from addressing the structural and systemic issues that contribute to such oppression (Chomsky, 2011). In the midst of this are numerous disenfranchised and marginalized communities including LGBTQs, who over the past two decades have become increasingly split. On the one hand are some LGBTs who, as has been highlighted, ascribe to a homonormative narrative and seek acceptance and respectability within normative heterosexual sites (read same-sex marriage and the corporatization of pride festivities). On the other hand are radical queers who celebrate being different from straight people and contribute to society's diversity by questioning the social order (read challenging restrictive binary notions of sexual orientation, gender identity, and gender expression) (Duggan, 2003; Mulé, 2006). Assimilationist LGBTs are more readily "tolerated" if not actually "accepted" in a heterosexist society, provided that they abide by heteronormative conditions (Seidman, 1997; Vaid, 1995; Warner, 1999). Politicized queers engage in the "progressive," sometimes considered "radical," act of troubling and challenging heteronormative and cisgendered precepts of the social order.

An informed social worker needs to recognize that LGBTQ communities are non-monolithic and that the political perspectives therein can be quite varied. Here I am focusing on two perspectives in particular (noting there are others), with specific attention placed on politicized queers who, due to our very progressive nature, find ourselves pushed to the margins by assimilating LGBTs who more readily position themselves within the mainstream, shaping their lives to heteronormative expectations. Politicized queers are distinguished by the critical questions we pose to society. For example:

- Why is heterosexuality seen as normal or even superior to other forms of sexuality?
- Why does society limit the definition of sex to a biomedical one?

- Why does society subscribe to restrictive binary notions of gender identity and expression?
- Why is the institution of marriage held up above all other types of relationships in terms of benefits, social sanctioning, and responsibility?

In the view of politicized queers our current social order is seen as disordered. A "social order" that is engaged in a myopic state of ignorance, avoidance, and denial regarding its own cisgendered and heterosexist functioning can, from a subversive psychiatric perspective, be seen as a form of societal narcissism. The NPIC contributes to this functioning by focusing attention on the problemed individuals and communities, not the restrictive, hierarchical, and discriminating structures that marginalize the very individuals who question it. Uninformed social workers within the NPIC become quickly identified by politicized queers as agents of social control (read oppressors) rather than agents of social change (read emancipators). Social workers actively engaging with the status quo or passively remaining silent while consciously recognizing NPIC-induced oppression and marginalization are complicit in the perpetuation of the social disorder. Engaging in this role is the antithesis of a critical social worker and rightly makes us vulnerable to critique for failing to do our jobs.

Re-Ordering the Social Order

In order to re-order the social order, social workers need to conscientiously listen to the critiques of radical queers, a marginalized segment of the LGBTQ movement who offer a critical, progressive, and nuanced politicized perspective. Social workers need to make the connections between queer liberationist ethos and the values and principles of the social work discipline: for example, between the queer liberationist tenet that we live our lives as we choose and not constrained by heteronormative and cisgendered notions (Altman, 1971) and the social work principle of respecting personal agency (CASW, 2005). Social workers need to, as queer liberationists do, take responsible action by questioning, resisting, and challenging from within in an attempt to effect systemic change—a critical social work approach.

Yet engaging in critical social work practice requires us to consider the issue of power. The settings in which social workers are practising and their professional position therein (hierarchical status, seniority, specialized experience, collegial respectability) will have a direct impact on the degree to which critical praxis can be engaged. Settings such as social work–dominated social service agencies versus multidisciplinary environments such as hospitals, prisons, and schools, in which social work ranks lower in the hierarchy of professions, often predetermine the extent to which critical practice can even be approached. Further layered in the complexity of how power can be manifested is the social worker's social location and positioning (e.g. race, ethnicity, age, (dis)ability, class, gender, sexual orientation, gender identity, and gender expression). Our socially disordered society lends credence, hence power, to some (e.g. the white, able-bodied, middle-class, cisgender heterosexual) over others, whose life experiences may represent a micro countercultural presence in a well-oiled NPIC. This intersectionality is further layered in highly complicated ways when one considers personal (whether private or public) social positioning and the myriad ways this is taken up or not. There is also the publicly imposed social locating and positioning of the individual by the system, often based on visible minority status or via self-disclosure by the individual. An example of this would be social status as symbolized by postal code, in which one's socio-economic status (often intersecting with racialized status) is stereotyped by location within one's city or town. In any of these cases, there is the very real possibility that individuals become sites of tension in which the exercising of power from a responsible critical perspective can be highly curtailed systemically.

Herein lies the challenge of the critical social worker to not only be informed, but to practise responsibly and ethically regarding the needs and issues of politicized queers who, for being so, are marginalized. As informed critical social workers (whether politicized queer or not), we should consider the following:

- Is it not our responsibility to listen to the voices of politicized queers and also to work with them toward effecting change, utilizing our positions from within?
- Is it not an obligation of ours to educate colleagues, and even superiors, who may not have contact with politicized queers, how they (we) are marginalized and importantly what they (we) have to contribute in addressing social inequities?
- Having the experience (whether lived or via practice) of being informed by a politicized queer perspective, are we not required to bring forth such specialized knowledge as an alternative approach to better meet the needs of those we serve?
- As a discipline and profession, is it not part of our role, regardless of the setting and environment in which we work, to assert our specialized knowledge as an alternative perspective in the altering of the social disorder and restructuring of systems away from oppression and toward emancipation?

To answer in the affirmative to all of the above would require conscientious, informed social workers exercising critical praxis at the level of practice they are engaged in. At the micro level, social work practice addresses various issues of individuals, couples, families, groups, and communities. Here, liberationist notions linked with personal agency allow social workers to raise consciousness, develop self-awareness, inform individuals of rights, and provide appropriate and sensitized resources and referrals. In essence, this means offering support toward the development of personal agency in service recipients and facilitating recipients' empowerment so they might define for themselves how they choose to create change in their lives, communities, and society. Mezzo level social work places social workers in positions of middle or senior management and policy making in various significant fields (e.g. social welfare, child welfare, corrections, health care, education, housing, settlement services). The informed social worker is in a unique position at this level to help influence the development of policies and programs, determination of funding priorities, and setting of standards and procedures. A liberationist/personal agency perspective brings with it the promise of a powerful influence on frontline work. Social workers at the macro level address the systemic/structural social order of society. Work at this level provides the informed social worker the opportunity to undertake broad sweeping analyses that are formulated into guidelines, policy, legislation, and funding that can be highly influential on the ultimate provision of services. Once again, the infusion of a liberationist/personal agency ethos to such work on the part of an informed social worker can assist in shifting the frameworks that inform society's social order. This is not to say that a singular informed social worker will have the capacity to effect such comprehensive changes, but rather that an informed human service worker or group of them (social workers among them), engaging in critical praxis informed by the worldviews of politicized queers, can cause a rupture, even if slight, to a system that has long been entrenched in disordered heterosexist and cisgendered notions of normativity.

Hankivsky's (2012) intersectionality-based policy analysis (IBPA) framework is a model that can assist informed social workers in re-ordering the social order at both the mezzo and macro levels. Premised on a series of guiding principles, the framework addresses intersecting categories that are not merely additive, but rather in interaction and in co-constitution with each other. It employs a multi-level analysis that centres power as a concept and engages in reflexivity to acknowledge its existence at micro and macro levels. It situates time and place in a fluid manner with regard to social location and position, and recognizes a diversity of knowledges to capture the worldviews of typically marginalized people as a means of disrupting exclusionary forces of knowledge production. This framework places a particular emphasis on social justice, closely tied to the principle of equity, in addressing how the multiple positions of privilege and oppression intersect. The IBPA framework provides two sets of questions, one descriptive and the other transformative, in undertaking intersectionality-based policy analysis designed to have an impact on systemic structures. The former questions the policy "problem," how it is represented, and how, in turn, this representation impacts the affected; the latter questions how best to address the policy "problem," from the reduction of inequities to implementation and evaluation.

Such actions for social change are in keeping with the values, principles, and ethics of social work (CASW, 2005) and our role in effecting positive change in the lives of the most marginalized members of the queer populations. Yet undertaking advocacy within the discipline and more specifically in one's work setting can be met with power-based and structural barriers, the kind that will protect the charitable status of these settings, yet be depoliticizing in the process. Sometimes, the ripples made by throwing that first pebble into the pond are worth it. A further alternative is for social workers to effect change from the outside by transferring their skills to activist/community development work as private citizens with public concerns, freed of constraints from their employer. This approach, particularly with non-profits without charitable status, can afford the informed social worker a greater opportunity to actively participate in social justice initiatives, creating change from without.

Conclusion

The politicized queer and the critical social worker are not that far apart in their respective commitment to social change. What I argue is that the critical social worker needs to be informed on the nuanced politics of the LGBTQ communities, how politicized queers are marginalized both within and outside these communities, and how vulnerable the worker is in contributing to this marginalization in the absence of such knowledge. Yet for the informed social worker to be meaningfully effective, they need to use this knowledge to advocate and activate change. Nevertheless, this presents numerous challenges for social workers ensconced in the NPIC where negative intersectionality (i.e. multiple challenging social locations that result in compounded oppression) is produced, linking directly to structural restrictions on systemic advocacy work. In presenting a subversive play on psychiatry's pathologizing work by disordering the current social order through the positing of a progressive, radicalized re-ordering of the social order that returns self-determination, agency, and autonomy to the systemically oppressed, the ethos of queer liberation is linked to principles of the social work profession including personal agency. Informed social workers with a critical, progressive perspective are challenged to activate it toward effecting social change for politicized queers and other politicized populations who are doubly marginalized in creating a new more inclusive and diversified social order.

Notes

1. See 2012 federal budget, in which the Government of Canada enacted new measures, tax penalties, and reporting requirements that impose tighter regulations on charities, further restricting their advocacy, at www.budget.gc.ca/2012/home-accueil-eng.html.

References

Allen, R. L. (2007). Black awakening in capitalist America. In INCITE! Women of Color Against Violence (Ed.), *The revolution will not be funded*. Cambridge, MA: South End Press.

Altman, D. (1971). *Homosexual oppression and liberation*. New York, NY: Outerbridge & Deinstfrey.

American Psychiatric Association (APA). (2013). Gender dysphoria. *Diagnostic and statistical manual of mental disorders (DSM-5)*. Retrieved from www.dsm5.org/Documents/Gender%20Dysphoria%20Fact%20Sheet.pdf

Anheier, H. K. (2009). What kind of non-profit sector, what kind of society? Comparative policy reflections. *American Behavioral Scientist, 52*(7), 1082–1094.

Baines, D. (2004), Caring for nothing: Work organization and unwaged labour in social services. *Work, Employment and Society, 18*(2), 267–295.

Barnoff, L., & Coleman, B. (2007). Strategies for integrating anti-oppressive principles. In D. Baines (Ed.), *Doing anti-oppressive practice: Building transformative, politicized social work* (pp. 44–63). Halifax, NS: Fernwood Books.

Brown, G. (2007). Mutinous eruptions: Autonomous spaces of radical queer activism. *Environment and Planning, 39*(11), 2685–2698.

Canadian Association of Social Workers (CASW). (2005). Code of ethics. Retrieved from www.caswacts.ca/sites/default/files/attachements/CASW_Code%20of%20Ethics.pdf

Canadian Rainbow Health Coalition (CRHC). (2013). Links—LGBT health and wellness. Retrieved from www.rainbowhealth.ca/english/links.html

Chomsky, N. (2011). *How the world works*. Berkeley, CA: Soft Skull Press.

Croatoan. (2012). Who is Oakland: Anti-oppression activism, the politics of safety, and state co-optation. *Escalating Identity*. Retrieved from escalatingidentity.wordpress.com/2012/04/30/who-is-oakland-anti-oppression-politics-decolonization-and-the-state

Crosby, C., Duggan, L., Ferguson, R., Floyd, K., Joseph, M., Love, H., … Villarejo, A. (2012). Queer studies, materialism and crisis: A roundtable discussion. *GLQ: A Journal of Lesbian & Gay Studies, 18*(1), 127–147.

Daley, A., & Mulé, N. J. (2014). LGBTQs and the DSM-5: A critical queer response. *Journal of Homosexuality, 61*(9), 1288–1312.

Duberman, M. (1991). *Cures*. New York, NY: Dutton.

Duggan, L. (2003). *The twilight of equality?: Neoliberalism, cultural politics, and the attack on democracy*. Boston, MA: Beacon Press.

Evans, B., Richmond, T., & Shields, J. (2005). Structuring neoliberal governance: Emerging new modes of control and the marketization of service delivery. *Policy and Society, 24*(1), 73–97.

Fook, J. (2012). *Social work: A critical approach to practice* (2nd ed.). London, England: Sage Publications.

Hankivsky, O. (Ed.) (2012). An intersectionality-based policy analysis framework. Simon Fraser University: Institute for Intersectionality Research and Policy. Retrieved from www.sfu.ca/iirp/ibpa.html

Helmig, B., Jegars, M., & Lapsley, I. (2004). Challenges in managing nonprofit organizations: A research overview. *International Journal of Voluntary and Nonprofit Organizations, 15*(2), 101–116.

INCITE! Women of Color Against Violence (Ed.). (2004). Beyond the non-profit industrial complex. Retrieved from www.incite-national.org/index.php?s=100

INCITE! Women of Color Against Violence (Ed.). (2007). *The revolution will not be funded: Beyond the non-profit industrial complex.* Cambridge, MA: South End Press.

Jagose, A. (1996). *Queer theory: An introduction.* New York, NY: New York University Press.

Jagose, A. (2000). Queer world-making. *Genders, 31.* Retrieved from www.genders.org/g31/g31_jagose.html

James, S. (1975). Sex, race and class. Retrieved from libcom.org/library/sex-race-class-james-selma

Jeppesen, S. (2010). Queer anarchist autonomous zones and publics: Direct action vomiting against homonormative consumerism. *Sexualities, 13*(4), 463–478.

Kivel, P. (2007). Social service or social change? In INCITE! Women of Color Against Violence (Ed.), *The revolution will not be funded: Beyond the non-profit industrial complex* (pp. 1–39). Cambridge, MA: South End Press.

Mananzala, R., & Spade, D. (2008). The nonprofit industrial complex and trans resistance. *Sexuality Research and Social Policy, 5*(1), 1–19.

Mulé, N. J. (2006). Equality's limitations, liberation's challenges: Considerations for queer movement strategizing. *Canadian Online Journal of Queer Studies in Education, 2*(1). Retrieved from jqstudies.library.utoronto.ca/index.php/jqstudies/article/view/3290

Mulé, N. J. (2011). Advocacy limitations on gender and sexually diverse activist organizations in Canada's voluntary sector. *Canadian Journal of Nonprofit and Social Economy Research, 2*(1), 5–23.

Mullaly, B. (2007). *The new structural social work* (3rd ed.). Don Mills, ON: Oxford University Press.

Queer Ontario. (2010). Queer liberation. Retrieved from queerontario.org/about-us/foundational-ideas/queer-liberation

Queer Ontario. (2013). Mission & vision. Retrieved September 22, 2013 from queerontario.org/about-us/mission

Queerupture. (2010). Diagnosis. Retrieved from queerupture.wordpress.com/2010/03/07/diagnosis

Robert, M. S., & Kelly, L. P. (2011). The effects of perceived funding trends on non-profit advocacy. *The International Journal of Public Sector Management, 24*(5), 435–451.

Rodriguez, D. (2007) The political logic of the non-profit industrial complex. In INCITE! Women of Color Against Violence (Ed.), *The revolution will not be funded* (pp. 21–40). Cambridge, MA: South End Press.

Ruiz, J. (2008). The violence of assimilation: An interview with Mattilda aka Matt Bernstein Sycamore. *Radical History Review, 100*(1), 237–247.

Sachdev, V. (2012). The implications of privileged gay politics on queer aberrations: Interrogating South Africa's nongovernmental industrial complex. Retrieved from digitalcollections.sit.edu/isp_collection/1410/?utm_source=digitalcollections.sit.edu%2Fisp_collection%2F1410&utm_medium=PDF&utm_campaign=PDFCoverPages

Salamon, M. L. (1999). The nonprofit sector at a crossroads: The case of America. *International Journal of Voluntary and Nonprofit Organizations, 10*(1), 5–23.

Samimi, J. (2010). Funding America's nonprofits: The nonprofit industrial complex's hold on social justice. *Columbia Social Work Review, 1*, 17–25. Retrieved from cswr.columbia.edu/wp-content/uploads/2012/10/2010_vol1_pg17_samimi.pdf

Seidman, S. (1997). *Difference troubles: Queering social theory and sexual politics*. Cambridge, MA: Cambridge University Press.

Smith, M. (1999). *Lesbian and gay rights in Canada: Social movements and equality-seeking, 1971–1995*. Toronto, ON: University of Toronto Press.

Sullivan, N. (2003). *A critical introduction to queer theory*. New York, NY: NYU Press.

Sycamore, M. B. (2004). Gay shame: From queer autonomous space to direct action extravaganza. In M. B. Sycamore (Ed.), *That's revolting: Queer strategies for resisting assimilation* (pp. 237–262). New York, NY: Soft Skull Press.

Thunder Hawk, M. (2007). Native organizing before the non-profit industrial complex. In INCITE! Women of Color Against Violence (Ed.), *The revolution will not be funded* (pp. 101–106). Cambridge, MA: South End Press.

Turner, W. (2000). *A genealogy of queer theory*. Philadelphia, PA: Temple University Press.

Vaid, U. (1995). *Virtual equality: The mainstreaming of gay and lesbian liberation*. New York, NY: Doubleday.

Warner, M. (1999). *The trouble with normal: Sex, politics, and the ethics of queer life*. New York, NY: The Free Press.

Warner, T. (2002). *Never going back: A history of queer activism in Canada*. Toronto, ON: University of Toronto Press.

CHAPTER 2
"We Are Expected to Work As If We Are Not Who We Are": Reflections on Working with Queer Black Youth

Marie-Jolie Rwigema, Onyinyechukwu Udegbe, and David Lewis-Peart

Building on existing literature (Daley, Solomon, Newman, & Mishna, 2007) that identifies the importance of recognizing the concept of "intersectionality" when working with queer Black youth, this chapter aims to articulate social work practice approaches that demonstrate a recognition of the mutually constitutive nature of intersecting/interlocking systems of oppression, such as racism and heterosexism.

This chapter emerges from a discussion between three queer Black social work practitioners and graduate students who work primarily with queer youth of colour in Toronto, Canada. David Lewis-Peart is a graduate student whose research is centred on the experiences of young Black men who have sex with men (YBMSM). As a social work practitioner, he facilitates the modified Many Men, Many Voices (3MV)—a three-day retreat-based sexual health intervention program for YBMSM. Onyii Udegbe is the program coordinator at a children and youth mental health agency, and is responsible for case management services and drop-in groups for a range of queer youth, including queer youth with disabilities, queer youth of colour, and queer immigrant and refugee youth. M.J. Rwigema is currently a doctoral student in social work, active in research on lesbian, bisexual, and queer (LBQ) women in Toronto, and was formerly a program facilitator for two groups serving queer youth of colour in community and mental health settings.

This chapter is written in a reflexive manner, with M.J.'s voice articulating our exploratory conversation. In our conversation, we began to think through two issues: (1) How does the concept of "intersectionality" manifest in our practice with queer Black youth? and (2) How do we respond to intersectional oppression with "intersectional interventions"? In other words, what does effective and meaningful work with queer Black youth look like and what does it require?

Background

There is consensus in the literature (Akerlund & Cheung, 2000; Crisp & McCave, 2007; D'Augelli & Hershberger, 1993; Holmes & Cahill, 2004; Russell, 2002) that queer youth experience a range of struggles including, but not limited to, homophobic violence and harassment, challenges associated with coming out, mental health issues including depression and suicidal ideation, substance use, and sexually transmitted diseases. For racialized youth, these typical struggles are compounded by racism, racist homophobia, homophobic racism, and class-based and immigration status–based oppression (Daley et al., 2007). Racialized identities are constructed as heterosexual, while queer sexuality is constructed as raceless or white, which constrains the ability of queer youth of colour to find communities of belonging (Daley et al., 2007; Grov, Bimbi, Nanin, & Parsons, 2006; McCready, 2004). In addition, a number of key institutions create barriers in the citizenship development of queer youth, including family, faith institutions, and educational institutions (Russell, 2002). Finally, there is the idea that homophobia is a "raced" construct, meaning that the ways in which racialized queer youth experience homophobia/heterosexism differ from the ways in which white queer youth experience homophobia/heterosexism (Daley et al., 2007; Garofalo, Deleon, Osmer, Doll, & Harper, 2006; McCready, 2004). However, while the literature argues that we should recognize that there

are differences in the experiences of racialized
ciently articulate how to effectively work with qu
a way that recognizes the multiplicity of their exp
hopes to make a contribution in this area.

What Do “Intersecting Oppressions” Look Like in ces?

> Well, in my experience, it looks like “spiralling crises.” … It looks like the youth coming to you to get help around obtaining refugee status. Their aunt’s family will no longer host or help them because they have been found out as gay. If and when the status issue gets resolved, they have difficulty obtaining a job for lack of “Canadian experience,” because they have a Caribbean accent, and because they don’t know how to do basic things like make [Canadian] small talk before the interview. Without employment, they seek social service support from a shelter where they face racism and/or homophobia or transphobia from staff and/or other residents. When they seek shelter at the homes of friends, who are often in similarly precarious circumstances, the stress and pressure experienced by both parties erupts into a fight. One friend calls the police and the one with precarious residency status ends up with a police record that further compromises his or her status. If a youth doesn’t seek help from peers, they sometimes end up in “relationships of convenience” with older predatory adults, who may exploit them in a variety of ways in exchange for helping them meet their survival needs. So where you may have started off with one issue, getting residency status or access to shelter, the issues end up spiraling very quickly for young people who do not have the socio-cultural capital to navigate systems in Canada. In addition, they are dealing with very stressful high pressure situations that compromise their mental health and often lead to substance misuse as they attempt to cope. This is what facing “intersecting oppressions” looks like. (Onyii)

The description above is Onyii's example of a "not too extreme" composite of the experiences of some of the youth she has worked with. In our collective attempt to articulate what "intersecting oppressions" has looked like when we've encountered it in practice, we have identified a number of recurring issues faced by youth. Along with the issues faced by queer youth in general, we've observed a number of additional struggles faced by queer Black youth: racism from institutions such as schools, police, workplaces, social services, health care services, and religious institutions; precarious immigration and residency status; precarious housing situations; experiences of racist violence in queer communities; experiences of homophobic violence in ethno-culturally specific communities; and vulnerability to exploitative relationships within queer communities.

The chapter entitled "I Could Have Killed Myself: A Narrative Inquiry into the History and Strategies of Coping for YBMSM from Black Cap's 3MV Intervention," in David's major research paper for his master's degree (Lewis-Peart, 2013), offers an equally complex picture of the experiences of YBMSM. Among the three young men he interviewed, who were prototypical of 40 participants included in his evaluation of the program, the issues faced included navigating the refugee system and the related insecurity of being without status; coping with HIV infection and subsequent HIV-related stigma and discrimination; issues of minority stress, in particular sexual orientation concealment and prejudicial events; familial violence and neglect; experiences of institutional abuse in the shelter and foster-care system; sexual assault; and exclusion from familial, social, and religious networks as a result of sexuality and gender role performance. The compounding effects of these experiences led the young men to struggle with mental health issues such as anxiety, depression, and suicidal ideation, as well as self-medicating substance use.

Despite these factors, as David argues, these young men—who, as one youth states, "could have killed themselves"—also managed to cope with their circumstances through what David refers to as the "performance of outsider role identities." He claims that through "creating identities from their exile and outcast status"—exploring in particular "the analyst, the activist, and the fighter" roles—these youth were able to restore their sense of agency. Our experience is similar in that the queer youth of colour we've encountered, by necessity, demonstrate resilience and find myriad ways to cope, ranging from creating their own families of choice complete with a "house mother" and "house father" (e.g. in Toronto's Black queer ballroom scene) to creating many spaces in which they enact and celebrate Black queerness. Thus, our reflection on how to do effective work with queer Black youth starts by recognizing the resilience of the youth we've encountered. At the same time, our own positioning as young queer Black individuals, from a range of backgrounds inclusive of low-income and/or refugee and immigrant histories, layered by experiences of oppression, force us to begin our analysis of "multiply-oppressed" queer Black youth with an analysis of ourselves.

Situating Ourselves: "Being Expected to Work As If We Are Not Who We Are"

> It's been a trip working in the agency I work at, ... sometimes when people are talking about social work theory they don't expect you [a young queer person with a disability] to be in the room. It's been a trip ... sitting in a room and hearing a case for example that sounds very much like me; but I'm supposed to act as if it's not me, I'm supposed to respond as if it's not me. We have to question where these ideas of service delivery are coming from, the whole basis rests on the assumption that the person is not in the room. (Onyii)

I (M.J.) initially approached David and Onyii to contribute to the theorizing in this book chapter because as a facilitator of two drop-in programs for queer youth of colour, I had heard a lot of positive feedback from some of the youth I worked with about each of their programs. From YBMSM who had participated in the 3MV retreat, I had heard on more than one occasion that they believed the program had saved their lives and/or re-oriented them in a positive direction. I had also heard from youth that Onyii's organization was very helpful in meeting a range of needs from mental health to housing to refugee settlement services.

Wanting to put words to what worked (and what did not) in providing services to queer youth of colour, David, Onyii, and I continually circled back to three interconnected themes that inform our practice: (1) self-reflexivity regarding our positionality vis-à-vis the youth we work with; (2) making sense of how racism and heterosexism are mutually constitutive and de-centring whiteness in queer social work practice; and (3) healing communities holistically.

Self-Reflexivity and Positionality

The first theme that resonated for the three of us was how we are positioned as queer "youth" (David and Onyii) and relatively young (M.J.) social work practitioners working with/for queer youth of colour who are often our age peers, and with whom we share similar social and cultural circles. As young Black queer social service providers working with queer youth of colour, we frequently found ourselves operating from a position of dual consciousness that mirrored the various "passing" strategies employed by the youth we worked with. In our collective case, we discussed the reality that in order to reach our respective leadership positions in organizational settings and ascend the academic ladder, we had to access and develop socio-cultural capital and discursive fluency in a number of different settings. In our ethno-cultural communities of origin, we not only speak other languages and dialects (Igbo, Nigerian Pidgin, Jamaican Patois, Toronto Black slang) but understand how to operate according to a complex system of cultural codes. Similarly, we understand how to engage and navigate in Black queer and queer people of colour communities, and then again, how to engage and navigate in social service and academic settings. Each of these settings demands different ways of being and speaking, presentations of self, and discursive strategies. We collectively agreed that it wasn't so much anything exceptional about ourselves as individuals, or as David stated "an ability to pull one's self up by the bootstraps," that differentiated us from the queer youth of colour we worked with. Rather, we decided that what differentiated us from the youth we worked with was our access to cultural capital and our encounters with individuals who chose to "train" us in dominant modes of being and engaging, and our own abilities to absorb and enact this training. While performing our training has benefitted us in terms of mitigating our experiences of personal struggle and has allowed us to "move on up," we also realized that our enactment of "passable" identities as social workers/academics of the dominant mould comes at a cost to us that may also be limiting the transformative possibilities of the work that we do.

On the first issue, Onyii reflected on participating in staff meetings in which "case presentations" of client issues were not dissimilar from her lived experience. David and I also echoed being in meeting spaces where the clients who were being described could have easily been ourselves or our friends and family members. I should add that, given the power dynamics inherent in social work practice, these case presentations and discussions about clients are often paternalistic. Practitioners are not referring to "their people" when they discuss clients, they are referring to people who are implicitly separate from them. Yet, because the organizations in which we've worked were run by racially and class privileged individuals who did not relate to clients as members of their community, we, who did relate to and identify with clients, were forced to pretend that we did not. "Passing" in those settings, in Onyii's words, required that we work "as if we are not who we are." In response to Onyii, David explained, "I've been in meeting situations [with older non-racialized staff] when I realized that wow, I must be performing so well that they do not see that I'm racialized and young.... Where I've realized ... do they know who I am though? No ... they don't see me!"

As we reflected on what it meant for us to "pass" by performing according to dominant white upper-middle-class "standards of professionalism," we realized that our sense of unease emerged from the knowledge that, to the extent that we participated in organizational practices that implicitly centred "whiteness," we necessarily put limits on the transformative possibilities of our work. This realization came from our understanding that helping queer Black youth requires challenging the centring of whiteness, in much the same way that challenging heterosexism requires challenging the normalization of heterosexuality.

De-Centring Whiteness: "It's All a Lie ... There Has Never Been Any Separation"

> I'm thinking about de-centring whiteness and it makes me think of my own stuff.... This whole idea of living in the peripheries and seeing power in the peripheral place. I think it is really important for human service professionals to see that the peripheries are where we need to go to do our work. I think that the centre is really the source of problems, whether or not we call it whiteness or whatever ... the centre is a construct, based on history and old ways of being and doing. The role of social workers is to begin to allow ourselves to exist in the not knowing places. (David)

Writing about whiteness and white supremacy is challenging. It is challenging, on the one hand, because the concept of race and the idea of racial superiority are ideological constructs with no basis in reality. At the same time, this "lie" has material consequences, as evidenced by the systemic marginalization of people of colour all over the world. It is also hard to write and talk about whiteness and white supremacy in social work and queer communities in an era when anti-oppressive discourse is standard.

Few people are overtly racist, and most in the helping professions are at least intellectually aware that people experience "intersecting" oppressions. In this context, talking about whiteness and white supremacy feels like harping about it. It feels offensive to speak about it.

Yet queer community spaces (in Toronto, for example) remain visibly racially segregated. At pride celebrations, there are the Black, and brown, and trans, and people of colour spaces, and the unnamed-as-such white spaces. In the gay villages, east and west, there are bars and parties that are known to be for people of colour and those known to be predominantly white. In the social service sector, there are organizations that are generally thought to be LGBTQ, but are usually headed by white folks, and there are people of colour–specific organizations and programs. There are divisions between different groups of LGBTQ people, with many lines of separation, including the colour line.

It is also challenging to write about how social work organizations, the field of social work practice, and LGBTQ social work practice are spaces where whiteness is the norm. However, when we discussed what was effective in our work with queer youth of colour—what approaches "reached" them—we found ourselves describing ways of relating and practice approaches that we thought of as "disrupting whiteness." For example, Onyii describes the anti-homophobia workshops she conducts:

> Because for instance when you talk about when we do workshops on queerness, we actually don't start by talking about white queerness ... so we do a lot of education about the history of queerness in Africa for example, and people are shocked. I have a relationship to queerness that is not necessarily western, that is based on for example, the fact that Igbo women have always been considered masculine and that gender has not always been a binary, and that dates back before the invention of what we know as white queerness. It's about fighting the erasure of our histories defining queerness for ourselves, shaping definitions of

our identity that don't centre whiteness at all, that is a core piece of what we are trying to do. (Onyii)

Similarly, the 3MV retreats delivered by David incorporate elements of what can be described as "Afrocentric spirituality," including a closing ceremonial circle in which young men are guided by a spiritual and community leader in a collectively witnessed process of releasing emotional and spiritual baggage. While certain youth, in post-program evaluations, express discomfort with the spiritual elements of the program, particularly because they feel these practices do not fit with their identification with Christian religion, other youths consider these circles as the most powerful and transformative of moments in the retreat. David described these circles as moments in which young people, in front of one another and program facilitators, verbally, emotionally, and spiritually begin the work of acknowledging and releasing the pain of internalized oppression. This process culminates with what is an intensive weekend of exploration and unpacking what it has meant for them to be Black, gay, and Black and gay; what they have lost in the process; and what they have seen and what they have faced, so that they can celebrate who they are and what they have gained. Reaching such a moment is facilitated throughout a weekend of creating spaces for authentic connections among youth and older Black LGBTQ and straight mentors. The youth described the mealtime connections as among the most powerful moments.

If we were to articulate our understanding of "whiteness" as manifested in social work, one of its core features would be the practice of creating and reifying separateness. Whiteness as a construct, white supremacy, and colonialism are implicitly based on notions of dividing and creating separations between people, and then enacting domination based on those separations. Social work practices that believe in and maintain separations and barriers between workers and clients are the types of practices that we've experienced as problematic. We feel that our abilities to deconstruct and disrupt separateness through practices of bridging have been the key to engaging in meaningful, effective, and transformative social work with queer Black youth. As individuals who are able to engage in the discourses of the youth we work with and the power brokers who provide them services, to some extent, we ourselves act as bridges. A large part of our work—those of us who do the work of "bridging"—is not only to teach the language of both those in power and those disempowered to each other, but to challenge the myth—held by both, and often ourselves—that one way of being, knowing, seeing, speaking is (1) separate from and (2) better than the other.

Healing Communities Holistically

> The problem with queer black youth is that they have been disconnected from their communities of origin, their families, society. The problem is they've been made to feel separate and apart. The solution is to bridge that gap, the way to do that is to have youth themselves understand, and have yourself understand, that that's all a lie. The separation itself is a lie ... there has never been any separation. So the problem is the idea of separation that has been imposed on the young people by churches, families, by workers. White queer theory thinks homophobia is a problem on its own; it's not. Homophobia is very much a product of white supremacy, and part of the work of healing black queer youth involves healing whole black communities, it involves addressing white supremacy. (David)

For Onyii, David, and me, it goes without saying that we view our social work practice (of counselling, social support, education, case management, etc.) as located in a broader project of social justice and liberation for all people. Our understanding of what constitutes "effective" work is that it is liberatory. For queer youth of colour, our understanding of liberation—based primarily on our own embodied knowledge, lived experience, and self-work—consists of releasing the pain of multiple forms of oppression, while transforming dominator forms of relating. At the same time our work involves creating equitable meeting spaces—being bridges at the periphery—where the myth of separation is shattered. Being a bridge requires, first of all, working through the idea that we are separate and different from the youth we work with. To the extent we are able to work through this separation, we can connect authentically with these youth.

Onyii describes how many of the (white) social workers she knows have admitted to being afraid of the (Black) youth they work with. David and Onyii both argued that this fear of the "other" (even among those with relative similarities) is an important issue that is unacknowledged in the literature. That power dynamics, histories, and practices of oppression inform this mutual fear and distrust is a given. The work of transcending this fear, hatred, and separation and replacing it with new ways of being: that is the work of bridging. But in order to transcend the fear, hatred, and separation that are the product of false constructs such as white supremacy and hetero-supremacy, we need to have certain kinds of knowledge and skills. These include, but are not limited to (1) understanding where ideas of supremacy (of race, gender, sexuality, ability, class)—all fundamentally connected to bodies—originate and connect to one another; (2) recognizing that if we buy into any one of these ideas, we buy into all of them; (3) doing the work of unravelling how we've internalized these ideas and how we enact them; and (4) deliberately training ourselves to engage in bridging and healing work, which is also the work of disruption and transformation. With queer youth of colour, the work involves figuring out where we've created barriers in our ability to relate to them, and finding ways to communicate where and how we connect.

In thinking through places where people feel connected, one of my mentors, Randi-Lee, a woman who has done a lot of between-communities bridging work, offered the idea that "the place where people feel safe are the places where they do not have to explain; where they know the other person 'gets it' (often because of shared backgrounds and similar experiences)." Sometimes, we get to a place of feeling connected and safe because we don't have to explain; certain experiences are shared and we know they are shared with little more than the exchange of a few identifiers (the ability to speak in certain languages, references to certain geographies, the way we are dressed). Thus, to a great extent, David, Onyii, and I felt that we were able to connect with the Black youth we've worked with because of shared languages and lived experiences. At the same time, because we've learned to perform in the ways of power brokers, most of the youth we've worked with have also recognized that we are different from them. Thus, "connecting" also involves learning how to communicate authentically and honestly about how we are "different" and where that difference positions us. From there we are able to offer up what we've learned from our journeys to "other villages." Some of what we can offer includes the skills required to navigate these other villages. In anti-oppressive social work language, this would be understood as educating service users in how to navigate systems. However, at the same time that we teach youth and clients how to navigate oppressive systems so that they can challenge and transform these systems, our bridging work involves challenging the legitimacy and superiority of the normative practices in these systems (including social work agencies, queer communities, and academic institutions). Bridging involves stretching the centre in every direction until it no longer exists.

Conclusion

Stretching the centre in social work practice includes de-centring whiteness by bringing other approaches to healing beyond what is recognized as legitimate in Western-centric helping modalities. The approaches might include interventions that integrate Afrocentric spirituality and community witnessing (e.g. the modified 3MV) or approaches to "case management" that start from relating to clients as though they are members of one's own family and community. Stretching the centre involves not only learning how to engage with the languages, ideas, and ways of others, but in having done the work that would enable one to truly appreciate their value. Stretching the centre, in queer activism, involves recognizing that homophobia and heterosexism are products of white supremacy, racism, and colonialism and that, therefore, queer liberation is intrinsically linked with the liberation of people of colour and vice versa. There are certainly many more ways than those we've named in which we can "stretch the centre" in order to do "transformative" work. Our goal was to offer a few examples of how we've learned to do this in our work. We will certainly face barriers to doing this type of work in an increasingly conservative neoliberal practice context where evidence-based approaches, managerialism, and professionalism reign and resources (including time) are made scarce. One challenge, for example, as Onyii articulated, is "How do you create an indicator for whether or not somebody can understand their identity outside of whiteness? How do you create an indicator and evaluate the long-term impact of that? How can you measure it when it hasn't yet been done? And you don't know what you are measuring against?" At this stage, our answer to that question is that it is important to ask the question itself, whether or not we can answer it. Why? In the simple act of asking such a question, we begin the process of stretching the centre.

References

Akerlund, M., & Cheung, M. (2000). Teaching beyond the deficit model: Gay and lesbian issues among African Americans, Latinos and Asian Americans. *Journal of Social Work Education, 36*(2), 279–292.

Crisp, C., & McCave, E. L. (2007). Gay affirmative practice: A model for social work practice with gay, lesbian, and bisexual youth. *Child Adolescent Social Work Journal, 24*, 403–421.

Daley, A., Solomon, S., Newman, P. A., & Mishna, F. (2007). Traversing the margins: Intersectionalities in the bullying of lesbian, gay, bisexual and transgender youth. *Journal of Gay and Lesbian Social Services, 19*(3/4), 9–29.

D'Augelli, A. R., & Hershberger, S. L. (1993). Lesbian, gay, and bisexual youth in community settings: Personal challenges. *American Journal of Community Psychology, 21*(4), 421–448.

Garofalo, R., Deleon, J., Osmer, E., Doll, M., & Harper, G. W. (2006). Overlooked, misunderstood and at-risk: Exploring the lives and HIV risk of ethnic minority male-to-female transgender youth. *Journal of Adolescent Health, 38*, 230–236.

Grov, C., Bimbi, D. S., Nanin, J. E., & Parsons, J. T. (2006). Race, ethnicity, gender and generational factors associated with the coming-out process among gay, lesbian, and bisexual individuals. *The Journal of Sex Research, 43*(2), 115–121.

Holmes, S. E., & Cahill, S. (2004). School experiences of gay, lesbian, bisexual and transgender youth. *Journal of Gay & Lesbian Issues in Education, 1*(3), 53–66.

Lewis-Peart, D. (2013). *Fall where they may: A qualitative exploration of the impact of many men, many voices (3MV) intervention on YBMSM in Toronto.* Unpublished master's thesis, York University, Toronto.

McCready, L. T. (2004). Some challenges facing queer youth programs in urban high schools: Racial segregation and de-normalizing whiteness. *Journal of Gay and Lesbian Issues in Education, 1*(3), 37–51.

Russell, S. T. (2002). Queer in America: Citizenship for sexual minority youth. *Applied Developmental Science, 6*(4), 258–263.

CHAPTER 3
Queer Disability and the Reality of Homo-Ableism

Lawrence Shapiro

I recall years ago presenting a workshop on the sexual functioning of lesbian amputees at the 2002 Queer Disability Conference, a remarkable two day gathering at California State University, San Francisco, focusing on issues for people with disabilities who identify as gay, lesbian, bisexual, or transgender (Shapiro, 2002a). From lectures to poetry readings to legal analysis, it was a truly remarkable weekend in the Bay area, the historic hotbed of both gay culture and the disability rights movement in the United States. Attendees were asked "How do we include the depth and breadth of queer disabled experience, politics, art, and theory?" and "Who are we including as queer and disabled and who are we excluding?" But perhaps the most fundamental question asked was "What is queer disability?"

The word *disability* has such a plethora of meanings and definitions that it alone is complex even without the sexual context. According to the Convention on the Rights of Persons with Disabilities (United Nations, 2006), "Persons with disabilities include those who have long-term physical, mental, intellectual or sensory impairments which in interaction with various barriers may hinder their full and effective participation in society on an equal basis with others." The concept of disability has been utilized by people with such limitations as a self-ascribed identity and a vehicle for their own political liberation. Today, *disability* is no longer a medical term but a social and political dynamic that has transformed lives and perceptions about what it means to be "disabled." The maturation of the disability rights movement, combined with the new impetus of disability studies, has liberated disability from a medical model into a proud and unrelenting force of personal and political empowerment.

At the time of the Queer Disability Conference in San Francisco, I was enrolled in Ryerson University's School of Disability Studies program in Toronto and had recently published a policy paper in *Disability Studies Quarterly* espousing the need of sexual surrogates for disabled lesbians (Shapiro, 2002b). I had interviewed sex workers in Toronto who had worked with disabled gay and lesbian clients. Throughout my research and interaction within the disability community, I could not ignore an unspoken almost disdain for gay culture, despite so many people with disabilities identifying as queer.

As I arrived in San Francisco, I found myself meeting myself through one of the performers at the conference. The woman's description in the program read, "Ms. Nomy Lamm is a bad ass, fat ass Jew dyke amputee, writer, performance artist and activist." Like Ms. Lamm, I am an amputee and, although not a dyke, I am positively bisexual. Truth be told, I am a bad ass, fat ass, Jew bi amputee, writer, performance artist, and activist as well as a former child amputee and long-term cancer survivor. The Queer Disability Conference was an historic event. After years of endless dissonance between the disabled and the gay/lesbian worlds, my community had finally arrived at both a physical and emotional environment of commonality and respect. At the end of the conference, everyone got a T-shirt that said "Disabled Queers." I was elated.

Body Image, Accessibility, and Popular Gay Culture

As a bisexual who is adamantly not gay, not heterosexual, and at the same time not "disabled enough" to be so labelled in mainstream society because "he's not disabled; he can walk," I find myself in a neverending maze of confusion around identity and social function. Sumi

Elaine Colligan (1999), a disabled lesbian writing in the *Journal of Gay, Lesbian and Bisexual Identity*, argued that "scholarship with personal narrative" can be a powerful way to understand and demystify the parallel worlds of gay and disability culture. Like me, Ms. Colligan came from a "medicalized childhood" in which she saw her body as a text being continuously written. She reflected on points of contention in her bisexual history:

> While in the past I had enjoyed several heterosexual relationships, as a woman with a disability, I could not simply expect to partake of heterosexual privilege. When it was suggested to me that I place an ad in the personals, I resisted packaging myself with the label "damaged goods." At the same time I also understand that persons with disabilities cannot simply expect to partake of gay privilege since gays and lesbians may hold exclusionary appearance norms as well. (p. 80)

I find Ms. Colligan's words haunting. Regardless of whatever historic persecution needs to be acknowledged, I have never encountered any cultural group as preoccupied with physical appearance as gay men.

In reaction to the historic oppression they have had to endure, many gay white men in major urban centres in North America display an attitude of elitism: an idealization of what a perfect body should be. These bodies are normally under the age of 25, with all four limbs, no body fat, total sensory ability, and sexual appendages in full bloom. Acts of homo-ableism have the same impact on disabled people who identify as queer as homophobic acts against gay people.

How do we define *homo-ableism*? In the same way the term *homophobia* has come into common usage in the last few decades, *homo-ableism* introduces a new lexical item into the dialogue of social prejudice. It is ableism in a specific sexual context. It is oppression within oppression. Homo-ableism is a set of attitudes and actions whose end result is the subjugation of gays and lesbians with disabilities by gays and lesbians without disabilities. Consider the following personal ad found on a gay website:

> VGL ("Very Good Looking"), masc, musc, 30-something guy, sensitive and intelligent Gym tight body, seeking same for LTF ("Long Term Friendship") or good times. I keep myself in shape by hitting the gym 3–5x/week. Not interested in guys without pecs—hey, it's only fair I showed you mine. NO FATS, FEMS, guys with baggage or guys on PROZAC!

Am I being unfair in offering the above piece of vulgarity as emblematic of the dynamic that is gay culture? I think not, for a variety of reasons, not the least of which is the day-to-day reality I face as a disabled queer in mainstream gay culture and media.

The social reality is clear: gay culture is predicated on body image. Yes, pioneers of social justice like Harvey Milk and James Baldwin sought an identity to counter their victimization; after the birth of the gay rights movement in the 1960s and the legalization of same-sex marriage in Canada, we have arrived in a new era of social recognition. But this new era, this erosion of legislated homophobia, has resulted in the expression of a largely cavalier attitude by many younger gay men who believe that most if not all of the battles have been won. Within white middle-class male subculture, gay media cater to the worst instincts of its least enlightened, that is, that gay culture equals gay sex, which equals a sexually available body. Where the young man's personal ad states "not interested in guys without pecs," let's substitute "without pecs" for anything that challenges widespread gay values, such as obesity, being older, or sexual ineffectiveness. There is nothing more contrary to middle-class white gay culture than the disabled body. Gay media and gay sensibility dictate that the disabled body can never be attractive and can never be sexual, though as I will illustrate, there are "proud" individuals and organizations who courageously challenge this prejudice. How many times must I hear endless stories of homophobia from gay men, while at the same time I know none of these men has ever been denied entry to a building that is not wheelchair accessible? Are they aware of their able-bodied privilege?

For years I attended bisexual support group meetings in Vancouver. The last Monday of every month was a ritual I looked forward to as I sat in a room with more than a dozen men and women discussing their lives and lifestyles. How fortunate I was that the meetings did not take place at Qmunity, the gay and lesbian community centre of Vancouver, as that venue was not wheelchair accessible. Our gatherings were in another building with an elevator. Had the queer community recognized the moral imperative of accessibility and offered me entrance? At least Vancouver's yearly pride parade has a sectioned-off area for people with disabilities who require the use of wheelchairs or other assistive devices.

Homo-ableism was also present at World Pride 2014, held in Toronto, Canada's largest city and the country's biggest gay/lesbian community. World Pride is an international celebration of LGBT culture and human rights hosted by various cities around the world since 2000. The 10-day event incorporated a human rights conference, interviews with LGBT rights activists visiting from numerous countries, including Uganda, as well as a myriad of cultural events and parades. One of the events provided an example of the worst form of homo-ableism I have experienced within the LGBT community. Despite World Pride's focus on social inclusion, an all-day cultural event (a spoken word, literary, and performance gathering) was held at a venue inaccessible for people with physical disabilities. Within LGBT communities and in Toronto, it is still a challenge to accommodate people with disabilities, which frustrates and does not speak well for either. This is of further concern when existing policy still falls short of addressing such barriers.

The lesser achievement of physical accessibility in fact denies and distracts attention from the broader, more important objective of social integration for people with disabilities. If the centre had had an elevator and our group had met there, I would have been in an environment completely surrounded by my culture, but more importantly would have access to the added services at the centre, especially the gay/lesbian library. Access to a once-a-month support group pales in comparison to addressing this larger social failure. Yes, the powers that be in Vancouver gay leadership are aware the building is inadequate. Yes, "accommodations" can be made for offsite meetings associated with the centre. But the bottom line remains that I, as a disabled bisexual man, am at once embraced and ostracized. But the elevator works … lucky me.

We have now arrived in an era where entire marketing strategies are devised to appeal to the gay male community, which is widely perceived to be well educated and economically empowered. Contrast that to the disability community, with a 50 percent unemployment rate and a tragically higher rate of sexual violence against its women (Brownridge, 2006). The reality of LGBT people with a disability is of an economically stigmatized group. The "inspiring" media images of disability conceal the institutionalized ableism found in every corner of society including, sadly and no less obviously, gay culture.

The Learned Political Correctness of a Younger Generation

I recently visited a high school Social Studies class. I was informed, proudly I believe, that students heard calling another student "fag," might very well find themselves in the principal's office. Homophobia is not accepted or acceptable at this school. I thought about those teenagers, young people who are taught to be respectful of gays and lesbians, young people who could be sent to the principal's office for uttering an obscene homophobic remark. I thought to myself how far the society has come when not only is alternative sexuality nothing to be ashamed of, it is in fact something to be studied and celebrated.

I asked the students if they ever used the *term* lame to derogatorily refer to another student. Yes, not surprisingly, I was told *lame* is socially acceptable language among young people. I was compelled to inform them that *lame* was essentially the equivalent of *fag* for disabled people. "We're not referring to disabled people when we say that word," an earnest 16-year-old protested. I never suggested they were, but the word in question is associated with hostile ableism to such an extent that the target of the scorn might just as well be a disabled person. *Fag* is a put-down. *Lame* is a put-down. Whether or not the scorn is consciously directed toward those minority groups the words seek to debase, the bottom line is that both these minority groups, gay and disabled, are themselves being degraded. I told the students that if an injured horse was seen struggling down the hallway, they could rightfully describe the animal as "lame" but to use a term historically connected to disabled people in referring to someone they didn't care for, was to persecute an entire segment of the society.

The irony is that a disciplinary framework is in place for these young people at the utterance of a homophobic comment and yet their use of language degrading to disabled people is not only tolerated, it is not even recognized as offensive. While the teacher felt comfortable revealing to the students her own sexual orientation—as a straight woman she comes from a position of power—she was correctly articulating that her own sexual orientation does in fact place her in a position of power. I, on the other hand, resisted sharing information regarding my own sexual orientation and instead told the students that gays and lesbians are a proud and often persecuted group but to remember that oppression is not practised solely by members of a dominant culture. Even minority groups have the capacity to oppress less powerful groups within the society. If you meet gay people who champion social justice, I said to the students, ask the individuals if their community centre is accessible. If it is not, you are dealing with a form of social hypocrisy if the commitment to positive change does not motivate them to address the inequity of their organization.

Issues in Same-Sex Disability Relationships

Same-sex relationships in the context of disability are rarely studied and even less often understood. Same-sex couples where one or both individuals have a disability represent a special aspect of queer culture. I am moved by Sara Axtell's (1999) groundbreaking study in which she interviewed dozens of lesbian and bisexual couples dealing with the issue of disability. Axtell recognized such relationships as being at the intersection of identities related to both disability and queer sexuality.

Couples questioned in the study spoke of joys and challenges in their relationships, for example being public and non-conformist: "We want very consciously to be a queer couple. We are making a serious effort to not fall into the stuff that gets called straight privilege, both of us are way too out and way too radical" (Axtell, 1999, p. 63). Here the couple articulates a political identity that resonates very strongly with same-sex disabled couples, that is, there is a uniqueness about this community that has only recently been recognized. Axtell went on to state that "for some participants their view of disability was parallel to their view of sexual orientation ... participants who expressed the strongest views against assimilation as it related to sexual orientation expressed similar views about disability" (p. 63). What is clear is that same-sex disabled couples have created a framework within their queer identity. The experience of both disability and alternative sexuality results in a unique and positive way of seeing self and a unique and positive way of relating to fellow members of this distinct community.

Disability and Sexual Functioning

The impact of disability on sexual functioning can be real and should not be dismissed. Many couples dealing with disability, both gay and straight, understand and recognize the impact of disability on their sexual interactions. Another of Axtell's (1999) participants commented on disability-related issues a couple must address regarding sexual expression:

There was a lot of discussion and exploration we did about how we could be sexual ... partly because ... the PTSD (post traumatic stress disorder) affected when we could be sexual. And if she was too tired, it was too late, or she hadn't eaten enough, her body got to the point where flashbacks ... could happen much easier. (p. 63)

As this participant articulated, sexual activity among couples where one is disabled cannot always be as spontaneous as it may be with able-bodied couples. The need to have an open discussion and understanding about one or both individuals' physical and/or psychological issues around the opportunity to be sexual becomes a necessary part of communication. Axtell (1999) identified that for many of the lesbian and bisexual couples interviewed, the disability strengthened their relationships: "by increasing their sense of interdependence, by prompting them to more fully enjoy their time together ... by presenting challenges they met together and by deepening their commitment to one another" (p. 64).

Axtell (1999) observed a distinction between the value of "independence" in mainstream American society and what she saw as a value within disabled lesbian relationships, namely the role of "interdependence," particularly when both partners are disabled. And yet the reality of ableism in the society of which all these women were a part persists, namely structural barriers and lack of accessibility. The "subtle racism" I articulated to a high school class finds its cousin in the not so subtle ableism within the gay community. Given that gay and bisexual men living with HIV/AIDS may have related disabilities, the gay community could be expected to have greater sensitivity to ableist prejudice than other minority groups; however, that is not necessarily so.

Social Function and Artistic Expression

Today, in both gay and disability cultures, resisting the threat of assimilation performs a vital role in relation to the self-preservation and self-respect of these groups. The creation of state-sanctioned "disability arts officers" (i.e. The Canada Council for the Arts recently created the position of a disability arts advocate, addressing the need for greater recognition and support of disabled artists in the country) attests not only to the Canadian value of multiculturalism but a genuine commitment by the state to recognize minority groups as real, vibrant, and legitimate entities. This cultural authenticity, for me, finds its best expression among sexual minorities with disabilities. Disabled queers are able to effectively identify themselves from outside the dominant gay and able-bodied culture. The uniqueness of being both queer and disabled and their desire to resist assimilation from the dominant gay culture defines them as a meaningful and unique cultural minority.

A few years ago I had the extraordinary experience of attending an all-day symposium on sex and disability, conducted at the Society of Medicine in London, England. Sex workers from across the United Kingdom who worked with disabled clients spoke of the professional gratification their service imparts. An unforgettable moment during that day focused on a stripper doing a striptease for a man who was blind/deaf (Solitaire & Lucia-Wright, 2009). He could not see her or hear the music playing as she stripped. What gratification could this man take from a stripper performing in front of him to prerecorded music? Needless to say, there was no point in her becoming naked in front of the 50 of us in the audience, but the real significance of the experience followed. After the performance, the gentleman was asked (through palm/hand communication) how he felt about the striptease. "Very nice," was his translated response. That sense of social function, that sense of "personhood" that comes with erotic interaction plays perfectly into the gay/disability dynamic.

One group that challenges conventional notions of disability and sexuality is Sins Invalid, a remarkable disability/alternative sexuality performing arts group out of San Francisco. How do they describe themselves?

Sins Invalid is a performance project that incubates and celebrates artists with disabilities, centralizing artists of color and queer and gender-variant artists as communities who have been historically marginalized. Our performance work explores the themes of sexuality, embodiment and the disabled body. Conceived and led by disabled people of color, we develop and present cutting-edge work where normative paradigms of "normal" and "sexy" are challenged, offering instead a vision of beauty and sexuality inclusive of all individuals and communities. (Sins Invalid, 2013)

I had the good fortune of attending three days of performance that Sins Invalid provided in San Francisco a few years ago. On the stage before me was a kaleidoscope of theatre, music, and spoken art elevating what it means to be disabled and queer ... and it was there again, on that stage, that I remet the fat ass dyke amputee whom I had encountered years earlier through the Queer Disability Conference at California State University, San Francisco.

She sang beautifully. As I sat there, surrounded by hundreds of disabled queer artists in that San Francisco theatre, celebrating what it means to be a disabled queer artist, in a city defined through its alternative sexuality, I couldn't help but feel tremendous pride and elation, although not because we as an artistic community were "fighting oppression" per se. I felt that the creative energy of a group like Sins Invalid was on the front lines of showing the world the utter uniqueness of queer disability culture.

Pride only has meaning when all are respected and all are valued. More than the seduction of working elevators, inclusion must incorporate a mentality of awareness of minority perspective within minority perspective, whether that awareness is fostered in a high school Social Studies class, a university conference, or a performance piece where disabled queers exchange erotic energy on stage and translate it into political action and personhood.

Into the Future

How can organizations and service providers best address the reality of homo-ableism that their clients may be facing? Obviously, accessibility, both physical and for those with sensory disabilities, at their workplace is paramount. Places to meet offsite can no longer be seen as an effective accommodation because "accommodation" by its very nature implies second-rate status. Clients should be able to access service regardless of their disability.

But the larger question is conceptual. How can we effect change in the queer community regarding inherent ableism? The answers begin with the very real need for education within the community about the reality of ableism and ingrained attitudes about body image that are so prevalent among white middle-class gay men and are further exacerbated by gay media. As well, gay, lesbian, and bisexual people with disabilities need to be reassured that their reality is recognized and respected. Workshops focusing on their shared concerns, the organized presence of queer people with disabilities at pride parades, a continual effort to make gay and lesbian businesses accessible, as well as a focus on gay youth with disabilities are all essential steps in this journey of social recognition.

Homo-ableism can only be challenged if gay, lesbian, and bisexual people with disabilities are in positions of leadership. Until that day arrives, what is most critical is constructive dialogue between service agencies and gay leadership to ensure the rights of sexual minorities with disabilities are protected, respected, and vindicated.

References

Axtell, S. (1999). Disability and chronic illness identity: Interviews with lesbian and bisexual women and their partners. *Journal of Gay, Lesbian and Bisexual Identity*, 4(1), 53–72.

Brownridge, D. A. (2006). Partner violence against women with disabilities: Prevalence, risk, and explanations. *Violence Against Women, 12*, 805–822.

Colligan, S. E. (1999). Wherein lie the "secrets of life"? An argument against biological essentialism. *Journal of Gay, Lesbian and Bisexual Identity, 4*(1), 73–85.

Shapiro, L. A. (2002a). *Media images of the amputee and sexual functioning of the lesbian amputee.* Paper presented at the Queer Disability Conference, California State University, San Francisco.

Shapiro, L. A. (2002b). Incorporating sexual surrogacy into the Ontario Direct Funding Program. *Disability Studies Quarterly, 22*(41), 72–81.

Sins Invalid. (n.d.). Sins invalid: An unashamed claim to beauty in the face of invisibility. Retrieved from www.sinsinvalid.org

Solitaire, J., & Lucia-Wright, J. (2009). *Dancing in the dark.* Paper presented at Disability: Sex, Relationships and Pleasure, a joint meeting of the Royal Society of Medicine and the Sexual Health and Disability Alliance, Nov. 13, 2009, London, England.

United Nations. (2006). Convention on the Rights of Persons with Disabilities. Retrieved from www.un.org/disabilities/convention/conventionfull.shtml

CHAPTER 4

The Invisibility Paradox: Oppression and Resilience in the Context of LGBT Aging

Louise Stern

Jack's Story

When I met Jack, he was 87 and had resided in a long-term care facility for two years. We encountered each other every morning and I often found him sitting in the lounge after breakfast, looking bored. I would fetch him a cup of coffee and we would switch on the television, watch the home decorating channel, and comment about how good or bad each design or room looked. Under his gruff exterior, Jack had a great sense of humour and loved company. Not that he got much. At that time, I had been a practising social worker with older adults for 15 years, and Jack was the first "out" gay older person I had worked with. I say the "first" only because I did not know if I had worked with others who were out. For me and many other social workers in the field of aging, these individuals were invisible or hidden. Being the only out gay man in the facility, Jack was unique. I could understand why people would want to remain invisible, as Jack frequently faced derisive and homophobic comments from staff, often disguised as humour. He dealt with them stoically, having spent a lifetime dealing with stigma, I suppose.

To situate myself in this chapter and to acknowledge my own complicity in the oppression of others, I admit that as a young heterosexual white woman, my understanding of the experiences of Jack and other LGBT people was limited. I simply did not acknowledge their existence or understand that the issues they encountered were relevant to non-heterosexual aging. In health care settings such as hospitals and long-term care facilities where I worked, the focus was on the aging and broken bodies. Within this context, older adults were not considered sexual, let alone gay, lesbian, or transgender. Social workers have a tendency to recognize older clients' ethno-racial backgrounds, gender, religious orientations, and class membership because these are considered essential to our assessments, interventions, and services, while sexuality, sexual orientation, and gender identity are often ignored (Donahue & McDonald, 2005).

Jack's story illustrates some of the dominant themes regarding aging, sexual orientation, and gender identity that have a bearing on social work practice. First, older LGBT adults often live their lives under a cloak of invisibility that has impacts on the aging process, especially as it relates to health and social care utilization and outcomes (Brotman, Ryan, & Cormier, 2003). Second, the experience of aging for older LGBT adults cannot be understood without an exploration of how oppression has shaped and formed these experiences on a personal and structural level. Third, to become knowledgeable about the impact of heterosexism and homophobia on LGBT individuals and to practise anti-oppressively requires awareness of one's own values and assumptions regarding sexual orientation and gender identity. And fourth, as Canada's population both ages and diversifies, social work practitioners can no longer "lump" together all older adults in one category. Singular identity categories do not contribute to understanding the depth, complexity, contradictions, and tensions inherent in the multiplicity of ways in which older adults experience and live their lives.

The objectives of this chapter are to explore how an intersectional lens can assist social workers to explore alternative storylines that challenge mainstream assumptions about the experiences of non-heterosexual aging. Emergent research indicates that there may be unique consequences and outcomes depending on intersections with other identity positions as older LGBT adults negotiate aging (Price, 2008). To illustrate this reality, the focus will be on the concept of *invisibility*. While invisibility is applicable to all LGBT people's experiences, it is uniquely evident in the lives of older LGBT people in the ways in which it occurs at the intersections of ageism, heterosexism, and other social processes (Calasanti & Slevin, 2006; Fish, 2008).

An Intersectional Lens

Intersectionality is a theoretical and methodological lens used to examine how social, cultural, and biological categories such as race, gender, class, sexual orientation, and other identity positions interact on multiple levels to inform and shape social inequality. Intersectionality addresses two important and interrelated themes. First, it acknowledges the problematic nature of understanding and representing experiences through a singular analytic category (McCall, 2005). Established within the feminist tradition as a way in which to develop a theoretical perspective that takes into account the complexity of the experiences of women of colour, an intersectional lens allows for more inclusiveness when exploring a singular category, in this case of women, which had traditionally been explored through a white, heterosexual, middle-class lens.

Gender cannot be seen as singular analytic category without exploring how class, race, (dis)ability, and sexual orientation intersect and overlap to construct a diversity of women's experiences (Samuels & Ross-Sheriff, 2008). According to McCall (2005), the questioning of singular, monolithic categories allows for the possibility of deconstructing normative assumptions that inform and control it and making visible alternative discourses and narratives that represent the diversity that exists within them. Within the context of LGBT aging, this means attempting to address intra-category diversity by reaching marginalized and excluded groups whose numbers and voices are not represented in either dominant or queer systems and institutions of knowledge.

The second theme intersectionality addresses is the recognition that organizations of oppression such as racism, sexism, ableism, and heterosexism do not act independently of one another, but interact to reinforce and construct systems of domination and subordination. Because they act together, there cannot be a prioritization of one identity position over the other. The interdependent and mutually constituted nature of inequalities requires an intersectional analysis that does not focus on the description of differences and similarities between and within groups, but on how these multiple identities and systems of oppressions interconnect. When applied to older LGBT individuals, researchers, theorists, and practitioners are interested in how the aging experience is contextualized by the intersection of various forms of oppression (ageism, sexism, racism, ableism, heterosexism, and classism), rather than how one oppression may be more oppressive than others (Calasanti & Slevin, 2006).

Social workers who are committed to social justice and anti-oppressive practice must begin to explore in greater depth the unique experiences of individuals whose voices may be missing from wider discourses on aging, such as those illustrated by my interactions with Jack. They require a theoretical framework that takes into account larger structural inequities and constructs in order to understand the challenges older LGBT adults face and that brings to light the strengths and capacities they draw on as they navigate their aging experience.

The Socio-Historical Context of Invisibility

Understanding invisibility in the context of LGBT aging is important because being "hidden" or "in hiding" makes identifying actual numbers impossible to ascertain. This limitation can influence the understanding of problems and needs, policy and resource development, service and program allocation and delivery, and the inclusion of their experiences within practice and research-based knowledge (Crisp, Wayland,

& Gordon, 2008). But before exploring invisibility, it is important to understand the socio-historical context in which it is constructed. The current cohort of aging LGBT adults is often practised at the art of concealment because of the institutionalized homophobia and oppression under which they came of age and lived their lives (Frederiksen-Goldsen & Muraco, 2010; Witten & Eyler, 2012). Many older LGBT adults grew up when homosexuality was illegal, their employment could be terminated if their identities were disclosed, and their so-called life choices were classified as mental illness. The institutionalized discrimination of LGBT people was inscribed in the legal, religious, educational, and health and social care institutions of the day. Social workers and other health and social care practitioners should be aware that they have been historically complicit in the suppression of LGBT identities and have contributed to the reluctance of many LGBTQ individuals to the disclose their identities (Addis, Davies, Greene, MacBride-Stewart, & Shepard, 2009). Accordingly, LGBT people kept their private lives "hidden" and "invisible," or "passed" by presenting a public image of heterosexuality (Averett & Jenkins, 2012).

It was not until the late 1960s and 1970s, post–Stonewall protests (the iconic 1969 uprising by LGBT people in New York City's Greenwich Village in response to systematic police harassment), that progress was made in gay rights/liberation. During this time, homosexuality was removed from the DSM-III and was no longer designated as a mental disorder and, in Canada, homosexuality was in effect decriminalized (O'Neill, 2006). Even though there have been recent changes in LGBT legal and citizenship rights, many social norms and cultural biases against homosexuality and non-normative gender identity continue to be embedded in the dominant culture and its institutions.

Coming of age in a social and political era when their identities and lifestyles were medicalized and criminalized predisposed LGBT people to internalize negative messages about who they were, and these continue to impact them as they age (Langley, 2001). Feeling unsafe, people may still be reluctant to "come out," resist traditional forms of aging supports, and draw on traditional coping strategies that further reinforce their invisibility. Invisibility, while viewed as something that is imposed on older LGBT people, can also be considered "intentional"—as a protective device against social oppression and discrimination. It is important for practitioners to be aware of how the effects of social stigma and prejudice in the past and present continue to mediate older LGBT adults' experiences through the aging process in ways that are much different from the experiences of their heterosexual counterparts.

While this dynamic is specifically pertinent to this generation of older LGBT adults, there is evidence that Baby Boomers' relationship to their sexual orientation, gender identity, and aging may be different from that of earlier cohorts. A MetLife study (MetLife Mature Market Institute, 2006) states LGBT Baby Boomers are at the convergence of two important social changes: a large demographic shift to an aging society (Employment and Social Development Canada, 2014) and a cultural shift that is increasingly acknowledging the civil and legal rights of LGBT individuals. The impact of this convergence should be recognized because, unlike earlier cohorts, many Baby Boomers tend to be "out," celebrate their sexual orientation, and have more positive representations of these experiences than earlier generations did. The aging experience has also vastly changed and there are different expectations as to what "getting older" means for this generation in general. Unlike heterosexual Baby Boomers, though, some key challenges still revolve around health and social care disparities, limited government supports, the exclusion of "families of choice," and a lack of gay-friendly supports and services.

The Categorization of the Older LGBT Adult

The ways in which the category of older LGBT adult has been represented does not acknowledge its heterogeneous nature and the diverse lived experiences of those people living in and around its boundaries. The use of an all-encompassing acronym creates an impression of false unity amongst diverse individuals whose only commonality may be membership in a sexual and gender minority. Often it is the primary (if not the only) one that receives attention when exploring identity (Price, 2008). Although this categorization has proved useful in the field of LGBT advocacy, it has led to understandings that masked the diversity of LGBT people. Categories cannot be ignored, due to the way they are used as part of everyday discourse, but they need to be challenged in respect to whom they represent and the knowledge base that informs them (McCall, 2005).

Traditional quantitative gerontological research on LGBT people tends to focus on inter-group differences, or how LGBT people are different from their heterosexual counterparts, rather than on intra-group differences, or differences within based on gender, race, disability, and age (Fish, 2008). Research samples are commonly drawn from a narrowly defined population of younger, middle-class, white, urban, and male participants' experiences (Averett & Jenkins, 2012). Problems emerge when findings from such non-representative samples are generalized to all LGBT people within a category. The small amount of research on transgender seniors, for example, critiques the presumption that older transgender individuals' experiences can be understood based on studies of lesbians and gay men (Williams & Freeman, 2007). Transgender is a complex amalgam of gender and sexual identity, gender expression, and sexual orientation that creates unique needs and challenges for older people, which may be completely different from those of their gay and lesbian counterparts.

These methodological problems are directly related to the levels of invisibility of older LGBT adults in mainstream society and the LGBT community. People who have been studied are those who are "out," visible, willing to self-identify, and who tend to be politicized and active in LGBT organizations. They are more accessible, while others may choose to hide or be compelled to hide, through marginalization and discrimination. Some may have complex relationships to being "categorized." There are multiple explanations for how and why this type of invisibility and inaccessibility occurs.

There is a marked diversity in the degree to which individuals' LGBT identities are central to their self-identity and to the ways in which they may be connected with the LGBT community (Butler, 2004). Sexual orientation and gender identity are not static entities and, for many older adults, identification with being LGBT may not necessarily be straightforward (Calasanti & Slevin, 2006). People who are multiply marginalized tend to resist being considered only in terms of their sexual orientation (Cronin & King, 2010). They may not identify with male/female or homosexual/heterosexual binaries, with bisexual and transgender individuals particularly resisting attempts at categorization (Price, 2008). The LGBT label is also seen as "stigmatizing" within the historical context of pathology and repression or, it may be political resistance to heterosexist labelling of LGBT people as "other."

Another reason for invisibility is closely linked to early critics of the women's movement and their observation of the exclusion of a diverse representation of women within the movement. Gay organizations and movements have been seen as limited to the young, urban, white, (and largely male) community. These organizations and movements have little relevance to older lesbians and racialized gay men, and this exclusion is attributed to patriarchy, gender oppression, and racism in the LGBT community (Kimmel, Rose, & David, 2006). Diversity of experience is further ignored by the failure to recognize the influence of cultural expectations of "silence," "disclosure," and stigmatization within different cultural communities. These expectations can significantly impact experience, regardless of age. David and Knight (2008) found that older Black gay men perceived greater homo-negativity within their racialized communities and were less likely to disclose their sexual identity than white men. Conversely, Parks, Hughes, and Matthews (2004) found Black lesbians were less likely to disclose to non-family groups than their white counterparts. It appears that the intersection of gender, race, age, and sexual orientation may construct fluid and shifting invisibility—within mainstream society, the LGBT community, and cultural communities—that impacts disclosure and identity.

Little is known about the intersection of aging with those individuals who are more marginalized within the categorical confines of the older LGBT adult label. This includes transgender (Persson, 2009), bisexual (Keppel, 2006), lesbian (Averett & Jenkins, 2012; Traies, 2009), and lesbians and gay men of colour (David & Knight, 2008; Hall & Fine, 2005; Parks et al., 2004). Less well-explored groups include the "old-old" (Cronin & King, 2010), individuals living in rural settings (Lee & Quam, 2013), and LGBT individuals who live in poverty and experience classism.

Invisibility: The Intersection of Heterosexism and Ageism

The invisibility of older LGBT adults is a result of the impact of the uncontested and intersecting nature of homophobia, heterosexism, and ageism (and other oppressions), which puts individuals at higher risk for marginalization and exclusion. The primary way that ageism and heterosexism impact older LGBT adults is within the cultural construct of sexuality and aging. A common ageist assumption posits that older adults are not sexual beings and that sexuality is not an essential component of the aging experience. Given that LGBT people are often stereotypically defined mainly by their sexual identity, this makes the notion of LGBT seniors ontologically impossible and invisible. My initial reaction to Jack's identity as "the first older LGBT person I worked with" is evidence of this conundrum, and it is further confirmed by the findings in the research literature.

Dickey's (2013) study in nursing homes found that care aides articulated surprisingly low levels of homophobic attitudes toward their residents. Rather than attributing this to the acceptance of homosexuality, Dickey (2013) believed it related to the workers' belief that residents did not have a sexual nature. In their study of predictors of heteronormativity in the same settings, Tolley and Ranzijn (2006) reported that some directors of nursing declined participation in their study because they believed that the residents' sexuality was not relevant to the operation of the facility or the care the residents received.

Heterosexism and homophobia impact the experiences of LGBT individuals because they construct and reinforce oppression on a personal and systemic level, and are deeply ingrained and institutionalized within aging care systems, resulting in discriminatory actions and practices (Cahill, 2002). Research on heteronormativity and heterosexism, and their impacts on older LGBT adults and the systems these individuals interact with, illustrate these biases. Willis, Ward, and Fish's (2011) study on older LGBT care givers focused on the heterosexist responses and heteronormative assumptions that caregivers encountered from health and social care professionals. The historical focus in the caregiving literature and research within the field of aging starts from the premise that caregiving is performed primarily by family members (often opposite-sex spouses or children), and fails to acknowledge the nature of support (families of choice) older LGBT adults draw upon (Hash & Netting, 2009). Policies such as "spousal priority" for long-term care placement of a couple in the same facility, for example, are generally applicable to those in "legalized" heterosexual marriage relationships, and exclude LGBT individuals from services and supports that heterosexual caregivers may have access or rights to.

A consistent thread running through the literature on LGBT aging is the fear of institutionalized forms of homophobia and heterosexism in long-term care facilities. Placement often brings up fear of dependence, social isolation, and powerlessness for older adults, and this can be particularly scary for people who have lived through a lifetime of oppression and discrimination. Older LGBT adults and their caregivers express fear that they will be the focus of discriminatory practices by administrators, workers, and other residents because of their sexual or gender orientation (Hovey, 2009; Johnson, Jackson, Arnette, & Koffman, 2005). These concerns are not unfounded, as research shows there is limited training for staff at all levels regarding sexual orientation of residents and their partners (Bell, Bern-Klug, Kramer, & Saunders, 2010) and that homosexuality is perceived more negatively than heterosexuality by staff in these settings (Hinrichs & Vacha-Haase, 2010). For many "out" LGBT older persons, entry into long-term care is particularly feared. It may entail re-entering the closet, denying who they are to appear "straight," and isolating themselves from their chosen support systems (Hughes & Kentlyn, 2011).

Long-term care facilities represent what Harrison (2001) calls the "hetero-sexing of spaces," where care takes place within a heterosexually dominant and heteronormative space. It becomes enacted in the silencing of non-heterosexual activities, in the absence of representation of non-heterosexuals in promotional and educational literature, and through the assessment and intervention tools used within these facilities (Phillips & Marks, 2006). Information gathered regarding an individual's sexuality is often relegated to biological functions and understandings or behavioural issues, and not as a component of one's multifaceted identity (Harrison, 2001). Sexual orientation is frequently based on marital status: *widowed*, *divorced*, and *married* are assumed to indicate heterosexuality, rather than any other alternative. This may begin to change in the future with the legalization and acceptance of same-sex marriage.

The stigmatization and marginalization of one's sexuality may be a new experience for many aging heterosexuals, but for LGBT people this is further problematization of a pre-existing stigma. Ageist attitudes are not exclusive to mainstream society; they are prevalent in the LGBT community, which has been critiqued as being overly focused on youthfulness and youth-based issues and for its reluctance to contest ageist discourses within it (Brotman et al., 2003; Witten & Eyler, 2012). Some age groups, especially those who are "not old," benefit from ageism at the expense of those who are "old," through the monopolization of resources. This is reflected in the focus on issues related to LGBT youth, such as suicide, harassment in schools, rejection by family, homelessness, HIV/AIDS and other health issues, and supports for "coming out" and "transitioning," which may be less pertinent for older adults (Addis et al., 2009).

Ageism, and the youth-centric nature of mainstream society in general, is prevalent in discourse within the LGBT community. It implies that gay life is primarily for young people (Kimmel et al., 2006) and that young and middle-aged members of the LGBT community particularly fear old age as a time of loneliness, obsolescence, and exclusion (Harrison, 2001). The idea that old age is a time of social isolation is reinforced by heteronormative research agendas that are based on the assumption that older LGBT adults are lonely and depressed due to a lack of social and family connections. Butler (2004) and other researchers challenge this assumption by differentiating between being "alone" and being "lonely," as aging LGBT adults have been shown to be no lonelier than their heterosexual counterparts and to have developed alternative forms of mutual support and assistance.

Contradictory Discourses of Oppression and Resilience

The exploration of the intersections of gender, ethnicity and race, and class with age, sexual orientation, and gender identity can be used to understand oppression and privilege, but also make visible the unique, complex, and contradictory experiences each individual can have. The use of a gender lens, for example, shows how experiences of oppression and privilege differ between gay men and lesbians. For example, Schope (2005) found gay men had more negative views on growing old and were more ageist than lesbians, and internalized an ageist focus on youth and beauty prevalent in society and the gay community. These beliefs have particularly negative consequences for older gay men. While they are considered sexless in the LGBT community, many try to emulate youthfulness, which ultimately makes growing older harder to accept and navigate.

Lesbians are perceived to be less burdened by the challenges to self-esteem posed by aging because of the impact of the feminist movement and their historical rejection of male-based judgments and biases, and/or rejection of societal definitions of beauty and femininity (Schope, 2005). Emerging research suggests older lesbians tend to be more careful about visibility and disclosure, especially in the context of health and social care, and are less likely to be "out" than older gay men (Butler, 2004; MetLife, 2006; Traies, 2009). While this could be seen as reinforcing their invisibility, it is too simplistic an explanation. Within the context of invisibility, lesbians often demonstrate resilience and ways of coping with oppression that make the aging process a less jarring and debilitating time than youth.

Resilience is identified as a possible outcome for individuals who experience discrimination and marginalization in a variety of domains over a lifetime, such that aging comes to be "just another hurdle to overcome" (Hulko, 2009). Resilience appears to allow older LGBT adults to enter old age with specific coping skills that have emerged in part from experiences such as navigating the "coming out" process, managing societal perceptions of difference and marginalization, facing family rejection, and developing supportive communities. Although significant, there are concerns resilience may reinforce invisibility of groups and individuals who are already dealing with discrimination and marginalization, which means we cannot understand it in the absence of oppression. An exploration of resilience and oppression in the context of older LGBT adults makes evident how the barriers and coping strategies of aging are strongly based on intersections with other identity positions (Witten & Eyler, 2012).

O'Connor, Phinney, and Hulko's (2010) case study of an older Aboriginal woman in a same sex-relationship, who has dementia and struggles with poverty, posits that different aspects of one's identity may support one another or work together to reinforce marginalization and/or privilege. For example, the intersection of her age, sexual orientation, and socio-economic status combined to increase her invisibility and limit her accessibility to formal supports. However, her Aboriginal ancestry assisted her in resisting more traditional biomedical decline narratives of having dementia. The emerging pattern is one in which individuals who, over a lifetime, deal with multiple oppressions based on gender, race, and sexual orientation, for example, tend to perceive a greater adaptive capacity for dealing with the challenges of aging (Hulko, 2009).

Hall and Fine's (2005) portrait of the friendship between two older Black lesbians illustrates how the intersection of age, race, gender, socioeconomic status, and sexual orientation creates a social space within multiple oppressions and marginalizations that allows for the resistance and reconceptualization of categorization, and the ability to develop transgressive strategies for survival. The subjects' marginalization did not lead to feelings of disempowerment per se, but instead led to what the authors label as "positive marginality." Deconstructing categories can reveal alternative storylines and new understandings that challenge heterosexist assumptions of sexual orientation and aging. A lifetime of managing "difference" appears to aid in the aging experience, specifically when it comes to stress, coping, adaptability, and advocacy (David & Knight, 2008). Social workers, then, must not only focus on the barriers to aging that many LGBT people may face, but also be aware of and make explicit the many strengths they draw on.

Resistance to Ageism in the LGBT Community

There are activist movements within the LGBT community that have been proactively resisting dominant essentialist understandings of aging that construct invisibility (Brown, 2009). An aging society and the growing activism in the LGBT community have created opportunities to unveil invisibility and to explore many topics of concern to aging LGBT adults. These include caregiver support; institutionalization; health care needs; and pensions, benefits, and support. The emergence of diverse narratives that reflect the contradictions, complexities, and tensions that constitute older LGBT identities will hopefully point the way toward the development of inclusive supports for individuals as they age. The goal of many activist organizations is to address ageism in the LGBT community and its services and programs, as well as the homophobia often inherent in mainstream aging supports and services. National organizations such as SAGE (Services and Advocacy for GLBT Elders, www.sageusa.org) in the United States offer support and advocacy to older LGBT adults at the legislative, legal, and social level. Many LGBT resource and support centres in larger North American cities have programs and services specific to the needs of aging members, and senior pride networks have become important subgroups within the larger pride networks.

This shift is also evident in mainstream social and health care supports. In Canada, CARP (Canadian Association of Retired Persons, www.carp.ca) now has a Pink Chapter that focuses specifically on LGBT issues and concerns, such as housing and long-term care access, health care, and legal rights. This type of advocacy work draws attention to the specific needs of aging LGBT people who demand the restructuring of health and social care systems and institutions to become more inclusive. In Toronto, Ontario, for example, city-run nursing homes have implemented an LGBT Diversity Steering Committee and Toolkit to assist in making their facilities more LGBT inclusive and accessible. They focus on LGBT-positive care, through staff training and education, and sensitivity and responsiveness to LGBT issues that may impact residents (www.toronto.ca/ltc/lgbt_toolkit.htm). While these are important steps forward, they remain the exception rather than the rule.

Unfortunately, what appears to be missing is attention to the diversity of those whom these advocates represent. With the increasing emergence of visibility and diversity in aging LGBT communities, how will these needs be acknowledged and addressed? Many organizations and services continue to be most accessible for individuals who are out and engaged in the LGBT community, and are less so for those who remain invisible. Research highlights some glaring gaps in knowledge about people who reside in the older LGBT category, bringing into question the extent to which their needs are met within many of these organizations. For example, transgender and bisexual individuals, those from racialized groups, and those of a lower socio-economic status remain missing from emerging narratives. Heteronormative and ageist discourses continue to dominate and inform mainstream health and social care organizations that provide services for older LGBT citizens and are considered highly suspect by them. Social workers, therefore, must not only enhance their clinical skills when working with older LGBT adults, but also consider the many historical and current structural barriers each individual LGBT person has encountered and will encounter in the future.

Conclusion

The use of an intersectional lens demonstrates that, as social workers, we need to be aware of ways in which we contribute to the categorization of older LGBT adults as an homogenous group without taking into account the impacts of social location, oppression, and privilege. The complex and shifting nature of the intersecting stigmatized identities older LGBT adults occupy and negotiate not only contributes to their invisibility and marginalization, but also fosters increased resilience, strength, and coping skills that other individuals may not have. Social work interventions and interactions should reflect the uniqueness of each older LGBT adult's lived experiences, while embedding them within a socio-historical and cultural context that acknowledges wider social processes. This is pertinent to the present-day cohort of older LGBT adults, but even more so for the future needs of an increasingly diverse, aging population who may have completely different experiences based on the shifting and fluid natures of their identities.

References

Addis, S., Davies, M., Greene, G., MacBride-Stewart, S., & Shepherd, M. (2009). The health, social care and housing needs of lesbian, gay, bisexual and transgender older people: A review of the literature. *Health and Social Care in the Community, 6,* 647–658.

Averett, P., & Jenkins, C. (2012). Review of the literature on older lesbians: Implications for education, practice and research. *Journal of Applied Gerontology, 31*(4), 537–561.

Bell, S. A., Bern-Klug, M., Kramer, K. W. O., & Saunders, J. B. (2010). Most nursing home social service directors lack training in working with lesbian, gay and bisexual residents. *Social Work in Health Care, 49*(9), 814–831.

Brown, M. T. (2009). LGBT aging and rhetorical silence. *Sexuality Research and Social Policy Journal, 6*(2), 65–78.

Brotman, S., Ryan, B., & Cormier, R. (2003). Health and social service needs of gay and lesbian elders and their families in Canada. *The Gerontologist, 443*(2), 192–202.

Butler, S. (2004). Gay, lesbian, bisexual and trans elders: The challenges and resilience of this marginalized group. *Journal of Human Behavior in the Social Environment, 9*(4), 25–44.

Cahill, S. (2002). Long-term care issues affecting gay, lesbian, bisexual and transgendered elders. *Geriatric Care Management Journal, 12*(3), 4–8.

Calasanti, T. M., & Slevin, K. F. (2006) *Age matters: ReAligning feminist thinking.* New York, NY: Routledge.

Crisp, C., Wayland, S., & Gordon, T. (2008). Older gay, lesbian and bisexual adults: Tools for age-competent and gay affirmative practice. *Journal of Gay and Lesbian Social Services, 20*(1/2), 5–29.

Cronin, A., & King, A. (2010). Power, inequality and identification: Exploring diversity and intersectionality amongst older LGB adults. *Sociology, 44*(3), 876–892.

David, S., & Knight, B. G. (2008). Stress and coping among gay men: Age and ethnic differences. *Psychology and Aging, 23*(1), 62–69.

Dickey, G. (2013). Survey of homophobia: Views on sexual orientation from certified nursing aides who work in long-term care. *Research on Aging, 35*(3), 563–570.

Donahue, P., & McDonald, L. (2005). Gay and lesbian aging: Current perspectives and future directions for social work practice and research. *Families in Society, 86*(3), 359–366.

Employment and Social Development Canada. (2014). Canadians in context—Aging population. Retrieved from www4.hrsdc.gc.ca/.3ndic.1t.4r@-eng.jsp?iid=33

Fish, J. (2008). Navigating Queer Street: Researching the intersections of LGBT identities in health research. *Sociological Research Online, 13*(1). Retrieved from www.socresonline.org.u/13/1/12.html

Frederiksen-Goldsen, K. I., & Muraco, A. (2010). Aging and sexual orientation: A 25-year review. *Research on Aging, 32*(3), 372-413.

Hall, R. L., & Fine, M. (2005). The stories we tell: The lives and friendship of two older black lesbians. *Psychology of Women Quarterly, 29,* 177-187.

Harrison, J. (2001). "It's none of my business": Gay and lesbian invisibility in aged care. *Australian Occupational Therapy Journal, 48,* 142-145.

Hash, K. M., & Netting, E. (2009). It takes a community: Older lesbians meeting social and care needs. *Journal of Gay and Lesbian Social Services, 21*(4), 326-342.

Hinrichs, K. L. M., & Vacha-Haase, T. (2010). Staff perceptions of same-gender sexual contacts in long-term care facilities. *Journal of Homosexuality, 57*(6), 776-789.

Hovey, J. E. (2009). Nursing wounds: Why LGBT elders need protection from discrimination and abuse based on sexual orientation and gender identity. *Elder Law Journal, 17*(1), 95-124. Retrieved from heinonline.org

Hulko, W. (2009). The time and context contingent nature of intersectionality and interlocking oppressions. *Affilia, 24*(1), 44-55.

Hughes, M., & Kentlyn, S. (2011). Older lesbian, gay, bisexual and transgendered people's care networks and communities of practice. *International Social Work, 54*(3), 436-444.

Johnson, M. J., Jackson, N. C., Arnette, J. K., & Koffman, S. D. (2005). Gay and lesbian perceptions of discrimination in retirement care. *Journal of Homosexuality, 49*(2), 83-102.

Keppel, B. (2006). Affirmative psychotherapy with older bisexual women and men. *Journal of Bisexuality, 6*(1/2), 85-104.

Kimmel, D. C., Rose, T., & David, S. (2006). *Lesbian, gay, bisexual and transgender aging: Research and clinical perspectives.* New York, NY: Columbia University Press.

Langley, J. (2001). Developing anti-oppressive empowering social work practice with older lesbian women and gay men. *British Journal of Social Work, 31*(6), 917-932.

Lee, M. G., & Quam, L. K. (2013). Comparing supports for LGBT aging in rural versus urban areas. *Journal of Gerontological Social Work, 56*(2), 112-126.

McCall, L. (2005). The complexity of intersectionality. *Signs, 30*(3), 1771-1800.

MetLife Mature Market Institute. (2006). Out and aging: The MetLife study of lesbian and gay baby boomers. Retrieved from www.metlife.com/assets/cao/mmi/publications/studies/mmi-out-aging-lesbian-gay-retirement.pdf

O'Connor, D., Phinney, A., & Hulko, W. (2010). Dementia at the intersections: A unique case study exploring social location. *Research on Aging, 24*(1), 30–39.

O'Neill, B. J. (2006). Toward inclusion of gay and lesbian people: Social policy changes in relation to sexual orientation. In A. Westhues (Ed.), *Canadian social policy: Issues and perspectives* (4th ed., pp. 331–348). Waterloo, ON: Wilfrid Laurier University Press.

Parks, C. A., Hughes, D. L., & Matthews, A. K. (2004). Race/ethnicity and sexual orientation: Intersecting identities. *Cultural Diversity and Ethnic Minority Psychology, 10*(3), 241–154.

Persson, D. I. (2009). Unique challenges of transgender aging: Implications from the literature. *Journal of Gerontological Social Work, 52*(6), 633–646.

Phillips, J., & Marks, G. (2006). Coming out, coming in: How do dominant discourses around aged care facilities take into account the identities and needs of aging lesbians? *Gay and Lesbian Issues and Psychology Review, 2*(2), 67–86.

Price, E. (2008). Pride or prejudice? Gay men, lesbians and dementia. *British Journal of Social Work, 38*(7), 1337–1352.

Samuels, G. M., & Ross-Sheriff, F. (2008). Identity, oppression and power: Feminism and intersectionality. *Affilia, 23*(1), 5–9.

Schope, R. D. (2005). Who's afraid of growing old? Gay and lesbian perceptions of aging. *Journal of Gerontological Social Work, 45*(4), 23–39.

Tolley, C., & Ranzijn, R. (2006). Predictors of heteronormativity in residential aged care facilities. *Australasian Journal on Aging, 25*(4), 68–86.

Traies, J. (2009). "Women like that": Older lesbians in the UK. In R. Ward, I. Rivers & M. Sutherland (Eds.), *Lesbian, gay, bisexual and transgender ageing: Biographical approaches for inclusive care and support* (pp. 67–84). London, England: Jessica Kingsley.

Williams, M. E., & Freeman, P. A. (2007). Transgender health: Implications for aging and caregiving. *Journal of Gay and Lesbian Social Studies, 18*(3/4), 93–108.

Willis, P., Ward, N., & Fish, J. (2011). Searching for lesbian, gay, bisexual and transgender carers: Mapping a research agenda in social work and social care. *British Journal of Social Work, 41*(7), 1304–1320.

Witten, T. M., & Eyler, A. E. (2012) *Gay, lesbian, bisexual and transgender aging: Challenges in research, practice and policy.* Baltimore, MD: Johns Hopkins University Press.

CHAPTER 5
Cross-Dancing as Culturally Restorative Practice

Jeffrey McNeil-Seymour

If decolonization is about creating spaces for Indigenous peoples and valuing their diverse gifts (Awâsis, 2012), as an Indigenous person, a member of the Secwépemc Nation, I view inclusion of this chapter in this volume as poignant and timely. Social workers and other helping professionals need to be knowledgeable regarding the continua of sexuality and gender expression, and their intersections with race and class, regardless of their own locations with respect to these issues. This volume attempts to address the learning needs of straight people, assuming these may be different from those of lesbian, gay, bisexual, trans-identified, queer, and Two-Spirit (LGBTQTS) people. The overall approach is similar to that taken in books dealing with racism for white people. Recognizing its inherent intersectionality (Tatonetti, 2010), Alex Wilson (2008) describes the Two-Spirit identity as encompassing all aspects of who Indigenous peoples are, including our culture, sexuality, gender, spirituality, community, and relationship to the land. My concern is that the use of the term *Two-Spirit* creates the impression that sexuality and gender identities are understood in the same way across the many First Nations.

At one end of the spectrum, Two-Spirit, as it is located within the LGBTQTS acronym, symbolizes equal treatment and access. As we move further away from the acronym as a destination, however, we arrive in spaces and places of dislocation, exclusion, rejection, and death (Brotman,

Ryan, Jalbert, & Rowe, 2002). The Two-Spirit concept has a wide range of meanings and interpretations across Turtle Island (North America). At present, there is a movement to reclaim respected places for Two-Spirit people in communities, through the use of analogous Indigenous words to articulate our roles, responsibilities, and experiences on our own terms. In my opinion, *Two-Spirit* has been colonized in the sense that it is often used as "just a way" to identify LGBT Aboriginal people. It is important to remember that, as noted above, the term refers to various aspects of identity, not only sexuality and gender. Two-Spirit people are faced with challenges on two counts, the first being the limited (but expanding) resources for Two-Spirit persons and those working with other Aboriginal persons in rural/urban communities; the second being hetero and homosexual hegemony (both within and outside of Aboriginal communities), as evidenced by the stories of my research participants found below.

I use the term *Two-Spirit* in this chapter because of its widespread use in current discourse and the fact that some Aboriginal people do identify with this terminology. For some, *Two-Spirit* can provide language for First Nations lacking terms that address diversity in sexuality and/or gender identity and/or expression. The term may not resonate with others as well as terms that more closely align with their gender and sexual experience and identity, such as *transgender* and *lesbian, gay* and *bisexual*. Ultimately, as I argue below, I am sensitive to others self-identifying with their own Indigenous-based identity that may or may not include Two-Spirit.

This chapter begins with an introduction to pow-wows and cross-dancing as culturally restorative practice. I then identify challenges attached to present articulations of Two-Spirit and decolonization using the lens of cross-dancing. Next I share findings of a study I conducted in British Columbia that explores experiences of LGBTQTS Aboriginal residents, revealing first-hand experiences of colonization and the challenges associated with terminology use. I then look at the indelible effect the media have on self-identified Aboriginal LGBTQTS people and their lack of positive representation therein, and subsequently interrogate the resulting power imbalances. The chapter includes recommendations for social workers and social work educators, both Aboriginal and non-Aboriginal.

Pow-Wows, Social Work, and Visibility

Pow-wows are socio-cultural gatherings of Indigenous nations that are imbued with spiritual and cosmological significance to Indigenous persons across Turtle Island. Pow-wows are also spaces for dance competitions between men and women. They are celebratory spaces for fun and laughter. A cross-dance (or switch-dance in some nations) is a pow-wow special (a dance held in honour of age, marriage, and other lifespan markers) in which dancers swap regalia. For example, women don grass-dancing regalia usually worn by men, and men don women's fancy dancing regalia.

While visiting a small rural pow-wow in British Columbia, I witnessed my first cross-dance and noticed that, although some in attendance were uncomfortable, the majority were visibly engaged and enjoying themselves, cheering on the dancers. I observed a trans Two-Spirit woman who did not swap regalia—nobody was excluded; everyone was welcomed, accepted, and encouraged. As a person who has participated in predominantly heteropatriarchal pow-wows, this moment was restorative from my experience, as there was a trans Two-Spirit woman troubling and problematizing the norms of gender performativity, but it also signified the restorative capacities such representation in the arena can have for not only Aboriginal youth, but the entire community.

Challenges faced by Aboriginal peoples, such as family violence, addiction, high rates of children in child welfare care, missing and murdered women, disproportionate incarceration of adults, gangs, and trauma related to residential schools, to name but a few, have been repeatedly reinforced in the imaginations of Aboriginal and non-Aboriginal social work students nationwide. Social work has attempted to address its participation in the subjugation of Turtle Island (Baskin, 2011) through adopting cross-cultural/anti-racist/anti-oppressive/decolonizing practice and other social justice approaches. However, these initiatives have been criticized as reproducing and maintaining the colonial present. Bell hooks (2004) reminds us of the danger of the academic industrial complex and being taught in a culture of domination by those who dominate. In contrast, pow-wows are important places of socialization with powerful cultural influences. Two-Spirit people who have experienced them do not find anything similar in Western LGBTQ communities, as there are no recognizable spaces to practise culture within the dominant LGBTQ community, resulting in a cultural divide between Indigenous and non-Indigenous people with same-sex sexual orientation and transgender identities.

Taking an intersectional approach to social work and understanding the lives of LGBTQTS people is an attempt to work toward social justice and peace. However, considering the necropolitical history of Turtle Island (Morgensen, 2010), I would caution that by using terms such as *Two-Spirit* in social work practice and education, social workers can unwittingly reinforce homonormative hegemony (Kinsmen & Gentile, 2011). The risk is that in employing this terminology as a simple categorization of Indigenous LGBT people for their own convenience and based on their perspectives, social workers fail to recognize the complexity of Indigenous experiences of gender and sexuality. Engaging Two-Spirit as it has evolved privileges Western concepts over Indigenous understandings and can be read as a successful colonial technology: divide and conquer, surveillance (Harris, 2002), or, as I suggest, sexual colonization.

Cross-Dancing as Culturally Restorative Practice

Estelle Simard (2009) shares from her Anishinaabe worldview that culturally restorative child welfare practice was developed out of attachment theory and indigenized through a conceptual framework based in the cultural teachings of her nation. Her model is structured as a circle of protection (individual, family, community, world); it is defined by the specific roles and responsibilities of members within their nation, which contribute to secure cultural attachment. The model is based on recognition of the cultural developmental milestones of a nation, with the goal of full integration of these concepts into an individual's identity. Cross-dancing as a culturally restorative practice (although not necessarily taken up in all First Nations), then, is about troubling heteropatriarchy embedded in Aboriginal communities and locating the specific roles and responsibilities for Two-Spirit members of a nation. It is an opportunity for Indigenous people experiencing their sexuality or gender identity or expression as outside the norm to see, observe, and experience an accepting space. As part of culturally restorative practice, social workers could make Indigenous clients aware that cross-dancing is performed at pow-wows for some nations.

To think about cross-dancing as culturally restorative practice, I draw attention to three pieces of work. Qwo-Li Driskill (2010) argues that the concept of Two-Spirit draws on Native traditions as precedents for understanding gender and sexuality, and asserts that Two-Spirit people are vital to tribal communities. Further, Driskill holds that the Two-Spirit identity concept incorporates recognition of relationships with ceremonial and spiritual communities and traditions, as well as with medicine and the land, marking it as distinct from dominant constructions of GLBTQ identities. With regard to sexuality and gender, Tafoya (1997) states that if one takes the line between male and female, or gay and straight, and bends it into a circle, theoretically, there are an infinite number of gender and sexual identities that may shift for an individual over time and location. This line of thinking erases margins and creates space for those who do not identify with any of the fixed constructs included in the LGBT acronym. Robinson and Watt (2001) suggest that the terms *gay* and *straight* do not have the same meaning in an Aboriginal context as in non-Aboriginal contexts because they represent elements of experience that fluctuate and influence each other, as opposed to representing polar opposites.

Indigenous and settler imaginations have been shaped by hetero/homo-centric, hegemonic notions of gender and sexuality, and have therefore been colonized. Traditional knowledge matters in the modern world; the works of Driskill (2010), Tafoya (1997), and Robinson and Watt (2001) create space for cultural remembrance; although not used by all Indigenous populations, the use of terms such as *LGBTQ* is particularly impactful, as it overrides Aboriginal ways of knowing.

"Ta7us k sllépen-c xétéqs re7 Sécwepmc-k." — "Don't Forget You're Secwépemc First"

The construct Two-Spirit may be used to acknowledge the specific roles, responsibilities, and contributions of members of a First Nation who express their gender and sexuality in ways other than the male/female and straight/gay binaries within the Indigenous context. The title of this section is a reminder from Secwépemc Elders shared with me by my friend Carl Archie. Following that principle, I humbly suggest to my Two-Spirit relations that they can reclaim their Indigenous identities by taking up their traditional roles and responsibilities within their communities, giving them precedence over their gender and sexual identities. Consider a Secwépemc word referring to Two-Spirit roles and responsibilities: *yucamin'min* means "protect the Earth and protect the people." Yucamin'min is an opportunity for all people to nurture solidarity with each other and the land, through the actions of Two-Spirit people carrying out their roles and responsibilities. Secwépemc teachings instruct people how to live in harmony with nature and with one another (Coffey, Goldstrom, Gottfriedson, Matthew, & Walton, 1990) assuming the gender binary. I have yet to receive teachings of stories that contain evidence of more than one gender. However, a morphological figure central in our creation stories is the "trickster" Ske'lep (Coyote), who is understood to be between the two genders. Ske'lep, in some stories, shape-shifts into either gender, sometimes for the purpose of seduction. I interpret this to mean we have the responsibility, if not the expectation, to move fluidly between the two roles and beyond, and to help where and when we are needed.

GLBT/Two-Spirit Voices: A Study

These teachings inspired me to undertake a study[1] that would provide an opportunity for Aboriginal self-identified GLBT/Two-Spirit persons who are visitors in or Indigenous to the Secwépemc'ulw (the name of the territory where the study was conducted) to express their understandings of identity, gender, and sexuality. I hoped to trouble binaries and homophobia through this research, while also interrupting the hegemonic dominant constructions of LGBTQTS.

Methods

I interviewed 15 individuals between the ages of 18 and 54 (five women and 10 men), 11 of whom self-identified as LGB and four as Two-Spirit. Participants were recruited using snowball sampling; all were from nations in the interior of British Columbia. As the work began, I learned the importance of following the correct protocol and asking the right questions. As I was raised off-reserve, I did not know these. It took three years of being observed for how I contributed to community to be given the word analogous to *Two-Spirit* in the Secwépemc language. Some questions addressed were how participants identified themselves, where they learned the terms for their identity, whether the term *Two-Spirit* represented their experiences, and what was needed in community to better their experience. The recurring themes revealed complex intersections of exclusion and sexual identity confusion, racism, homo/transphobia, and classism.

Experiences Related to Identity

Participants described experiencing exclusion and a lack of safety in relation to both their sexual and Aboriginal identities on-reserve and in non-reserve settings. With respect to being open about sexuality on-reserve, one person commented, " ... it ends up destroying you in the end." Several participants knew friends who were conflicted about their sexual identity and were involved in substance abuse and self-harm, such as cutting; some had even taken their own lives. The majority of participants themselves had had substance use issues in the past, some to such a degree that residential treatment was necessary.

Off-reserve, participants also experienced a lack of safety. They stated that the local LGBT youth group was not a safe space for Aboriginal people. For example, a participant shared an experience of racism through identity enforcement by a white lesbian who asserted, "You aren't Two-Spirit, you're a lesbian." This experience took power away from the participant during a sensitive time of her identity formation by dismissing her Aboriginal identity as inconsistent with being lesbian. This comment suggested identifying as lesbian or gay in the queer community provides a better opportunity for social inclusion than identifying as Two-Spirit. In contrast, participants felt lesbian-identified persons experience greater social acceptance on-reserve.

Challenges of Identifying as Indigenous and a Sexual Minority

Some participants recognized that "something" was missing when they identified as gay or lesbian: they didn't experience their Indigenous selves through these lenses; there was a loss of cultural connection. Other participants perceived strong ties between their LGB identities and their Native identities without embracing the "traditional" framing of Two-Spirit.

Some of the research participants experienced disconnection from community and family when they "came out." For the Indigenous person, coming out, while empowering, also asserts individuality, distancing them from the Indigenous community through embracing a queer (settler) identity. There is also a Secwépemc belief that we are born with just one spirit. Thus, in the interior of British Columbia, some First Nations people are reluctant to embrace the construct of Two-Spirit, reasoning that the term itself is offensive, as it implies that one embodies "two spirits," suggesting a loftier status than members of the rest of the community.

Impacts of Residential Schools

Homophobia, transphobia, and heteropatriarchy (Simpson, 2012) are now commonplace and problematic in reserve communities, another legacy of heteronormative (Smith, 2010) framings of our communities. In part, this negative climate is seen as a legacy of the residential schools. One reason suggested for resistance to accepting LGBT and Two-Spirit people on reserves is that pedophilia and homosexuality are conflated, as a result of the multiple traumas experienced by survivors of residential schools. One of the younger participant's insight into the issue was, "[residential school survivors] were taught [being homosexual] was wrong. It's not a lifestyle choice, we were born this way, it's how our body is wired. If it's so wrong, why did the Creator make us this way?" A participant who was a residential school survivor wouldn't talk about the experience in detail, but corroborated the residual colonial impacts of residential schools, such as rewriting Indigenous ways of knowing gender and sexuality.

One of the most haunting stories I was gifted from a study participant was of a little girl in a residential school who enjoyed the company of her sisters until it was discovered at puberty that she was endowed with a penis. The nuns quickly cut off her hair and moved her to the boys' dormitory. Unfortunately, this truth was the only fragment of her story my participant knew. The complete story has been forgotten forever, but it demonstrates the ways residential schools extinguished Indigenous understandings of gender and sexuality, an omission further compounded by the omission of this reality from the truth and reconciliation discourse (Regan, 2010; Truth and Reconciliation Commission of Canada, 2012). Even though there were also calls for Elders to take the lead in establishing Two-Spirit acceptance in community, some participants perceived that the "spiritual" or "traditional" people were another barrier to community participation, perhaps in part due to residential school experience. If the truth about residential schools is contingent to reconciliation, so too then is restoring Two-Spirit roles, responsibilities, and experiences on our own terms.

Participants' Recommendations

A number of changes that could contribute to recognition of LGBT/TS people as respected members of First Nations were suggested. There was a consensus on the need for more visibility of Aboriginal LGBT people at events both on- and off-reserve. For instance, the desire for a pride parade, as well as eventually hosting the International Two-Spirit Gathering, was expressed. The traditional places of Two-Spirit peoples could be made visible in ceremonies or in pow-wow specials such as cross-dancing. Cross-dancing as culturally restorative practice could assist with dialoguing about roles and responsibilities. It could create space for acceptance consistent with the physical, psychological, spiritual, and cultural identity development milestones, thus providing opportunities for secure cultural attachment in ways that are recognizable and respected—in essence, to "come in" to community (Wilson, 2008). It could counter norms in dominant LGBT communities of having to "choose" or having to "come out." Alex Wilson (2008) indigenizes the hegemonic queer coming of age, "coming out," with the concept of "coming in." Coming in, however, asserts and reaffirms one's place in Indigenous communities. A place to begin such changes would be community education around Two-Spirit and LGBTQ peoples.

When participants discussed reserve spaces, there was consensus that "There should be services and places for young kids to talk, more openness and welcoming of Two-Spirit community members." The reserve health service was identified as a place where such resources could be located. Inclusion of knowledge regarding sexual and gender diversity in sex education was also recommended. The need to teach appropriate terminology and knowledge regarding Two-Spirit roles was identified. One way suggested to achieve this was the development of opportunities for mentorship.

Media as a Colonial Technology

Considering the interpellation that has occurred, as evidenced by my research participants, what also needs to be considered is the powerful impact of modern technology, advertising platforms, film, and social media in particular. It is important that social work have an understanding of the assimilationist and co-opting impacts such media outlets have. Ezra Redeagle Whitman (2012, p. 89) reflects on and ultimately rejects the term *Two-Spirit*:

> Inside, a voice tells me to retain some sort of integrity, to try, try again and resist the obscure pressure to succumb to generalized norms of gender and sexual identity as they have been molded from both my Native upbringing and the remarkable control of white gay culture.

Whitman speaks of shared experience and internalized conflict when it comes to negotiating the subjectivity of Indigenous and settler impositions. The continued struggle for social justice would therefore seem a good place to start when acknowledging the relationships between LGBTQTS politics and indigeneity.

On the surface, LGBTQTS appears to be inclusive, but when viewed across various social media and advertising platforms, the acronym reinforces the margins of gender and sexuality, and smooths away the lines of class and race (Gross, 2001). LGBTQTS media and advertising, therefore, assert a politic of homonormativity and homonationalism (Morgensen, 2010). An example of co-optation was identified by Daniel Francis (2011) in *The Imaginary Indian*, which notes that Chief Pontiac's image was usurped by General Motors. Pontiac, having led successful campaigns protecting the land and his people, became a symbol of that (settler) civilization in which his image was used to push an economic agenda to sell cars.

Advertising platforms and social media undeniably play a huge role in how our children and youth come to know self and each other. The gatekeepers of both heterosexual and LGBTQ discursive formations that manufacture white lesbian, gay, and straight desires through these platforms support sexual colonization. We have to ask, where do Two-Spirit people observe positive examples that mirror our image, our skin, our diversity? What are the impacts on identity formation when landscapes (such as gay and lesbian villages) have been rewritten with settler narratives imagined into them (Chamberlin, 2003)?

When it comes to the heteronormative (Smith, 2010) framing of our community spaces, which unknowingly dismisses and silences Two-Spirit experiences, there is a lack of positive or well written sexuality and gender fluid role models or examples for Indigenous youth to look up to through Indigenous media and film (Tatonetti, 2011). It is a point shared and problematized by Tsu'tina filmmaker Beric Manywounds:

> The absence of queer Indigenous youth visibility in cinema troubles and motivates me. I remember how much life and excitement and validation and inspiration the films in my youth gave me, and yet they were laced with problems in that they never represented an image/opinion/comment on the real root things pertaining to my own identity, verifying in cinema culture, the erasure and oppression of Two-Spiritedness in the colonial world. Today I walked down Vancity streets to the café to do my writing, and reflect with fondness and sadness, the moments of romance and sensuality and breakthrough, as well as the isolation, self non-existence, and immobilization in my "gay" youth that were indeed the moments that great films are usually made of. As that (gay) part of my life comes to a close for the opening of a new chapter, I am left with a residual and sincere pursuit of creating on screen cinema images that hold more of the truths that we as Two-Spirits would more relate

and understand, and that would shed light and begin discourse about what our paths forward are. I'm really excited to do the work, and help set the weird record (not) straight that "gay" was not a social defect that arrived with the "Whiteman." (Personal communication, January 12, 2013)

For instance, if we take a look at relationships and sexualities in dating services, as well as the current gay marriage equality human rights campaign in some countries, as manufactured through advertising and media hegemonic depictions of white gay culture, why not imagery of trans-identified or racialized queer persons of colour and other-gendered relationships? These examples reveal the maintenance of how gay stays white and what kind of white it stays (Berube, 2001). A contemporary version of LGB social justice and its successful campaign around the marriage debate is noteworthy here, due to a recent moment when the gay marriage agenda appropriated the Imaginary Indian. For instance, two recent memes (short, often politicized sayings or statements that get posted and shared on social media sites) to consider are "Gay marriage, ha! Back in my day we just called it marriage" (memegenerator.net/instance/29105214), and the following:

> Christian leaders, stand on our soil and claim: gay marriage has never occurred here. Over 130 tribes in every region of North America performed millions of same sex marriages for hundreds of years. Their statements are both hateful and ignorant. Your "homosexual" was our "Two-Spirit" people ... We considered them sacred. (nsaney.blogspot.ca/2012/10/two-spirit-people-we-considered-them.html)

These postings represent blatant co-optation of an historical Indigenous cultural concept that is simply non-translatable to meet the needs of the white LGBT pro-marriage agenda. Although these memes were well intentioned, to suggest that contemporary understanding of terms like *gay, homosexual,* and *same-sex* were understood in the same way as how "over 130 tribes" (a rather arbitrary number to arrive at) understood their Two-Spirit people, erases the complexities and responsibilities of the relationships to community, spirituality, and the land. It suggests that each linguistically analogous word that is tribally unique and still used to describe space for sexually and gender fluid Indigenous persons is the same as LGBTQTS. These memes fall short in that they overshadow present "Two-Spirit" activisms, maintain that our accepted spaces are in the past, and, like the use of Pontiac's image, indigeneity has once again become a face for the justification of contemporary gay marriage's dominant international imagery. This is not acceptable. I have yet to witness major LGBTQ organizations and foundations coming out to support Aboriginal/Native American/Inuit/Métis struggles for basic human/Aboriginal rights to be recognized on the lands settlers have come to prosper in.

In a similar vein, Allan Berube (2001) makes an excellent point with his critique of the 1993 American senate hearings on gays in the US military, where gay white men were recast in the roles of African American civil rights leaders. Berube (2001) argues,

> The extended race analogy compensates for this weightlessness by first invoking the moral authority of the civil rights movement (while erasing its actual history), and then transferring that unearned moral authority to a white gay movement, without giving anything back. (p. 244)

It is important to recognize these gaps in various queer and Indigenous modern technology, film, advertising platforms, and social media. Their ensuing interpellation is detrimental to Two-Spirit people. Appropriation is a very real problem, as the above memes found their way onto Indigenous and non-Indigenous Facebook walls, I observed with very little question or debate. These examples are connected to how LGBT is positioned in front of Aboriginal (as I've outlined above) and is a caution for social work practice to consider power and assimilation through sexuality and (cis)genderism. Furthermore, Indigenous media and social action platforms could reconcile the situation by acknowledging spaces beyond the binary that exist on Turtle Island, especially during discussions of violence against *all* women and *all* masculinities, and ultimately Aboriginal rights, title, and nationhood. There is urgency in the development of culturally restorative practice through media to assist Two-Spirit youth as recognized by Manywounds (2013), to (re)imagine ourselves into the present.

Recommendations for Social Work

It is essential that schools of social work place more emphasis on finding confluence with Indigenous epistemology and research methods, or risk the continued production of colonized minds. It is important to note here the reminder from Margaret Kovach (2010) that while decolonizing perspectives are important and useful, they are centred in settler discourses, whereas Indigenous paradigms are centred in Indigenous knowledges. In using social justice/anti-oppressive/anti-racist/decolonizing paradigms in social work practice with Indigenous peoples, social workers could unknowingly be (1) imposing Western understandings of gender and sexuality and (2) excluding people due to the wide range of meanings and interpretations in and around the concept of Two-Spirit itself.

It is time to start imagining beyond strict LGBTQTS constructs. Indigenous social work requires an Indigenous-led, culturally restorative practice and strong allies for Two-Spirits. Cross-dancing as culturally restorative practice can counter the multiple issues as presented in this chapter through supporting Indigenous persons, whether rural or urban. Restorative practice is about reconnection: reconnection to culture, spirituality, identity, community, and the land. Indigenous relationships to the land are important for us to note, as they are connected to our bodies. There is no blanket approach to practice with Aboriginal peoples. We must consider cultural safety (Brascoupe & Waters, 2009) for sexually and gender fluid Indigenous persons who find themselves outside of dominant definitions of LGBTQTS by limiting their self-expression or incorrectly reproducing and regulating Two-Spirit identity.

Conclusion

In reflecting on the younger participants' experience in a LGBT youth group, it was evident they saw no semblance of self through participating in it. We should be careful with the language we use and the invocation of Indigenous culture. Although I still come back to how to create a space for non-Indigenous practitioners to utilize and incorporate our tools (including that of modern technology) in service to Indigenous populations, appropriation and, above all else, harm are of the utmost concern. When and how will these opportunities manifest, and what is it going to take for this line of thought to be realized?

Cross-dancing as a culturally restorative practice is about visibility. It is an effort toward engaging with the acronym and thinking of practice in terms of social justice, fairness, equality (O'Brien, 2011), and equity. What does practice look like and how do we avoid erasing the complexities of those imagined to be included under the LGBTQTS umbrella? I would like to caution students of social work on the grounds that we're perpetually and sometimes effervescently seeking social justice and solidarity through multiple approaches to sites of practice. Simard (2009) brings up a crucial point in turning theory into practice: the absence of leadership by the Indigenous Nation could prove disrespectful in relation to the goal of culturally restorative practice, which is nationhood empowerment. Nationhood empowerment can only occur when everyone has been invited back into the circle; this means that cross-dancing as culturally restorative practice is but one piece in the effort to empower Two-Spirit people via roles and responsibilities. At present, there is an overwhelming need for mentors and role models, as well as positive media representation of Two-Spirit peoples, to achieve nationhood empowerment across all of Turtle Island. It is my opinion that cross-dancing as culturally restorative practice is a necessary modus operandi to further inspire interruptions of heteropatriarchy in Indigenous communities, as well as homonormativity across Turtle Island. In this way, we can have multiple tools to engage the restorative capacities of embracing diversity in our communities, as well as create opportunity for expanding nationhood empowerment via Indigenous approaches to social work.

Note

1. I would like to thank the Tk'emlups te Secwépemc First Nation for giving me permission to conduct this research on Secwépemc territory. I would also like to thank Thompson Rivers University's Undergraduate Student Research Experience Award and my research supervisor, Dr. Lisa Cooke, for providing me the opportunity to contribute to the growing body of knowledge around indigeneity, sexuality, and gender. And of course, I would like to thank those who have shared their stories with me.

References

Awâsis, S. (2012, October 23). Why we need indigenous feminism. *KWE Today*. Retrieved from www.kwetoday.com/2012/10/guest-post-why-we-need-indigenous.html

Baskin, C. (2011). *Strong helpers' teachings: The value of Indigenous knowledges in the helping professions*. Toronto, ON: Canadian Scholars' Press.

Berube, A, (2001). How gay stays white and what kind of white it stays. In B. B. Rasmussen, E. Klineberg, I. J. Nexica, & M. Wray (Eds.), *The making and unmaking of whiteness* (pp. 234–256). Durham & London England: Duke University Press.

Brascoupe, S., & Waters, C. (2009). Cultural safety: Exploring the applicability of the concept of cultural safety to Aboriginal health and community wellness. *Journal of Aboriginal Health, 5*(2), 6–41.

Brotman, S., Ryan, B., Jalbert, Y., & Rowe, B. (2002). Reclaiming space-regaining health. *Journal of Gay and Lesbian Social Services, 14*(1), 67–87.

Chamberlin, J. E. (2003). *If this land is your land, where are your stories? Finding common ground.* Toronto ON: Vintage Canada.

Coffey, E., Goldstrom, E., Gottfriedson, G., Matthew, R., & Walton, P. (1990). *Shuswap history: The first 100 years of contact.* Kamloops, BC: Secwépemc Cultural Education Society.

Dennis, D. (2005). *Darrell Dennis: Two plays.* Toronto, ON: Playwrights Canada Press.

Driskill, Q. (2010). Doubleweaving Two-Spirit critiques: Building alliances between native and queer studies. *GLQ: A Journal of Lesbian and Gay Studies, 16*(1/2), 5–39.

Francis, D. (2011). *The imaginary Indian: The image of the Indian in Canadian culture* (2nd ed.). Vancouver, BC: Arsenal Pulp Press.

Gross, L. (2001). *Up from invisibility: Lesbians, gay men and the media in America*: New York, NY: Columbia University Press.

Harris, R. C. (2002). *Making Native space: Colonialism, resistance and reserves in British Columbia.* Vancouver, BC: UBC Press.

hooks, b. (2004). Choosing the margin as a space of radical openness. In S. Harding (Ed.) *The feminist standpoint theory reader: Intellectual and political controversies* (pp. 153–159). New York, NY: Routledge. (Originally published in hooks, b. (1990). *Yearning: race, gender, and cultural politics* (pp. 145–153). Cambridge, MA: South End Press.)

Kinsmen, G., & Gentile, P. (2011). *The Canadian war on queers: National security as sexual regulation.* Vancouver, BC: UBC Press.

Kovach, M. (2010). *Indigenous methodologies: Characteristics, conversations, and contexts.* Toronto, ON: University of Toronto Press.

Morgensen, S. L. (2010). Settler homonationalism: Theorizing settler colonialism within queer modernities. *GLQ: A Journal of Lesbian and Gay Studies, 16*(1/2), 105–131.

O'Brien, M. (2011). Equality and fairness: Linking social justice and social work practice. *Journal of Social Work, 11*(2), 143–158.

Regan, P. (2010). *Unsettling the settler within: Indian residential schools, truth telling, and reconciliation in Canada.* Vancouver, BC: UBC Press.

Robinson, T. L., & Watt, S. K. (2001). "Where no one goes begging": Converging gender, sexuality, and religious diversity. In D. C. Locke, J. E. Myers, & E. L. Herr (Eds.), *The Handbook of counseling* (pp. 589–599). Thousand Oaks, CA: Sage.

Simard, E. (2009). Culturally restorative child welfare practice—A special emphasis on cultural attachment theory. *First Peoples Child and Family Review, 4*(2), 44–61.

Simpson, L. (2012, June 1). Queering resurgence: Taking on heteropatriarchy in Indigenous nation-building. *Mamawipawin.* Retrieved from 130.179.14.66/blog/queering-resurgence-taking-on-heteropatriarchy-in-indigenous-nation-building

Smith, A. (2010). Queer theory and Native studies: The heteronomativity of settler colonialism. *GLQ: A Journal of Lesbian and Gay Studies, 16*(1/2), 42–67.

Tafoya, T. (1997). Native gay and lesbian issues: The Two-Spirited. In B. Greene (Ed.), *Ethnic and cultural diversity among lesbians and gay men: Vol. 3. Psychological perspectives on lesbian and gay issues* (pp. 1–10). Thousand Oaks, CA: Sage.

Tatonetti, L. (2010). Visible sexualities or invisible nations: Forced to choose in *Big Eden, Johnny Greyeyes,* and *The Business of Fancydancing. GLQ: A Journal of Lesbian and Gay Studies, 16*(1/2), 157–181.

Truth and Reconciliation Commission of Canada. (2012). *They came for the children: Canada, Aboriginal peoples, and residential schools.* Winnipeg, MB: Public Works & Government Services Canada.

Whitman, E. R. (2012). Straightening the shawl. In M. B. Sycamore (Ed.), *Why are faggots so afraid of faggots?: Flaming challenges to masculinity, objectification, and the desire to conform* (pp. 85–90). Oakland, CA: AK Press.

Wilson, A. (2008). N'tacimowin inna nah': Our coming in stories. *Canadian Woman Studies, 26*(3/4), 193–199.

CHAPTER 6
The Silent *B*: The Erasure of Bisexuality

Ron Goodine

This chapter is a personal reflection on my experiences as a bisexual man. I share it for the purpose of demonstrating how the cultural assumption that only heterosexual and homosexual identities are valid contributes to the erasure of bisexuality within heterosexual and gay/lesbian communities. By sharing these reflections, I hope to provide helping professionals with insight into the diversity of those who identify as bisexual and demonstrate how the erasure of bisexuality is perpetuated, highlighting the unique struggles bisexuals face as a consequence. Using a combination of an intersectional framework and a queer studies approach, I will deconstruct normative identity categories that silence bisexuality. Fotopoulou (2012) claims hybridity can facilitate an understanding of shifting borders and can operate as a political mode of destabilizing complex social structures to expose oppression. The purpose of this chapter is not only to find interrelations between class, gender, and sexuality, but to deconstruct and examine complex social locations and the inherent privileging and subordination within those locations. In addition to my experience of shifting identities within an LGBT context, the analysis is informed by my perspective as a middle-class helping professional in his fifties.

Bisexuality and Coming Out

What does it mean to be bisexual and what are our attitudes toward bisexuality? As will become evident, the term *bisexuality* itself is problematic in an era of identity politics because there is no one bisexual identity; rather, there is a fluid continuum of sexualities that are neither exclusively heterosexual nor exclusively homosexual.

Coming out is a process queer folk are intimately acquainted with. It is a process of identifying as non-heterosexual and working toward maintaining a stable sexual identity. This process is contextual and evershifting. Every time I have come out it has been different—sometimes joyful, sometimes painful; it is an act of bravery repeated over and over again by many.

The coming out process for the individual is best understood in a cultural and historical context. I came out for the first time as a gay man in the early 1980s after a period of identifying as bisexual. The 1980s was not an easy decade for the maintenance of bisexual identities, and my own coming out process was strongly influenced by two cultural/historical factors: the invalidating of bisexuality as a legitimate and maintainable sexual orientation by psychology and other social sciences, and the AIDS crisis. Speaking to the first factor, Paul (2001) indicates that from the 1960s through the 1980s, social scientists defined the culmination of the coming out process as the adoption of a stable lesbian or gay identity. Coming out was framed as an acceptance of one's homosexuality. Bisexuality was regarded as a transitory stage on the way to becoming gay or lesbian—a phase in one's psychosexual maturation.

Early in the AIDS crisis, the second significant influence in my coming out process, little was known about the nature of the epidemic other than that it predominantly affected gay men in North America. It was believed gay men would bring AIDS to the general population. Accordingly, *AIDS* became synonymous with *gay*, and all gay men were feared. The message for bisexuals from within heterosexual populations was similar. They could not be trusted because they too could infect heterosexuals. At the time, there was within the gay community a rallying cry to come out and join the struggle to end the epidemic and demand social justice for gays and lesbians. The message for bisexuals from the gay community was to stop sitting on the fence. The message I heard was to pick a team—either straight or gay. There was no middle ground in the polarized 1980s.

Feeling forced to choose, I picked the gay team, largely because I was never going to fit into or maintain a normative heterosexual identity. I maintained a gay identity with little difficulty and found a supportive community. Within this historical and cultural context it was far easier to maintain a stable gay identity than to ever consider living as a bisexual. Nearly 30 years later, after some soul searching and exploration, I found myself coming out again as a bisexual man.[1]

Bisexuality is a troublesome term for many who identify as neither heterosexual nor homosexual. The term *bisexuality* itself is deeply problematic—it connotes that bisexuality is the hybrid of two distinct sexualities at opposite ends of a pole. There is also the problem of how sexuality is measured and categorized. Yoshino (2000) states "there are three axes along which sexual orientation is conventionally defined: desire, conduct, and self-identification. Definitions can rely on a single axis, or on a combination of the axes" (p. 371). I employ *bisexual* as an umbrella term for individuals who are neither exclusively heterosexual nor exclusively homosexual, whether cisgender or transgender[2], and who define themselves as bisexual in terms of desire, conduct, self-identification, or a combination of the three.

To understand my experience in relation to gender and sexuality, it is important to also consider the intersection of my class and gender identity. I knew from a very early age that I was different, being a feminine boy in the 1960s growing up in a working class family. Maynard (1989) describes working-class masculinities as comprising characteristics that support "manliness," measured by pride in one's physical labour, technical skills, and risk-taking in the service of industry and the nation state. Walker (2011) states "exaggerated masculinity is an integral part of being working-class and male. The working-class male has become the national benchmark for what it means to be an American man" (p. 2).

One episode that captures the influence of gender stereotypes and my sense of otherness occurred when I was eight years old. For some reason I was pulled from class to have a conversation with the school psychologist, who must have been tipped off that there was a "sissy" boy in one of the classrooms. I am not certain my parents had any knowledge of this session. The psychologist asked me a battery of questions regarding the types of activities my father and I pursued, and about my interest in sports and things boys pursued. Even at this young age I was aware of the "right" answers and how to give them in an official setting like school. I responded to the questions and to the best of my ability provided the "right" answers—not the truthful ones. I knew telling the psychologist I preferred to play with girls or other "sissy" boys in my neighbourhood and that I had no interest in sports would mean more visits to her office and grilling about my participation in "boyhood" activities. I must have answered "correctly" because there was only ever one session. The session reinforced normative messages of how boyhood is gendered and is probably my first memory of being the subject of some sort of gender policing. Shortly after, I learned how to pass for "normal" and fly under the radar like the other boys who were different, whether they were to identify as gay, bisexual, or straight later in life.

Perhaps one of the earliest lessons for boys is that masculine gender roles are clearly defined and enforced. Boys who deviate from the normative expectations of gender roles often experience a great deal of institutional pressure and even violence, whether within the classroom or other institutional setting, or outside the classroom where peers actively police and punish them for a failure to conform. Gender role and sexuality are conflated, and boys who demonstrate non-masculine gender roles are often targeted and labelled gay.

The Erasure of Bisexuality—Theoretical and Personal Considerations

Continuing to draw on my coming out story, I will demonstrate how bisexuality is erased and silenced in both the dominant heteronormative culture and mainstream lesbian and gay communities. I employ an intersectional framework and a queer studies approach to critique essentialized concepts of sexuality and gender. Fotopoulou (2012) states "[Q]ueer theory alongside intersectionality can be fruitful ... queer theory questions the assumptions of identity politics, that sexuality constitutes a stable identity" (p. 25). This approach is anti-categorical in that it challenges identity categories.

McCall (2005) defines an anti-categorical approach as one that deconstructs and exposes categories as arbitrary constructs of history and language that contribute little to understanding the ways in which people experience their lives in society. She claims inequalities are rooted in our definitions of race, class, sexuality, and gender, and that an anti-categorical approach works to eliminate oppression in society by eliminating or making problematic categories used to define classes of persons. The author maintains society is too complex to be reduced to finite categories. Using an anti-categorical approach, I examine the social and cultural construction of sexuality and gender by the dominant society, and privilege bisexuality and non-normative sexuality perspectives to demonstrate how monosexuality[3], the categorizing of sexuality into singular sexual orientations of either homosexual or heterosexual, erases bisexuality and bisexual identities.

DeLamater and Hyde (1998) maintain that a classic essentialist perspective is characterized by a belief in an underlying true form or essence within sex and gender. Essentialists would argue that there are recognizable biological and medical categories and explanations when it comes to sexuality and gender identity. Further, they would contend that there are fixed identities regarding sexuality and gender identity, which are innate, and that these identities have been constant throughout history and across cultures—that sexualities and gender identities are transhistorical and transcultural. Essentialists assume that these fixed sexual orientations and gender identities are polar opposites: heterosexual or homosexual, male or female. Essentialism denies the existence of fluid sexual identities.

In contrast, a social constructivist perspective challenges the idea that sex and gender have a true form or essence, and consider both as continua influenced by multiple variables in individuals' lives and the social context in which they live. Hemmings (2007) claims social constructivism rejects the notion that sex and gender identities are discrete categories, arguing that they refer to behaviours played out in social contexts and that they are historical and cultural, as opposed to transhistorical and transcultural.

The very existence of bisexuality presents all kinds of challenges for essentialist constructions of sexuality and gender identity, including the role of choice and the idea of fluid sexual identities and continuous categories. This queer viewpoint challenges the normative construction of fixed sex and gender identities and renders "categories" a meaningless concept. This critique asks others to engage in the difficult work of suspending their assumptions regarding sexuality and gender, and to view sexuality and gender as fluid and so much more than straight/gay, male/female.

Witnessing Bisexual Erasure—Personal and Theoretical Considerations

The most profound experience I have had since coming out as bisexual was witnessing this erasure of bisexuality. Bisexual erasure or bisexual invisibility dismisses, minimizes, and, in its most extreme form, denies the existence of bisexuality. Yoshino (2000) argues that monosexuals have a vested interest in bisexual erasure in order to stabilize their own sexual orientation and identity. He holds that both straight and gay populations value monosexuality because it relieves them of anxiety they experience around their own sexual identity.

Based on a survey of popular news sources, Yoshino found that the number of articles on homosexuality far exceeded those that addressed bisexuality. His online search for the words *homosexuality* and *bisexuality* in mainstream newspapers, newsmagazines, and academic abstracts revealed a striking discrepancy in the incidence of the two terms. For example, he found that *The Wall Street Journal* had 396 documents mentioning "homosexuality" and only nine documents mentioning "bisexuality" during a period from January 1, 1990, to November 30, 1999. Other media and academic sources produced similar results (For a more detailed discussion of the findings, please see Yoshino, 2000). By comparison, I recently conducted an online search for the words *homosexuality* and *bisexuality* in *The Wall Street Journal* that spanned the four years from June 9, 2009, to June 9, 2013. I discovered 385 items that mentioned "homosexuality" and 17 items that mentioned "bisexuality." It would appear little has changed.

Yoshino (2000) maintained that bisexuality is rendered invisible, and theorized that monosexuals, both heterosexual and homosexual, have an "epistemic contract" to erase the recognition of bisexuality in culture. More specifically, he argued monosexuality erases bisexuality in three ways: through class erasure, dismissing bisexuals as a distinct class of persons; through individual erasure, dismissing the individual's claim of bisexuality; and through delegitimization, invalidating the individual's claim for legitimacy and recognition.

Because of the power and privilege it affords them, straight-identifying people have an investment in the stability of heterosexuality and in preserving normative roles of what it means to be a man or to be a woman in contemporary North American society in terms of both gender identity and sexual orientation. Gay-identifying people also have an interest in guarding the belief in fixed sexual orientations and of "homosexuals" as a distinct class of persons, arguing that as a group with an immutable identity, they should be afforded the same rights as other people in immutable categories, such as racial minorities.

Yoshino (2000) notes that the immutable defence as a legal and political argument asserts that sexual orientations are unchangeable, and therefore people who share a sexuality are part of a recognizable class of persons. This defence has been a focal point for politicization, to the point where the argument about whether to extend rights to gay and lesbian people appears to hinge on it. This was evident in the November 2008 California ballot Proposition 8, passed during a state election, which added a new provisional constitutional amendment to the California Constitution that stated "only marriage between a man and a woman is valid or recognized in California" (retrieved from ballotpedia.org/California_Proposition_8,_the_%22Eliminates_Right_of_Same-Sex_Couples_to_Marry%22_Initiative_(2008), para. 2). According to Talbot (2010) the debate about the proposition centred on whether sexual orientation was a choice or immutable. In this case the argument that sexuality was a choice worked against gay and lesbian populations and their struggles toward marriage equality, based on the argument people do not deserve special rights because of the choices they make. Here the immutable defence was a logical and necessary response, because of the argument that rights should not be denied to members of a group if those people are part of a distinct and recognizable group deserving of rights.

Bisexuality threatens the interests of both straight and gay identities. It undermines heterosexual privilege as well as the notion of a recognizable and stable homosexual identity. As noted above, Yoshino (2000) argues that, in response, monosexism encourages the erasure of bisexuality in order to protect heterosexual and homosexual categories that privilege the primacy of sex in the selection of partners, and normalize and preserve monogamy—at least in the heterosexual mainstream.

The following personal experiences further and more concretely demonstrate bisexual erasure in both the dominant heterosexual society and the mainstream homosexual community. Three years ago I joined a bisexual social and support group at the local LGBT centre. I was looking for a community to join, a tribe to belong to. Shortly after joining I was asked to take over as the group facilitator. One of the first issues that came forth was the lack of visibility and confusion about the times and locations of the group's meetings. Volunteers at the centre either didn't know who we were, or of our existence as a group. What little information there was about the group was misleading. I took it upon myself to change this situation, arranging to meet with programming staff. As I walked through the centre, I scanned the space for visible representations of bisexual identities. I had walked through this centre many times before and it never dawned on me that there were no images of bisexuals. In the space there were multiple posters with images of gay and lesbian folk and one lonely poster drawing awareness to sexual health issues for female to male transsexuals. At the time there was an HIV awareness campaign specifically targeting gay-identified men. The campaign did not represent any non-gay male identities; rather, it very specifically promoted safe sex and well-being amongst those who assumed recognizable gay identities. What about the other men at risk, including bisexual men, transmen (transgender men, female to male transsexuals), or men who have sex with other men and who don't identify as either gay or bisexual? It was an odd experience walking through the space and sensing what it feels like to be part of an invisible minority within the LGBT community. I had the sense of being an outsider despite having thought I was a member of the tribe for all those years.

I addressed my concerns about the lack of visibility of bisexual identities within this LGBT space with the program staff. The response I received was "we did have a bisexual health pamphlet" and an exhausted shrugging of the shoulders. In fairness, this is a resource centre that attempts to provide support and resources for sexual minorities on a shoestring budget with overworked and underpaid staff. The service needs are great and the resources are limited. However, I learned this was not a local issue, but rather systemic. I became aware of the erasure of bisexuals as distinct class of persons, my own erasure as a bisexual individual, and the absence of any recognition of bisexual identities within a queer space.

I later discovered that addressing bisexual erasure within an LGBT community setting was contentious. The recognition of bisexual identities continues to be a sticking point for some within gay and lesbian communities. Twenty years ago I would have rallied around the identity politics of the 1980s and 1990s, given my belief in a just world and the claim to human and civil rights. I saw non-normative sexuality and gender identities as less nuanced than I do today. I still believe sexuality is innate, but rather than fixed at one of two points, I see it as moving along a continuum for each person as they respond to the culture they live in and the events and people that come into their lives.

Current Erasure within Gay and Lesbian Communities

The immutable defence continues to be well guarded and policed in the general culture and within gay and lesbian communities. A recent example demonstrates how this defence plays out in popular culture. Cynthia Nixon, an actor in the popular television series *Sex and the City*, which ran from 1998 to 2004, announced in a *New York Times Magazine* article (Witchel, 2012) that, for her, sexuality was a choice. The media firestorm that erupted afterward demonstrates the tensions between gay/lesbian and bisexual communities. Nixon responded to critics' skepticism, which branded her midlife switch in sexual orientation (living with a man, having previously lived with a woman) as disingenuous. In the interview she commented,

> I gave a speech recently, an empowerment speech to a gay audience, and it included the line "I've been straight and I've been gay, and gay is better." And they (the event organizers) tried to get me to change it, because they said it implies that homosexuality can be a choice. And for me, it is a choice. I understand that for many people it's not, but for me it's a choice, and you don't get to define my gayness for me. (Witchel, 2012, para. 3)

Gay and lesbian activists were quick to jump on Nixon's pronouncement. Four days after the interview was published, John Aravois (2012), blogger for AmericaBlog.com, tweeted "Dear Cynthia Nixon, hurting own community is a choice too" with a link directing readers to his blog in which he wrote the following:

> It's not a "choice," unless you consider my opting to date a guy with brown hair versus a guy with blonde hair a "choice" ... It's only a choice among flavors I already like ... every religious right hatemonger is now going to quote this woman every single time they want to deny us our civil rights. (para. 6)

At the time of Nixon's "choice" firestorm I asked gay friends for their response. What ensued was telling. I had a hard time convincing any of them that it was even remotely possible that sexuality could be a choice. Every time I challenged this position within a gay setting, I was met with a visceral, knee-jerk response—a quick rebuke, an immediate defence, and my argument was hastily rejected. I didn't have the opportunity to ask that question in a lesbian setting, but I would be interested to see if there would be a noticeable difference. Although this is anecdotal, it highlights my position that the immutable defence is used within the gay community to protect hard-won rights at all costs. Unfortunately, the cost for bisexuals is that it contributes to bisexual erasure in the process.

Erasure in the Dominant Culture

Psychological research reflected in the popular culture sets sexuality up as a heterosexual or homosexual binary, using biological explanations to validate fixed heterosexual and homosexual identities. It creates a tableau to validate common assumptions about sexuality. The effect is to dismiss bisexuality as a valid and maintainable sexuality (Barker & Langdridge, 2008). Research regarding bisexuality is similarly framed within mainstream media. For example, on July 5, 2005, the *New York Times* published an article titled "Straight, Gay or Lying? Bisexuality Revisited" by Benedict Carey. Even though Carey's article was fair and balanced and raised questions about a 2005 study by Rieger, Chivers, and Bailey titled "Sexual Arousal Patterns of Bisexual Men," the wording of the headline raised doubt about the existence of bisexuality among men and framed those who claim to be bisexual as lying. In so doing, it supported assumptions that dismiss bisexuality as a legitimate sexuality.

In a July 14, 2005, column, gay activist Dan Savage also weighed in on the issue of the existence of bisexual men using this study to dismiss male bisexuality. Savage did not question any aspect of the study itself. In his column, Savage stated,

> I don't think the study can be dismissed out of hand. At the very least it jibes with, er, [sic] field observations I've made of male bisexuals. The sad fact is that male bisexuality is rare, much more so than female bisexuality. While there are a lot of guys out there having bisexual experiences—probably more than ever, God bless them—there's a difference between someone's true sexual orientation and their sexual capabilities. (Savage, 2005, para. 14)[4]

Rather than critically examining this study, Savage perpetuated the erasure of bisexuality, reinforcing dominant beliefs, and highlighting his own assumption that male bisexuality does not really exist. Three words underscored his essentialist bias: "true sexual orientation." He succumbed to cultural assumptions that erase sexual categories other than straight and gay.

On a final note regarding this study, the *New York Times* published an article titled "No Surprise for Bisexual Men: Report Indicates They Exist" by David Tuller on August 22, 2011. The article reports on a follow-up to the aforementioned study by Rieger and colleagues (2005). Rosenthal, Sylva, Safron, and Bailey (2011) changed the sampling methods to better screen for bisexual male participants. In this new study they found evidence to confirm bisexual identities amongst bisexual-identified participants. I highlight these comparative studies not to validate any claim that bisexual men are a definable and recognizable class of persons, but rather to illustrate how sexuality is framed and constructed as fitting into categories and how cultural assumptions, in this case that bisexuality doesn't exist, inform the public discourse and influence social research that define sexual identities.

Biphobia

Research suggests that bisexual erasure often presents itself as biphobia: hostility toward or irrational fear of bisexuals. In their study of gender and binegativity[5], Yost and Thomas (2012) found that both gay and straight male populations were inclined to dismiss the existence of male bisexuality. Straight women tended to be more accepting of bisexuality amongst men, in that they recognized bisexual men as distinct from gay men. However, they rated gay men more favourably than bisexual men. Straight men were less accepting of bisexual men than of bisexual women. The acceptance of bisexual women among straight-identifying men can be explained by the eroticization of female same-sex sexuality. Among straight-identifying populations, bisexual men were negatively perceived as gender non-conforming and labelled "really gay," whereas female bisexuals were perceived more positively by straight men and regarded as sexy and labelled as "really heterosexual" (Herek, 2002; Yost & Thomas, 2012).

Conflation of Bisexual and Gay/Lesbian Populations

Another example of bisexual erasure is the conflation of bisexual and gay/lesbian populations in research. In reviewing the literature, I discovered a dearth of research regarding bisexuality and bisexual identities, particularly in epidemiological research exploring health outcomes of various populations. There are few population studies that parse out specific health outcomes and issues for bisexual populations. In the case of HIV epidemiological research, bisexual men are usually lumped into a unified gay and bisexual cohort, making it difficult to draw any conclusions about bisexual men's behaviour and health. Further, conflating these populations skews data regarding behaviour and safe sex practices for both populations. Conflation serves neither homosexual nor bisexual populations. It fails to recognize the differences between the circumstances of bisexual men and women and those of lesbians and gay men (Dodge & Sandfort, 2007; Miller, André, Ebin, & Bessonova, 2007).

Health Care Impact of Erasure on Bisexuals' Health

The cost of bisexual erasure is significant for bisexuals. Their identities are rendered invisible and silenced—they are marginalized. Bisexuals face significant stressors related to their marginalized sexuality including dismissal, isolation, oppression, and internalized oppression. These stressors affect the well-being of bisexual populations. For example, many who identify as bisexual experience poorer health than gay and lesbian or heterosexual populations (Tjepkema, 2008). In terms of mental health, bisexuals experience higher rates of depression, anxiety disorders, and suicidal ideation (Jorm, Korten, Rodgers, Jacomb, & Christensen, 2002; King, Semlyen, Tai, Killaspy, Osborn, Popelyuk, & Nazareth, 2008), which contribute to higher rates of hypertension and other poor health outcomes (Brennan, Ross, Dobinson, Veldhuizen, & Steele, 2010). There are also higher reported rates of alcohol and substance use amongst bisexuals. For example, researchers have found connections between multiple stressors and substance use amongst bisexual women (Koh & Ross, 2006; McCabe, Bostwick, Hughes, West, & Boyd, 2010; Steele, Ross, Dobinson, Veldhuizen, & Tinmouth, 2009). Additionally, Case and colleagues (2004) indicate that bisexual women in relationships with monosexual partners experience a higher rate of domestic violence than lesbians or heterosexual women.

The weight of being invisible also has a significant impact on health care for bisexuals. A 2011 San Francisco Human Rights LGBT Advisory Committee report states,

> Many, if not most, bisexual people don't come out to their health care providers. This means they are getting incomplete information (for example, about safer sex practices). Most HIV and STI prevention programs don't adequately address the health needs of bisexuals, much less those who have sex with both men and women but do not identify as bisexual. (p. 20)

I conclude this discussion by sharing a recent experience I had when consulting a health care provider. He asked me a series of questions at the beginning of the consult, including questions about my sexuality: "Are you heterosexual or homosexual?" My response was "Neither, I am bisexual." I am not sure what box he ticked. I imagine this particular episode is typical of situations bisexuals face when dealing with health care providers and mental health professionals. Luckily, I was able to correct the health care professional, but what about other bisexual people who remain silent?

Conclusion

Bisexual erasure makes bisexuality invisible and silences bisexuals. The stigmatization and discrimination bisexuals face have serious consequences for their health and well-being. Clearly, significant changes are required in the health care system to address the erasure of bisexuality at a cultural/institutional level and by those who provide service.

Returning to my experiences facilitating the bisexual support group, one meeting stands out as encapsulating the collective frustration bisexuals experience in regard to being rendered invisible. One of the participants spoke up about the silencing he experienced in a LGBT setting. He was upset and frustrated by the lack of recognition he experienced as a bisexual in the LGBT community—he said "the 'B' is silent." Everyone in the room nodded their heads in unison.

As helping professionals, we need to ask some difficult questions, the first and most difficult being: how do we contribute to the erasure of bisexuality? Also, what assumptions do we have in terms of sexuality and gender? How do we bring an intersectional framework to our work that allows us to examine and deconstruct the normative categories of sexuality that oppress bisexual people with diverse intersecting identities? When working with bisexual clients, how do we change the conversation and confront the cultural assumptions that silence bisexual individuals and render many different bisexual identities invisible? How do we reframe coming out so the culmination of that process is more than just assuming a stable homosexual identity? How do we make room for non-normative sexualities? More specifically, how can helping professionals address the social, psychological, and health issues that result from erasure and biphobia and affect the individual in their care?

Notes

1. For me, being bisexual means that biological sex and gender identity are irrelevant in my selection of partners—it is the person that matters most.
2. "A cisgender person is someone who identifies as the gender/sex they were assigned at birth. For example, your birth certificate says female, and you identify as a female woman." See "Cisgender," retrieved June 30, 2013 from Queer Dictionary: queerdictionary.tumblr.com/post/9264228131/cisgender-adj. A transgender person is "one whose gender identity is different from the gender assigned at birth." See "Transgender," retrieved June 30, 2013 from Queer Dictionary: queerdictionary.tumblr.com/post/15456066827/transgender-adj
3. *Monosexuality* is defined as romantic and/or sexual attraction to members of one sex or gender only. A monosexual person may identify as heterosexual or homosexual. In discussions of sexual orientation the term is chiefly

used in contrast to bisexuality and other non-monosexual orientations, such as pansexuality.
4. On May 30, 2013, Dan Savage, at the Bryant Park Reading Room in New York City, spoke about bisexuality, recanting earlier claims made by him as found in this chapter. He was interviewed by Mark Oppenheimer, *New York Times* journalist who profiled him for the *New York Times Magazine* (Oppenheimer, 2013).
5. Yost and Thomas designed a Gender-Specific Binegativity Scale, based on Mulick and Wright's Biphobia Scale that measured study participants' biphobic responses to a series of questions. Yost and Thomas rewrote the scale to refer to bisexual men and bisexual women, and thus renamed it the Gender-Specific Binegativity Scale. Binegativity measures heterosexual-identifying male and female raters' negative response toward male and female bisexual targets. Results confirm the importance of considering gender (of both the target and the rater) when assessing sexual prejudice.

References

Aravois, J. (2012, January 23). Cynthia Nixon on being gay: "For me it's a choice." *Huffington Post: Gay Voices*. Retrieved from www.huffingtonpost.com/2012/01/23/cynthia-nixon-wit-being-gay_n_1223889.html

Barker, M., & Langdridge, D. (2008). Bisexuality: Working with a silenced sexuality. *Feminism & Psychology, 18*(3), 389–394.

Brennan, D. J., Ross, L. E., Dobinson, C., Veldhuizen, S., & Steele, L. S. (2010). Men's sexual orientation and health in Canada. *Canadian Journal of Public Health, 101*(3), 255–258.

California Proposition 8. (n.d.). Ballotpedia. Retrieved from ballotpedia.org/wiki/index.php/California_Proposition_8,_the_%22Eliminates_Right_of_Same-Sex_Couples_to_Marry%22_Initiative_(2008)

Carey, B. (2005, July 5). Straight, gay or lying? Bisexuality revisited. *New York Times*. Retrieved from www.nytimes.com/2005/07/05/health/05sex.html?pagewanted=all&_r=0

Case, P., Austin, S. B., Hunter, D. J., Manson, J. E., Malspeis, S., Willett, W. C., & Spiegelman, D. (2004). Sexual orientation, health risk factors, and physical functioning in the nurses' health study II. *Journal of Womens' Health, 13*(9), 1033-1047.

DeLamater, J. D., & Hyde, J. S. (1998) Essentialism vs. social constructionism in the study of human sexuality. *The Journal of Sex Research, 35*(1), 10-18.

Dodge, B., & Sandfort, T. G. M. (2007). Mental health among bisexual individuals when compared to homosexual and heterosexual individuals: An introductory review. In B. A. Firestein (Ed.), *Becoming visible. Counseling bisexuals across the lifespan* (pp. 28-51). New York, NY: Columbia University Press.

Fotopoulou, A. (2012). Intersectionality, queer studies and hybridity: Methodological frameworks for social research. *Journal of International Women's Studies, 13*(2), 19-32.

Hemmings, C. (2007). What's in a name? Bisexuality, transnational sexuality studies and western colonial legacies. *International Journal of Human Rights, 11*(1/2), 13-32.

Herek, G. M. (2002). Heterosexuals' attitudes toward bisexual men and women in the United States. *Journal Of Sex Research, 39*(4), 264-274.

Jorm, A. F., Korten, A. E., Rodgers, B., Jacomb, P. A., & Christensen, H. (2002). Sexual orientation and mental health: Results from a community survey of young and middle-aged adults. *British Journal of Psychiatry, 180*(5), 423-427.

King, M., Semlyen, J., Tai, S. S., Killaspy, H., Osborn, D., Popelyuk, D., & Nazareth, I. (2008). A systematic review of mental disorder, suicide, and deliberate self harm in lesbian, gay and bisexual people. *BMC Psychiatry, 8*(70). Retrieved from www.ncbi.nlm.nih.gov/pmc/articles/PMC2533652/#__ffn_sectitle

Koh, A. S., & Ross, L. K. (2006). Mental health issues: A comparison of lesbian, bisexual and heterosexual women. *Journal of Homosexuality, 51*, 33-57.

Maynard, S. (1989). Rugged work and rugged men: The social construction of masculinity in working class history. *Labour/Le Travial, 23*, 159-169.

McCabe, S., Bostwick, W. B., Hughes, T. L., West, B. T., & Boyd, C. J. (2010). The relationship between discrimination and substance use disorders among lesbian, gay, and bisexual adults in the United States. *American Journal of Public Health, 100*(10), 1946-1952.

McCall, L. (2005). The complexity of intersectionality. *Signs: Journal of Women in Culture and Society, 30*(3), 1771-1800.

Miller, M., André, A., Ebin, J., & Bessonova, L. (2007). Bisexual health: An introduction and model practices for HIV/STI prevention programming.

National Gay and Lesbian Task Force Policy Institute, the Fenway Institute at Fenway Community Health. Retrieved from www.outforhealth.org/files/all/bisexual_health_tf.pdf

Oppenheimer, M. (2011, June 11). Married, with infidelities. *New York Times Magazine*. Retrieved from www.nytimes.com/2011/07/03/magazine/infidelity-will-keep-us-together.html?pagewanted=all

Paul, J. P. (2001). Bisexuality: Reassessing our paradigms of sexuality. In P. C. Rodríguez Rust (Ed.), *Bisexuality in the United States: A social studies reader* (pp. 15–18). New York: Columbia University Press.

Rieger, G., Chivers, M. L., & Bailey, J. M. (2005). Sexual arousal patterns of bisexual men. *Psychological Science: A Journal of the American Psychological Society, 16*(8), 579–584.

Rosenthal, A. M., Sylva, D., Safron, A., & Bailey, J. M. (2011). Sexual arousal patterns of bisexual men revisited. *Biology Psychology, 88*(1), 112–115.

San Francisco Human Rights LGBT Advisory Committee. (2011). Bisexual invisibility: Impacts and recommendations. Retrieved from sf-hrc.org/sites/sf-hrc.org/files/migrated/FileCenter/Documents/HRC_Publications/Articles/Bisexual_Invisiblity_Impacts_and_Recommendations_March_2011.pdf

Savage, D. (2005). Just a piece on the side. *The Stranger*. Retrieved from www.thestranger.com/seattle/SavageLove?oid=22160

Steele, L. S., Ross, L. E., Dobinson, C., Veldhuizen, S., & Tinmouth, J. (2009). Women's sexual orientation and health: Results from a Canadian population-based survey. *Women & Health, 49*(5), 353–367.

Talbot, M. (2010, January 25). Is sexuality immutable? *New Yorker*. Retrieved from www.newyorker.com/online/blogs/newsdesk/2010/01/is-sexuality-immutable.html

Tjepkema, M. (2008). Health care use among gay, lesbian and bisexual Canadians. Statistics Canada. Retrieved from www.statcan.gc.ca/pub/82-003-x/2008001/article/10532-eng.htm

Tuller, D. (2011, August 23). No surprise for bisexual men: Report indicates they exist. *New York Times*. Retrieved from www.nytimes.com/2011/08/23/health/23bisexual.html?_r=0

Walker, M. (2011). Manliness is the backbone of our nature: Masculinity and class identity among nineteenth century railroad workers in West Oakland, California. *Anthropological Studies Center, Sonoma State University, SCA*

Proceedings, 25, 1–11. Retrieved from academia.edu/1053945/Manliness_is_the_Backbone_of_Our_Nature_Masculinity_and_Class_Identity_among_Nineteenth-Century_Railroad_Workers_in_West_Oakland_California

Witchel, A. (2012). Life after "sex." *New York Times Magazine.* Retrieved from topics.nytimes.com/topics/reference/timestopics/people/w/alex_witchel/index.htm

Yoshino, K. (2000). The epistemic contract of bisexual erasure. *Stanford Law Review, 52*(2), 353. Retrieved from www.kenjiyoshino.com/articles/epistemiccontract.pdf

Yost, M., & Thomas, G. (2012). Gender and bnegativity: Men's and women's attitudes toward male and female bisexuals. *Archives Of Sexual Behavior, 41*(3), 691–702.

PART II
Fields of Service, Practice, and Organizational Change

CHAPTER 7
Transfeminist Theory and Action: Trans Women and the Contested Terrain of Women's Services[1]

Jake Pyne

> "This space is for women, that guy has a dick, so he ain't no woman."

The above statement, made by a cisgender (non-trans) woman shelter resident about a transgender (trans) woman, is recalled by Vachon (2006) in his account of doing trans inclusion work as a shelter service provider in Toronto. In his essay, Vachon describes the difficulty of navigating between the competing claims to comfort and safety made by trans and cisgender residents. Vachon comes to understand that his role as a pro-feminist service provider was not, as he had first thought, to protect female residents from potentially dangerous trans women (male to female) residents, but to create a safer space for both cisgender women and trans women to access services with dignity.

In recent years, studies have increasingly found alarming levels of violence and poverty impacting trans communities (Bauer, Boyce, Coleman, Kaay, Scanlon, & Travers, 2010; Grant, Mottet, Tanis, Harrison, Herman, & Keisling, 2011). In turn, studies have also found the services that might ameliorate these conditions, like shelters and anti-violence programs, are in fact excluding trans communities (Grant et al., 2011; Namaste, 2000). Multiple reports have demonstrated trans women's ongoing exclusion from feminist-based services since the 1970s (Califia, 1997; Denny, 2006; Elliot, 2010; Namaste, 2000, 2005; Scott-Dixon, 2006). A growing transfeminist movement has challenged this exclusion, yet debate has largely taken place among online activists and within the field of women and gender studies. As the discipline most directly concerned with the just provision of social services, the absence of a social work voice on this issue is glaring.

With the upsurge of North American trans activism and scholarship since the 1990s (Stryker, 2008), accounts of the barriers facing trans communities have slowly made their way into social work literature (Burdge, 2007; Mallon, 1999; McGihon, 1998; McPhail, 2004; Nagoshi & Brzuzy, 2010; Pyne, 2011). Authors have typically employed a wide scope, resulting in relatively broad proposals for change, including calling on social workers to educate themselves about trans communities (McPhail, 2004), to empower and advocate for trans people (Burgess, 1999), to infuse social work pedagogy with queer (McPhail, 2004) and transgender theory (Nagoshi & Brzuzy, 2010), and to engage in training and policy work to better serve trans clients (Mallon, 1999). While helpful, I argue these broad proposals are insufficient for attending to the specificity of feminist-based services where a bitter struggle over the inclusion/exclusion of trans women has taken place for more than three decades.

As a trans man and community worker, I coordinated a project for many years that provided trans-access training and policy assistance to social service agencies in Toronto and other parts of Ontario.[2] Though the service providers I encountered were highly skilled, many lacked a framework for responding to conflicts over trans women's inclusion in women's spaces—conflicts in which those opposed to such inclusion have attempted to establish the justification for exclusion by making recourse to feminist ideology. As someone who worked on a variety of feminist projects prior to transitioning to male, I remain invested in the success of both trans and feminist movements. I acknowledge that I do not share the experience of being targeted in the ways in which trans women have been, and I continue to learn from trans women's sophisticated theorizing and activism. This chapter is an attempt to build on their important work in order to spark a discussion about transfeminism within social work. Tracing the political history of the conflict over trans women's access to women's services, I argue that transfeminism holds the potential to clarify contradictions in feminist thought as they manifest in barriers to service for trans women. Transfeminism, specifically when informed by an intersectional framework, enables new ways of conceiving of and creating safer spaces, ultimately providing a necessary resource for social work practitioners and educators navigating this contested terrain.

Language and Terminology: *Trans, Cis,* and *Feminism(s)*

Scott-Dixon (2006) notes that *feminist* and *trans* are not mutually exclusive groups, as there may be trans, non-trans, and anti-trans individuals who align themselves with feminism, as well as feminist, non-feminist, and anti-feminist individuals who align themselves with trans communities (p. 16). In this chapter I intend the term *trans* to be inclusive of identities such as transgender, transsexual, genderqueer, transitioned, and some Two-Spirited people—individuals who also occupy other social identities along lines of race, class, sexual orientation, disability, and more. During some historical moments described in this chapter, the only term used to describe a form of trans subjectivity was *transsexual*, popularized in the 1950s to describe those who sought medical technologies to change their sex (Stryker & Whittle, 2006). The term *transgender* emerged in the 1990s to capture a growing political movement devoted to challenging gender norms, at times at odds with some transsexuals' political goals. Whittle (in Stryker & Whittle, 2006) describes the development of the term *trans* as an attempt to unify the varied interests of transsexuals, transgender people, and others. For the sake of consistency, I use *trans* throughout and use the term *cisgender* to refer to people who are not trans (Serano, 2007).

Though I focus on trans women's relationship to feminism, this intersection is relevant to other trans people as well. Trans men (female to male) and genderqueer individuals (those whose identities are not contained within male or female) also require shelter and anti-violence services and also have stakes in feminist movements (Goldberg & White, 2006). The challenges in securing services for these groups are substantial and some have called for new services, not organized on the basis of gender, to augment existing gender-specific services (Denomme-Welch, Pyne, & Scanlon, 2008; Pyne, 2011; White & Goldberg, 2006). Yet a focus on trans women remains important as they are disproportionately targeted for violence and exclusion—a phenomenon recently named *trans-misogyny*—in particular racialized and Black trans women (Democracy Now, 2014). In contrast, the overvaluing of masculinity functions to offer trans men, particularly white trans men, comparatively greater safety and social inclusion. As both the exclusion of trans women from feminist services and the social action response have been unique, I focus this discussion accordingly.

North America has seen multiple waves of feminism, including its first wave (from the nineteenth to early twentieth centuries), second wave (beginning in the early 1960s), and third wave (beginning in the 1990s) which gave rise to competing streams of feminist thought including liberal, radical, socialist, Black, lesbian, and post-modern feminism (Freedman, 2007). All of these feminisms may operate simultaneously in a feminist-based organization; however, women-only services emerged specifically out of second wave radical feminism and many retain features of this analysis, discussed further below (Goldberg & White, 2006). The term *transfeminism* developed in the late 1990s to describe a movement led by trans women and allies who located themselves at the intersection of feminist and trans politics (Koyama, 2001). Transfeminist action strategies have included online activism and self-published writing (Koyama, 2001, 2006; Riddell, 2006; Ross, 1995;

Stone, 1996); academic scholarship (Namaste, 2000, 2005; Salah, 2007; Scott-Dixon, 2006; Stryker & Whittle, 2006); and training and policy development (Darke & Cope, 2002; The 519 Church Street Community Centre, 2013; White, 2003). Though not all authors use the term, for the sake of consistency I use *transfeminism* to refer to the scholars, activists, and texts that have advocated for trans inclusion within feminist communities and spaces.

A History of Trans Women and North American Feminism

As White (2003) notes, the second wave of feminism was an era of tremendous momentum and the issue of violence against women became a central focus for the movement. Out of shared experiences exchanged in radical feminist consciousness-raising groups, feminists began to build a theoretical framework for confronting the pervasive phenomenon of male violence. One of the crowning accomplishments of the second wave was the creation of woman-specific services such as rape crisis centres and shelters, an accomplishment that cannot be overstated given the paucity of government support at the time (Rebick, 2009). Radical feminist theory emphasized translating private experiences into broad political analyses. As Goldberg and White (2006) note, this methodology allowed for a profound challenge to male domination in the private sphere, yet at the same time also led the radical feminist movement to develop theories that reflected the limited life experience of its leadership (often white, middle-class, heterosexual, able-bodied, and cisgender women).

During the same decades, what would come to be called the trans rights movement was beginning in North America. In the US, after Christine Jorgensen's 1950s debut as the first highly publicized transsexual, more privileged cross-dressers and transsexuals began to organize quietly in suburban private clubs to express themselves, free from the restrictive laws and stigma of the time (Stryker, 2008). During the same period, racialized trans people were becoming highly visible members of street and urban culture in major American cities and were often targeted for harassment and violence by police (Stryker, 2008). A number of well-publicized clashes took place in the 1960s when these communities physically fought against authorities for public space, for example the 1966 Compton Cafeteria Riot in San Francisco and the 1969 Stonewall Inn Riot in New York. From this new visibility emerged the first networks of formal and informal social services for trans people in American urban centres.

The history of trans activism in Canada remains more challenging to report. Accounts of trans history are absent from important Canadian gay and lesbian texts (Smith, 1999; Warner, 2002), while texts focusing on Canadian trans activism have only recently begun to be published (Irving & Raj, 2014). The history of trans activism in Toronto and Montreal during the 1990s has been documented in some self-published work (Phillippa, 1993; Ross, 1995) and academic publications (Namaste, 2005). These accounts suggest that organizing goals reflected the subject positions of those engaged. For example, Ross (interviewed in Namaste, 2005) details the 1990s social action of Canadian transsexual women in the sex trade who prioritized the decriminalization of sex work, access to housing, and HIV/AIDS prevention and treatment, rather than the identity-based activism common to more privileged trans people.

White (2003) notes that it was predictable that emerging trans and radical feminist movements would collide over access to the new 1970s women's communities and services. While some trans women were welcomed in radical women's spaces in the 1960s and 1970s (Stryker, 2008), hostility toward trans people increased throughout the 1970s. Some have attributed this to the substantial investment in androgyny among lesbian and feminist activists of the time (Green, 2006). Groups perceived to embody aberrant types of femininity or masculinity, such as butches, femmes, drag queens, and trans women, were denounced. However, the condemnation of trans women was particularly severe and led to a number of active trans feminists being publically ousted from women's organizations. For example, Stryker (2008) notes that Beth Elliott, a trans woman, lesbian, and feminist musician, was singled out from the stage of the 1973 West Coast Lesbian Feminist Conference by keynote speaker Robin Morgan, who called for 1,200 attendees to vote on whether Elliott should be permitted to remain at the conference, even though she was a scheduled performer and a member of the organizing committee.

Transphobia within feminism was both exemplified and propelled by Janice G. Raymond's 1979 book *The Transsexual Empire: The Making of the She-Male*, which argued "all transsexuals rape women's bodies by reducing the real female form to an artefact, appropriating this body for themselves" (p. 104). With endorsements from influential feminists (Mary Daly, Germaine Greer, Andrea Dworkin, Adrienne Rich), Raymond's work left a legacy tainting subsequent feminist thought on transsexuality (Califia, 1997; Stone, 1996; Stryker & Whittle, 2006). Reading like a blueprint for the conflicts that would unfold in women's spaces, Raymond (1979) claimed transsexual women were not "real" women, their use of medical technology was detrimental to other women, and they posed a physical or sexual danger to cisgender women. The *Kimberley Nixon vs. Vancouver Rape Relief* case, outlined below, is one example of the codification of these biases within women's service provision.

In 1995, trans woman and survivor of gender-based violence Kimberley Nixon was dismissed on her first day of volunteer training at a women-only rape crisis centre (Vancouver Rape Relief) when staff members perceived her to be trans. Nixon was told that only women who had been born female and who had lived their entire lives as women could volunteer with the centre. She successfully filed a complaint with the British Columbia Human Rights Commission and was awarded the highest level of compensation for damages to date in that province (Namaste, 2005). Vancouver Rape Relief subsequently filed a petition to the Supreme Court of British Columbia to overturn the decision and met with success in 2003. Nixon lost a final bid to appeal the decision at the Supreme Court of Canada in 2007. The final ruling upheld the right of Vancouver Rape Relief to decide who *is* and who *is not* a woman, for the purposes of their organization (Denike, 2006). Though Nixon sought entry as a service provider, not a service user, the ruling had far-reaching implications and continues to threaten the provision of just services to trans women.

Feminist Contestation and Transfeminist Social Action

Debates stemming from the *Nixon vs. Vancouver Rape Relief* case erupted for more than a decade within feminist communities and scholarship. Those who were opposed to trans inclusion viewed Nixon's claim as a violation of women's space (Lansberg, 2000) and expressed concern for the well-being of cisgender women survivors of violence and for the future of women's organizing (Nolan, 2000). Those who were in favour of trans women's access understood the debate as an attack on trans women's personhood (Nolan, 2000) and the case took on a larger symbolic meaning (Elliot, 2010). It continues to focus Canadian transfeminist debates around terrain similar to that staked out by Raymond (1979). Below I discuss transfeminist responses to these key areas of contestation, which include the nature of sex and gender; the concept of a shared woman's experience; bodies and bodily sovereignty; and violence and safety. I conclude with a discussion of the implications for social work.

The Nature of Sex and Gender

Elliot (2010) remarks that the issue for those who oppose trans women's access to women's spaces is the threat of being forced to admit men into their organizations—a valid concern for a women's service. Yet Elliot (2010) argues this concern lacks validity with respect to trans women, unless one regards them as men. Of course, the key claim used to refute trans women's access to women's services is that they are not real women. Indeed, Lee Lakeman, of Vancouver Rape Relief, has stated so explicitly (Groocock-Renshaw, 2001). Califia (1997) notes those who make this claim often conflate sex and gender, and oscillate, sometimes within the same text, between citing trans women's biology and their socialization as that which makes them unsuitable (p. 87). These are both curious positions considering feminist history, and transfeminists have responded by revisiting basic feminist principles.

Trans women have often been refused women's resources on the basis that they were not born female. Yet in her groundbreaking work *The Second Sex*, Simone de Beauvoir (1949/1973) wrote, "One is not born a woman, but becomes one" (p. 301). A radical statement at the time, Beauvoir laid the groundwork for the theory of the social construction of gender and the now fundamental tenet of feminism: *biology is not destiny* (Scott-Dixon, 2006, p. 16). Thus women are not biologically determined to embody any of the traits oppressively associated with them. However, concerns about trans women do not end with biology, as they are also accused of not being real women due to their early *socialization* as males. As with biological arguments, exclusion based on presumed prior socialization is inconsistent with feminist principles. Serano (2007) points out that just as cisgender women might transcend their socialization to become feminists, or in fact to become what they choose, so might trans women transcend theirs (p. 241). Exclusion on the basis of "realness" is illegitimate, as neither biology nor socialization is a final determinant of human identity and potential.

Women's Experience

Intimately connected to the question of whether trans women are women, is another area of contestation: the concept of "woman's experience" and whether trans women can be said to share in it. Speaking for Vancouver Rape Relief, Lakeman stated trans women "don't know what it's like to be treated like a woman" (Groocock-Renshaw, 2001). Transfeminists (Goldberg & White, 2006; Koyama, 2006; Namaste, 2005) have responded to these claims by calling attention to the way in which the discourse of "women's experience" has been erroneously resurrected from second wave feminism, despite the work of racialized and lesbian feminists who argued decades ago that not all women shared the white middle-class heterosexual woman's experience at the centre of second wave feminism (hooks, 1984; Moraga & Anzaldua, 1981). More recently, Koyama (2006) has challenged the assumption that women's spaces ever welcomed all women, referring to this as "the unspoken racism in the trans inclusion debate" (p. 698). Stryker (in Stryker & Whittle, 2006) highlights early African American feminist Sojourner Truth's famous question "Ain't I a Woman?" noting that the battle for marginalized women to be recognized as women is not a new struggle for feminism.

Addressing the issue of a shared woman's experience has required some engagement with the claim that trans women possess male privilege, widely refuted by transfeminists. Cox (as cited in Romano, 2014) disputes this charge by pointing to the injustices young trans women face as feminine and gender non-conforming youth. Koyama (2001), who acknowledges her past male privilege as a stated act of solidarity with cis women, calls for an appreciation of the complexity of a *history* with male advantage and a *present* with both female and trans disadvantage (p. 3). Finally, the discourse of women's experience has been used to justify the exclusion of trans women service providers by suggesting that those who are not assigned female at birth are unfit to work with survivors of violence (Nolan, 2000). However, Hornick (2006) points out that if women naturally possessed counselling skills, this would render social work education and social service worker training unnecessary for all women. Recognizing multiple axes of social difference, transfeminists argue that women's experience is diverse and overlapped with many identities and interconnected forms of oppression and privilege.

Bodies and Bodily Sovereignty

Trans women seeking entry into women's spaces have often been regarded as suspect on the basis of how they embody their gender identity, including their personal style choices and/or the medical interventions that they do or do not seek (Daly, 1978; Greer, 1999; Hausman, 1995; Raymond, 1979). Indeed, Hausman (1995) views trans women as powerful agents who have convinced physicians to perform procedures she thinks highly problematic, while Jeffreys (1997) imagines transsexuality as a human rights violation with trans people as the victims of their own gender transitions. Further, gender transition has been described within feminism as a form of mutilation (Jeffreys, 1997; Raymond, 1979). Noting women's bodies are frequently battlegrounds for religious fundamentalism and medical science, Stone (1996) adds feminist theory to the list of battles waged on trans women's bodies (p. 230).

Trans women are often charged with over-subscribing to femininity (Jeffreys, 1997; Sweeney, 2004). Hausman (1995), for example, argues that trans women reproduce stereotypes so harmful to cisgender women that all access to transition ought to be discontinued. An image of trans women as caricatures of femininity has emerged consistently within public debate regarding access to women's space, including media coverage of the Kimberley Nixon case, which included references to "oversized heels" (Jacobs, 2000) and "feather boas and sequins" (Lansberg, 2000). Summarizing a common assumption within some threads of feminism, Sweeney (2004) declares, "Trans-women have a deep investment in defending femininity, and consequently, represent the antithesis to feminist social change" (p. 75). Yet not only does this statement inaccurately characterize all trans women as feminine, it also redraws the boundaries of feminism to curiously exclude "femininity." Serano (2007) suggests one of the contributions of transfeminism is a more empowering perspective on femininity.

Ironically, trans women have also been characterized as insufficiently feminine, and in some settings, expected to undergo the medical interventions that are regarded in such low esteem above. Indeed, some women's shelters have opted not to exclude trans women outright, but to make admission contingent on criteria such as completion of genital surgery (Namaste, 2000; Pyne, 2011). This has occurred in spite of the fact that many trans women do not desire such procedures, cannot afford them, or are medically ineligible to access them (Namaste, 2000).

Serano (2007) notes that with the overwhelming focus on trans women's bodies and appearances, rather than their characters and identities, the trans inclusion debate has a distinctly sexist feel to it. Moreover, absent from this discussion is an analysis of the societal forces that influence gender presentation for many trans women, including but not limited to public violence and the requirements of mental health professionals who confer or withhold approval for medical transition. Also absent from this discussion is an analysis of trans women's agency to consider and contest these and other forces. Transfeminism draws on the feminist analysis of reproductive choice, including the doctrine of "our bodies, our choice," to support trans women's claims for sovereignty over their bodies (Koyama, 2001, p. 9). Koyama (2001) calls on feminists to reserve scrutiny for the institutions that limit women's choices, rather than attack the choices that women make within these limitations (p. 3).

Violence and Safety

At the heart of the trans inclusion debate is the notion that trans women make women's spaces unsafe. Indeed, prominent second wave feminist thinkers quite openly stated that trans women are inherently comparable to rapists (Daly, 1978; Raymond, 1979). In the absence of any evidence that trans women pose such a threat to cisgender women, this notion was built on unsupportable theoretical foundations. For example, Raymond (1979) proposed that trans women were a patriarchal invention designed to infiltrate and destroy the women's movement (p. 135). Describing the process of male to female transition, Greer (1999) states, "When a man decides to spend his life impersonating his mother (like Norman Bates in *Psycho*) it is as if he murders her ..." (p. 74). Lansberg (2000) made similar discursive links to violence, describing Kimberley Nixon's human rights case as an "unwanted advance" and an "assault" on Vancouver Rape Relief.

My own experience with anti-violence service providers suggests that many do not consider trans women to be violent; rather, they are concerned that a trans woman who has not had sex reassignment (genital) surgery will trigger a survivor's past experience of violence and make her feel unsafe. To be clear, survivors' trauma from violence is very real and the importance of support is not in question. But to juxtapose trans women and survivors of violence constitutes a powerful discursive move, as a trans woman's own experiences and status as a survivor are obscured in this rendering of survivors and trans women as mutually exclusive groups. Subsequently, trans women's comfort and safety is positioned as less significant than that of cisgender women, though presumably most trans women would not find having their body scrutinized for suitability, to be comfortable or safe. While some cisgender women service users may express disapproval or even fear of trans women's bodies (as the opening quotation suggests), for a service provider to prioritize one woman's feelings about another woman's body is to reassert who owns a space and who must make application for entry. As Serano (2007) notes, in the debate over the acceptability of trans women's bodies, trans women appear to be expected to acquiesce to what their bodies signify to others.

As Namaste (2005) points out, the conception of safety and violence in the trans inclusion debate seems to preclude an awareness of, or appropriate response to, violence against trans people. However, the widespread and shocking nature of transphobic violence has received increasing attention as annual "Transgender Day of Remembrance" events publically mark this violence in a growing number of jurisdictions (Kennedy, 2011). Further, as many have noted, the violence in trans communities is not evenly distributed and instead overwhelmingly impacts racialized trans women who work in the sex trade (Namaste, 2005; White & Goldberg, 2006). Indeed, some have critiqued the public remembering practices within trans communities, charging that this violence ought to be remembered not simply as transphobic but also as racist, misogynist, and anti–sex worker, with a greater focus on the interlocking nature of oppression (Lamble, 2008; Namaste, 2005). Through the recent public activism of racialized trans women, the convergence of anti-Black racism and transphobia is more widely acknowledged than ever before (Democracy Now, 2014; Mock, 2014). Overall, transfeminism rejects the claim that trans women pose a disproportionate threat to cisgender women, rejecting as well any reductive analysis that neglects the intersecting realities of trans women with multiple marginalized identities.

Implications for Social Work

Transfeminist activism continues to have a profound impact on women's organizational policy and service provision. Findlay indicates that after transfeminist mobilizing around the Kimberley Nixon case, 80 percent or more of women's organizations in Canada developed trans inclusion policies (findlay, 2006, p. 152). Twenty-one women's organizations in British Columbia formed the Trans Alliance Society in opposition to Vancouver Rape Relief's stance, and a sister organization of Vancouver Rape Relief, the Toronto Rape Crisis Centre/Multicultural Women Against Rape, openly disagreed with their practice in a national newspaper (Nolan, 2000). Policy manuals and training resources were developed to assist women's organizations in writing inclusive policy (Darke & Cope, 2002), and widespread training has taken place within women's services in a number of Canadian cities, including Toronto and Vancouver. Yet despite this substantial progress, trans women continue to have very little voice in feminist organizations. There remains an absence of representation among the staff, board members, and volunteers in women's services, prompting Goldberg and White (2006) to state there is still much work to do.

A transfeminist analysis, informed by an intersectional framework, has implications for a number of streams of social work, including direct practice, research and policy, and professional education. For those in direct practice, transfeminism provides a framework to navigate conflicts over women's spaces in a manner that can do justice to both trans and cisgender women's multiple intersecting identities. The historical exploration of the trans inclusion debate demonstrates that trans women's struggles have not occurred in isolation but within the context of broader organizing by racialized women in particular, who have called attention to the dominance of more privileged women's voices within feminism. Social work practitioners using a transfeminist and an intersectional lens can respond to instances of transphobia within women's services using similar tools employed to respond to expressions of other forms of social violence such as racism, homophobia, and ableism. Important steps include education for staff and service users, programming to address the needs of diverse groups of trans women, and a commitment to seeking the representation of diverse trans women at every level of an organization. In residential services, a discussion of the organization's commitment to welcoming all women can be included within the intake process, and conflicts among residents can be addressed in a manner that affirms the diversity of trans women's experiences and their entitlement to service. Further, this analysis may assist practitioners in understanding why some trans women may not attempt to access service, thus guiding more effective outreach to trans communities. Lastly, practitioners should be aware that those trans women who may be most in need of services are those facing the convergence of multiple forms of social violence including racism, trans-misogyny, poverty, and sex worker stigma.

Focusing a research lens on trans women's experiences can also function to unsettle assumptions about who is included in feminist research. In research design, researchers might avoid making assumptions about women's "common" physiological characteristics, health-related needs, and social upbringing. Further, researchers can devote attention to how to best facilitate inclusive agencies, particularly for trans women whose gender identities intersect with other marginalized identities. For social workers engaged in organizational policy development, transfeminist thought illustrates that trans women's claims to women's spaces are deeply grounded in feminist principles and consistent with the mandates of feminist-based organizations. Policy change efforts can benefit from existing transfeminist resources (Darke & Cope, 2002).

In addition, transfeminism also offers important pedagogical opportunities for social work educators. Critical discussion of feminist theory can be enriched by raising questions about who speaks for women and for feminism. Course content on family violence and gender issues can better prepare students for the struggles over access to women's services that they may encounter in the field. Social work educators can use these debates to reveal tensions within anti-oppressive practice regarding competing claims to oppressed positions, while highlighting the importance of working in coalition. Educators can teach about interlocking forms of oppression by exploring how transphobia, racism, sex worker stigma, and misogyny work together to endanger groups on the margins, such as trans women. Lastly, the trans inclusion debate presents opportunities for educators to explore links between theoretical positions and the policies and practices these positions manifest in service provision.

In closing, social work literature increasingly addresses the marginalization of trans communities, often proposing interventions that reflect a less binarized and deterministic view of sex and gender (Burdge, 2007; McPhail, 2004). I have argued that, while helpful, this analysis does not capture the specificity of the feminist-based anti-violence service sector where the inclusion/exclusion of trans women has been bitterly debated for decades. Social work engagement in these debates has been markedly absent, impeding the ability of social work practitioners to respond in practice or in classroom settings to conflicts over safety and space. I have proposed transfeminism, informed by intersectionality, as a resource for social workers to navigate this contested terrain. Grounded in feminist principles, this framework holds the potential to transform women's services to truly welcome all women.

Notes

1. The author would like to thank Dana Baitz, Trish Salah, Morgan Page, Ken Moffatt, and Akua Benjamin for their helpful comments on earlier drafts, in addition to thanking the many trans women activists and writers who have fought to articulate these issues.
2. The Trans Access Project is a project of The 519 Church Street Community Centre in Toronto. This project began in 2001, thanks to the grassroots activism of Mirah Soleil Ross, Christina Strang, and Kyle Scanlon. I was personally involved in this work from 2001 to 2008.

References

Bauer, G., Boyce, M., Coleman, T., Kaay, M., Scanlon, K., & Travers, R. (2010). Who are trans people in Ontario? *Trans PULSE E-Bulletin, 1*(1). Retrieved from www.ohtn.on.ca/Documents/Publications/didyouknow/july28_10/E-Bulletin.pdf

Beauvoir, S. (1949/1973). *The second sex.* New York, NY: Vintage Books.

Burdge, B. (2007). Bending gender, ending gender: Theoretical foundations for social work practice with the transgender community. *Social Work, 52*(3), 243–250.

Burgess, C. (1999). Internal and external stress factors associated with the identity development of transgendered youth. *Journal of Gay & Lesbian Social Services, 10*(3), 35–47.

Califia, P. (1997). *Sex changes: The politics of transgenderism.* San Francisco, CA: Cleis Press.

Daly, M. (1978). *Gyn/ecology: The metaethics of radical feminism.* Boston, MA: Beacon Press.

Darke, J., & Cope, A. (2002). *Trans inclusion policy manual for women's organizations.* Women and Trans Dialogue Planning Committee/Trans Alliance Society. Retrieved from www.transalliancesociety.org/education/documents/02womenpolicy.pdf

Democracy Now (2014, February 19). "Black trans bodies are under attack": Freed activist CeCe McDonald, actress Laverne Cox speak out. Retrieved from http://www.democracynow.org/2014/2/19/black_trans_bodies_are_under_attack

Denike, M. (2006). Inclusion and exclusion. In K. Scott-Dixon (Ed.), *Trans/forming feminisms: Trans/feminist voices speak out* (p. 140). Toronto, ON: Sumach Press.

Denny, D. (2006). Transgender communities of the United States in the late twentieth century. In P. Currah, R. Juang, & S. Minter (Eds.), *Transgender rights* (pp.171–191). Minneapolis, MN: University of Minnesota Press.

Denomme-Welch, S., Pyne, J., & Scanlon, K. (2008). *Invisible men: FTMS and homelessness in Toronto*. Toronto, ON: The Wellesley Institute.

Elliot, P. (2010). *Debates in transgender, queer and feminist theory: Contested sites*. Surrey, England: Ashgate Publishing.

findlay, b. (2006). Acting queerly: Lawyering for trans people. In K. Scott-Dixon (Ed.), *Trans/forming feminisms: Trans-feminist voices speak out* (pp. 145–153). Toronto, ON: Sumach Press.

Freedman, E. (2007). *The essential feminist reader*. New York, NY: Modern Library.

Goldberg, J., & White, C. (2006). Anti-violence work in transition. In K. Scott-Dixon (Ed.), *Trans/forming feminisms: Trans-feminist voices speak out* (pp. 217–226). Toronto, ON: Sumach Press.

Grant, J., Mottet, L., Tanis, J., Harrison, J., Herman, J., & Keisling, M. (2011). *Injustice at every turn: A report of the national transgender discrimination survey*. Washington, DC: National Center for Transgender Equality and National Gay and Lesbian Task Force.

Green, E. (2006). Debating trans inclusion in the feminist movement: A trans positive analysis. *Journal of Lesbian Studies, 10*(1/2), 231–248.

Greer, G. (1999). *The whole woman*. London, England: Doubleday.

Groocock-Renshaw, N. (2001). Relief mission. *Elle Canada, 5*, 76–78.

Hausman, B. (1995). *Changing sex: Transsexualism, technology and the idea of gender*. Durham, NC: Duke University Press.

hooks, b. (1984). Black women: Shaping feminist theory. In b. hooks, *Feminist theory: From margin to center* (pp. 1–15). Boston, MA: South End Press.

Hornick, J. P. (2006). *For all women*. Brochure published by The 519 Church Street Community Centre, Toronto, ON.

Irving, D., & Raj, R. (2014). *Trans activism in Canada: A reader*. Toronto, ON: Canadian Scholars' Press.

Jacobs, M. (2000, December 17). Should transsexuals counsel rape victims? *Edmonton Sun*. Retrieved from www.fact.on.ca/news/news0012/es001217.htm

Jeffreys, S. (1997). Transgender activism: A lesbian feminist perspective. *Journal of Lesbian Studies, 1*(3/4), 55–74.

Kennedy, N. (2011, November 20). The balancing act of Transgender Remembrance Day. *Guardian*. Retrieved from www.theguardian.com/commentisfree/2011/nov/20/transgender-remembrance-day

Koyama, E. (2001). Transfeminist manifesto. Retrieved from minism.org/readings/epdf-rdg/tfmanifesto.pdf

Koyama, E. (2006). Who's feminism is it anyway? The unspoken racism of the trans-inclusion debate. In S. Stryker & S. Whittle (Eds.), *The transgender studies reader* (pp. 698–705). New York, NY: Routledge.

Lamble, S. (2008). Retelling racialized violence, remaking white innocence: The politics of interlocking oppressions in Transgender Day of Remembrance. *Sexuality Research & Social Policy, 5*(1), 24–42.

Lansberg, M. (2000, December 23). Rape crisis centre in BC endures assault. *Toronto Star*. Retrieved from www.fact.on.ca/news/news0012/ts001223.htm

Mallon, G. P. (1999). A call for organizational trans-formation. *Journal of Gay & Lesbian Social Services, 10*(3/4), 131–142.

McGihon, C. L. D. (1998). "Outside and inside, male and female" reconsidered. *Clinical Social Work Journal, 26*(4), 385-396.

McPhail, B. (2004). Questioning gender and sexuality binaries: What queer theorists, transgendered individuals, and sex researchers can teach social work. *Journal of Gay & Lesbian Studies, 11*(2), 3–21.

Mock, J. (2014). *Redefining realness: My path to womanhood, identity, love and so much more*. New York: Atria Books.

Moraga, C., & Anzaldua, G. (1981). *This bridge called my back: Writings by radical women of colour*. Watertown, MA: Persephone Press.

Nagoshi, J. L., & Brzuzy, S. (2010). Transgender theory: Embodying research and practice. *Affilia, 25*(4), 431–443.

Namaste, V. (2000). *Invisible lives: The erasure of transsexual and transgendered people*. Chicago, IL: University of Chicago Press.

Namaste, V. (2005). *Sex change, social change: Reflections on identity, institutions and imperialism*. Toronto, ON: Women's Press.

Nolan, S. (2000, December 9). Fighting to do a woman's work. *The Globe and Mail*. Retrieved from www.fact.on.ca/news/news0012/gm00120d.htm

Phillippa, X. (1993). *Gender Trash, 1*(1). [Out of print]

Pyne, J. (2011). Unsuitable bodies: Trans people and cisnormativity in shelter services. *Canadian Social Work Review, 28*(1), 129–137.

Raymond, J. (1979). *The transsexual empire: The making of the she-male*. Boston, MA: Beacon Press.

Rebick, J. (2009). *Transforming power: From the personal to the political*. Toronto, ON: Penguin Group.

Riddell, C. (2006). Divided sisterhood: A critical review of Janice Raymond's *The Transsexual Empire*. In S. Stryker & S. Whittle (Eds.), *The transgender studies reader* (pp. 144–158). New York, NY: Routledge.

Romano, T. (2014). Laverne Cox: I absolutely consider myself a feminist. *Dame Magazine*. Retrieved from http://damemagazine.com/2014/06/01/laverne-cox-i-absolutely-consider-myself-feminist

Ross, M. (1995). Investigating women's shelters. *Gendertrash, 3*, 7–10.

Salah, T. (2007). Transfixed in lesbian paradise. *Atlantis, 31*(2), 24–29.

Scott-Dixon, K. (2006). *Trans/forming feminisms: Trans/feminist voices speak out*. Toronto, ON: Sumach Press.

Serano, J. (2007). *Whipping girl: A transsexual woman on sexism and the scapegoating of femininity*. Emeryville, CA: Seal Press.

Smith, M. (1999). *Lesbian and gay rights in Canada: Social movements and equality-seeking, 1971–1995*. Toronto, ON: University of Toronto Press.

Stone, S. (1996). The empire strikes back: A posttranssexual manifesto. In K. Straub & J. Epstein (Eds.), *Body Guards: The Cultural Politics of Sexual Ambiguity*. New York, NY: Routledge.

Stryker, S. (2008). *Transgender history*. Berkley, CA: Seal Press.

Stryker, S., & Whittle, S. (2006). *The transgender studies reader*. New York, NY: Routledge.

Sweeney, B. (2004). Trans-ending women's rights: The politics of trans-inclusion in the age of gender. *Women's Studies International Journal, 27*, 75–88.

The 519 Church Street Community Centre. (2013). Trans Access Project. Retrieved 2013 from www.the519.org/programsservices/researcheducationandtraining/transaccessworkshops

Vachon, W. (2006). Transforming values/Engendering policy. In K. Scott-Dixon (Ed.), *Trans/forming feminisms: Trans-feminist voices speak out* (pp. 227–234). Toronto, ON: Sumach Press.

Warner, T. (2002). *Never going back: A history of queer activism in Canada.* Toronto, ON: University of Toronto Press.

White, C. (2003). *Re/defining gender and sex: Educating for trans, transsexual, and intersex access and inclusion to sexual assault centres and transition houses.* Unpublished master's thesis, University of British Columbia, Vancouver, Canada.

White, C., & Goldberg, J. (2006). Expanding our understanding of gendered violence: Violence against trans people and their loved ones. *Canadian Woman Studies, 25*(1/2), 124–128.

CHAPTER 8
Beyond Stress and Burden: Exploring the Intersectionality of Gay Caregiving

Hossein Kia

The study of informal caregiving, in the context of chronic illness, has expanded significantly in recent years as a recognized area of academic inquiry. A number of writers have attributed this heightened interest in caregiving research to increases in populations of older or ailing adults across the developed world (Cahill, 2007), as well as the growing reliance of Western welfare states on "informal care" to address issues accompanying this population trend (Kadushin & Egan, 2005; Globerman, White, & McDonald, 2002). Despite general interest in studying issues related to caregiving, few attempts have been made to examine phenomena of informal care among lesbian, gay, and bisexual (LGB) minority groups (Fredriksen-Goldsen & Hoy-Ellis, 2005).

In this chapter, I outline the findings of a study initially aimed at exploring how five caregiving partners of gay men "story" their experiences, or construct their subjective realities in narrative form, and revisit these findings with attention to intersectionality as a relevant frame of analysis. More specifically, I consider the applicability of intersectionality as a lens with which to reconceptualize the findings of the study, present new insights that an intersectional framework provides, and highlight different ways such a focus can contribute to social work knowledge. An intersectional lens facilitates an analysis of how various components of identity interact at the interface of personal narrative and social context (Davy, 2011; Yuval-Davis, 2006). I utilize this framework to illustrate how the complex array of intersecting identities and experiences of power, privilege and disadvantage, and interrelated structural factors, influence and are reflected in each of the caregiver's personal narratives. I then consider the implications of such analysis for social work practice and policy.

Positioning the Study: Identifying Gaps in Past Caregiving Literature

In recognizing bodies of literature associated with the study of informal care, writers linked with three foundational theoretical traditions have historically conceptualized the constructs of informal "caring" and "caregiving." Those concerned with studying "stress" and "burden" in the realm of informal care have primarily examined the prevalence of stress, as well as factors that influence the presence of this phenomenon, in contexts (e.g. illness) that force the "burden of care" to be disproportionately distributed on one or more persons in a relational field (Knight, Lutzky, & Macofsky-Urban, 1993; Pearlin, Mullan, Semple, & Skaff, 1990; Sorensen, Pinquart, & Duberstein, 2002; Zarit, Reever, & Bach-Peterson, 1980). Critical feminist writers, in contrast, have drawn attention to the invisibility of caring labour often performed by female kin-based caregivers, and some have argued an exclusive focus on "stress" and "burden" may be inadequate to address issues of power that are located in gendered contexts of care (Hankivsky, 2004; Ruddick, 1989; Tronto, 1993; Ward-Griffin, Brown, Vandervoort, & McNair, 2005). Constructivist writers concerned with the study of care have, in contrast to both "stress" and "burden" researchers and feminist theorists, focused primarily on how caring experiences are constructed within a variety of relational contexts. In so doing, they have explored substantively how language and discourse factor into caregiving as a process of social construction (Adams, 1998; Adams, 2000; O'Connor, 2007).

All three bodies of literature have been criticized, either explicitly or implicitly, for predominantly failing to address the realities of LGB caregivers (Hash, 2001; Ward-Griffin et al., 2005). In light of such shortcomings in traditional caregiving literature, some have started to examine non-heterosexual care as a phenomenon that is uniquely situated in contexts marked by homophobia and heterosexism (Brotman, Ryan, Collins, Chamberland, Cormier, Julien, Meyer, Peterkin, & Richard, 2007; Fredriksen, 1999; Fredriksen-Goldsen, 2005; Grossman, D'Augelli, & Dragowski, 2005; Hash, 2001; Hash & Cramer, 2003; Kayal, 1993; King, 1995; Omoto & Crain, 1995; Shippy, 2005). The studies broadly suggest non-heterosexual caregivers often lack appropriate support, are met with homophobic hostility by health care providers, and, among other realities, hide the nature of their same-sex caring partnerships from health professionals for fear of being discriminated against (Brotman et al., 2007; Hash, 2001; Hash & Cramer, 2003; Shippy, 2005).

Regardless of the limited body of research on the realities of LGB caregiving, theoretical frameworks that appropriately capture issues specific to LGB care have yet to be developed. As already noted, a lens of intersectionality will be introduced as a framework that could facilitate a conceptualization of experiences evident in the narratives of gay caregivers (Davy, 2011; Yuval-Davis, 2006). Hulko (2009) describes intersectionality as a paradigm that draws attention to the ways in which varying social identities interact with one another in the realm of individual experience, and specifically discusses its applicability in analyzing processes of subordination and domination within which these interactions are often based. As I will illustrate in subsequent sections of this chapter, this framework is well suited to examining the complexity of interfaces between subjective experience and structural context that appear to be salient in the stories of gay carers.

Adopting a Constructivist Epistemological Position

Though I have thus far provided theoretical and conceptual bases for pursuing research on gay caregiving, it is also important to delineate my own social location as a frame of reference that has shaped the parameters of the research being discussed and my understanding of the participants' narratives. Being myself a gay social worker employed in health care, I have often been sensitized to scenarios in which caregiving partners of gay patients have explicitly discussed the challenges of providing care in social contexts that they describe as being homophobic and/or heterosexist. Accordingly, I understand that the rationale for conducting the study was not only based in external realities associated with gay caregiving, but was also influenced by my own subjectivity as a gay social worker and researcher. Similarly, I acknowledge that the results of the research may have been products of co-construction that likely arose in my interaction with research participants, since elements of shared experience potentially framed how respondents' realities were understood and conceptualized.

Because I also identify as Middle Eastern, middle-class, and able-bodied, and often participants did not share realities that would pertain to these components of my identity, I recognize that the dynamic process of co-construction required reflection and clarification with the participants. This position is consistent with a constructivist orientation in qualitative research that, in accordance with its critiques of objectivity, conceptualizes reality as a "co-construction" between researchers and participants whose subjectivities may comprise elements of both shared and discrepant social location, the contents of which often necessitate careful acknowledgment, reflection, and analysis (Clandinin & Rosiek, 2007; Creswell, 2006).

Methods

As indicated above, the qualitative study on which the chapter is based was originally designed to explore how five Canadian caregiving partners of gay men "story" their experiences or construct their subjective realities in the form of narratives. The research was conducted in a large Canadian urban centre, and received approval from the Behavioural Research Ethics Board at the University of British Columbia.

Five participants partook in the study, all of whom were recruited with assistance from personal contacts and local social service agencies serving lesbian, gay, bisexual, and transgender (LGBT) clients. Purposive sampling strategies were used to invite participants who were of adult age, who were fluent in the English language, and, most importantly, who identified as same-sex caregiving partners of gay men with chronic illness. Table 8.1 provides a detailed overview of participant characteristics.

All five respondents participated in two in-depth (one- to one-and-a-half-hour) semi-structured interviews. During initial interviews, I encouraged the caregivers to share their stories by specifically asking them about

1. how they had come to self-identify as caregivers;
2. the unique challenges and rewards they had experienced in their stories as gay caregivers; and
3. their overall stories as caregiving partners of gay men.

Follow-up interviews were primarily left unstructured, and were conducted as a member check, in order for participants to review the authenticity and trustworthiness of my interpretations of the interviews (Hollingsworth & Dybdahl, 2007).

Subsequent to each interview, I would analyze the data by reading and rereading transcriptions of the interviews. I used Clandinin and Connelly's (2000) three-dimensional model of narrative analysis to guide this process. This model is premised on the notion that the content of stories is not only structured temporally, but is also organized according to elements of interaction (both personal and social) and physical space. This approach enabled a thematic analysis of "storied"

Table 8.1: Participant Characteristics

Alias	Age	Current or Past Caregiver (Length of Time Since Experience)	Legal Nature of Partnership with Care Recipient	Nature of Care Recipient's Illness	Length of Partnership
Pedro	39	Current	Married	HIV	7 years
Rob	22	Current	Common-law*	Arthritis and nystagmus/astigmatism	8 years
Nick	44	Past (10 years)	Legally undefined	HIV/AIDS	7 months
Joseph	55	Past (1 year)	Married	Gastric cancer	27 years
Mylo	44	Current	Common-law*	CVA/stroke/aphasia	15 years

* In both cases above, participants identified the status of their respective relationships as "common-law," which would legally refer to relationships characterized by two years' cohabitation in their provincial jurisdictions.

experience that focused specifically on how participants referred to each of these dimensions literally and/or figuratively when structuring their narratives, which then facilitated an exploration of the content located within these categories of storied account.

The Stories

Pedro

Pedro, a self-identified gay Latino man in his late thirties, immigrated to Canada several years ago after meeting Andrew, his HIV-positive partner, in Mexico. Pedro indicated Andrew had communicated his HIV status to him soon after the couple had met, and had given the respondent some time to decide whether or not he would commit to a relationship that would likely involve care and support. Pedro consciously decided to enter into a relationship with Andrew, believing it to constitute an "opportunity" and a "challenge," and was assured by his partner that the commitment could be revisited "day by day." He explained that, once he was in Canada, his caring role with Andrew primarily entailed assisting him with daily activities such as cooking, and occasional support with personal care. While acknowledging that the couple had predominantly experienced positive interactions with health professionals, Pedro also indicated they had often felt uncomfortable with some service providers who appeared hostile to them on the basis of their sexual orientation and Andrew's HIV status. He additionally indicated expressions of homophobia at times combined with manifestations of racism. Pedro suggested this was particularly evident when it appeared service providers suspected him of exploiting his ill white partner because he was a younger Latino man. He stated,

> In [Canadian] health [settings], you are with more open-minded people. At the same time, it doesn't mean everybody's gay, but yes, you need to be [more] open [to issues of sexuality]. I think the thing that moves [Canadian service providers] more, or shocks them more ... is when they see the difference of age.... They really jump a little bit.... In my mind it's like, they think "oh, this is the hot Latino who is taking advantage of this sick Canadian guy," sometimes. I cannot say that I'm 100 percent sure, but sometimes you have that feeling.

Rob

Rob met Allan when they were both still adolescents. The participant explained to me that his partner had developed chronic arthritis and visual impairments, the combination of which had eventually prompted Rob to accept caregiving responsibilities with Allan. Similar to Pedro, Rob had been given some time to reconsider his commitment at the onset of Allan's symptoms, and he had consciously chosen to maintain a relationship with his partner because of their strong relational ties. Rob's caring activities primarily included organizing Allan's medical appointments and accompanying him to these meetings when necessary. Rob spoke at length about perceiving homophobic discrimination in health care settings, particularly during instances in which he would be denied entry into medical spaces as Allan's partner:

> If Allan wants me to come in [to see the doctor] with him, we have to expressly say so and be really firm about it and push the issue, which is ridiculous. When I need to follow my female friends, I literally just follow them in and nobody says a word about it. And then I see this happen to me, and that's sad.

Rob also described encountering ableist attitudes in his interactions with other gay men, particularly when he asserted his commitment to a partner with functional impairments in the context of his social network. For instance, he indicated that the couple's gay acquaintances would often comment on Rob's commitment to Allan as being marked by "burden" and cumbersome responsibility, which Rob in turn perceived as a delegitimization of the couple's relationship on the basis of Allan's abilities. He explained that to mitigate and attempt to resist these sexuality- and ability-related sources of marginalization, both he and Allan placed great significance on the strength of their bond, and believed themselves to constitute "family," regardless of the lack of legitimacy granted to them as a couple by the health care system and by the mainstream gay community.

Nick

Ten years prior to the study, Nick had cared for William, a gay man who eventually died of HIV/AIDS in a rural region of Canada. Nick indicated to me that he had made an agreement with William, following the end of a brief dating relationship between the two men, to provide him with care should his health condition decline at any point. At least in part, Nick had agreed to assist William with his care because he was aware William was reluctant to seek formal support from rural health care providers, whom he feared would stigmatize him as a gay man with HIV:

> [William] knew the hospital had no awareness or no understanding of [HIV]. Cause when he had pneumonia, before, when he was outed by HIV, that happened I believe in [the city]. So he was aware that HIV hadn't really hit the [rural] hospital. ... And William was the first in that hospital.

William did eventually begin developing symptoms related to the progression of HIV, at which point Nick started providing him with instrumental support (e.g. cooking and cleaning), some personal care, and eventually, assistance with medical decision-making during the care recipient's final days at a local hospital. Nick described his caring experience as a profoundly spiritual one, and attributed the presence of such spiritual meaning, among other factors, to his reality as a gay man who had helped another non-heterosexual man die amid the HIV/AIDS epidemic with only minimal reliance on formal systems of care.

Joseph

Joseph and Edwin, a retired married couple based in a large urban centre, had been together for more than 25 years when the latter was diagnosed with gastric cancer. Joseph's interviews were conducted approximately two years after Edwin first received his diagnosis, and one year after his death. The participant explained to me that he had started identifying as a caregiver immediately following his partner's diagnosis, but had seldom articulated his identification with this role. Instead, he had often believed his caregiving position to constitute an extension of his existing relational role as Edwin's legal spouse, and had not, therefore, consciously reflected on the realities of giving care while engaged in this capacity. As a caregiver, Joseph provided his partner with the full range of care support: he accompanied Edwin to medical appointments, provided personal care, and contributed to medical decision-making. Although anticipating some homophobia during the course of the couple's many encounters with health care professionals, Joseph suggested he had been treated exceptionally well, and had been relieved of such concerns after being explicitly and appropriately recognized as Edwin's partner in medical settings:

> [Health care providers] took the initiative [of asking about our relationship to one another] in a very nice way. They'd say to Edwin, "I'm doctor so and so," and then they'd turn to me and say "oh, and who are you?" Or they'd introduce themselves, and I would say "Joseph," and they'd say, "what's your relationship?" in a nice way. It's training. Providers should learn how to, in a respectful way, discern who is this person standing beside the patient.

A central theme in Joseph's story included the profound grief he experienced over the loss of his partner, as well as his perceived need to identify sources of support and meaning as a single gay man following this challenging event in his life.

Mylo

Mylo began identifying as a caregiver after Diego, his partner of approximately 15 years, became hospitalized for a stroke. He informed me Diego's hospitalization had been lengthy, and that he had stayed at his partner's bedside nearly full-time for three months in the span of this relatively longer-term admission. The interview was conducted two years after Diego's hospitalization, when the couple was once more living at home. At the beginning of his caregiving story, Mylo described how he had started experiencing his relationship with Diego differently upon the couple's transition into an institutional setting. He expressed fearing that, because of Diego's post-stroke speech impairment, his partner would be unable to resist potential hostility by service providers. Mylo was also concerned about the discrimination Diego might encounter as a sexual minority. He specified Diego's functional limitations, together with his sexual identity, contributed to his vulnerabilities, and these were located at the interface of sexuality and issues of ability:

> You always wonder how he's going to be treated when you know that he can't talk or he can't talk for himself. Like, he can't tell [professionals] what he wants.... At one point, [the gay issue] didn't really play a whole lot in my head, but at first, when we first went into the hospital, it did. I thought, "oh okay, here we are, a gay couple going into the hospital, we'll have issues".... And you know, we really didn't.

Mylo also shared that he would often have to correct heterosexist assumptions made by other patients and their family members about the couple's relationship to one another. Additionally, he indicated he had experienced conflict with Diego's sister over retaining his role as a primary medical decision-maker. The remainder of Mylo's story revolved around the value he placed on informal networks of friendship, which he described as "a different kind of family." These networks were important sources of support in his partner's ongoing recovery, particularly in light of relatively limited involvement by the couple's families of origin.

Discussion

Intersectionality as a Lens for Conceptualizing the Study's Findings

In exploring the narratives of the five gay caregivers featured in this study, a number of common themes were originally apparent. These included (1) participants' perceptions of "choice" and conscious decision-making in committing to caregiving roles within non-conventional relational contexts; (2) carers' experiences of anticipated, felt, and overt expressions of homophobia and heterosexism; (3) the value respondents appeared to place on gay-friendly sources of support; and (4) caregivers' unique constructions of "family" and "partnership" in the realm of same-sex caring partnerships. However, significant differences in each of the stories also reflected the possibility that the themes had distinct meanings for each of the participants, depending on the varied intersecting identities each occupied. Some of the participants' stories, in particular, revealed how structural factors other than homophobia and heterosexism intersected alongside issues of sexual orientation to produce complex interfaces of personal narrative and social context. More specifically, culture, race, (dis)ability, age, and geographic and historical location appeared to influence how different participants constructed and narrated their stories.

Research on caregiver stress and burden (Pearlin et al., 1990; Zarit et al., 1980), as well as feminist (Hankivsky, 2004; Ward-Griffin et al., 2005) and constructivist (Adams, 1998; Adams, 2000; O'Connor, 2007) literature on care, may present both opportunities and shortcomings in conceptualizing the findings of the current study. "Stress" and "burden" constructs may be useful in explaining experiences of distress recounted by many of the participants, but this framework may also be limited in addressing the systemic/structural contexts in which such realities appear to have been located. Though feminist lenses on care, which principally emphasize the construction of gendered care, may be used to conceptualize some of the structural and power-related issues invoked in the current study, earlier feminist perspectives have historically neglected issues of sexual orientation found in the context of care (Hash, 2001). Finally, constructivist frames of reference, which primarily attend to subjective realities found within diverse contexts of care (Adams, 2000), may be useful in situating the accounts of gay men whose caregiving experiences appeared to vary depending on relational and broader social factors. However, such lenses, on their own, fail to fully address structural issues specific to the lives of gay carers and, by extension, how different contexts influence each of the individual participants' subjective understandings of the structural issues experienced. Given the strengths and limitations of the three frameworks, specifically in relation to attending to both subjective and multifaceted structural factors associated with the stories of participants, I propose employing intersectionality as an additional framework that can serve to more comprehensively situate the findings of this study.

Under a framework of intersectionality, each person is said to comprise complex identities with multiple facets that intersect at the interface of personal narrative and social context, and each individual is therefore said to develop a complex and ever changing subjectivity that is in part shaped by both personal and political dimensions of the self (Cronin & King, 2010; Davy, 2011; Hulko, 2009; Yuval-Davis, 2006). Given the complex interplay of subjective experience and multidimensional structural context based on factors related to sexual orientation, race, age, and ability present in the narratives of the respondents, the use of such a lens may be applicable. I will revisit the experiences and stories of the five gay carers, and discuss how structural and systemic elements based on different aspects of their identities and subjective positions impacted how they constructed and made meaning of their experiences as caregiving partners of gay men. More specifically, I will consider differences in intersecting dimensions of sexual orientation, age, culture, race, geographic and historical location, and disability.

Pedro's and Rob's stories reflect the suitability of using intersectionality as a lens for addressing and theorizing the realities invoked in this study, specifically given the framework's emphasis on recognizing multiple structural factors that are likely to co-exist within individual narratives (Cronin & King, 2010; Davy, 2011). Although Pedro discussed experiencing homophobia and heterosexism in his story, he indicated his social location as a younger Latino man had exposed him to vulnerabilities specifically located at the intersection of race and age. These dimensions of his identity—and the experiences that related to them— at times appeared more salient to him in his caregiving relationship with an older white HIV-positive man. Similarly, despite the pronounced presence of homophobia and heterosexism in Rob's story, this participant indicated he and his partner also encountered ableist attitudes in their interactions with other gay men, particularly following the onset of the care recipient's impairments. These experiences of ableism intersected with issues surrounding sexual identity, and were influential in shaping Rob's realities as a caregiving partner of a man with functional impairments. The narratives, when analyzed through the framework of intersectionality, illustrate that structural issues related to sexual orientation may co-exist with other sources of marginalization in the stories of gay caregivers, often depending on individual social location.

Mylo's story, when analyzed using a lens of intersectionality, enables a consideration of how multiple systemic issues, rather than simply co-occurring, can at times combine to construct unique realities within the realm of subjective experience. In his narrative, the respondent indicated he had anticipated experiencing homophobia when he and his partner had first entered a hospital setting at the onset of the latter's stroke, and that he particularly feared his partner's stroke-related speech impediment would render him more vulnerable to possible homophobic hostility by service providers on the basis of his new functional limitations. A framework of intersectionality, with its focus on how structural factors can combine to produce entirely unique realities in the scope of subjective experience (Yuval-Davis, 2006), would highlight this particular expression of interfacing sexuality and ability-related factors as grounds for recognizing complex idiosyncrasies that may surface in the unique relational contexts of some gay caregivers.

Employing intersectionality to attend to experiences highlighted in Nick's and Joseph's stories yields yet different insights, particularly when considering the attention that this theoretical orientation draws to geographic, historical, and/or institutional factors that exert significant influence on the lived experience of privilege and marginalization (Cronin & King, 2010). Whereas Nick was located in a rural setting while caring for William, Joseph resided in a large urban centre, and the otherwise comparable (white, able-bodied, and gay) participants' experiences appeared to be distinguished and differentiated by geographic context, among other factors. Because William was concerned he would be stigmatized on the basis of a disease linked with gay sexuality (King, 1995), Nick avoided exposing him to a hospital setting whenever possible. William's concerns and Nick's response were strongly influenced by the rural geographic location of the hospital where health care professionals had limited knowledge of HIV and few resources for professional education. In contrast, Joseph explained that he had had access to service providers he believed were informed on matters related to same-sex sexuality and therefore felt he had encountered few systemic barriers as a gay carer. Accordingly, Nick and Joseph, regardless of identity-based factors that appeared similar on the surface, described vastly different structural realities that marginalized and privileged their experiences of giving care distinctively.

In addition to geographic location, it is important to consider the influence of the dominant culture and the historical context at the time when William and Nick were exposed to the stigma they experienced. Nick had been William's caregiver 10 years prior to bring interviewed, at a time when HIV knowledge was limited and HIV stigma was pervasive in dominant culture (King, 1995). The couple's experiences contrasted with the positive encounters Joseph presented, where he was actively involved in discussing his partner's care with health professionals. Analyzing Nick's and Joseph's stories, using a lens of intersectionality, brings the geographic, historical, cultural, and institutional factors into focus and demonstrates how these dimensions influence the experiences of gay caregivers with apparently similar bases for privilege and marginalization in vastly different ways.

Based on the above application of intersectionality to the participants' narratives, it is apparent the use of this framework generates insight into how multiple structural factors can co-exist alongside homophobia and heterosexism in individual experiences of gay carers. Intersectionality also highlights how these systemic factors can combine to produce entirely unique realities in LGB individuals, and how gay caregivers' geographic, historical, cultural, and institutional contexts can exert significant influence in the construction of their experiences. In the next section, I outline implications of this analysis on social work practice and policy.

Intersectionality: Implications for Social Work Practice and Policy

When conceptualized using a framework of intersectionality, the study's findings provide new insight into how social workers could practise with gay carers whose lives approximate some resemblance to those involved in the study. One direct practice implication includes the need for practitioners to be cognizant of the possibility that some gay caregivers may anticipate or experience systemic homophobia and heterosexism, along with other sources of oppression such as racism and ageism, as their personal caregiving narratives come to be situated in institutional contexts historically perceived as stigmatizing on multiple grounds. In recognizing marginalization on the basis of sexual orientation, social workers engaged in clinical practice must be conscious that they could make heterosexist assumptions about relationships between caregivers and care recipients of the same sex. In addition to engaging in reflexive practice, they can specifically ask open-ended questions that enable same-sex couples to define the nature of their relationships in language they deem appropriate. While being cognizant of the potential impact of structural and systemic factors that perpetuate heterosexism and homophobia, it is also important for social workers to adequately acknowledge the presence of other intersecting dimensions that impact the lives of gay carers. To meaningfully address the impact of intersecting forms of oppression based on diverse grounds, practitioners need to thoroughly explore the influence of structural and systemic forms of oppression, such as racism and ageism, with caregivers. Through a mutual exploration of the caregiver's experiences from his unique perspective, then, comes the foundation to address these experiences, and in working together, the provision of care. As an example, Mylo's challenges of giving care, some of which were located at an interface of sexuality and issues of ability, could have been mitigated to some extent if service providers had thoroughly explored his concerns surrounding Diego's perceived vulnerabilities within the health care system, and would have assisted him in setting parameters for his partner's care in a hospital setting.

In outlining macro-level implications for social work practice based on a framework of intersectionality, it may be important for social workers devising policy at the institutional level to recognize that conventional standards for establishing kinship may unfairly disadvantage some gay carers whose partnerships diverge from heterosexist and cultural norms. In response, social workers may need to develop policy and mechanisms for ensuring gay caregivers' ability to be primary decision-makers for their partners is recognized, especially in the absence of formal legal arrangements such as marriage or common-law status. They may also need to take steps to influence organizational contexts, for instance by encouraging LGBTQ-positive signage, and by challenging policies that systemically oppress caregivers and their partners on the basis of sexuality and other intersecting dimensions of their lives.

Another implication for social work at the policy level includes the need for practitioners to advocate for—and develop—formal structures and opportunities for health care providers to receive training on recognizing and responding to issues of marginalization apparent in the lives of gay carers. Importantly, given that systemic issues evident in the study appeared to relate not only to homophobia and heterosexism, but also to realities of race, culture, ability, and geographic and historical location, social workers may advocate for the creation of training mechanisms that seek to educate health care providers on the range of structural factors that affect sexual minorities and other disadvantaged groups as they access formal systems of care. Such education may, for instance, enhance the capability of service providers in health care to ask appropriate open-ended questions to sexual minority patients and caregiving partners about their relationships to one another, while simultaneously acknowledging the possible influence of issues specific to race, culture, and other factors in their experiences of accessing care. Given notable differences in the stories of Joseph and Nick, many of which could be attributed to distinctions in the extent of training and knowledge of social issues among health care providers in disparate geographic and historical contexts, such a recommendation may be particularly salient.

Conclusion

In this chapter, I outlined a study initially aimed at exploring how five caregiving partners of gay men "story" their experiences, and then discussed the applicability of intersectionality as a frame of reference for conceptualizing aspects of the study's findings. As noted in the latter sections of the chapter, although respondents appeared to construct their caregiving experiences by ascribing significance or meaning to their relational realities as gay carers, these accounts were often situated in complex structural contexts defined by multiple factors related to sexual orientation, race, ability, and other sources of influence. Accordingly, a lens of intersectionality enabled a conceptualization of the findings that attended both to the role of subjective reality and the multitude of structural issues located in the realm of the participants' narratives. This analysis, in turn, provided a comprehensive foundation for determining implications of the study for social work practice and policy.

References

Adams, T. (1998). The discursive construction of dementia care: Implications for mental health nursing. *Journal of Advanced Nursing, 28*(3), 614–621.

Adams, T. (2000). The discursive construction of identity by community psychiatric nurses and family members caring for people with dementia. *Journal of Advanced Nursing, 32*(4), 791–798.

Brotman, S., Ryan, B., Collins, S., Chamberland, L., Cormier, R., Julien, D., Meyer, E., Peterkin, A., & Richard, B. (2007). Coming out to care: Caregivers of gay and lesbian seniors in Canada. *The Gerontologist, 47*(4), 490–503.

Cahill, S. (2007). The coming GLBT boom. *Gay and Lesbian Review Worldwide, 13*(7), 19–21.

Clandinin, D. J., & Connelly, F. M. (2000). Narrative *inquiry: Experience and story in qualitative research.* San Francisco, CA: Jossey-Bass.

Clandinin, D. J., & Rosiek, J. (2007). Mapping a landscape of narrative inquiry: Borderland spaces and tensions. In D. J. Clandinin (Ed.), *Handbook of narrative inquiry: Mapping a methodology* (pp. 3–34). Thousand Oaks, CA: Sage.

Creswell, J. W. (2006). Qualitative *inquiry and research design: Choosing among five traditions.* Thousand Oaks, CA: Sage.

Cronin, A., & King, A. (2010). Power, inequality and identification: Exploring diversity and intersectionality amongst older LGB adults. *Sociology, 44*(5), 876–892.

Davy, Z. (2011). The promise of intersectionality theory in primary care. *Quality in Primary Care, 19*(5), 279–281.

Fredriksen, K. (1999). Family caregiving responsibilities among lesbians and gay men. *Social Work, 44*(2), 142–155.

Fredriksen-Goldsen, K. (2005). HIV/AIDS caregiving: Predictors of well-being and distress. *Journal of Gay and Lesbian Social Services, 18*(3/4), 53–73.

Fredriksen-Goldsen, K., & Hoy-Ellis, C. (2005). Caregiving with pride: An introduction. *Journal of Gay and Lesbian Social Services, 18*(3/4), 1–13.

Globerman, J., White, J., & McDonald, G. (2002). Social work restructuring in hospitals. *Health and Social Work, 27*(4), 274–283.

Grossman, A. H., D'Augelli, A. R., & Dragowski, E. A. (2005). Caregiving and care receiving among older lesbian, gay and bisexual adults. *Journal of Gay and Lesbian Social Services, 18*(3/4), 15–38.

Hankivsky, O. (2004). *Social policy and the ethic of care.* Vancouver, BC: UBC Press.

Hash, K. (2001). Preliminary study of caregiving and post-caregiving experiences of older gay men and lesbians. *Journal of Gay and Lesbian Social Services, 13*(4), 87–94.

Hash, K., & Cramer, E. (2003). Empowering gay and lesbian caregivers and uncovering their unique experiences through the use of qualitative methods. *Journal of Gay and Lesbian Social Services, 15*(1/2), 47–63.

Hollingsworth, S., & Dybdahl, M. (2007). Talking to learn: The critical role of conversation in narrative inquiry. In D. J. Clandinin (Ed.), *Handbook of narrative inquiry: Mapping a methodology*. Thousand Oaks, CA: Sage.

Hulko, W. (2009). The time- and context-contingent nature of intersectionality and interlocking oppressions. *Affilia, 24*(1), 44–55.

Kadushin, G., & Egan, M. (2005). Managed care in home health: Social work practice and unmet client needs. *Social Work in Health Care, 41*(2), 1–18.

Kayal, P. M. (1993). *Bearing witness: Gay men's health crisis and the politics of AIDS*. Boulder, CO: Westview.

King, N. (1995). HIV and the gay male community: One clinician's reflections over the years. In G. M. Herek & B. Greene (Eds.), *AIDS, identity and community: The HIV epidemic and lesbians and gay men* (pp. 1–18). Thousand Oaks, CA: Sage.

Knight, B. G., Lutzky, S. M., & Macofsky-Urban, F. (1993). A meta-analytic review of interventions for caregiver distress: Recommendations for future research. *The Gerontologist, 33*(2), 240–248.

O'Connor, D. (2007). Self-identifying as a caregiver: Exploring the positioning process. *Journal of Aging Studies, 21*(2), 165–174.

Omoto, A. M., & Crain, A. L. (1995). AIDS volunteerism: Lesbian and gay community-based responses to HIV. In G. M. Herek & B. Greene (Eds.), *AIDS, identity and community: The HIV epidemic and lesbians and gay men* (pp. 187–209). Thousand Oaks, CA: Sage.

Pearlin, L. I., Mullan, J. T., Semple, S. J., & Skaff, M. M. (1990). Caregiving and the stress process: An overview of concepts and their measures. *The Gerontologist, 30*(5), 583–594.

Ruddick, S. (1989). *Maternal feminism: Toward a politics of peace*. Boston, MA: Beacon Press.

Shippy, R. A. (2005). We cannot go it alone: The impact of informal support and stressors in older gay, lesbian and bisexual caregivers. *Journal of Gay and Lesbian Social Services, 18*(3/4), 39–51.

Sorensen, S., Pinquart, M., & Duberstein, P. (2002). How effective are interventions with caregivers? An updated meta-analysis. *The Gerontologist, 42*(3), 356–372.

Tronto, J. (1993). *Moral boundaries: A political argument for an ethic of care*. New York, NY: Routledge Press.

Ward-Griffin, C., Brown, J. B., Vandervoort, A., & McNair, S. (2005). Double-duty caregiving: Women in the health professions. *Canadian Journal on Aging, 24*(4), 379–394.

Yuval-Davis, N. (2006). Intersectionality and feminist politics. *European Journal of Women's Studies, 13*(3), 193–209.

Zarit, S. H., Reever, K. E., & Bach-Peterson, J. (1980). Relatives of the impaired elderly: Correlates of feelings of burden. *The Gerontologist, 20*(6), 649–655.

CHAPTER 9
Child Welfare Practice with Sexual Minority and Gender-Diverse Youth: A Social Justice Perspective

D. Margo Nelson

Canadian social workers in child welfare work with young people and families of diverse cultural, ethnic, religious, and socio-economic backgrounds. Many of these youth and families have experienced social isolation and marginalization resulting from racism, prejudice, and Canada's colonial past. While racism is a pernicious harm, children and youth affected by racism can often acquire positive self-identities and survival strategies from parents, families, and community members who share a common racial identity (Tatum, 2004). The social isolation experienced by children and youth who are gay, lesbian, bisexual, or who have atypical gender behaviours or identities, is just as harmful, but is different in one important respect. In many instances, these youth experience marginalization within their family, among their peers, at school, and in the community, and they often are unaware of, or do not have access to, positive sexual and gender minority role models (Little, 2001; Sullivan, 1994).

The consequences of this are observed in elevated risk profiles for these youth with respect to social, health, and psychological outcomes, in their over-representation in child welfare settings, and in the high percentage of LGBTQ youth found among homeless and street-entrenched youth, as well as youth engaged in survival sex (Walls & Bell, 2011; Woronoff, Mallon, & McHaelen, 2006). Canadian society has become more inclu-

verse sexualities and gender identities, with the legalization of same-sex marriage, the inclusion of sexual orientation in human rights legislation, and the increased visibility of LGBTQ people in many public social institutions. Nevertheless, for many children and youth, the disadvantages that may accrue due to a non-heterosexual orientation or a non-conforming gender identity persist (Taylor & Peter, 2011).

Terminology

Before discussing the risk and resilience of sexual and gender minority youth, it is necessary to consider terminology and language. It is difficult to identify a single term that accurately and respectfully encompasses the breadth of gender expressions and sexual orientations that affect the experiences and opportunities of diverse individuals. In practice, I think it most respectful to ask people how they prefer to identify or to be described. As this is not possible in the context of a written chapter, I have chosen to use the term *LGBTQ* to encompass people of varying sexual orientations and gender identities, including people who are gay, lesbian, and bisexual, as well as people who identify as transgender, transsexual, gender-variant, or as questioning or queer. *Queer* is a term often used by people who identify as a gender or sexual minority other than LGBT (such as intersex, Two-Spirit, or genderqueer), or by people who are questioning their gender or sexual identity.

With respect to describing the social/cultural context within which discrimination, bias, and stigmatization occur, I prefer to refer to heterosexism, as it describes "a systematic process of privilege toward heterosexuality relative to homosexuality based on the notion that *heterosexuality* is normal and ideal ... [and] implies that all other sexual orientations and related practices are abnormal or deviant" (Dermer, Smith, & Barto, 2010, p. 325). I use this term because I believe that much (although unfortunately not all) of the bias and poor social work practice that occurs in child welfare settings with sexual minority children and youth is the result of heterosexual assumption rather than explicitly hateful or discriminatory attitudes among workers. I also use the term *cisgenderism*, referring to beliefs and assumptions about gender identity and expression that exclude and discriminate against people who do not conform to or identify with their societally recognized sex.

In this chapter, I argue that the risks and disadvantages experienced by LGBTQ children and youth are located in heterosexist and cisgendered culture, rather than in LGBTQ identities, and identify legal instruments that attempt to secure the human rights of LGBTQ youth. I suggest that social work practice should embody human rights perspectives and remain cognizant of the implication of child welfare systems and workers in the violation of those rights. This model of practice, grounded in an ethic of care, offers a useful framework for meeting the developmental needs of, and mitigating risks to, LGBTQ children and youth. While many social workers can readily identify moral, humanitarian, and ethical reasons to reduce risk and improve outcomes for sexual minority youth, Mallon (2001) notes that social workers sometimes perpetrate, or fail to mitigate, the bias, stigma, and discrimination that contribute to these poor outcomes. It seems clear that efforts to meet the needs of LGBTQ youth must not be solely dependent on the good intentions of workers.

Risk and Resilience

Over the past two decades, increasing attention has been directed at the needs of LGBTQ children and youth in the child welfare system (Wilber, Reyes, & Marksamer, 2006). A review of that literature points to the unique vulnerabilities of LGBTQ youth, who experience an increased risk of numerous health, social, and psychological difficulties (Friedman, Marshal, Guadamuz, Wei, Wong, Saewyc, & Stall, 2011; Saewyc, Poon, Wang, Homma, Smith, & the McCreary Centre Society, 2007; Saewyc, 2011). Numerous studies have demonstrated that LGBTQ youth, when compared to gender-conforming heterosexual youth, have a higher risk of being subjected to or participating in a spectrum of harmful or risky experiences. These children and youth experience higher rates of physical and sexual abuse in their family homes (Saewyc et al., 2007) and are more likely to experience family rejection (Friedman et al., 2011; Tharinger & Wells, 2000). LGBTQ youth have sexual relationships at an earlier age on average than do heterosexual youth (Saewyc et al., 2007), are more likely to be sexually exploited (Walls & Bell, 2011), are more likely to use alcohol and drugs (Little, 2001; Saewyc, 2011), and are more likely to be forced to leave or to run away from their homes and to then become homeless (Little, 2001; Woronoff et al., 2006). They are more likely to be bullied or physically assaulted at school and in the community (Saewyc et al., 2007; Taylor & Peter, 2011), are more likely to experience academic difficulties or to leave school prematurely (Tharinger & Wells, 2000), are more likely to become pregnant or to impregnate somebody during adolescence (Saewyc, Poon, Homma, & Skay, 2008), and are more likely to report suicidal ideation (Saewyc, 2011). As a result of these difficulties, they are more likely than other youth to come to the attention of social workers in schools, health settings, and child welfare and protection systems (Phillips, McMillen, Sparks, & Ueberle, 1997; Wilber et al., 2006). Once LGBTQ youth are in these systems, particularly if they become wards of the state, they are more likely to experience minority-related stress, including harassment, bullying, and assault by other youths; rejection, verbal abuse, and physical assault by carers; multiple breakdowns of foster home placements; and running away from placements (Mallon, 2001; Ragg, Patrick, & Zeifert, 2006).

It is important to note that the risk factors for various outcomes are layered and intersecting: for instance, being a LGBTQ child or youth is a risk factor for parental maltreatment, which is a risk factor for becoming homeless, which is a risk factor for sexual exploitation. Being LGBTQ does not inevitably result in the poor social and psychological outcomes enumerated above. Rather, being a LGBTQ child or youth *in the context of a society that is often hostile, hateful, or unsafe* is the risk factor (D'Augelli, 2003; Mays & Cochran, 2001; Tharinger & Wells, 2000). Travers and colleagues (2010) point out that an over-emphasis on risk factors associated with a LGBTQ identity fails to locate risk in the social environment, instead identifying LGBTQ status as the source of risk, and obscures the concrete steps that can be taken by social workers and other service providers to promote wellness and positive relationships with family, peers, and in the various communities to which youth belong.

Factors associated with resilience for LGBTQ youth include family attachment; school connectedness; school policies explicitly prohibiting discrimination against LGBTQ people; access to accurate human sexuality education including material on LGBTQ identities; and positive representations of LGBTQ people in the community, media, and classroom (D'Augelli, 2003; Shilo & Savaya, 2011). Other sources of resilience are found in the intersecting identities of LGBTQ youth.

Although this chapter focuses on LGBTQ identities, all people have multiple and intersecting identities, including class, culture, gender, ethnicity, religion, geographical community. These intersecting identities mediate both risk and resilience for LGBTQ children and youth (Walls & Bell, 2011; Travers, Guta, Flicker, Larkin, Lo, McCardell, & van der Meulen, 2010). Travers and colleagues point to the need to recognize that cultural and religious identity may represent risk factors for some LGBTQ youth because they influence the willingness and ability of LGBTQ youth to access sexual health and other social services, as well as the willingness and ability of community organizations to meet the needs of these youth. Intersecting identities may also be a source of resilience. For example, youth may acquire positive self-perceptions based on racial identity and/or access to positive racialized LGBTQ role models (Tatum, 2004). Despite often-significant experiences of stigma and discrimination, most LGBTQ youth do arrive at adulthood with health and well-being that is comparable to that of their peers (Saewyc, 2011). It is the task of the social workers and agencies involved with these youth to help them do so.

The Rights of LGBTQ Children

There are a number of international, federal, and provincial legal and human rights mechanisms that secure and protect the rights of all children, the rights of LGBTQ people, and/or the rights of children who are in the care of the state. It is useful to examine the ways in which these various charters, conventions, laws, and policies intersect, and to consider their legal and practical limitations.

International documents include United Nations Convention on the Rights of the Child (UNCRC) (United Nations, 1989) and the *International Covenant on Civil and Political Rights* (United Nations, 1966). In Canada, the Canadian Charter of Rights and Freedoms (Constitution Act, 1982) and the Canadian Human Rights Act (current version, 1985) have secured sexual orientation as a protected status; gender identity is not currently protected. Table 9.1 enumerates rights and protections that are particularly salient to LGBTQ youth.

The UNCRC represents a significant departure from the socio-legal conceptualizations of children and families that originated in British common law. It positions children as full citizens in possession of a set of identified universal rights—rights that are connected to, but distinct from, the rights of their parents. The UNCRC also recognizes that children have unique developmental needs and that states have an obligation to see that those needs are met.

The UNCRC does not make explicit mention of LGBTQ children, although it states in the preamble that all persons are entitled to human rights "without distinction of any kind, such as race, colour, sex, language, religion, political or other opinion, national or social origin, property, birth *or other status*" (emphasis mine). Of note with respect to LGBTQ children and youth, Article 39 asserts that children who have experienced neglect or abuse are entitled to "physical and psychological recovery and social reintegration" in an environment "which fosters the health, self-respect and dignity of the child." This article has particular resonance for LGBTQ children in care who, in my interpretation, require and are entitled to a caring environment that is respectful and supportive of their LGBTQ identities.

Although the UNCRC is a significant document that demonstrates some international consensus on the rights of children, the ideals of this document are clearly not realized, either in Canada, or in most other places in the world, as evidenced by the global ubiquity of child poverty, exploitation, and abuse. Further, the standards of care and human rights of children that are articulated in the UNCRC are not secured by any legal mechanisms of enforcement, internationally or in Canada.

Table 9.1: Canadian and International Rights

United Nations Convention on the Rights of the Child (United Nations, 1989)	Article 1	The right to life and the obligation of state to ensure survival and development of children
	Article 13	The right to freedom of expression
	Article 14	The right to freedom of thought, conscience, and religion
	Article 19	The right to be free from neglect, abuse, exploitation, and maltreatment
	Article 39	The right to physical and psychological recovery and social reintegration after the experience of abuse
International Covenant of Political and Civil Rights (United Nations, 1966)	Articles 2 and 26	Reference to "sex" is to be interpreted as including sexual orientation (Canadian Heritage, 2009)
Canadian Charter of Rights and Freedoms (Constitution Act, 1982)	Section 15	*Charter* affirms that sexual orientation (but not gender identification) is a protected category
Canadian Human Rights Act (1985)		Sexual orientation included in the act in 1996. Currently, efforts are being made to extend the protections of the act to transgender and transsexual people (Bill C-279, 2011).

Provincial Legislation

All of the provinces and territories in Canada have included sexual orientation as a protected category in their human rights legislation. In addition, several have included gender expression and/or gender identification as protected categories, or have interpreted existing gender protections to include gender identity (see Table 9.2) (Alberta Human Rights Commission, 2012; BC Human Rights Coalition, n.d.; Charter of Human Rights and Freedoms, 1975; Human Rights Act, 2009; Human Rights Code, 2012; New Brunswick Human Rights Commission, n.d.; The Human Rights Code, 2012). This means that provincial child welfare authorities are required to meet the needs of all children in the province without discriminating on the basis of sexual orientation or, in some provinces, gender identity.

The legal scope and requirements of child welfare services are delineated in legislation by each province and territory. In Canada, none of these specifically addresses the rights or needs of LGBTQ children and youth, although in some cases agencies have developed their own policies and programs in this area. Each of these affirms that the decisions of government must take into consideration the best interests of the child, including the child's physical, mental, and emotional needs.

Table 9.2: Provincial and Territorial Rights

Province/Territory	Sexual Orientation	Gender Identity	Gender Expression
Alberta	Included	Included	
British Columbia	Included	By interpretation	
Manitoba	Included	Included	
New Brunswick	Included	By interpretation	
Newfoundland and Labrador	Included		
Northwest Territories	Included	Included	
Nova Scotia	Included		
Nunavut	Included		
Ontario	Included	Included	Included
Prince Edward Island	Included		
Quebec	Included	By interpretation	
Saskatchewan	Included		
Yukon	Included		

I believe that in the case of LGBTQ youth, these needs include a social environment that affirms and supports the sexual orientations and gender identities of all children and youth.

Despite the legal entitlement to formal equality, accessing the justice system is difficult, expensive, and unlikely to take place within the developmental timescale of an individual child's life. As a result, social workers and agencies must find other ways to meet the complex safety and developmental needs of these young people, in the context of a profoundly heterosexist and transphobic society.

Barriers to Securing Rights through Judicial Processes

Although there is momentum with respect to recognition of the equality rights of LGBTQ people, there are significant barriers for children and youth who require assistance in realizing these rights, or protection against violations of them. In particular, it is difficult for professionals to assist LGBTQ children and youth if the existence of LGBTQ youth is not acknowledged. Mallon and Woronoff (2006) point out that although agencies serving homeless and street-entrenched youth have long been aware of the over-representation of LGBTQ youth in these populations, child welfare professionals have been reluctant to implement services specifically targeted at them. They note, "The affirmation and protection usually automatically afforded to most children, youth, and families are rights not guaranteed by child welfare agencies to most gay and lesbian children, youth, and families" (p. 118).

Because youth who are receiving services from child welfare systems are young and experience ageism, the majority have limited ability and opportunity to advocate for themselves. They also often lack committed and effective advocacy from parents or other adults in their lives and their access to the legal system is limited. In addition, human rights challenges in Canada are very costly and lengthy processes and, even if successful, are not likely to result in remediation that takes place in time to meet the plaintiff's developmental needs. The development of human rights perspectives has advanced the cause of social justice at a societal level; however, the legal remedies that are available to individuals whose rights have been violated are limited, cumbersome, and expensive, suggesting that a rights framework, while important and necessary, is insufficient as a framework for social work practice that meets the complex needs of LGBTQ youth. It is necessary to consider other approaches to conceptualizing care.

An Ethical Framework for Child Welfare Practice

Ethic of care is a moral theory that has evolved, in part, as a feminism-informed response to the perceived inadequacies of, and inequities that result from, the reliance on liberal Western jurisprudence, legislation, and policy as a means of enacting social justice (Hankivsky, 2004). It is a useful framework for child welfare practice because an ethic of care presupposes that "needs are products of social relations rather than properties of individuals who demonstrate some sort of deficiencies of character" (Hankivsky, 2004, p. 37). This is pertinent for social work with LGBTQ youth, whose sexual orientation and/or gender identity or expression—rather than enacted stigma within a heterosexist social environment—are often identified as the problem.

Hankivsky (2004) refers to three principles in her model of an ethic of care. First, practice grounded in an ethic of care is contextually sensitive, taking into consideration the complexity of people's lives, relationships, and environments. Different people require different types of care—and enough flexibility among workers and agencies to respond to this diversity. Second, an ethic of care embodies the quality of responsiveness. Hankivsky notes that this requires more than simple empathy or superficial efforts to understand the position of another person. Instead, it is necessary to take "seriously the perspective of citizens who may be experiencing inequality" (p. 36). She continues, "[this can] reveal that it is not necessarily human diversity that is the problem, but rather social constructs that render differences problematic" (Hankivsky,

2004, p. 36). This principle requires that social workers and their agencies adopt a structural critique as part of the practice at the agency, and understand that it is necessary to change hostile environments, rather than focus on changing clients. Finally, when attempting social work practice in the context of an ethic of care, the consequences of decisions need to be considered. It is not enough to provide the usual service and then shrug one's shoulders when that service does not meet the needs of, or worse, harms, the individual for whom care is being provided.

Child welfare social workers are called upon to not only circumnavigate the procedural constraints often seen in agencies, but to also challenge and work to transform the heterosexist and cisgendered environments representing a risk of harm to LGBTQ youth. It is easy to task social workers with the responsibility to mitigate biased practice habits, assumptions, or policies, but it is more difficult for them to fulfill these tasks, particularly in the context of high caseloads and agency environments that may not be sensitized to, or may be overtly hostile to, the needs of LGBTQ children and youth.

Social Work Practice with LGBTQ Youth

Sexual and Gender Identity Formation

Social workers in child welfare and protection agencies are required to safeguard children and youth, to support parents and families in their efforts to care for their children, and, when these efforts are unsuccessful, to arrange for the provision of out-of-home care that is safe, nurturing, and meets the developmental needs of the child. For LGBTQ youth, these include the need to be supported while managing the emergence of a LGBTQ identity in the context of a fundamentally heteronormative society (Sullivan, 1994; Tharinger & Wells, 2000). This process can start at a young age. Children typically become aware of same-sex attractions by about the age of eight or nine, although it may be another 10 years before the young person begins to make disclosures to other people.

It is worth noting that the typical age of disclosure to others is much younger now than was the case in previous generations, when it was more typical for young people to "come out" in early adulthood, after achieving independence, accounting in part for the increased need for services from child welfare workers (Woronoff et al., 2006). Many transgender children and youth become aware of their gender identities in early childhood (Kennedy & Hellen, 2010). The intersection of LGBTQ identity with other identities, including cultural, religious, linguistic, and physical or developmental ability may also mediate the timing and trajectory of the coming out process.

Saewyc (2011) discusses the evolution of theory concerning sexual identity formation, noting that early models of this process described a linear pathway from "sensitization," or awareness of same-sex attraction, through "identity confusion," a stage where young people grapple with stigma and distress about their emerging identity, to a gradual process of "coming out," to one's self and to others, and finally, "identity commitment" or "identity integration," a stage in which the individual solidifies his or her self-image and social identity as a gay, lesbian, or bisexual person. Saewyc describes emerging theoretical understandings of this process. First, sexual identity formation is not always linear and people may move back and forth between stages. Second, there may be differences in the trajectory of this process associated with gender, (dis)bility, culture, and age of awareness of same-sex attraction. Finally, coming out is rarely a singular event; it is more accurately described as a process of self-identification and then the selective sharing of that identity with family, peer groups, work colleagues, and members of the community. Kennedy and Hellen (2010) discuss the trajectory of identity formation for trans children, describing experiences of isolation and secrecy and the difficulty of developing a positive trans identity in a profoundly gender-normative environment. Of course, if social workers aspire to meaningfully support healthy processes of identity formation, it is necessary that LGBTQ youth be seen and recognized. Many continue to remain invisible and to fear coming out.

Invisibility

It is first important to recognize that it is only recently and reluctantly that the existence of LGBTQ youth has been recognized, and that this invisibility is among the more painful effects of heterosexism (Little, 2001; Mallon, 1997; Mallon & Woronoff, 2006). Along with a disinclination in society to acknowledge that children and youth have sexual identities at all, there is reluctance among many, including many social workers, to accept that some children and adolescents have non-heterosexual orientations or non-conforming gender identities (Mallon & Woronoff, 2006). Mallon and Woronoff (2006) note, "The welfare of LGBT children, youth, and families cannot be adequately enhanced as long as the larger society, heterocentrically oriented and heterosexually controlled, ignores their existence" (p. 118). This reality highlights the need of workers, managers, and administrators to develop the capacity individually and at the agency level to critically and reflectively examine the heterosexist, transphobic, and homophobic beliefs that reinforce the invisibility and oppression of LGBTQ youth.

Agency Characteristics that Support Ethical Practice with LGBTQ Youth

Although the Code of Ethics of the Canadian Association of Social Workers obligates social workers to "recognize and respect diversity" and to uphold human rights (CASW, 2005, Value 1), social workers and child welfare systems have often failed to mitigate, or have themselves perpetuated, stigma, bias, and discrimination against LGBTQ children and youth (Mallon, 2001). There are, however, models of policy and practice in child welfare that do affirm LGBTQ youth and explicitly require workers to engage in a process of challenging their internalized heterosexist assumptions, homophobia, transphobia, and/or cisgenderism. Reflective practice is an intentional process of challenging one's own assumptions and beliefs about the multiple intersecting identities of ourselves and the people with whom we work. Reflective practice with LGBTQ youth requires workers to critically examine and to address their own assumptions, areas of discomfort, biases, and prejudices. This allows social workers to engage in an active process of challenging not only homophobia, in the form of bullying and prejudice, but also the passive acceptance of heternormative and other assumptions in our agencies (DePalma & Atkinson, 2009).

The Children's Aid Society of Toronto (CAST) has developed a comprehensive policy framework that identifies the unique needs and vulnerabilities of LGBTQ youth and focuses on making service provision safe, accessible, and equitable (CAST, 2008). The Out and Proud program promotes LGBTQ-affirming practice and the development of LGBTQ-welcoming work and residential settings. Characteristics of LGBTQ-affirming practice environments include

- education, training, and support for workers around topics including one's own homophobia and heterosexism and the developmental needs of LGBTQ children and youth;
- the development in workers of a perspective that the acceptance of a LGBTQ identity is a positive outcome for youth;
- the use of inclusive and non-heterosexist language when speaking to youth, for example, asking a young person, whether male or female, if he or she has a boyfriend or girlfriend;
- not assuming that young people have a heterosexual orientation or conforming gender identity;
- displaying pamphlets, posters, and other materials depicting diverse youth and families, representing multiple cultures, ethnicities, religious affiliations, abilities, sexual orientations, and gender identities;
- core agency philosophies supporting and affirming the diverse identities of people working in and being cared for by agencies;
- a commitment to safety for all clients and zero tolerance for any physical aggression or verbal harassment;

- hiring supportive employees, including LGBTQ employees; ensuring that candidates will be able to positively affirm LGBTQ identities; and advocating for LGBTQ youth in other community settings, such as schools, residential facilities, and other community organizations by providing training, support, and educational materials. (CAST, 2008; Jacobs & Freundlich, 2006; Little, 2001; Mallon, 1997; Phillips et al., 1997)

Supporting Youth in the Family and Community

Research, human rights documents, and legislation with respect to the care of children all affirm that youth should, whenever possible, remain in the care of their parents. The point at which a child and his or her family become aware that the child may be developing a LGBTQ identity, or that a child is not conforming to gender norms in dress or behaviour, can represent a point of crisis, and in some families this results in the rejection or the verbal, physical, or sexual abuse of the LGBTQ child (Jacobs & Freundlich, 2006; Phillips et al., 1997; Woronoff et al., 2006). Social workers can help to prevent abuse by supporting families as they navigate the ambivalence, fear, and grief that are sometimes associated with the coming out of a family member. When a social worker is involved with a young person prior to his or her disclosure to family members, it can be useful to assist the child or youth by planning how to disclose to family members, establishing a safety plan in the event that family members react negatively, and gathering information and referrals to youth groups, parent support groups, and other supportive resources. When the emerging LGBTQ identity of a child or youth threatens the ability of parents to provide safe, nurturing, and identity-affirming care, social workers can help educate and support parents while foregrounding the right of the child or youth to be safe and supported, preferably in the home of his or her parents, or elsewhere if this is impossible.

Supporting Youth in Out-of-Home Care

While there are risks for all youth in out-of-home care, LGBTQ youth are more likely to endure frequent disruptions in placements, are often harassed and abused by peers and carers, are more likely than their peers to be placed in group settings rather than family homes, and often run away from placements that they perceive to be hostile or unsafe (CAST, 2008; Mallon, 2001). In order to mitigate the risk of these outcomes, social workers need to work to identify, create, and support care environments for youth, whether with foster carers or in group care, that are inclusive and supportive of diverse identities (Wilber et al., 2006). Work to support this goal might include the recruitment of LGBTQ carers, training and ongoing support for carers, ensuring that agency staff are not communicating or behaving in ways that reinforce bias, and ensuring that carers are aware that they may be caring for LGBTQ youth and are prepared to do so, so that youth do not experience rejection by carers as a result of their LGBTQ status (Wilber et al., 2006).

LGBTQ youth who experience multiple placements have the unenviable task of deciding at each new placement, in each new school, and with new carers, teachers, peers, and household members, whether, when, and how to disclose their LGBTQ identities. Although LGBTQ youth who have begun the process of coming out have demonstrated incredible resilience and courage, to have to do this repeatedly is an enormous burden for a young person already grappling with the difficulties associated with being a child in care. Just as young people may need support in coming out to parents, social workers can support young people in care as they decide when to disclose their orientations or identities, and how to do so safely.

Ongoing Challenges and Opportunities

A contextually aware model of practice requires that social workers be prepared to address the intersecting needs of LGBTQ youth. Some families and communities have cultural or religious affiliations that are hostile to non-heterosexual identities, making it difficult for both the youth and his or her family to seek support from family and community resources (Mallon, 1997). Sometimes, youth and families reside in rural or isolated areas where there is minimal access to supportive services, other LGBTQ youth, and positive adult role models. Some youth with disabilities, a population often in contact with social workers, will have LGBTQ identities. The social and sexual identity needs of this population are doubly invisible, as the sexuality and sex education needs of youth with disabilities are frequently neglected. Youth in these situations are faced with dilemmas that can seem intractable, and supportive social work practice can help them navigate the unique contexts of their lives.

Despite the difficulties faced by some LGBTQ youth, most do become healthy and happy adults (Saewyc, 2011). Youth are increasingly likely to reject the straight/gay binary and to self-identify with more nuanced identities (Savin-Williams, 2005). In addition, LGBTQ role models are increasingly visible and people are more likely than ever to report that they know someone who identifies as LGBTQ. There is some evidence that these factors, along with ongoing changes to the legal status of LGBTQ people, may lessen the heterosexist pressure that negatively affects the developmental process for LGBTQ youth (Saewyc, 2011). Social workers, who can provide identity-affirming support to youth and their families while also working in more public domains to challenge the hegemony of heternormative assumption, can further the cause of social justice by working to eliminate the most salient risk factors for LGBTQ youth: invisibility, bias, and enacted stigma.

References

Alberta Human Rights Commission. (2012). Protected areas and grounds under the Alberta Human Rights Act. Retrieved from www.albertahumanrights.ab.ca

BC Human Rights Coalition. (n.d.). Grounds of protection in B.C. Retrieved from www.bchrcoalition.org/files/GroundsProtection.html#Sex

Bill C-279. (2011). Retrieved from www.parl.gc.ca/HousePublications/Publication.aspx?Docid=5127590&file=4

Canadian Association of Social Workers (CASW). (2005). Code of ethics. Retrieved from www.casw-acts.ca

Canadian Heritage. (2009). Sexual orientation and human rights. Retrieved from www.pch.gc.ca/pgm/pdp-hrp/canada/sxrnt-eng.cfm

Canadian Human Rights Act. (1985, c. H-6). Government of Canada.

Charter of Human Rights and Freedoms. (1975, c. C-12). National Assembly of Quebec.

Children's Aid Society of Toronto (CAST). (2008). Board governance policy: Equitable child welfare services relating to sexual orientation and gender identity/expression. Retrieved from www.torontocas.ca/files

Constitution Act: Part I. (1982). Being Schedule B to the Canada Act 1982 (U.K.), c. 11 [*Charter*].

D'Augelli, A. R. (2003). Lesbian and bisexual female youths aged 14 to 21: Development challenges and victimization experiences. *Journal of Lesbian Studies, 7*(4), 9–29.

DePalma, R., & Atkinson, E. (2009). "No Outsiders": Moving beyond a discourse of tolerance to challenge heternormativity in primary schools. *British Educational Research Journal, 35*(6), 837–855.

Dermer, S. B., Smith, S. D., & Barto, K. K. (2010). Identifying and correctly labeling sexual prejudice, discrimination, and oppression. *Journal of Counseling & Development, 88*(3), 325–331.

Friedman, M. S., Marshal, M. P., Guadamuz, T. E., Wei, C., Wong, C. F., Saewyc, E. M., & Stall, R. (2011). A meta-analysis of disparities in childhood sexual abuse, parental physical abuse, and peer victimization among sexual minority and sexual nonminority individuals. *American Journal of Public Health, 101*(8), 1481–1494.

Hankivsky, O. (2004). *Social policy and the ethics of care*. Vancouver, BC: UBC Press.

Human Rights Act. (2009). Legislative Assembly of the Northwest Territories. Retrieved from nwthumanrights.ca/wp-content/uploads/2013/10/Human_Rights_Act_Ammended_2012.pdf

Human Rights Code. (2012, c. 7). Government of Ontario. Retrieved from www.e- laws.gov.on.ca/html/statutes/english/elaws_statutes_90h19_e.htm

Jacobs, J., & Freundlich, M. (2006). Achieving permanency for LGBTQ youth. *Child Welfare, 85*(2), 299–316.

Kennedy, N., & Hellen, M. (2010). Transgender children: More than a theoretical challenge. *Graduate Journal of Social Science, 9*(2), 25–43.

Little, J. N. (2001). Embracing gay, lesbian, bisexual, and transgendered youth in school-based settings. *Child & Youth Care Forum, 30*(2), 99–110.

Mallon, G. P. (1997). Basic premises, guiding principles, and competent practices for a positive youth development approach to working with gay, lesbian, and bisexual youths in out of home care. *Child Welfare, 76*(5), 591–609.

Mallon, G. P. (2001). Sticks and stones can break your bones: Verbal harassment and physical violence in the lives of gay and lesbian youths in child welfare settings. *Journal of Gay & Lesbian Social Services, 13*(1), 63–82.

Mallon, G. P., & Woronoff, R. (2006). Busting out of the child welfare closet: Lesbian, gay, bisexual, and transgender-affirming approaches to child welfare. *Child Welfare, 85*(2), 115–122.

Mays, V. M., & Cochran, S. D. (2001). Mental health correlates of perceived discrimination among lesbian, gay, and bisexual adults in the United States. *American Journal of Public Health, 91*(11), 1869–1876.

New Brunswick Human Rights Commission. (n.d.). The New Brunswick Human Rights Act explained. Retrieved from www.gnb.ca/hrc-cdp/18-e.asp

Phillips, S., McMillen, C., Sparks, J., & Ueberle, M. (1997). Concrete strategies for sensitizing youth-serving agencies to the needs of gay, lesbian, and other sexual minority youths. *Child Welfare, 76*(3), 393–409.

Ragg, D. M., Patrick, D., & Ziefert, M. (2006). Slamming the closet door: Working with gay and lesbian youth in care. *Child Welfare, 85*(2), 243–265.

Saewyc, E. M. (2011). Research on adolescent sexual orientation: Development, health disparities, stigma, and resilience. *Journal of Research on Adolescence, 21*(1), 256–272.

Saewyc, E. M., Poon, C. S., Homma, Y., & Skay, C. L. (2008). Stigma management? The links between enacted stigma and teen pregnancy trends among gay, lesbian, and bisexual students in British Columbia. *Canadian Journal of Human Sexuality, 17*(3), 123–139.

Saewyc, E., Poon, C., Wang, N., Homma, Y., Smith, A., & McCreary Centre Society. (2007). *Not yet equal: The health of lesbian, gay, & bisexual youth in BC.* Vancouver, BC: McCreary Centre Society.

Savin-Williams, R. C. (2005). *The new gay teenager.* Boston, MA: Harvard University Press.

Shilo, G., & Savaya, R. (2011). Effects of family and friend support on LGB youths' mental health and sexual orientation milestones. *Family Relations, 60*(3), 318–330.

Sullivan, T. R. (1994). Obstacles to effective child welfare service with gay and lesbian youths. *Child Welfare, 73*(4), 291–304.

Tatum, B. D. (2004). Family life and school experience: Factors in the racial identity development of black youth in white communities. *Journal of Social Issues, 60*(1), 117–135.

Taylor, C., & Peter, T. (2011). "We are not aliens, we're people, and we have rights." Canadian human rights discourse and high school climate for LGBTQ students. *Canadian Review of Sociology, 48*(3), 275–312.

Tharinger, D., & Wells, G. (2000). An attachment perspective on the developmental challenges of gay and lesbian adolescents: The need for continuity of caregiving from family and schools. *School Psychology Review, 29*(2), 158–172.

The Human Rights Code. (2012, c. H175). Government of Manitoba. Retrieved from web2.gov.mb.ca/laws/statutes/ccsm/h175e.php

Travers, R., Guta, A., Flicker, S., Larkin, J., Lo, C., McCardell, S., & van der Meulen, E. (2010). Service provider views on issues and needs for lesbian, gay, bisexual, and transgender youth. *Canadian Journal of Human Sexuality, 19*(4), 191–198.

United Nations. (1966). International Covenant of Political and Civil Rights. Retrieved from www2.ohchr.org/english/law/ccpr.htm

United Nations. (1989). Convention on the Rights of the Child. Retrieved from www2.ohchr.org/english/law/crc.htm

Walls, N., & Bell, S. (2011). Correlates of engaging in survival sex among homeless youth and young adults. *Journal of Sex Research, 48*(5), 423–436.

Wilber, S., Reyes, C., & Marksamer, J. (2006). The model standards project: Creating inclusive systems for LGBT youth in out-of-home care. *Child Welfare, 85*(2), 133–149.

Woronoff, R., Mallon, G. P., & McHaelen, R. (2006). Bridges, barriers, and boundaries. *Child Welfare, 85*(2), 407–438.

CHAPTER 10

Collaboration and Affirmation: Supporting Younger Lesbian and Bisexual Women and Transgender Youth in Small Cities and Rural Communities

Wendy Hulko[1]

In recent years, socio-cultural differences have been factored into research on queer youth (Gray, 2009; Haskell & Burtch, 2010; Saewyc, 2011) and those with sexual identities other than gay, lesbian, and bisexual; as well, young people whose gender expression is other than male or female have been included (Taylor & Peter, 2011; Toomey, McGuire, & Russell, 2012). Yet intersectionality has rarely been adopted as a theoretical lens through which to understand the lives of lesbian, gay, bisexual, transgender, transsexual, Two-Spirit (see McNeil-Seymour, this volume), intersex, queer, and/or questioning (LGBTTSIQ) youth (see Diamond & Butterworth, 2008; Gray, 2009 for notable exceptions). Transgender, Two-Spirit, intersex, and questioning youth have not been well represented, and research pertaining to geographic location has not treated small cities as distinct from either rural or urban areas (Hulko & Hovanes, under review). Thus, research on the experiences of youth who identify as LGBTTSIQ that directly seeks their insights and focuses on the social contexts in which they live (i.e. small cities or rural communities) is a new area of scholarly inquiry. The research upon which this chapter is based sought to elicit the experiences and views of younger and older women[2] who identify as sexual and/or gender minorities[3] and live in small cities and rural communities. Employing intersectionality, this chapter specifically highlights the experiences of younger lesbian and bisexual women, and transgender youth who identify as women.

Subsequent to presenting the theory and literature that informed the study and briefly describing the research design, the chapter presents findings on participants' experiences and insights into a variety of social supports in a small city, including high school and university student clubs, youth programs, the queer community, and social media. Analysis of their experiences highlights the significance of accessible and inclusive programming, and the importance of community collaboration to expand on these existing support services. The chapter concludes with recommendations that may assist service providers, educators, and members of the queer community to enhance the visibility or presence of younger lesbian and bisexual women and transgender youth, as well as assisting them in collaborative efforts to create more sources of support in small cities and rural communities.

Intersectionality

Theorists and researchers adopting an intersectional lens avoid isolating a particular aspect of a person's identity—such as gender expression—or prioritizing one form of oppression—like heterosexism—and instead consider various facets of a person's social location and treat oppressions (and privileges) as interactive and mutually reinforcing (Hulko, 2009). The connection between individual experiences and social structures is taken for granted in intersectional theorizing, which generally focuses on both structure and agency, or the micro and macro levels (see Hill Collins, 2000). This partly explains why intersectionality has become a key concept in social work practice, education, and research (Murphy, Hunt, Zajicek, Norris, & Hamilton, 2009), with naming of unearned privileges and sites of oppression occurring more often than in other scholarship (Hulko, 2009; Mehrotra, 2010; Murphy et al., 2009).

Sexual orientation was foregrounded in early writings on intersectionality (Combahee River Collective, 1977; Lorde, 2007), and women and queer people—as diverse, overlapping, or monolithic groups—have been the focus of much intersectionality research (Bowleg, 2008; Diamond & Butterworth, 2008). However, age and the ways in which it structures experiences of gender identity is addressed infrequently, as is geographic context (Hulko & Hovanes, under review). This study sought to fill a gap in intersectionality scholarship by investigating age and geographic context in relation to sexual orientation and gender expression.

Literature Review

While in the past, the voices and experiences of lesbians and bisexual women were less frequently sought or heard in research than those of gay and bisexual men (Diamond, 1998), it appears this pattern has shifted with respect to qualitative research based on convenience samples of youth (Elze, 2007). Queer research has expanded its focus beyond the "urban oasis" (Gray, 2009), yet qualitative studies of the experiences of LGBTTSIQ youth are not as common as large surveys. In British Columbia, surveys and needs assessments have highlighted the health concerns and service needs of lesbian, gay, and bisexual youth living in rural and remote regions (Poon & Saewyc, 2009; Saewyc, Poon, Wang, Homma, Smith, & the McCreary Centre Society, 2007) and identified ways that service providers and First Nation communities can support Two-Spirit youth (Urban Native Youth Association, 2004). In their analysis of rural and urban differences related to sexual orientation in the 2003 BC Adolescent Health Survey, Poon and Saewyc (2009) argued that "lesbian, gay, and bisexual adolescents in rural communities may need additional support and services as they navigate adolescence" (p. 118). They recommended "informal help networks [linking] LGB adolescents with peers and LGB adults" (p. 122), as well as interventions focused specifically on mental health, substance abuse, and sexual education. However, these support services and networks are not always available in small cities and rural areas where virtual communities may be the only sources of peer support and information about identity development and services (see Cohn & Hastings, 2010). Further, if programs for queer youth exist in rural settings, they may be staffed by one person tasked with serving a very large geographic area, necessitating the development of creative research/practice collaborations (Hulko, Bepple, Turco, & Clark, 2010).

The concept of community figures strongly in research on the role and impact of social networks on the lives of queer youth. These include family, friends, gay/straight alliances (GSAs), and other clubs that support their health and well-being (Gray, 2009; Poon & Saewyc, 2009; Saewyc, 2011; Taylor & Peter, 2011; Toomey et al., 2012; Walls, Kane, & Wisneski, 2010; Wilkinson & Pearson, 2009). For example, a comprehensive Canadian survey of queer high school students indicated homophobia, biphobia, and transphobia exist "in every class in every school" such that 64 percent of LGBTQ students and 61 percent of students with LGBTQ parents reported feeling unsafe at school. Findings also suggested female sexual minority and trans youth face worse situations than male sexual minority students (Taylor & Peter, 2011, pp. 8, 18; see also Grossman & D'Augelli, 2006; Haskell & Burtch, 2010; Meyers, 2009). An American survey with GLBTQ youth found that GSAs and the inclusion of LGBTQ issues in the curriculum made a positive difference in schools—whether or not LGBTQ youth were members (Walls et al., 2010).

Research Design

As noted, the purpose of this feminist anti-oppressive research was to explore experiences of women who identify as sexual and/or gender minorities and reside in small cities or rural communities. The study employed strategies to prioritize the voices of participants, and explicitly sought to change inequitable social relations (Brown & Strega, 2005). Additional features included a focus on social location and the practice of locating oneself in relation to the research participants

(Kirby, Greaves, & Reid, 2006). Consistent with feminist methodology, this research employed qualitative methods, namely focus groups and individual interviews. Three research questions guided the inquiry: self-identification, intersecting social identities, and geographic location. This chapter draws mostly on data generated from the third research question: "how does geographic location affect the identification of younger women and girls as sexual and/or gender minorities?"

Youth participants (n=13) were recruited through purposive sampling and consent was obtained directly from all participants, including those under the age of 16, maximizing queer youth participation. Data were collected through four individual interviews (two in person and two by email) and two focus groups (one with three younger lesbian women, another with six transgender and questioning youth), using a semi-structured interview guide. Subsequent to thematically analyzing the data and coding it, an intersectional lens was applied (see Bowleg, 2008; Diamond & Butterworth, 2008; Murphy et al., 2009). This chapter draws on findings coded under the categories of community, organizations, and media involvement. These are linked to Hulko and Hovanes's (under review) article, which includes further details on the methods, and presents an intersectional analysis of the experiences of LGBTQ youths who identify and find community.

The Small City Context

The small city where this research took place has a population of approximately 80,000 and serves as a transportation and service hub for rural communities and smaller cities surrounding it. The predominantly working-class residents have strong ties to resource industries, although this is changing due to the presence and growth of the university. Existing services and supports for queer youth include a group started in 1998 by a social service agency, and regular GSA meetings in at least two of five local high schools. Since 2011, Social Justice (SJ) 12, an elective course on understanding inequalities based on sexual orientation, gender expression, and other aspects of difference (Ministry of Education, 2008), has been offered in one high school. In the mid-1990s, an on-campus queer student club was started by gay faculty, and later became an official student club with decreased faculty involvement.

Research Participants: Intersectional Dimensions

At the time of the research, two of the thirteen participants lived in rural communities, and eleven resided in the small city described above. Five participants had previously resided in larger cities (e.g. Vancouver, Edmonton, Calgary) and six had lived only in small cities. When the data were collected in 2009, participants ranged in age from 15 to 25 years (with an average of 19.8 years). Two of the participants were Indigenous (First Nations and Métis), though neither identified as Two-Spirit; the rest were white anglo-Canadians. Four youth disclosed disability status (physical disability, mental illness, chronic health condition). Social class differences emerged when educational backgrounds, families of origin, and intersectionality were raised. Table 10.1 presents the area where the greatest diversity was seen: the gender identities/expressions and sexual orientations of the participants. Three of the five transgender participants identified as straight, while also identifying as belonging to the category of women or girls.

Table 10.1

Gender Identity/Expression	8 female, 5 transgender (3 female to male (FTM), 2 male to female (MTF))
Sexual Orientation	7 lesbian, 3 bisexual or pansexual, 3 straight (1 FTM, 2 MTF)

The following sections present and discuss the results of the data analysis relating to sources of support, starting with the views of the youth on safety and acceptance in the small city.

Safety and Acceptance in the Small City

Youth participants highlighted the degree to which their current, former, and ideal places of residence could be considered safe and accepting of queer people (Hulko & Hovanes, under review). They identified specific places they chose to frequent and tried to avoid in the small city (see Hulko, in press). Generally, the unsafe spaces were public ("downtown core," "buses," "parks late at night") and safer ones more private areas ("in bed," "this room," "friend's house"). Social service agencies and gay-oriented public events or organizations featured prominently, as did the Internet. Yet, as one lesbian youth noted, "it's not necessarily where we would and wouldn't go, [rather] it's more what we would and wouldn't do there," for example, engage in public displays of affection. Similar to many LGBTQ high school students in large urban settings, those participants who were in high school at the time or had been identified as lesbian or bisexual while in high school shared stories of harassment and discrimination in educational settings. In contrast, universities were identified as safe places.

Key public spaces queer youth felt were unsafe or safe were high schools and universities, respectively. Transgender participants told stories of "training [themselves] not to go to the bathroom at school" and changing schools during transition, while other queer youth spoke to harassment in schools. A bisexual participant stated "it got out that I was bi and people were hissing at me in the hallways," and a lesbian participant spoke of being called names "mostly from bullies." The ubiquity of the expression "that's so gay" was noted by a transgender participant—"everyone in grade eight was 'that's so gay, blah, blah, blah'"—who indicated even queer youth repeat this saying without knowing the meaning.

Some participants viewed universities as places where growth and acceptance could potentially occur and where one could be free to be gay. For example, a young lesbian indicated, "I'd left high school. I was starting something new and felt like I could start my life as being more of a gay person." Others asked if one had to be a student and/or 19 years or older to be a member of the campus pride club and to attend their events, seeking both peer support and opportunities to meet other queer youth.

Sources of Support for Queer Youth

In addition to peer-led clubs like GSAs and the campus student club, participants identified the queer youth group run by a social service agency, the local gay and lesbian association, and social media sites as sources of support.

The Queer Youth Group

Participants were extremely positive about the queer youth group run by a local social service agency: "You know there is someplace that you can go where you are not going to be judged." They highlighted the quality of their interactions with one another—"everybody's good to me, they are nice to me, they treat me right" —and the sense of belonging this engendered. This feeling of affinity and safety amongst the group members was carried into the community as they spent time with one another apart from the queer youth group and acknowledged one another at other events or places in the community. While participants also spoke positively of a weekly event sponsored by another youth agency, they noted that the heterosexual and gender-conformative youth who treated them well at this weekly event ignored them in other contexts: "Everybody is all friendly and they know my name and then I see them in town and they don't even give two shits that I am there."

The words of a transgender youth (FTM) who had recently moved to the small city attest to how the queer youth group enabled connection with other queer people, increased his knowledge of the language of gender identity and expression, and heightened his self-understanding:

Oh wow, there's actually more and more people, not just the couple of people that I've just met randomly ... they started to explain the words and I'm like "oh, that explains everything" because I didn't know what anything meant. I just knew [that] I wasn't who I was and that I felt at a young age that there was [a] huge problem [for other people] with me dressing in guy's clothes.

Another transgender youth (MTF) originally from a remote First Nations reserve, spoke of being confused and "trying new things and everything" before finding her way to the queer youth group and meeting youth dealing with similar issues. However, the move did not necessarily alleviate her confusion about her multiple identities—"I decided—I am like, I don't know who I am"—but it did provide her with a safe and supportive community of peers where she could explore her gender identity/expression and sexual orientation. Her continued confusion arose from being both First Nations and a sexual and gender minority, with this dual identity having led to her rejection by family and community, while providing a new community of peers.

Transgender participants felt it was very important to have a specific group "'cause gay issues and transgendered issues are completely different." This group, started by the queer youth group coordinator, consulted with the provincial transgender health program. Youth were observed to move between the two groups; for example, two lesbian youth attended the transgender youth group as well as the queer youth group when questioning their gender identity. The youth stressed the importance of having a member of the queer community as group facilitator, as they were "easier to relate [to]" and expanded the group in terms of size and opportunities.

The Local Gay and Lesbian Association

Another source of support was the local gay and lesbian association that held dances the majority of participants regularly attended; even the bisexual women who were not out reported going to the dances and "not [being] embarrassed to tell people [including] my coworkers, my family, friends and even acquaintances." For most of the participants, attendance at the gay dances contributed to a sense of inclusion in the local queer community and, by extension, to greater self-acceptance. The words of one participant captured the relevance of the dances: "seeing people that didn't fit into the norms I think helped a lot to figure out that I could be myself." Unfortunately, these dances are infrequent and there is neither a gay bar nor café in this small city; further, regular "bars" in the small city were reported to be unsafe places (see Hulko, in press).

GSAs or Peer-Led Student Clubs

Although not all participants were involved in GSAs while in high school, those who were spoke of their current or past experiences. The majority of the older youth attended high school in small cities where there were no GSAs and/or they were not "out" in high school. One of the lesbian youth recounted watching news coverage of the controversy in Utah over the first GSA every night when she was in grade seven, wishing a student club like this existed in her hometown. Another lesbian in university who was a volunteer with a local GSA was surprised at the size and composition of the group: "there was like 15 people in this classroom and I was just so shocked, like they're all here, they're gay or supporting a gay friend."

Despite the value of GSAs, there were challenges, for example, inconsistent attendance and competing/dissimilar purpose and goals. Some youth felt that GSAs did not make a difference and wanted more "education" and "awareness" type activities, in addition to providing a meeting place. One participant, speaking to her unsuccessful efforts to start a GSA, pointed to the age and diverse interests of the attendees and the need for an authority figure (i.e. a teacher) as the reason for its failure: "It worked good for the first couple of months, but then it got run over by a bunch of grade eight [students] and they wouldn't listen to me 'cause they knew [that] I wasn't a teacher." The challenges of building membership and maintaining a presence were also noted for the campus student club, with the lulls in activity and visibility being noted by at least one lesbian youth.

Social Media

Youth spoke of the importance of the Internet as a source of information and support, naming the specific social media sites Facebook, Pink Sofa, Gay.com, deviantart, Nexopia, Craigslist, and YouTube. One transgender (FTM) youth told us that he had started a forum on Nexopia called "transgeneration." A bisexual woman spoke of her pride in taking "a small step" toward being out when she accepted an invitation to join a local Facebook group:

> I think I stared at the computer for a good half hour debating whether or not to accept the invitation. Finally I decided I was being ridiculous and accepted. I know it is a small step, but I felt pretty proud of myself.

While most youth lauded the Internet, some expressed disappointment with social media sites:

> I have checked out [website] a couple times, but I can't navigate it very well and I don't really have a lot of time for online stuff and also it kind of depresses me a bit because they aren't real people, you know.

The limitations of existing sites that are "always dating oriented" were noted by another youth who wanted to find friends: "I just want to meet people that I can be friends with and stuff."

As noted, the Internet was a significant source of labels and information on the meaning of labels, especially for transgender youth exploring their gender identity. For example, one youth stated, "When I had gender issues, I spent hours on the internet trying to find labels for myself because without labels, I feel like I cannot learn more about myself and I can't kind of grow as that person." Social media, coupled with the queer youth group, student clubs, and the gay and lesbian association, were all forms of support accessed by younger lesbian and bisexual women and transgender youth in the small city. While the Internet is considered even more relevant for queer youth in the small city because potential resources and supports are more limited (see Gray, 2009), this was not the focus of the recommendations youth made for making the small city a better or safer place.

Making the Small City Better for Queer Youth

Participants indicated several ways in which the small city could be made a better or safer place for all queer youth, particularly those who identify as women. Their suggestions focused on educational settings and the importance of building a queer community of younger and older women, some of whom could be role models.

Educational Settings

Educational settings were identified as sites through which to effect change, by "starting off at a younger grade [because] the future is the younger ones" and arranging "activities for the school, not just [a] lecture." Youth recommended the campus student club be "established more [with] more support around it" through greater involvement of queer faculty. They stressed the importance of doing outreach and creating visibility and support for queer youth through hosting public events in high schools in conjunction with Day of Silence (www.dayofsilence.org):

> On International Day Against Homophobia [IDAH] there was this little tiny article in [free paper] and I was thinking why wasn't there something [bigger] ... and then in the school there

was Day of Silence and I heard that there was only three or four people participating [but] I guess three is better than no one.

Clearly there is a need for allies within schools and the community to assist with creating and maintaining GSAs, organizing events associated with IDAH and Day of Silence, and ensuring that SJ 12 is offered as an elective in local high schools. This would help to build a larger and more visible community of support for queer youth in the small city.

Building a Community of Queer Women

Fearing exposure, many women who were not out or selectively disclosed their identities avoided queer gatherings. At the same time, some participants who were out and proud, yet perhaps not visibly recognized to be queer in the small city, had difficulties accessing a community of queer women (Hulko & Hovanes, under review; see Rich, 1980; Sperling, 2010). The need for a means of tapping into the community was linked to the absence of space for LGBTQ community members to gather. The need for a small group specifically for queer women was also identified by a bisexual woman who wanted "to talk about sexual orientation, gender expression, experiences, struggles we have with coming out ... in a confidential and safe place." As one younger lesbian said, "I do think that having a community [is important] and ... I think that community is dependent on space. I think that those things together would create stronger individuals and create a stronger community for everybody." Underpinning the youth's desire for a community of queer women was a longing to meet and learn from out lesbian and bisexual women (see Snively, 2004). For example, a lesbian youth highlighted the significance of meeting a lesbian woman with a career in social services, a partner, and a child: "it was just so shocking to meet someone that has kind of what I want to have one day." Dedicated space—accessible and identifiable—for the queer youth program would increase the visibility of the existing community, potentially drawing other lesbian women and transgender persons as role models.

Discussion and Recommendations

Despite the impression queer youth "out yonder" are in greater need of support than those in urban centres (Poon & Saewyc, 2009; Wilkinson & Pearson, 2009), the participants in this research identified a number of opportunities for support and affirmation available through youth programs, schools and universities, the queer community, and the Internet. Further, their experiences of feeling unsafe in high school appeared no different than those of urban queer youth (Haskell & Burtch, 2010; Taylor & Peter, 2011). There is little research into the lives of queer youth in small cities and rural areas, and much of what exists focuses on barriers, risks, and gaps in service (Cohn & Hastings, 2010; Elze, 2007; Saewyc et al., 2007). While there certainly is a need for more formal support services in non-urban centres, there may be sources of support that youth are using or have already created that can be strengthened or formalized, including collaboration between members of different communities and groups in the small city, like those that research participants identified as sources of support, belonging, and identity affirmation.

While the movement of students active with GSAs and/or who have taken SJ 12 from high school to university has and will continue to strengthen the campus student club and allow for connections between high school and university queer youth, there are particular challenges associated with the dearth of openly queer role models in high schools and on university campuses in smaller cities or rural communities. Their limited number demands "major personal investment" by faculty members, including the need to be out in potentially hostile environments (D'Augelli, 2006; Siebecker, 2004). The lack of positive queer role models understandably impacts the ability to assign queer staff to work with the queer youth group or to recruit volunteers.

Making the small city a safer and affirming place will help more lesbian and bisexual women to openly identify as queer, freeing them to serve as role models for younger queer women (see Sperling, 2010).

Finding space to facilitate a queer women's group, for example, could provide an informal help network (Poon & Saewyc, 2009) and a means to counter compulsory heterosexuality (Rich, 1980) and the policing of gender (Wilchins, 2004) in the context of inter-generational support (Snively, 2004). Another way of building more inter-generational support could be through the creation of an adult/youth GSA like Snively (2004) did in a rural area of the United States. A first step would be to bring together representatives of the support services identified by youth—the queer youth group, the student clubs, and the local gay and lesbian association—and to make use of social media to promote this collaborative venture and report on the outcome or next steps. When building such an alliance, it will be important to acknowledge differences amongst queer youth based on their diverse intersecting identities.

Recommendations for Future Practice and Research with Queer Youth in Small Cities

This research suggests a number of ways in which social service workers and educators can improve their ability to serve queer youth in small cities and rural communities through collaboration and affirmation. Practitioners and policy makers must focus more attention on and devote more resources toward community building, including creating opportunities for queer youth to meet in accessible and safe environments and to connect with older lesbian and bisexual women and transgender persons, who can serve as role models and mentors. Further, programs should seek to reflect the diversity of queer youth and determine how best to honour these differences while seeking affinities (see Saewyc, 2011). For example, youth services could recruit and/or match openly queer staff with the queer youth program and match the identities of role models with those of the queer youth caught between two cultures. It has been argued that interventions "need to be adapted for different regions and ethnic groups, for males and females, and perhaps even for specific orientation groups" (Saewyc, 2011, p. 268). This research certainly indicates the need to offer trans-specific groups, and separate groups for lesbians and possibly also for bisexual women who are not out, in addition to women-only groups and groups for all queer youth. Additionally, youth programs could arrange training on sexual and gender diversity for their staff and offer workshops on being an ally for the youth who attend their programs. These steps might address the concerns younger lesbian, bisexual women, and transgender youth expressed about their participation in general youth programs.

GSAs should be created in more small cities and rural areas across Canada. Currently there are 100 GSAs registered on Egale Canada's website (Taylor & Peter, 2011), yet there are only two small cities in the interior of BC and two in the North listed as having GSAs (see educators.mygsa.ca/gsas-canada). In addition to assigning queer-positive teacher mentors to GSAs and stressing the critical role played by GSAs to parents, teachers, or straight students who question their existence (Walls et al., 2010), all high schools in BC should offer SJ 12 as an elective. This would mean encouraging teachers to take on the responsibility for SJ 12 and supporting those who do, while also encouraging students to enroll and celebrate their collective efforts toward achieving social justice. Anti-bullying policies in schools are required as well (Meyers, 2009; Poon & Saewyc, 2009), as "actions to promote LGBTQ inclusion in the formal discourses of schools ... are among the strongest predictors of which schools are safer than others" (Toomey et al., 2012, p. 194). In order for these objectives to be achieved, boards of education, principals, and vice-principals need to demonstrate leadership by encouraging and supporting initiatives that seek to reduce heterosexism and homo/lesbo/trans/biphobia in schools.

Further, campus student clubs would benefit from assigned faculty mentors and a formal connection with both the GSAs in the area and the local gay and lesbian association. The latter could create a youth position on the board and sponsor community events other than dances.

In addition to more comprehensive studies on the experiences of queer youth in rural areas and small cities, future research needs to consider other dimensions of intersecting identities in greater depth, that is, to ensure that samples are diverse and that this diversity informs data analysis. Evaluative studies of the impact of support services and educational programs, including websites aimed at queer youth and the SJ 12 course in high schools, are also needed.

This chapter focuses on the challenges experienced by and supports available to queer youth who reside in small cities and rural communities, particularly those who identify as women. It demonstrates how geographic location impacts the lived experiences of LGBTQ youth and intersects with other social identity categories. The recommendations emphasize collaboration and affirmation that build on existing supports in the small city, while others speak to gaps that result from the sociocultural context of the participants' lives as residents of small cities and rural communities. These recommendations, if adopted, can enhance the well-being of queer youth in the small city, as well as their much-needed sense of belonging and community.

Notes

1. This chapter arose out of research conducted in collaboration with Natalie Clark and Jessica Hovanes, through funding from two SSHRC Aid to Small Universities grants, and two Michael Smith Foundation for Health Research grants (Women's Health Research Network and BC Rural and Remote Research Network). I would like to thank Natalie and Jessica, BSW student research assistants Erica Bouffioux and Megan Stevenson, and all the research participants and community partners for their contributions to this research project.
2. This chapter pertains only to the youth participants.
3. While the project focused on women and girls, both male to female and female to male transgender youth sought to participate. Three trans men—none of whom had transitioned—opted into the study, knowing the researchers were seeking "women and girls."

References

Bowleg, L. (2008). When black + lesbian + women = black lesbian woman: The methodological challenges of qualitative and quantitative intersectionality research. *Sex Roles, 59*, 312–325.

Brown, L., & Strega, S. (Eds.) (2005). *Research as resistance: Critical, Indigenous and anti-oppressive approaches.* Toronto, ON: Canadian Scholars' Press.

Cohn, T. J., & Hastings, S. L. (2010). Resilience among rural lesbian youth. *Journal of Lesbian Studies, 14*(1), 71–79.

Combahee River Collective. (1977). The Combahee River Collective statement. Retrieved from zinelibrary.info/files/Combahee3.pdf

D'Augelli, A. R. (2006). Coming out, visibility, and creating change: Empowering lesbian, gay, and bisexual people in a rural university community. *American Journal of Community Psychology, 37*, 203–210.

Diamond, L. M. (1998). Development of sexual orientation among adolescent and young adult women. *Developmental Psychology, 34*(5), 1085–1095.

Diamond, L. M., & Butterworth, M. (2008). Questioning gender and sexual identity: Dynamic links over time. *Sex Roles, 59*, 365–376.

Elze, D. E. (2007). Research with sexual minority youths. *Journal of Gay & Lesbian Social Services, 18*(2), 73–99.

Gray, M. L. (2009). *Out in the country: Youth, media and queer visibility in rural America.* New York, NY: New York University Press.

Grossman, A. H., & D'Augelli, A. R. (2006). Transgender youth: Invisible and vulnerable. *Journal of Homosexuality, 51*(1), 111–128.

Haskell, R., & Burtch, B. (2010). *Get that freak: Homophobia and transphobia in high schools.* Halifax, NS: Fernwood Publishing.

Hill Collins, P. (2000). *Black feminist thought: Knowledge, consciousness, and the politics of empowerment* (2nd ed.). New York, NY: Routledge.

Hulko, W. (2009). The time and context contingent nature of intersectionality and interlocking oppressions. *Affilia, 24*(1), 44–55.

Hulko, W. (in press). Being queer in the small city. In C. Walmsley & T. Kading (Eds.), *Power and possibility in the small city* [provisional title]. Edmonton, AB: Athabasca University Press.

Hulko, W., & Hovanes, J. (under review). Intersectionality in the lives of LGBTQ youth: Identifying and finding community in small cities and rural communities. *Journal of Homosexuality.*

Hulko, W., Bepple, K., Turco, J., & Clark, N. (2010). Safe spaces in BC's interior: Working with LGBT youth to promote mental health. *Visions: BC's Mental Health and Addictions Journal, 6*(2), 27–29. Retreived from www.heretohelp.bc.ca/sites/default/files/visions_lesbian_gay_bt.pdf

Kirby, S., Greaves, L., & Reid, C. (2006). *Experience, research, social change: Methods beyond the mainstream* (2nd ed). Peterborough, ON: Broadview Press.

Lorde, A. (2007). Age, race, class and sex: Women redefining difference. In A. Lorde, *Sister outsider: Essays and speeches by Audre Lorde* (pp. 114–123). Berkeley, CA: Crossing Press. (Original work published 1984.)

Mehrotra, G. (2010). Toward a continuum of intersectionality theorizing for feminist social work scholarship. *Affilia, 25,* 417–430.

Meyers, E. J. (2009). *Gender, bullying and harassment: Strategies to end sexism and homophobia in schools.* New York, NY: Teachers College Press.

Ministry of Education, Province of British Columbia. (2008). *Social Justice 12 integrated resource package 2008.* Victoria: Ministry of Education, Province of British Columbia.

Murphy, Y., Hunt, V., Zajicek, A. M., Norris, A. N., & Hamilton, L. (2009). *Incorporating intersectionality in social work practice, research, policy, and education.* Washington, DC: NASW Press.

Poon, C. S., & Saewyc, E. (2009). Out yonder: Sexual-minority adolescents in rural communities in British Columbia. *American Journal of Public Health, 99*(1), 118–124.

Rich, A. (1980). Compulsory heterosexuality and lesbian existence. *Signs, 5*(4), 631–660.

Saewyc, E. M. (2011). Research on adolescent sexual orientation: Development, health disparities, stigma and resilience. *Journal of Research on Adolescence, 21*(1), 256–272.

Saewyc, E., Poon, C., Wang, N., Homma, Y., Smith, A., & McCreary Centre Society (2007). *Not yet equal: The health of lesbian, gay, & bisexual youth in BC.* Vancouver, BC: McCreary Centre Society.

Siebecker, M. (2004). To be or not to be ... out in the academy. *Law & Inequality,* 22, 141–168.

Snively, C. A. (2004). Building community-based alliances between GLBTQQA youth and adults in rural settings. *Journal of Gay & Lesbian Social Services,* 16(3-4), 99-112.

Sperling, R.L. (2010). Conspicuously absent: Lesbians in professional social work. *Affilia,* 25(3), 250–263.

Taylor, C., & Peter, T. with McMinn, T. L., Elliot, T., Beldom, S., Ferry, A., Gross, Z., Paquin, S., & Schachter, K. (2011). *Every class in every school: The first national climate survey on homophobia, biophobia, and transphobia in Canadian schools. Final report.* Toronto, ON: Egale Canada Human Rights Trust.

Toomey, R. B., McGuire, J. K., & Russell, S. T. (2012). Heteronormativity, school climates and perceived safety for gender nonconforming peers. *Journal of Adolescence,* 35, 187–196.

Urban Native Youth Association. (2004, March). *Two-spirit youth speak out: Analysis of the needs assessment tool.* Vancouver, BC: Urban Native Youth Association.

Walls, N. E., Kane, S. B., & Wisneski, H. (2010). Gay-straight alliances and school experiences of sexual minority youth. *Youth & Society,* 41(3), 307–332.

Wilchins, R. A. (2004). *Queer theory/gender theory: An instant primer.* Los Angeles, CA: Alyson Books.

Wilkinson, L., & Pearson, J. (2009). School culture and the wellbeing of same sex attracted youth. *Gender & Society,* 23(4), 542–568.

CHAPTER 11
Collective Trauma as a Personal/Social Concern for LGBTTTSQ Persons

Susan McGrath, Bill Lee, Ken Moffatt, Mirna Carranza, and Andrea Lagios[1]

A growing body of literature addresses how emotional responses are tied to social relations, whereby the way people express affect is linked to their relationships with others. The emotional lives of individuals are not separate from their relational networks (see for example Fuss, 1991; Kristeva & Lotringer, 2002; Moffatt, 2004; Salzman, 2001; Zarowsky, 2004). Community practice literature explores the multiple social networks people participate in to contribute to the development of their emotional lives (see Kirmayer, Brass, & Tait, 2000; Kidron, 2003).

Queer theory has been at the forefront of conceptualizing emotional states such as shame (Halperin & Traub, 2009; Moffatt, 2012; Sedgwick, 2009) and rage (Cvetkovich, 2003; Halberstam, 2011) as socially constructed and public in nature. These emotional states are tied to the continual experience of domination and prejudice. At times, the experience of these emotions can be debilitating. Other times, they are "taken back" by lesbian, gay, bisexual, transgender, transsexual, Two-Spirited, and queer (LGBTTTSQ) persons in order to disrupt ever-present dominant gender and social conventions that have been used to construct dominant straight identities as "normal" (Halberstam, 2011; Moffatt, 2012; Noble, 2006). Toronto-based authors have specifically written about trauma as a socially shared experience felt in a personal manner (Burstow, 2003; Noble, 2006).

This chapter draws on a study by four professors from three Ontario universities, funded by the Social Science and Humanities Research Council of Canada (SSHRC). The focus on the experiences of collective trauma by three marginalized communities—Aboriginal, El Salvadorian refugee, and LGBTTTSQ—involved community leaders and activists from each of these groups. This chapter specifically explores the relationship of trauma, a shared injurious experience to which a community responds (Sztompka, 2004), to the experiences of members of the LGBTTTSQ community. Based on our findings, we argue that an LGBTTTSQ person does not have to experience a traumatic act personally in order to feel the emotional and social effect of that trauma. Canada's LGBTTTSQ community is diverse in terms of racial, ethnic, class, ability, and gender identities (Brotman & Lee, 2011; Poon, 2011); in Ontario, the community is widely dispersed while having a geographic centre in the City of Toronto (Lepischak, 2000). Our chapter offers a means to think about some relations that may bind a queer community while not minimizing differential experience due to prejudice based on race, gender, class, ethnicity, and ability.

Experience of Social Marginalization and Trauma

Marginalization represents a form of oppression that excludes entire groups of people from meaningful aspects of participation in society (McGrath, Moffatt, George, & Lee, 2007; Young, 2000). The social results may include material deprivation, social exclusion, and underemployment (Lee, 2011). Many marginalized communities constitute a growing underclass permanently confined to the fringes of society because the education system or labour market cannot or will not accommodate them. Members of marginalized communities are blocked from the opportunity to exercise their capacities in a socially defined way that is valued, recognized, and respected (Young, 2000). These experiences of marginalization can have traumatic impacts on the community and its members.

Various authors have expanded on the link between individual affect and relational systems by focusing on how trauma is a shared experience with social roots among marginalized communities (Alexander, 2004; Fuss, 1991; Noble, 2006). Specifically, the social relations associated with the process of marginalization are perpetuated by social forces outside the marginalized community and contribute to a sense of trauma (Antone, Miller, & Myers, 1986; Sonn & Fisher, 1998). Burstow (2003) notes that when community theorists discuss trauma within communities, the intention is not to imply that all people within a given community are traumatized, rather "the community as an integral whole is traumatized" by social forces that are sometimes beyond their control (p. 1297). This traumatization of an entire community results from the long-term oppressive conditions that dehumanize social relations among people (Martín-Baró, Aron, & Corne, 1996). Trauma is understood as a shared experience to which the entire community responds (Herman, 1992; Sztompka, 2004). Rather than a medicalized disorder to be controlled by psychiatry, trauma is conceptualized as a reaction to injurious social events and situations that cause people to be wounded. It is conceived as inherently political, given that traumatic events occur within specific contexts grounded in societal structures (Burstow, 2003).

The effects of social trauma can affect the identity of community members and social cohesion within the community. Eyerman (2004) argues the effects of collective trauma can be profound, resulting in "a dramatic loss of identity and meaning, a tear in the social fabric, affecting a group of people who have achieved some degree of cohesion" (p. 160). Scott (2000) states traumatic experiences lead to "a perennial mourning of an identity long-lost and a perpetual sense of victimization that continues to weigh heavily upon much of the group" (p. 13). Community trauma may be expressed through despair, loss of tradition, and the breakdown of people's connections with each other (Burstow, 2003). As a result, the impacts of trauma may also extend across generations (Brave Heart, 2000; Kidron, 2003; Salzman, 2001) and unhealed wounds may cause trauma to be experienced by various groups within the community on a daily basis (Coutin, 2001; James, 2004).

In spite of these tremendous pressures on marginalized communities, community relationships constitute a means of overcoming the effects of trauma. Herman (1992) observes that "those who have survived learn that their sense of self, of worth, of humanity, depends upon a feeling of connection to others. The solidarity of a group provides the strongest antidote to traumatic experience" (p. 214). The process of identifying a shared experience can help communities recognize a common cause of their pain, allowing them to further define and expand their solidarity (Alexander, 2004). Given that members of a community possess a unique understanding of their history and daily lives (Narayan, 1988), their knowledge can be conceptualized as a "resource"; it entails their implicit but rich understanding of the context in which their trauma emerged and developed, how it affected their community, and how they have attempted to deal with its effects (Fuertes, 2004, p. 492).

LGBTTTSQ community members have experienced marginalization through violence as well as through silencing and the ongoing historical refusal to acknowledge their existence (Duberman, 1999; Kinsman, 1996; O'Brien, 1999; Pyne, 2011). In addition, LGBTTTSQ persons in Ontario have been highly regulated through police surveillance, legal action, and social ostracism, such that many community members have not experienced full civic participation as valued citizens (Kinsman, 1996; Warner, 2002). Kinsman (1996) specifically illustrates how the Canadian LGBTTTSQ community is subject to moral regulation through a series of texts, language, institutions, policies, laws, and practices all put in place to regulate sexuality. Many professions, police, doctors, social workers, and psychologists have categorized, regulated, and disciplined LGBTTTSQ persons through social mechanisms that include essentializing and pathologizing LGBTTTSQ identities, suggesting they need intervention and repair (Foucault, 1991;

Kinsman, 1996; Pyne, 2011). A unique aspect of the marginalization of the LGBTTTSQ community is that it is expected to remain invisible or quiet (Kinsman, 1996).

Members of the community need to be vigilant in terms of the ongoing and persistent threat of prejudice, verbal abuse, and physical violence (Lepischak, 2000; O'Brien, 1994). In some cases, community members may lose the support of family members who also hold prejudicial views; the inability to draw on familial support, combined with inequitable access to discriminatory social services, places them in an especially vulnerable position. Some community members, especially youth and the elderly, do not have access to proper material care in terms of housing, health services, and food, and therefore are vulnerable to discrimination, exploitation, and poverty (Daley, 1998; Lepischak, 2000; O'Brien, 1994; Pyne, 2011).

Tensions within Resistance

The political organizing and advocacy tied to emotions such as shame, anger, and trauma within Ontario are complex. Organizing has focused on LGBTTTSQ rights (including the right to privacy) (Mulé, 2010), the LGBTTTSQ community as a minority group (Nash, 2005), and the creation and protection of queer space, cultures, and identities (Moffatt, 2012; Noble, 2006; Warner, 2002). The movement has ranged from assimilationist politics for individual rights to fit better into mainstream notions of family and community, to liberationist politics based on the idea that queers and their community are utterly different from the mainstream and current social structures must change, since the social mores and taken for granted social roles are oppressive in nature. This liberationist approach demands a restructuring of hegemonic social relationships (Mulé, 2006, 2010). The histories of queer persons in Ontario are complex due to the many racialized persons and ethnicities, and the multiple genders within the community (Goldie, 2001) and, at times, the tendency to replicate social relations of dominance within the community based on race and gender (Goldie, 2001; Poon, 2011). The politics of gay liberation and rights-based organizing are rife with tensions and contradictions. For example, the Campaign for Equal Families, while rights-based, was accused of being based on heteronormative assumptions and assimilationist politics (Mulé, 2010). Services for LGBTTTSQ people are often hidden within other services, such as health services for AIDS or women's services, which in fact continues to make the LGBTTTSQ community invisible. At times, this approach tends to universalize identities and at other times, reinforces dominance by class and race (Nash, 2005). Furthermore, as Ontario's LGBTTTSQ community became more visible, some critiques within the community became evident. Groups such as AIDS Action Now and Queer Nation, who took direct action, have challenged not only the dominant social and economic relations, but also some of the divisions within the queer community due to social location and dominance (Goldie, 2001). As well, groups who have organized around race, such as the Black Coalition for Aids Prevention (Black CAP), have challenged the dominant white assumptions about queer identity.

Along with the many forms of regulation and discrimination LGBTTTSQ persons experience daily (Moffatt, 2012), the community is under constant threat of physical violence and backlash against its advances. The infamous Toronto bathhouse raids by the police in 1981 (Kinsman, 1996; Warner, 2002) were particularly effective as a form of moral regulation, due to the public exposure and shaming enacted against persons who had been too fearful to acknowledge their LGBTTTSQ identities. Attempts to criminalize and morally regulate the gay community have been met with anger leading to rebellion; the bathhouse raids "served to politicize, radicalize, and further define the gay community" (Kinsman, 1996, p. 342). The community response to the raids may have prevented other acts of state repression by signalling a shift in the balance of power away from the police, in favour of the queer community (Warner, 2002).

AIDS has had a significant impact on the LGBTTTSQ community as a form of marginalization that allowed persons to elaborate an extant bias that LGBTTTSQ persons are morally suspect and diseased. With AIDS, the shunning of the community was overt and commonplace (Schulman, 2012); however, there was a community mobilization that occurred across gender and within racialized communities that resulted in the development of many community supports, such as the AIDS Committee of Toronto, Hassle Free Clinic, Black CAP, and Asian Community AIDS Service. While histories of the LGBTTTSQ community are often characterized through big events, advocates, and a linear progression to improvement, in fact the histories are complex due to the intricate makeup of the community and individual subjectivities.

Research Method

Our research sought to explore the notion of collective trauma and to demonstrate that one does not have to experience trauma personally in order to feel its effect socially. To this end, we utilized a research method that reflects the recent trend in interpretive and reflective research designs as a means of opening space to examine issues related to community experiences of marginalization (Coady & Wolgien, 1996; Fook, Ryan, & Hawkins, 1994). An advisory group that included LGBTTTSQ community members provided consultation on the purpose and direction of the research, the interview guide, and preliminary findings. The interview schedule sought to explore community members' understandings of the concept of collective trauma, asking questions to determine what the notion of a shared trauma means to them, what the internal and external sources of trauma for the community are, what collective trauma looks like manifested within the community, whether historical events have an impact on the community, and how trauma affects efforts to organize within the community.

Participants were recruited using a snowball technique drawing on the researchers' existing social networks (Trevillion, 2000). We interviewed nine LGBTTTSQ community members who are involved with social service organizations and/or are community leaders, spokespersons, or activists in urban centres across Southern Ontario where there are sizable queer populations. Each of these participants is representative of diverse identities within the LGBTTTSQ community and also occupies various points of intersection with other marginalized communities.

Throughout the research, the team, which includes both gay-identified and straight-identified members, took an inductive approach, looking for major themes that emerged from transcribed interviews (Martínez-Brawley, 2001; Schon, 1983, 1987). The advisory group challenged some of the conclusions we had reached, while at other times we reached easy consensus on the themes drawn from the data (Moustakas, 1990). We reflected on how the conclusions of the research could best be understood for the community and looked to those with the greatest experience with the particular community, drawing on their lived experience and insight to interpret our findings.

Findings: You Do Not Have to Experience Trauma Personally to Be Affected

Through our longitudinal multi-year study of community practice within urban marginalized communities, we discovered that the term *marginalization* did not best represent some of the emotional responses that influence the nature of community relations and, therefore, community practice. The following findings about the shared nature of trauma are part of the exploration of community processes in marginalized communities. A key finding of our research on trauma is that individual and collective acts of prejudice or political violence that happen to one member of the community have a traumatic effect on the other members, regardless of individuals' personal proximity to the traumatic event, including their geographical distance or whether they experienced the trauma personally and directly.

COLLECTIVE TRAUMA

LGBTTTSQ community respondents noted the shared nature of trauma and explained some of the sources of that trauma, which included political discipline by the state, prejudicial reactions to the disease AIDS, the effects of AIDS, and physical violence. Simon, a gay Black social worker in an agency that serves people who are HIV-positive, spoke to the pervasiveness of the sources of trauma.

> I think as queer people we experience the collective experience about homophobia and heterosexism that really contributes to our shared trauma. There's no doubt. I think also sexual violence as well is something that we don't talk about. In queer communities it's something that we have collectively experienced. I think sexual violence could be classified in a number of different ways. And obviously people can be traumatized by words, by ideas, by social conditions right, in direct and indirect ways.

Simon illustrated that not only does a shared trauma exist within the queer community, but it is perpetuated in various ways that contribute to its insidious nature. Steven is a married man in a same-sex relationship, a gay, Black Jamaican-Canadian father who works with youth and families. His words demonstrated how injurious acts can affect a person across national borders:

> At the same time many—there was a vote in California about gay marriage right? And it was decided that they would ban gay marriage and in fact one state even banned adoption. One of the American states also had a referendum on whether or not gays should be able to adopt children. It's a huge issue in my life. So does that matter to me? Does it affect me? I think it does.... Of course, well I adopted a kid. There's no ban here but I was very hurt.... Wherever that ban is, yeah I'm connected. It has

everything to do with me. Maybe it's about identity right? You know, the experience of oppression.

Steven spoke further about the intrinsic and transnational impacts of such decisions:

> It means some part of the state in California doesn't believe I'm a person, or there's something evil, intrinsically evil about me that I would be banned from raising children. There's something intrinsically evil about me being around children or raising children, instilling my values on, or whatever gifts that I have.... There's something wrong. I think it is traumatizing. I think it is traumatizing.

Solomon, a Jewish transgender female to male, is an activist who works with youth. He explained how AIDS in Canada has historically been closely associated with the LGBTTTSQ community and the traumatic effect on community members:

> I think also, the things that happen on a community level ... that have ramifications for everybody, even if they haven't necessarily had a personal, individual experience of it. So things like ... HIV/AIDS that have a traumatic experience on the community level. In some ways regardless, they have different impacts on different people, for sure.... but also have a community level effect.

He suggested that the trauma of HIV/AIDS occurs at the community level, having an effect on many individuals in a community that is diverse.

Barb, a lesbian mother of Ukrainian-Canadian descent in a same-sex marriage, administers a large LGBTTTSQ-focused community-based health program. She concurred with Solomon about the historical significance of AIDS as a traumatic community event:

I think the AIDS crisis especially in the early years when people didn't know what was going on and the response was really small and very blaming and victimizing ... sort of intensified all the homophobia that existed in society at that time. And people were experiencing incredible personal trauma through all the deaths that they had to deal with on a day-to-day basis.

Saul, a single, gay Jewish male who works with an LGBTTTSQ anti-violence and counselling program, highlighted how violence experienced by one member of the community can affect another member who has not experienced it directly:

For me the term collective trauma implies, I guess, how we each experience trauma in one way or another, either from our own personal trauma that we've experienced or from those that we know. And certainly, you know, there is unfortunately an abundance of violence and harassment that the LGBT community faces. And so if you yourself haven't experienced a bashing or verbal harassment of one form or another it would seem very likely, it's not impossible, but you know of somebody who has ... and so I think we all sort of experience, experience it in different ways, but I think unfortunately it's something that's very familiar to us, to us all.

Barb was explicit in explaining that you need not have experienced the traumatic event itself to understand it. She indicated that the sources of trauma are multiple and entail insecure employment, violence, legal actions, as well as the use of police force and abuse of authority against community members. Highlighting the historical event of the bath-house raids, she stated,

Okay. I feel like ... to be someone who experiences that sense of collective trauma in a community doesn't mean that you individually have to have experienced trauma, that you individually have to have been fired from a job or assaulted or threatened or anything like that. It's about knowing that you are a member of a group to whom that happens a lot and where political decisions sometimes happen that are traumatizing, where legal decisions happen that are traumatizing ... so I would define the bathhouse raids as a situation where collective trauma was created.

Barb also indicated,

The whole sense of integrity of the whole group, that's my sense of what collective trauma is. ... It is a constant reminder that you still are really vulnerable ... hated and despised. And it's not just one person, it is as a group.

Participants also spoke about the extent to which a shared experience of collective trauma contributes to a sense of group affinity or solidarity, whereby a collective experience of harm serves to connect members of a marginalized community with each other. Steven stated,

Even though it's not happening to me, because I have a connection with or affinity with or some, I identify myself ... with the same potential to be oppressed as the folks who are experiencing that, then everybody, I guess we're not free until all of us are free right? So if something horrible can happen over here, yeah, I can feel that pain over here even though I'm not where it happens because ... there's some collective whatever that connects us.

Barb also spoke to the concept of solidarity through a shared experience of trauma, noting the potential for overcoming traumatic histories through this connection:

It's also the kind of thing that as a community it's very important to recognize it as such and not simply look at individual situations and assume that the only thing that's happening out there is those individual acts of whatever victimizations; that it's political to recognize this as an assault on a whole community and that's both, I mean, I think it creates solidarity and it's the only way to move out of staying in a traumatized state.

Simon noted the importance of healing and supports found within the community:

I think organizations like this are really I think big sources of healing and resilience. I remember my first pride parade and marching in the parade.... I didn't but a lot of folks had to leave our families because it wasn't a safe space for them. And I think our chosen families are incredible sources of healing and resilience in terms of opportunities for mentorship. You know just learning how to be gay and learning how to live that healthy gay life, having a social network place that's engaged in your health and one that's I think a really important thing. I think activism as well is really an important source of incredible power in reclaiming what's been taken away from us.

He went on to point out the empowering impact of activism and how individual acts of resistance address the collective impact of trauma upon the community:

Yeah and then we're also finding ... it empowers another group, empowers 10, empowers 10 more and I think that's one of the beautiful things about the queer community is that we're a community of activists and even if you're only a person who is, you know, willing to live with your boyfriend. And even if you're doing that and your family doesn't even know you're gay, I think that's an act of resistance, you know. Walking down the street with your partner and just, you know, holding his hand, that's an act of resistance. It's a public act, it's not an active act but it's still an act of resistance. And I think we've got this incredible tradition in the queer community.... We've all experienced this collectively. We all have a collective role in revisiting the conditions that contribute to this trauma and there's a little thing that I can do.

Discussion

The position taken by Eyerman (2004) and Scott (2000), that trauma becomes part of the identity of the community, is clear. Participants often referred to how trauma was a crucial aspect of their connections with each other. Further, Burstow's (2003) assertion of the notion of trauma as a political phenomenon is also echoed throughout the responses. Many people continue to live in fear and silence, experiencing still the need to protect themselves through dominant demands for invisibility. As in any community, there are people who deal with a multiplicity of marginalizing processes, such as individuals who are racialized.

The participants do not minimize their differences or the power struggles within the community through being aware of how trauma is shared or imagining other people's struggles. In fact, they speak quite specifically of their own social locations within the community, while imagining a broader community or interlocking communities. More than one person spoke to the particular vulnerability of trans people to violence and prejudice at this moment in Ontario. While one should not minimize the differing experiences of trauma due to social location and multiplicity of identities within the community and the ways with which dominant social relations are replicated in the community due to gender, race, class, and ability, this sense of affinity is a hopeful moment for community practice engagement.

Implications for Social Work Practice

Understanding the experiences of marginalized communities through a lens of collective trauma presents social work practitioners with opportunities to appreciate the nuanced realities of shared harm. Beyond focusing on the extent to which communities are victims of ongoing trauma, viewing marginalization among collective groups also suggests the extent to which these communities have worked through traumatic experiences to shape a shared identity that opposes the oppressive conditions they have faced. Community reactions to oppression and marginalization influence how members constitute their identity (Moffatt, George, Lee, & McGarth, 2005), while that same collective identity, despite being injured, may underpin a community's efforts aimed at recovery and resistance to trauma and oppression (Alexander, 2004; Burstow, 2003, 2005; Herman, 1992; Sztompka, 2004). By examining forms of trauma that are widespread and recur over time, we call on social work practitioners to adequately incorporate an understanding and appreciation of trauma in their work with diverse members of marginalized communities. What we learn from viewing trauma as an ongoing collective experience is that we must attend to much more than a single traumatic event; in fact, we must recognize the way in which trauma continues to affect individuals and communities over time. Social workers must recognize and address persistent elements of marginalization and its relationship with ongoing trauma.

Part of this recognition of ongoing collective trauma also entails being attuned to the risk of retraumatization, particularly as major events affect community members. As social workers, we must be aware of how ongoing events will have an impact upon those with whom we work, drawing the link between current social forces and histories of widespread trauma.

There is also a need to increase public awareness about both the achievements and challenges experienced by the LGBTTTSQ community. We argue that while it is important to acknowledge advancements—such as the attainment of same-sex marriage in some jurisdictions (Bill C-38, 2005), access to benefits (Department of Justice, 2012), the recent Ontario legislation ensuring the right to have gay/straight alliance clubs in schools (Bill 13, 2012), among others—marginalization may not actually be decreasing, but rather may be taking on many new forms in advancing social contexts (such as the continued and changing need for access to health care, and random acts of violence) (Mulé, 2010).

Our respondents clearly stated that trauma persists in many forms due to troubling social relations of dominance. It is thought of as a daily occurrence, as well as one that is enacted through extraordinary acts of prejudice and violence. Further studies could consider the very specific manner in which trauma is experienced in specific social locations. How shame, as a defining feature of LGBTTTSQ identities based on prejudicial dominant relations (Eribon, 2004; Munt, 2008; Sedgwick, 2009) relates to trauma, could also be explored. Viewing marginalization and collective trauma historically and generationally helps us to understand that as achievements are made, new challenges also arise. We challenge social workers to move beyond, for instance, mythologies of a "safe space," so that we do not assume the contexts we work within are inherently "safe" for LGBTTTSQ community members. We challenge social workers to work toward creating respectful and supportive environments in a constantly changing social context, while recognizing how affective states change with shifting social relations.

Notes

1. Contact person: Susan McGrath, smcgrath@yorku.ca

References

Alexander, J. C. (2004). Collective trauma and collective identity. In J. C. Alexander, N. J. Smelser, R. Eyerman, B. Giesen, & P. Sztompka (Eds.), *Toward a theory of cultural trauma* (pp. 1–30). Berkeley, CA: University of California Press.

Antone, R., Miller, D., & Myers, B. (1986). *The power within people: A community organizing perspective.* Toronto, ON: Tribal Sovereignty Associates.

Bill 13: Accepting Schools Act. (2011) First reading Nov. 30, 2011. Legislative Assembly of Ontario. Retrieved from ontla.on.ca/web/bills/bills_detail.do?locale=en&BillID=2549&detailPage=bills_detail_the_bill

Bill C-38: The Civil Marriage Act. (2005). First Reading Feb. 1, 2005, 38th Parliament, 1st session. Retrieved from www.parl.gc.ca/About/Parliament/LegislativeSummaries/bills_ls.asp?ls=c38&Parl=38&Ses=1

Brave Heart, M. (2000). Wakiksuyapi: Carrying the historical trauma of the Lakota. *Tulane Studies in Social Welfare, 21*(22), 245–266.

Brotman, S., & Lee, E. O. U. (2011). Exploring gender and sexuality through the lens of intersectionality: Sexual minority refugees in Canada. *Canadian Social Work Review 28*(1), 151–156.

Burstow, B. (2003). Toward a radical understanding of trauma and trauma work. *Violence Against Women, 9*(11), 1293–1317.

Burstow, B. (2005). A critique of posttraumatic stress disorder and the DSM. *Journal of Humanistic Psychology, 45*, 429–445.

Coady, N. F., & Wolgien, C.S. (1996). Good therapists' views of how they are helpful in cross-cultural clinical practice. *Clinical Social Work Journal 24*(3), 311–322.

Coutin, S. B. (2001). The oppressed, the suspect, and the citizen: Subjectivity in competing accounts of political violence. *Law & Social Inquiry, 26*(1), 63–94.

Cvetkovich, A. (2003). *An archive of feelings: Trauma, sexuality and lesbian public cultures.* Durham, NC: Duke University Press.

Daley, A. (1998). Lesbian invisibility in health care services: Heterosexual hegemony and strategies for change. *Canadian Social Work Review, 15*(1), 57–71.

Department of Justice. (2012). Marriage and legal recognition of same-sex unions—A discussion paper. Retrieved from www.justice.gc.ca/eng/dept-min/pub/mar/2.html

Duberman, M. B. (1999). *Left out: The politics of exclusion. Essays 1964–1999.* New York, NY: Basic Books.

Eribon, D. (2004). *Insult and making of the gay self.* Durham, NC: Duke University Press.

Eyerman, R. (2004). The past in the present: Culture and the transmission of memory. *Acta Sociologica, 47*(2), 159–169.

Fook, J., Ryan, M., & Hawkins, L. (1994). Expertise in social work practice: An exploratory study. *Canadian Social Work Review 13*(1), 7–22.

Fuertes, A. B. (2004). In their own words: Contextualizing the discourse of (war) trauma and healing. *Conflict Resolution Quarterly, 21*(4), 491–501.

Foucault, M. (1991). *The history of sexuality, Volume 1*. London, England: Penguin.

Fuss, D. (1991). *Inside/out: Lesbian theories, gay theories*. New York, NY: Routledge.

Goldie, T. (2001) Queer Nation? In T. Goldie (Ed.), *A queer country* (pp. 7–26). Vancouver, BC: Arsenal Pulp Press.

Halberstam, J. (2011). *The queer art of failure*. Durham, NC: Duke University Press.

Halperin D. M., & Traub, V. (Eds.) (2009).*Gay shame*. Chicago, IL: University of Chicago Press.

Herman, J. L. (1992). *Trauma and recovery*. New York, NY: Basic Books.

James, C. (2004). Urban education: An approach to community-based education. *Intercultural Education, 15*(1), 15–32.

Kidron, C. A. (2003). Surviving a distant past: A case study of the cultural construction of trauma descendant identity. *Ethos, 31*(4), 513–544.

Kinsman, G. W. (1996). *The regulation of desire: Homo and hetero sexualities*. Montreal, QC: Black Rose Books.

Kirmayer, L., Brass, G., & Tait, C. (2000). The mental health of Aboriginal peoples: Transformations of identity and community. *Canadian Journal of Psychiatry, 45*(7), 607–616.

Kristeva, J., & Lotringer, S. (2002). *Revolt, she said*. New York, NY: Semiotext(e).

Lepischak, B. (2000). Supporting out youth: Building community for queer youth in Toronto. Practice-based research paper, Graduate Program in Social Work, York University, Toronto, ON.

Lee, B. (2011). *Pragmatics of community organization* (4th ed.). Toronto, ON: Common Act Press.

Martín-Baró, I., Aron, A., & Corne, S. (1996). *Writings for a liberation psychology*. Cambridge, MA: Harvard University Press.

Martínez-Brawley, E. E. (2001). Searching again and again: Inclusion, heterogeneity and social work. *British Journal of Social Work 31*, 271–285.

McGrath, S., Moffatt, K., George, U., & Lee, B. (2007). Seeking social justice: Community practice within diverse marginalized populations in Canada. *Social Development Issues 29*(2), 77–91.

Moffatt, K. (2004). Beyond male denial and female shame: Learning about gender in a sociocultural concepts class. *Smith College Studies in Social Work, Special Issue on Teaching, 74*(2), 243–256.

Moffatt K. (2012). Shame and men: A queer perspective on masculinity. *C Magazine, 114*(Summer), 5–8.

Moffatt, K., George, U., Lee, B., & McGrath, S. (2005). The subjective encounter in community practice research. *British Journal of Social Work, 35,* 89–104.

Moustakas, C. E. (1990). *Heuristic Research: Design, Methodology and Applications.* Newbury Park, CA: Sage.

Mulé, N. J. (2006). Equality's limitations, liberation's challenges: Considerations for queer movement strategizing. *Canadian Online Journal of Queer Studies in Education, 2*(1). Retrieved from jqstudies.library.utoronto.ca/index.php/jqstudies/article/view/3290

Mulé, N. J. (2010). Same-sex marriage and Canadian relationship recognition—One step forward, two steps back: A critical liberationist perspective. *The Journal of Gay and Lesbian Social Services* (special issue), *22*(1/2), 74–90.

Munt, S. (2008). *Queer Attachments: The cultural politics of shame.* Aldershot, England: Ashgate Publishing.

Narayan, U. (1988). Working together across difference: Some considerations on emotions and political practice. *Hypatia, 31*(2), 31–47.

Nash, C. J. (2005). Contesting identity: Politics of gays and lesbians in Toronto in the 1970s. *Gender, Place and Culture, 12*(1), 113–135.

Noble, J. B. (2006). *Sons of the movement: FtMs risking incoherence on a post-queer cultural landscape.* Toronto, ON: Women's Press.

O'Brien, C. A. (1994). The social organization of the treatment of lesbian, gay, and bisexual youth in group homes and youth shelters. *Canadian Review of Social Policy, 34,* 37–57.

O'Brien, C. A. (1999). Contested territory: Sexualities and social work. In A. Chambon, A. Irving, & L. Epstein (Eds.), *Reading Foucault for social work* (p. 131). New York, NY: Columbia University Press.

Poon, M. K. L. (2011). Writing the racialized queer bodies: Race and sexuality in social work. *Canadian Social Work Review, 28*(1), 145–150.

Pyne, J. (2011). Unsuitable bodies: Trans people and cisnormativity in shelter services. *Canadian Social Work Review, 28*(1), 129–137.

Salzman, M. B. (2001). Cultural trauma and recovery. *Trauma, Violence, and Abuse, 2*(2), 172–191.

Schon, D. (1983). *The Reflective practitioner: How professionals think in action.* New York, NY: Basic Books.

Schon, D. (1987). *Educating the reflective practitioner: Toward a new design for teaching and learning in the professions.* San Francisco, CA: Jossey-Bass.

Schulman, S. (2012). *The gentrification of the mind: Witness to a lost imagination.* Berkeley, CA: University of California Press.

Scott, K. (2000). A perennial mourning: Identity conflict and the transgenerational transmission of trauma within the African American community. *Mind and Human Interaction, 11*(1), 11–26.

Sedgwick, E. (2009). Shame theatricality and queer performance. In D. Halperin & V. Traub (Eds.) *Gay shame* (pp. 49–62). Chicago, IL: University of Chicago Press.

Sonn, C. C., & Fisher, A. T. (1998). Sense of community: Community resilient responses to oppression and change. *Journal of Community Psychology, 26*(5), 457–472.

Sztompka, P. (2004). The trauma of social change. Collective trauma and collective identity. In J. C. Alexander, N. J. Smelser, R. Eyerman, B. Giesen, & P. Sztompka (Eds.), *Toward a theory of cultural trauma,* (p. 155). Berkeley, CA: University of California Press.

Trevillion. S. (2000). Social work, social networks and network knowledge. *British Journal of Social Work 30,* 505–517.

Warner, T. (2002). *Never going back: A History of Queer activism in Canada.* Toronto, ON: University of Toronto Press.

Young, I. (2000). *Inclusion and democracy.* New York, NY: Oxford University Press.

Zarowsky, C. (2004). Writing trauma: Emotion, ethnography, and the politics of suffering among Somali returnees in Ethiopia. *Culture, Medicine and Psychiatry, 28*(2), 189–209.

CHAPTER 12

Roadblocks and Pathways to Settlement: Experiences and Needs of Lesbian, Gay, and Bisexual Newcomers

Brian J. O'Neill and Hossein Kia

Canada's Multiculturalism Act (1985) states that it is the policy of the federal government to "promote the full and equitable participation of individuals and communities of all origins in ... all aspects of Canadian society ..." (section 3.1 [c]); as well, the 1982 Canadian Charter of Rights and Freedoms and provincial human rights codes recognize the rights of lesbian, gay, and bisexual (LGB) citizens to full inclusion in society (Nierobisz, Searl, & Theroux, 2008). Settlement services for immigrants and refugees aim to contribute to the achievement of these policies for newcomers. While the importance of responding to settlement needs specific to racialized, female, and young immigrants and refugees has been recognized (Omidvar & Richmond, 2005), and the need to address additional barriers encountered by migrants in smaller communities identified (Drolet & Robertson, 2011), the settlement needs of LGB newcomers have been largely overlooked. In addition to facing challenges similar to those experienced by many other immigrants and refugees, including discrimination related to race and ethnicity, LGB newcomers are likely to face prejudice associated with their sexual orientation, both within their ethnic communities and throughout society at large. This chapter reports on a Metropolis BC–funded study (O'Neill

& Kia, 2012) focused on LGB newcomers' settlement experiences in cities of various sizes in the Canadian province of British Columbia (BC), and their perceptions about immigrant settlement services. The views of settlement service workers and LGB community organization members about responding to LGB newcomers' settlement needs are also presented.

Importantly, the findings of the study are analyzed using an intersectional framework. This lens is premised on the notion that varying social identities often interact with one another at the level of individual experience, and it therefore facilitates an exploration of how subjective reality interfaces with structural context when multiple sources of privilege and disadvantage appear salient in the phenomena under study (Hulko, 2009; Yuval-Davis, 2006). Applied to the findings of the study, this framework enables an analysis of the complex relationships between participants' personal experiences relating to settlement and the multifaceted systemic issues often underpinning these realities, some of which pertain to marginalization based on sexuality, race, and gender identity, among others. In the sections that follow, this lens is used as a means for drawing attention to the array of interrelated structural factors underpinning the settlement experiences of lesbian, gay, and bisexual newcomers.

Settlement, in the context of this study, refers to processes of adaptation and integration among those who relocate permanently to Canada from another country, under varying circumstances. Accordingly, the term *settlement services* is used to refer to the broad range of resources designed to facilitate newcomers' settlement, including those providing information about and orientation to Canada, language training, employment programs, and community integration (CIC, 2012c). *Newcomers* refers to the full array of new arrivals, including immigrants, those who voluntarily choose to migrate to Canada, and refugees, those who do so to escape persecution. The terms *lesbian*, *gay*, and *bisexual* (or *LGB*) are used to refer to variations of same-sex sexual attraction. Although this language is used for convenience, it is done so with the recognition that these terms are not used across many cultural contexts when referring to same-sex sexual attraction.

Homophobia, Heterosexism, and Immigration in Canada

Whereas the term *homophobia* has grown over time to broadly refer to discrimination or prejudice against sexual minority groups (Dermer, Smith, & Barton, 2010; Herek, 2000), the construct of *heterosexism* has been developed to describe the systemic privileging of heterosexuality: the ideological premise that "straightness" is ideal and preferred (Herek, 2004; Walls, 2008). Similar to many other jurisdictions across the world, expressions of homophobia and heterosexism have remained pervasive in Canada, despite the constitutional and legislative reforms that have arisen to address these realities. Although Canada's Charter of Rights and Freedoms has been interpreted to include issues of sexual orientation in its scope of recognized protections, and full marriage rights are now afforded to same-sex couples in all provinces and territories across the nation, all sexual minorities in Canada (gay, lesbian, bisexual, Two-Spirit, transgender, intersex, and queer people) continue to encounter sexuality- and gender-based discrimination. For example, police reports indicate that hate crimes continue to be committed against non-heterosexual and gender-variant groups, and that they are the most violent of those perpetrated against all minorities (Dowden & Brennan, 2012).

Nonetheless, due to the legal protections currently available to LGB people in Canada, it is important to note that the social context of non-heterosexuals in this country differs to some extent from that of sexual minorities located in other regions of the world. For instance, because fundamental protections and human rights are still not afforded to non-heterosexuals in the majority of non-Canadian jurisdictions (GLAD, 2010), it is necessary to emphasize that Canadian LGB groups may experience homophobia and heterosexism differently than their non-heterosexual counterparts in other regions of the world, whose experiences may more directly reflect the lack of legislative recognition and protection.

Within the context of immigration policy specifically, Canada recognizes same-sex partners of Canadians as eligible for sponsorship, provided that relationships between sponsors and prospective newcomers are marriages recognized by law in Canada or elsewhere, are common-law relationships of 12 consecutive months or longer, or are "conjugal relationships" in which exceptional circumstances prevent cohabitation (CIC, 2012b). In addition, Canada recognizes sexuality-based persecution as grounds for pursuing refugee status and frequently validates the legitimacy of such claims from individuals who have experienced discrimination on the basis of sexual orientation in their countries of origin (CIC, 2012a). However, although the rate of acceptance of refugee claims based on sexuality-based persecution parallels that of claims made on non-sexual grounds, it is important to note that sexual-minority asylum seekers nonetheless face countless systemic barriers in justifying the validity of their claims. Rehaag (2008), to note one example, has described the challenges that bisexual refugee claimants experience with a refugee determination system that often requires these asylum seekers to conform to "folk" definitions of gay/lesbian identity in legitimizing their claims and gaining refugee status in Canada.

Research Design

LGB newcomers' settlement experiences in BC, as well as their perceptions of how their needs could be met by settlement agencies, were the primary areas of investigation in the research process. Service providers' views of the needs of these populations, as well as their insights on how LGB and settlement organizations could be more welcoming of newcomers, were also considered. All respondents participated in in-depth semi-structured interviews or focus groups designed to elicit insight into the experiences and potential needs of LGB newcomers. A qualitative descriptive approach (Sandelowski, 2000), loosely informed by tenets of grounded theory (Strauss & Corbin, 1998), was used to gather and analyze data.

Participants were recruited from three cities of various sizes in BC, on the assumption that people living in larger cities generally have more accepting attitudes regarding same-sex sexual orientation than people in smaller towns and rural areas (see also Hulko, this volume). Participants meeting eligibility criteria were recruited with assistance from settlement agencies, LGB organizations, and personal contacts.

Interviews were conducted with a total of 87 participants, including 19 self-identifying LGB newcomers (13 men and six women), three of their family members, 40 settlement agency service providers, and 25 members of LGB community organizations. LGB immigrants and refugees participating in the study came from an array of countries, including Iran, Mexico, Ukraine, China, Malaysia, and Israel. The settlement needs and experiences of transgender newcomers were purposely excluded from the scope of this study, primarily to acknowledge the need for a separate study that adequately addresses the uniqueness of gender identity issues (Williams & Freeman, 2005).

In both individual and focus group interviews, issues specific to LGB newcomers were explored with questions addressing

- the meanings of same-sex sexual orientation and associated identifiers (e.g. *gay, lesbian,* and other terms) held by participants;
- issues and possible settlement needs of LGB newcomers;
- experiences either accessing or delivering settlement services in relation to issues of same-sex
- sexual orientation (depending on the participant group being interviewed); and
- aspects of settlement services that were identified as either helpful or ineffective for LGB newcomers.

In addition, participants associated with settlement agencies and LGB organizations were asked to comment on

- the relevance of considering the interface of sexual and ethnic diversity in the context of program planning and service delivery;
- the knowledge base and skill set required for serving LGB newcomers; and
- organizational factors that appeared to either welcome or deter non-heterosexual newcomers in accessing services, factors that may have historically affected responses to LGB immigrants and refugees in organizational settings.

Qualitative content analysis (Hsieh & Shannon, 2005) was used to examine and conceptualize the data. This method is characterized by identifying patterns and regularities that appear in a body of qualitative data, and then summarizing this information in descriptive terms. Themes were subsequently interpreted using an intersectional lens.

Findings

An overview of themes prevalent across all participant groups is presented below, with a focus on identifying patterns that provide insight into the experiences and needs of LGB newcomers.

"Mediating Is Part of It": Issues of Identity among LGB Newcomers

Same-Sex Attraction across Diverse Ethnic Contexts: Recognizing Variations

A theme common among all participant groups included the acknowledgement that expressions and understandings of same-sex sexual attraction vary across social contexts, and that recognition of this reality may be necessary in order to appropriately situate the experiences of sexual-minority newcomers. Perhaps the issue most commonly highlighted by participants was the labelling of same-sex sexual attraction and orientation. For instance, a newcomer stated "the minute you say 'gay,' it creates a particular image, usually very Western." Some newcomers preferred to keep issues of sexual orientation private, rather than coming out and publicly identifying as members of a sexual minority. For example, one participant believed coming out could threaten his family relationships: "[coming out is] not something I want for myself ... I don't think the possibility of losing your family or having some kind of dislocated family relationship is worth risking everything and saying 'this is who I am.'"

Settlement agency workers reported some newcomers choose not to come out explicitly, even when describing same-sex relationships. Similarly, a member of an LGB organization perceived that some same-sex attracted newcomers were reluctant to identify as LGB and therefore avoided mainstream LGB groups. It is important to note that, in spite of the above findings, some newcomers recognized the terms *lesbian*, *gay*, and *bisexual* as descriptors of same-sex sexual attraction, regardless of social context.

A refugee newcomer indicated that although he considered himself gay in his home country, coming out there had markedly different implications than doing so in Canada:

> The difference [between my country of origin and Canada] is the culture, the religion, [and] the law ... to have more freedom [here]; that's really, really different. When I was raised, as a gay person I had to hide everything from everybody around myself, and it was the worst torture. So that's really different [in Canada].

However, a member of an LGB organization indicated that even within Canada, LGB newcomers living in smaller communities could encounter social pressures to stay in the closet. Although some newcomers and service providers rejected use of terms such as *LGB* as "Western" constructions of non-heterosexuality, others adopted these identifiers in referring to issues of same-sex sexual orientation. The fluidity of self-identification is important to recognize in understanding matters of same-sex sexual orientation among newcomers.

The Context of Marginalization: Intersections of Racism, Ethnocentrism, Sexism, and Heterosexism

Some participants believed non-heterosexual newcomers suffered greater disadvantage than either heterosexual newcomers or non-newcomer LGB Canadians by virtue of experiencing discrimination on multiple bases, particularly surrounding issues of race and sexuality. A racialized newcomer commented, "you're less likely to be accepted by your own community and by the larger community. So you face double discrimination, triple discrimination ... a lot of people are closeted for those reasons." Another participant described impacts of sexuality-based discrimination on his mental health: "I didn't feel supported by my culture, my community, and I was really depressed and suicidal when I was younger." While he had received support around his experiences of anti-gay discrimination, this participant had been subjected to prejudice on the grounds of his identity as South Asian in both mainstream and LGB communities. For example, he noted that within LGB social contexts, South Asians could be stereotyped as intolerant with relation to issues of sexual orientation: "If there's a gay bashing and the person responsible is South Asian, [the mainstream gay community blames] all South Asians for being intolerant and says 'send them back home.'"

That LGB newcomers may experience multiple bases of discrimination was also highlighted by participants from settlement agencies and LGB organizations. A settlement worker at an immigrant-serving agency, for instance, noted that identification with a stigmatized sexual minority group could render the settlement process, already laden with practical barriers to integration, even more complex: "it's just seen as an additional problem on top of everything else ... integrating is already hard enough ... without having to ... talk about sexual orientation."

Illustrating the intersection of oppression based on gender as well as sexual orientation, one newcomer perceived that her lesbian identity was often rendered invisible because the existence of sexual relationships between women was denied in her home country and women's status was often based on their relationships with men:

> My mother ... told me lesbians don't exist, ... the lesbian thing is not talked about, [not like] being gay.... [P]eople ask "does she have a boyfriend?" and so she makes up boyfriends to tell her friends.

With respect to the impact of geographic location on settlement, another newcomer pointed out that sexuality-related discrimination may be more pronounced in smaller towns with fewer supports for LGB newcomers than in larger centres with more resources.

Identity-related oppression may also lie in the realm of the personal or private. Specifically, some findings suggested that such marginalization, rather than arising solely in interpersonal or institutional interactions, could also be understood as a primarily subjective or intra-personal experience. One newcomer provided an example of this type of struggle:

> I didn't recognize I was ... attracted to men ... [until I came to Canada]. It was kind of a curiosity ... I was trying to suppress until I [came] to Canada and [had] enough space from my family to delve deeper into that one issue ... finding out who you are as a person when you try to suppress so many things ... there's ... stress associated with that.

This participant's identity-based crisis was related to his struggle to find a safer environment in which he could explore his same-sex attractions. Given this finding, it is important to be aware that some newcomers may consider their sense of marginalization as stemming from personal limitations rather than systemic influences.

"A Lot of Roadblocks": Settlement Experiences and Needs of LGB Newcomers

Navigating the Unknown in Isolation

Although lack of information regarding support services may be common among newcomers regardless of their sexuality, several participants identified challenges in locating information on LGB-friendly settlement support. For instance, it can be particularly difficult for LGB newcomers to find information on meeting other same-sex attracted people, which can result in feelings of isolation: "There is a very important thing we need when we come here. It's to see ... gays and lesbians who are friendly ... the worst thing ... is being alone." Some newcomer participants explained that the difficulty of locating information on informal LGB support groups or networks can be exacerbated by language barriers.

Elements of Danger and Safety: Negotiating the Realm of Settlement

Some participants feared their access to support would be impacted if they revealed their same-sex sexual orientation to settlement workers. For example, a newcomer was afraid to ask for information on sexuality-related resources "my biggest fear was, if I speak up ... would there be rejection. That's why I pulled back from revealing my sexuality." Other participants feared being stigmatized if members of their communities and families became aware they had accessed LGB-specific resources. A participant suggested it would be preferable for all settlement services to become LGB-friendly, minimizing the need for newcomers to come out in order to access services relevant to their sexuality: "they have to provide [services to LGB newcomers] in a way that is confidential, is discreet, and [ensures] that people don't necessarily have to disclose their sexuality to get services."

As a settlement worker in a smaller centre noted, because safety issues were pronounced for all queer people in his region, LGB newcomers may have a heightened fear of accessing sexuality-related resources in such communities. It appears that same-sex attracted newcomers' reticence in approaching both settlement agencies and LGB organizations regarding sexuality-related issues may be related to the risk they perceive in seeking help.

Lacking Access to Services: Health Risks and Socio-Economic Impacts

Barriers to accessing sexuality-specific information and gay-friendly support services can put newcomers at risk. A participant recounted how a friend (also a newcomer) was put in a particularly vulne situation:

> [His] parents found out he was gay ... [he was] kicked out of the house and had nowhere to go. He didn't have [access to] support services, and I felt ... [he] might try something drastic, like kill himself, or ... prostitute himself because he [had] nowhere to go [or] stay, no money for food.

A number of newcomers underscored health issues associated with resource inaccessibility. One immigrant thought newcomers may feel reluctant to disclose matters of sexuality to health professionals: "doctors ask 'have you had sex with men?' What are closeted gay guys going to do there?" Newcomers may feel reluctant to access testing for sexually transmitted infections—which in turn could increase their risk for exposure to such conditions, including HIV—if they believe they would be asked to disclose their sexual orientation during the testing process. Although this barrier to testing may exist for many same-sex attracted individuals, regardless of their immigration status, such fears may be particularly pronounced for newcomers who already experience heightened sexuality-related stigmatization within their ethnic communities and broader social contexts, as described earlier. The following sections present participants' perceptions of how such marginalization could be mitigated to better address the needs of newcomers.

Improving Pathways to Settlement for LGB Newcomers

Enhancing Safety: Universalizing Access to Appropriate Settlement Services

Given that safety was frequently raised as an issue, safer access to appropriate services is clearly a need for many newcomers. One suggestion to address this need was making information on LGB issues and resources available to all newcomers, thus mitigating the fear that asking for such information would implicitly label them as LGB. This strategy would facilitate sexual minority newcomers' access to appropriate services without them having to self-identify. A settlement worker hypothesized that as his organization did not mention sexual orientation in describing its services, newcomers seldom requested help in relation to LGB issues. Newcomers, settlement agency workers, and members of LGB organizations all suggested broadening settlement services' mandates to include provision of sexuality-related resources.

It is important to note that, in spite of the above, a small number of participants highlighted the possible need to designate specific information and resources for LGB newcomers, instead of universalizing these services. The need to "universalize" LGB services appeared to apply less to newcomers who strongly identified as LGB.

The Role of Education and Cross-Service Collaboration in Addressing Settlement Needs

Participants highlighted the importance of settlement workers possessing knowledge of issues surrounding same-sex sexuality. One participant emphasized the need for settlement workers to be trained on issues specific to sexual minorities:

> It was shocking to me that the [settlement] workers who really wanted to help people were so resistant to the idea of homosexuality, and had so much lacking [in terms of] knowledge about homosexuality.... In all immigrant settlement agencies, there should be regular presentations and regular workshops.

In addition to the above, a number of LGB community organization participants commented on the relevance of training on anti-racism and cultural awareness in local LGB organizations. Settlement workers and people associated with LGB organizations are influenced by their own life experiences; they may be native-born or foreign-born, fully or partially assimilated, racialized or not, and/or have some degree of same-sex attraction. Their own assumptions about racialized groups, gender, and LGB people need to be addressed in such training.

Cross-service collaboration was described as including the development of partnerships that would foster formal information-sharing and referral mechanisms, particularly between settlement agencies and LGB community organizations. One member of an LGB organization suggested that LGB organizations could provide education on issues affecting sexual minorities, while settlement agencies could offer training on working with newcomers. A settlement worker stated that it would be helpful for LGB organizations to create information in various languages that would assist LGB newcomers to connect with supportive resources and to ask settlement agencies to distribute it to their clients. Another notion discussed in the realm of cross-service collaboration included the need for referrals to take place consistently between settlement agencies and LGB organizations.

Newcomers and Service Providers: Exploring Differences in Perceptions of Experience and Need

Though most themes were discussed by members of each of the participant groups, there were some differences between service providers' and newcomers' perceptions. The most striking discrepancy was the importance some participants from settlement agencies and LGB organizations ascribed to either sexuality or ethnicity, whereas most newcomers expressed service needs relevant to both dimensions of identity. Use of an intersectional lens could help settlement agency workers and members of LGB organizations to respond more comprehensively to the needs of LGB newcomers.

Some service providers perceived that newcomers would place greater importance on either sexuality or ethnicity and race in their search for relevant resources. Interestingly, whereas many members of LGB organizations believed newcomers would experience their sexual orientation or identity as most salient in their quest for support, a small number of settlement agency workers believed the needs of newcomers would relate more closely to overcoming ethnic differences and language barriers, rather than matters of sexuality. One member of an LGB organization in a large urban centre, for instance, assumed that issues of same-sex sexuality would take precedence in newcomers' search for appropriate resources, primarily because less stigma is attached to a racialized or non-Western ethnic identity:

> I think it's much easier if you're looking for services as an ethnic [minority] person; there's less stigma ... the real taboo is being gay ... stigma is much stronger [for issues of sexuality], largely, than ... race or ethnicity.

This perception by a non-racialized participant may well be disputed by racialized people, whether gay or heterosexual. For example, a worker at a settlement organization expressed the belief that LGB organizations often seem to assign greater importance to matters of sexual orientation than newcomers do, questioning the suitability of referrals to LGB organizations as a result:

> The people associated with [a local LGB group], their sexual orientation is their whole identity, and that's who they are, and that's it. That's all they're interested in talking about. And for our clients, that's a small part of their identity, so ... it's not a match.

Clearly, there may be discrepancies between service providers' and newcomers' understandings of settlement needs. These distinctions point to the need for reassessment of service needs specific to LGB immigrants and refugees, keeping in mind the fluid nature of how people identify and how this can change in different social contexts. A number of service providers recognized the futility of basing the identification of service needs on a singular dimension of identity.

Discussion

In this section, the study's findings are discussed in relation to existing literature, using intersectionality as a theoretical lens to conceptualize these accounts and delineate their implications for policy, practice, and research. To start, however, a summary of the study's findings, emphasizing certain themes, is provided as a basis for more substantive analysis.

Issues of identity appeared to form a framework for understanding settlement experiences and needs among sexual minority immigrants and refugees. Same-sex sexuality, orientation, and identity had diverse meanings for LGB newcomers, many not identifying with Western constructs of *lesbian*, *gay*, and *bisexual*. Various dimensions of identity, including race, gender, ethnicity, and sexuality appeared to shape LGB newcomers' experiences of marginalization. For instance, newcomers recounted experiences of racism within mainstream LGB communities and heterosexism within their ethnic communities.

Many of the newcomers interviewed reported feeling isolated and lacking in knowledge regarding useful resources, seemingly as a consequence of not fully identifying with either their ethnic minority communities or sexual-minority social networks. Some participants did not seek support related to same-sex sexual orientation from settlement agencies because they did not see them as welcoming sexual minorities. Further, they feared that their same-sex sexual orientation could become known in their communities if they came out to settlement workers or became involved with local LGB organizations, thus exposing them to stigmatization. These safety issues were perceived to be more pronounced in smaller centres, because of the lack of anonymity possible in such milieus as compared to big cities.

Given their concerns about safety in accessing support, many newcomers suggested that information about the human rights of LGB people in Canada and relevant support services be provided to all migrants in order to minimize the need for newcomers to self-identify as sexual minorities. Refugee participants appeared to prefer specialized services for LGB newcomers, possibly because they had already come out in claiming refugee status on the basis of sexual orientation. Other participant-identified means of reducing barriers to relevant support services included collaboration among settlement agencies and LGB organizations in service delivery and staff development.

Importantly, there was one notable difference among perceptions of newcomers, settlement workers, and LGB organization members. Whereas newcomers consistently referred to multiple identity-based factors in discussing their settlement experiences and needs, settlement workers and LGB organization members often assumed newcomers' needs would be related either to their ethnic backgrounds or to their sexuality, respectively. This finding suggested that settlement agencies and LGB organizations may lack recognition of the complexity of sexual minority newcomers' settlement experiences, an issue that could be addressed by basing training on an intersectional approach.

Previous inquiry identified aspects of settlement experiences and needs specific to women and youth, and highlighted the importance of recognizing the complex and distinct needs of diverse newcomer populations (Dyck & McLaren, 2004; Omidvar & Richmond, 2005; Waters, 2011). Jordan (2010), as well as Lee and Brotman (2011), underlined that sexual minority refugees' experiences are often shaped by marginalization at the intersection of race, sexuality, gender, and other dimensions. The current study's findings reinforce these insights in describing the needs of LGB newcomers, particularly for protection from sexuality-related stigmatization. The concept of intersecting oppressions is highly useful in interpreting the current study's findings, for instance drawing attention to the need for service providers and LGB community organizations to understand newcomers' settlement needs as functions of multiple identity-based factors rather than, as found, attributing them to either ethnic or sexual differences alone.

Using a framework of intersectionality, each person is seen as having a complex identity, encompassing facets that intersect at the interface of personal narrative and social, political, and historical contexts (Cronin & King, 2010; Hulko, 2009; Yuval-Davis, 2006). This perspective challenges the assumption that focusing on oppression related to only one dimension of identity is adequate for a comprehensive understanding of marginalization. An intersectional approach facilitates a more in-depth appreciation of the experiences of LGB newcomers by recognizing the confluence of "othering" related to same-sex sexuality, as well as racial/ethnic identity and gender. For instance, identifying that the simultaneous interaction of both heterosexism and racism/ethnocentrism may underlie LGB newcomers' experiences can explain their sense of danger and consequent need for greater safety within the context of settlement. Such an understanding is needed in order to effectively address related social injustices. An interesting aspect of the findings is that participants did not allude to oppression specifically related to gender, although there were a significant number of female-identified participants. As well, issues related to bisexual identity or other aspects of identity, such as disability or age, never arose. These areas merit further study.

Conceptualizing the study's findings through an intersectional lens suggests ways in which LGB newcomers' settlement needs could be better met. Recognition in policy that multiple forms of oppression may shape the settlement experiences of LGB newcomers could translate into development of mechanisms that enhance access to resources, support, and services by mitigating this population's safety concerns. For instance, providing all newcomers with government-sponsored literature, including information regarding laws and resources relevant to LGB people in Canada, would eliminate the need for immigrants and refugees to self-identify as LGB in order to access such information. Another implication is the need to amend existing "best practices" documents intended for settlement service providers, primarily those created by federal government agencies (Parliament of Canada, 2010), so that they reflect the need for settlement agencies to include sexuality-related issues within the scope of their services. This expectation would encourage the development of support for immigrants and refugees with same-sex sexuality within the range of services offered to newcomer populations as a whole, again reducing barriers related to safety for LGB newcomers. More importantly, however, incorporation of sexuality-specific information in both newcomer orientation and settlement-related best practices documents would reinforce the understanding that multiple identity-based factors, including those related to sexual orientation, are relevant to the settlement process.

Recognition of the complexity of newcomers' settlement needs—be they related to race, ethnicity, sexuality, or gender—afforded by use of an intersectional framework would provide grounds for both settlement agencies and LGB organizations to address such needs in their programming. For instance, settlement services could provide all newcomers with information about local LGB resources and health services that address sexuality-related concerns non-intrusively and confidentially. Settlement agencies and LGB community organizations could form alliances that would facilitate referral of newcomers between them and contribute to the education of settlement staff and LGB organization members regarding the range of cultural, racial, and sexuality-related factors that influence the settlement experiences of LGB newcomers.

Given the diversity among subgroups of LGB newcomers, for instance in relation to dimensions of ethnicity, age, and gender, an intersectional framework is also useful in conceptualizing implications of the study's findings specific to program planning. Because it appeared that refugees preferred services targeted directly at sexual minority asylum seekers, whose needs may differ from those of LGB immigrants, the creation of specialized programs for these newcomers could be considered. In addition, as concerns regarding safety were voiced far more frequently in smaller, more rural centres, an intersectional lens taking into account geographical context could allow a more nuanced understanding of the needs of LGB newcomers located in these regions, particularly for programs that are confidential, non-intrusive, and safe.

Perhaps most importantly, given the apparent reluctance of many newcomers to raise sexuality-related concerns within settlement services, keeping in mind that newcomers may be subjected to intersecting, but not obvious oppressions, settlement service workers may be encouraged to interact with all clients in ways that indicate their awareness that some newcomers have same-sex sexual attraction. For example, they could use gender-neutral language (e.g. "partner") in discussing relationship concerns with all clients. This strategy could provide a subtle message to LGB newcomers that workers are open to addressing issues related to diverse sexual orientations. Settlement workers could also emphasize with all newcomers the confidentiality of information provided to the agency, thus reassuring LGB newcomers that it would be safe to raise matters of same-sex sexuality. Neither strategy entails asking direct questions related to newcomers' sexual orientation, and may contribute to newcomers feeling it is safe to discuss sexuality-related concerns.

Several issues arise from this study that could inform future inquiry. Perhaps most significantly, distinctions in the accounts of refugees interviewed in this study suggest a need for research specifically focused on the settlement experiences of newcomers who sought asylum on the basis of being persecuted for being LGB. Further, the omission of transgender individuals from the study points to a need for examination of the settlement experiences and needs of trans-identified newcomers. Similarly, because issues of gender, disability, class, and other social factors did not surface saliently in the study's findings, LGB newcomers' experiences of marginalization on such grounds may need to be explored further in order for the needs of sexual minority immigrants and refugees to be more comprehensively understood. Lastly, there is a need to evaluate initiatives or projects aimed at implementing any of the changes recommended for settlement services and LGB community organizations.

References

Citizenship and Immigration Canada (CIC). (2012a). Determine your eligibility—Refugee status from inside Canada. Retrieved from www.cic.gc.ca/english/refugees/inside/apply-who.asp

Citizenship and Immigration Canada (CIC). (2012b). Determine your eligibility—Sponsor your spouse, partner or children. Retrieved from www.cic.gc.ca/english/immigrate/sponsor/spouse-apply-who.asp#definitions

Citizenship and Immigration Canada (CIC). (2012c). Integration of newcomers and Canadian citizenship. Retrieved from www.cic.gc.ca/english/resources/publications/annual-report-2012/section4.asp

Cronin, A., & King, A. (2010). Power, inequality and identification: Exploring diversity and intersectionality amongst older LGB adults. *Sociology, 44*(5), 876–892.

Dermer, S. B., Smith, S. D., & Barton, K. K. (2010). Identifying and correctly labeling sexual prejudice, discrimination and oppression. *Journal of Counseling and Development, 88*(3), 325–331.

Dowden, C., & Brennan, A. (2012, April 12). Police-reported hate crime in Canada, 2010. Statistics Canada. Retrieved from www.statcan.gc.ca/pub/85-002-x/2012001/article/11635-eng.htm

Drolet, J., & Robertson, J. (2011). *Settlement experiences of family class immigrants in a small city: Kamloops, British Columbia.* Vancouver, BC: Metropolis British Columbia. Retrieved from mbc.metropolis.net/assets/uploads/files/wp/2011/WP11-19.pdf

Dyck, I., & McLaren, A. (2004). Telling it like it is? Constructing accounts of settlement with immigrant and refugee women in Canada. *Gender, Place and Culture, 11*(4), 513–534.

Gay and Lesbian Advocates and Defenders (GLAD). (2010). Equal justice under law: Marriage guide. Retrieved from www.glad.org/uploads/docs/publications/ri-marriage-guide.pdf

Herek, G. M. (2000). The psychology of sexual prejudice. *Current Directions in Psychological Science, 9*(1), 19–22.

Herek, G. M. (2004). Beyond "homophobia": Thinking about sexual prejudice and stigma in the twenty-first century. *Sexuality Research and Social Policy, 1*(2), 6–24.

Hsieh, H. F., & Shannon, S. E. (2005). Three approaches to qualitative content analysis. *Qualitative Health Research, 15*(9), 1277–1288.

Hulko, W. (2009). The time- and context-contingent nature of intersectionality and interlocking oppressions. *Affilia, 24*(1), 44–55.

Jordan, S. A. (2010). Un/convention(al) refugees: Contextualizing the accounts of refugees facing homophobic or transphobic persecution. *Refuge: Canada's Periodical on Refugees, 26*(2), 165–182.

Lee, E. O. J., & Brotman, S. (2011). Identity, refugeeness, belonging: Experiences of sexual minority refugees in Canada. *Canadian Review of Sociology, 48*(3), 241–274.

Nierobisz, A., Searl, M., & Theroux, C. (2008). *Human rights commissions and public policy: The role of the Canadian Human Rights Commission in advancing sexual orientation equality rights in Canada.* Ottawa, ON: Canadian Human Rights Commission.

Omidvar, R., & Richmond, T. (2005). Immigrant settlement and social inclusion in Canada. In T. Richmond & A. Saloojee (Eds.), *Social inclusion: Canadian perspectives* (pp. 155–179). Toronto, ON: Fernwood Publications.

O'Neill, B., & Kia, H. (2012). Settlement experiences of lesbian, gay and bisexual newcomers in BC. Working paper, Metropolis BC. Retrieved from mbc.metropolis.net/assets/uploads/files/wp/2012/WP12-15.pdf

Parliament of Canada. (2010). Best practices in settlement services. Retrieved from www.parl.gc.ca/content/hoc/Committee/403/CIMM/Reports/RP4388396/cimmrp02/cimmrp02-e.pdf

Rehaag, S. (2008). Patrolling the borders of sexual orientation: Bisexual refugee claims in Canada. *McGill Law Journal, 53*(1), 59–102.

Sandelowski, M. (2000). What ever happened to qualitative description? *Research in Nursing and Health, 23,* 334–340.

Strauss, A., & Corbin, J. (1998). *Basics of qualitative research: Grounded theory procedures and techniques.* Newbury Park, CA: Sage.

Walls, N. E. (2008). Toward a multidimensional understanding of heterosexism: The changing nature of prejudice. *Journal of Homosexuality, 55*(1), 20–70.

Waters, J. L. (2011). Time and transnationalism: A longitudinal study of immigration, endurance and settlement in Canada. *Journal of Ethnic and Migration Studies, 37*(7), 1119–1135.

Williams, M. E., & Freeman, P. A. (2005). Transgender health. *Journal of Gay and Lesbian Social Services, 18*(3/4), 93–108.

Yuval-Davis, N. (2006). Intersectionality and feminist politics. *European Journal of Women's Studies, 13*(3), 193–209.

CHAPTER 13
Resisting The Binary: The Role of the Social Worker in Affirmative Trans Health Care

X. Sly Sarkisova[1]

The subject of accessible trans health care is especially dear to me. I approach this topic as a whole individual, with the experience of identifying as a gender-variant[2] trans[3] person, as someone who does not adhere to a medically prescribed trans narrative, who is accessing medical health care in order to feel healthy and whole, and as someone who is a practitioner and clinician in the field. I have intimate knowledge of the disconnect between delivery systems of trans-specific health care vis-à-vis personal needs, and the resultant impacts on health, wellness, and wholeness. I have insider knowledge of the experiences of my peers and community members' attempts at accessing appropriate, affirmative, individualized health care. I am also at the frontlines of mental health, addictions, and trans health practice, providing therapeutic counselling, referrals, advocacy, and education.

As such, I, like many other social workers and health care providers, am directly implicated in systems keeping the boundaries of current models of health care intact. I am privy to the processes and power dynamics involved in the subjectification and psychiatrization of trans and gender-variant identified individuals through protocols, pathways of assessment, and diagnostics that restrict and control access to funding, hormones, and surgery, and thus, many of the possibilities for *being* a trans person. It is this regulation and production of trans histories, narratives, and realities by current modes of service delivery that I am concerned with—both as a trans-identified person and as a social worker practising therapy. Regardless of the focus of one's work, individuals who are engaged in social work, especially those who do not believe they will be working with Two-Spirit, trans, or gender-variant people, have an obligation to consider the impacts of restrictive service delivery systems limiting appropriate health care.

In writing this chapter, I acknowledge limitations in my capacity to deeply address issues related to intersecting oppressions such as physical-based ableism and Indigenous perspectives. I will be focusing on an introduction to the issues particular to trans folks who do not pass, nor wish to pass, as the "opposite" gender, or who identify outside of narrow understandings of gender endemic to legal, social, and health care systems. In order to consider the nuances of individual experiences in light of systemic oppressions, it is necessary to develop a critical awareness of the disproportionate impacts of racism and trans-misogyny—the specific misogyny that trans women face (Serano, 2007), and the cumulative impacts psychologically, emotionally, spiritually, and socioeconomically on trans women, Indigenous folks, and trans people of colour, specifically (Brotman, Ryan, Jalbert, & Rowe, 2002; Sanchez, Sanchez, & Danoff, 2009).

Practitioners who develop the capacity to understand these intricate experiences of multiple oppressions, along with strengths and resiliencies of diverse people, will be more apt to help individuals reflect upon, frame, and begin to deconstruct and externalize the shame, trauma, depression, guilt, transphobia[4], racism, classism, and ableism impacting health and spirits. This self-education and awareness-building on the part of service providers is key to developing conversations and spaces that begin to help people unpack the layered messages and negative associations that often become internalized narratives of defective personhood.

Social workers may play a role in facilitating or impeding trans-related care and may participate in the delegitimization of trans experiences.

The role of reflexive practice in addressing a lack of knowledge of trans-related issues and resources, cis-normative[5] thinking with regard to the gender binary, unwillingness to advocate on behalf of trans folks[6], and buying into current medical delivery systems will be explored. It is hoped readers and clinicians in the field may begin to develop the capacity to provide an expanded space for individuals to self-formulate and assert narratives, histories, needs (medical or otherwise), understandings, and desires that are ultimately respected.

Centrality of Self-Identification

There are many ways that the term *transgender* has been defined over space and time, with much individual variation in meaning in trans and gender-variant communities (Valentine, 2007). Not everyone agrees on what, exactly, it means to be trans, particularly given the Eurocentrism of the term (Walters, Evans-Campbell, Simoni, Ronquillo, & Bhuyan, 2006). While the definition of *trans* as some sort of umbrella term of various gender identities and expressions that do not fit neatly into the assigned gender binary can be useful, I would propose that the term is more than an articulation of a particular gender category. It is a space and place of liminality and subjective, contextual experience. In this space, individuals can come to understand that their body, spirit, gender preferences, or expression may fall outside typical Euro-American understandings and delineations of gender that presume individuals are biologically born masculine/males/men or feminine/females/women, with no variation thereof. While many people who seek medical or social modes of transition[7] may identify as cross-gendered and seek to align their bodies with their internal sense of gendered self in ways that society would recognize as conventional masculine maleness or feminine femaleness, many other trans folks do not fit neatly into such categories. It is important to make efforts to understand and resist the false social and biological constructs that render normative conceptualizations of gender identity, body, dress, behaviour, and roles exclusively legitimate. These constructs are deeply embedded in service structures, producing a singular medically approved and psychiatrically defined narrative ("one true narrative") for Two-Spirit, gender-variant, or trans individuals (Coleman et al., 2012).

Trans folks call into question the legitimacy of biological understandings of gender and social categories limiting gender expression and possibility, particularly those expressions that have been rendered oppositional and static in nature. Contrary to common assumptions, a trans identity does not necessarily—although it could—presuppose any sort of directionality or "crossing over" of experience. Rather, it can signify a place of existence that cannot easily be pinned down in terms of language, social codes, physical expression, and embodiment. As such, social workers who uphold cisnormative constructs and ideals of gender used to assess and verify trans-ness must take heed of the impacts on all those individuals who do not subscribe to a binary narrative or, indeed, even those who do, yet nevertheless seek counselling, referrals, advocacy, support, or medical health care to express their gender identities in ways most comfortable to them.

As someone who has experiences of being both a seeker and a provider of services, it is particularly important for me to identify that my social location of holding white, able-bodied, class, and masculine privilege is radically different from the experiences of racialized, Two-Spirit, or trans female or feminine people. There remains a wide variety of trans male or masculine privilege and experiences depending on the individual, intersections of oppressions related to race, the context in which one grew up and lives, the resources they had and do have access to, as well as the type of body, coherent legibility, and adherence to masculine norms they present. My social location and gender presentation enable me to gain employment much more easily than my counterparts; not be subject to transphobia based on my appearance alone; obtain housing without scrutiny; pay for surgery and avoid psychiatric evaluation for funding; and receive better overall care from supportive physicians who do not question my ability to be read as a conventional male by society at large. Access to trans health care and support is made easier by these privileges, regardless of my resistance to conform to medically reinforced gender narratives.

Due to systemic racism and trans-misogyny, trans women of colour disproportionately experience unemployment, criminalization and incarceration for sex work, systemic abuses, diminished health care, lack of food and shelter access, as well as protection of basic human rights such as safety, and child custody (Grant, Motett, & Tanis, 2011). Trans women of colour, and trans women, in general, are especially excluded from the financial means to access funding for surgeries and face deep stigma in the assessment process for hormone replacement therapy (Gehi & Arkles, 2007). Julia Serano (2007) has written about the magnified sexism, misogyny, and drastic role expectations of "womanhood" placed upon trans women vis-à-vis cis women as a result of patriarchy (see also Chapter 7). She argues that trans women experience particularly severe scrutiny, judgment, discrimination, and violence based on the complex power dynamics that occur when one is perceived to "give up" male privilege in order to embody femaleness. The setup of social service and legal systems as gender segregated and gender normative ensures that trans and gender-variant people are at high risk for physical and emotional violence, exclusion, and isolation (Nuttbrock, Hwahng, Bockting, Rosenblum, Mason, Macri, & Becker, 2010).

As reported in (in)visible (2012), a genderqueer-identified trans woman spoke out about the erasure of narratives and pressure to conform:

> I was once a boy. I have a lot of history there, some of which I absolutely cherish. Out of respect for myself, I own that and fiercely challenge any attempt made to assimilate my experience. My past is a part of my present; it's a path that brought me to this now. It's a path that I'm very much still on. To disavow that past would feel like lying to myself, lying to others. ((in)visible, 2012)

By way of introducing what can be perceived as an incongruous history, the author confronts normalizing forces outside of and within trans communities that seek to erase and consolidate differences. Similarly, another trans woman wrote about social forces restricting possibilities for being trans and her process of reclamation:

> Generally speaking, most people expect a trans person to assume a gender expression that is a very tight, stereotyped version of the gender that is not the one to which they were assigned at birth [because most people don't know of anyone who identifies "outside of the gender binary"; they only see gender as an either/or]. But that is not what I want for myself. And, as it should for anyone, what I want for myself takes infinite precedence over what other people expect of me. (charismatics are dangerous, 2012)

The regulation and psychiatric production of trans narratives have largely erased the possibilities and meaning-making of trans identities outside of Western, disease-based models, and have greatly impacted the wellness and wholeness of trans lives and experiences.

Current Practice Standards

The current and widely used revised Standards of Care (WPATH SOC7) have been agreed upon internationally by practitioners tasked with assessing and determining appropriate health care with trans community members (Coleman et al., 2012). The SOC7 have been refined significantly from the original Harry Benjamin Standards and play a guiding role as a major resource for clinicians, advocates, trans or gender-variant people, allies, and policy makers. The guidelines contain information related to health options, assessments, risks, and outcomes for providing health care to trans-identified clients. These standards and others such as "Transgender Primary Medical Care: Suggested Guidelines for Clinicians in British Columbia," developed and used by Vancouver Coastal Health (Feldman & Goldberg, 2006), as well as "Guidelines and Protocols for Comprehensive Primary Health Care for Trans Clients" developed and used by Sherbourne Health Centre (2009) have moved in recent years (Raj & Schwartz, 2013) to a more person-centred approach to determining readiness for medically assisted forms of transition, such as hormone therapy and various top and bottom surgeries.

These existing groundbreaking and widely used protocols, while ensuring the maximum available knowledge for health care providers in supporting primary trans health care access, also have major limitations in terms of the scope and criteria used for determining suitability of non-binary identified clients to access said care. Until recently, the standards of care did not make mention of the possibility of providing individualized care options to genderqueer, gender-variant, gender-fluid, Two-Spirit, or non-binary identified people seeking services that fall outside of protocol guidelines, expectations, or medically defined and psychiatrized narratives.

Many of the elements of the SOC7 still remain problematic for trans women, as well as non-binary identified folks, restricting their access to primary health care based on a specific narrative steeped in rigid notions of gender, and enforced by psychiatrically based mental health assessments. The following core elements of the SOC7 remain deeply limiting and damaging for trans folks, binary and non-binary alike, particularly since they are used prior to any medical interventions:

- Requirement to be diagnosed with mental illness in the form of gender identity disorder or gender dysphoria
- A one-year gender role test (formerly the "Real Life Test")
- Three-month mental health screening
- Having a coherent history and narrative of cross-gender affiliation

- Ability to "pass" in the "opposite" gender
- Exclusions based on mental health status—including depression, anxiety, trauma, and psychosis—homelessness, or substance use

What our medical, legal, and social systems do not seem to grasp is that there can be no distinction made between a "true" transsexual and a "fake" transsexual. Historically, transgender narratives have been medically constructed as synonymous with transsexual experience (HBGDA, 1979). Presenting one's trans narrative to medical and social service practitioners has called upon folks who seek medical technologies of health care or transition to present a congruent, cohesive, transsexual narrative—one based in cross-gender affiliation and focused on experiences of distress and suffering in one's assigned natal gender. The most understood story of transsexual experience has been one of being "born in the wrong body" and experiencing an early understanding of one's mis-fit with their body and gender role. In order to receive access to health care, trans people have to present a coherent, linear narrative of discovering their gender identity that can be reduced to the following formula:

"born in the wrong body" → desire to "cross-dress" from an early age → play preferences appropriate to "opposite" gender → heterosexual identity (i.e. trans men attracted to women and trans women attracted to men) → experience largely of suffering and suicidality → unbearable dysphoria → seeking physical and social transition to "opposite" gender

This singular understanding of transsexual narratives has functioned as the barometer of whether one should qualify for trans-specific health care (i.e. "are you trans enough?"). Recent revisions to trans health protocols and updated guidelines published via WPATH SOC7 and practice standards of various organizations[8] have somewhat broadened the criteria of assessment for suitable trans health care. However, the reliance on a singular, psychiatric construction and understanding of trans as a narrative of cross-gender affiliation and suffering with one's assigned natal sex is still widely employed, particularly by service providers who have limited understandings of gender identity and who rely on protocols that frame trans health in yet another dichotomy of MTF (male to female) or FTM (female to male), with emphasis on one path to transitioning via medical care. This employment and validation of "one true narrative" is not only a disservice to any trans individuals who do not understand their experience in this way, it is actually harmful (Bauer, Hammond, Travers, Kaay, Hohenadel, & Boyce, 2009).

This pathologizing psychiatric narrative narrows the possibilities for what it *means* or *can mean* to be trans. The use of this framework has resulted in trans people presenting a well-crafted standard narrative that suits the assessment needs of gatekeepers, but does not necessarily represent who trans people are or how we know ourselves to be. Current medical practices significantly restrict the possibilities for self-determination and expression, and largely erase personal experiences, forcing individuals to submit to an inauthentic psychiatrically defined and diagnosable gender identity in order to qualify for services. Medical and legal systems have been instrumental in regulating what it means to be trans, who may qualify for social, medical, and legal transition, and what trans can and should look like (Coleman et al., 2012; Hage & Karim, 2000).

The singular trans narrative, as backed by legal governance across North America and beyond, has limited the possibilities for those of us who know ourselves to be intrinsically non-binary, yet do not meet the assessment criteria for "transsexualism." Criteria for transsexualism have been shaped and crafted by medical and legal establishments to mimic and reinforce the existing cisnormative, socially constructed, and biologically inaccurate gender binary. This has resulted in a limited script of possibility for individuals who are trans and gender-variant, or genderqueer, and seeking medical interventions to induce feminization or masculinization of our bodies.

Transsexual/transgender health care has been enacted as the site of gender policing and upholding of cis-sexist[9] gender norms. Historically, and still today, access to health care has required one to become largely invisible: to seamlessly blend in with idealized notions of maleness or femaleness. Trans and Two-Spirit activists and allies have been working fiercely for years to increase the accessibility of medical care and legal status by de-pathologizing and expanding practitioner understandings of trans- and gender-related issues (Brotman et al., 2002).

In the province of Ontario, trans health care technologies have been tightly controlled by government funding guidelines that have resulted in one psychiatric assessment clinic at the Centre for Addiction and Mental Health being given the task of diagnosing and treating trans experiences. This model follows the original Harry Benjamin Standards (HBGDA, 1979), which psychiatrize and pathologize differently gendered people. It has resulted in a long history of trans people, especially trans women, being refused access to supportive means of embodiment and has contributed unnecessarily to distress, anxiety, trauma, and suffering (Rotondi, Bauer, Travers, Travers, Scanlon, & Kaay, 2011). Ironically, basing trans care in the realm and control of psychiatry and mental health has resulted in increased dysphoria of trans people—forcing trans women, men, and others to perform their gender roles publicly in all settings *before* qualifying for access to technologies that would fulfill their embodiment and expression. In other words, trans people have been forced to perform the "opposite gender" while still inhabiting space visibly as their assigned sex at birth. Furthermore, the clinic guidelines require one to be "out" in employment, school, or volunteer settings for a minimum of one year to qualify for funding. This entirely disregards the psychosocial risks involved in terms of losing employment, family, friends, social opportunities, and supports. This criterion further damages and restricts access to individuals who are unemployed, are dealing with mental health issues, are not in school, or who may have already been out to close friends and passing for years.

Current SOC7 protocols demand that trans people place themselves at increased risk for assault, violence, exclusion, and discrimination, while these same protocols dangle a loose carrot indeterminately at the end of practitioners' biased assessment of their ability to "pass" successfully as the "opposite" gender. For trans people who may already be experiencing increased distress, anxiety, and depression resulting from myriad factors erasing our identities, psychiatric-based assessments forcing us to out ourselves in ways that many of us are uncomfortable with, and to conform to a singular narrative only serve to increase depression, anxiety, and trauma. The use of mental health assessments and requirement for diagnosis of differences in gender identity or presentation are doubly ironic in that they create new, or exacerbate ongoing, mental health issues that then may serve as criteria for exclusion from access to care. It is unclear under what circumstances those who are determined to have active depression, anxiety, psychosis, or complex trauma presentations are deemed "fit" for medical care.

Ultimately, current assessments increase the distress of trans individuals, and possibly penalize individuals for presenting mental health issues as a result of cumulative experiences of transphobia. Further, folks who are homeless, under-housed, doing sex work, or using substances may be automatically screened out of the assessment process due to social systems that cannot provide adequate supports and resources (e.g. housing), yet require one to be "stable enough" to be approved for health care. Indeed, while the classification and designation of transsexual and transgender identities as pathological in and of themselves serve to bring trans identities, bodies, and expressions under the control of medical, legal, and psychiatric systems, this control does more to exclude and marginalize trans women, men, and others than to offer rights, support, assistance, or resolution. While there are no specific, agreed-upon protocols in place for addressing the needs of non-binary identified trans folks, access to appropriate supportive counselling for social transition and, if desired, medical care for feminization, masculinization, or surgeries can and should happen.

Alternative Practice: Increasing Knowledge, Reducing Barriers

Social workers take many and varied roles in the legal, social, and health care systems that trans people may access. We may be involved in any or all of the following: outreach to folks who are homeless or under-housed, mental health support, case management, advocacy in accessing social assistance, child custody, disability supports, legal support, temporary shelter, housing, health care, supportive counselling, and crisis de-escalation, to name a few. We may be directly involved in a person's reconciliation of gender identity and narrative via clinical counselling, assessment, and approval for gender-affirming procedures and health care.

In all of these roles, we directly impact the health and wellness of trans individuals, by way of our interactions, the safety and acceptance we provide, and the predetermined ideas we may or may not have about gender as it is socially constructed. As practitioners, we must take care to inform ourselves of the specific gender-based barriers individuals face in interaction with systems, people, and processes. In practice, we must be aware of the potential to, unintentionally or otherwise, participate in the delegitimization of trans bodies, experiences, and narratives by way of the spaces we help create.

Specifically, trans folks may face a lack of acceptance, understanding, and affirmation in their interactions with social workers that may alienate them from accessing potentially beneficial resources (Bauer et al., 2009; Hage & Karim, 2000). Cisnormative thinking—especially in social work practitioners' understandings of gender, sex, and bodies—buying into current medical and psychiatric narratives, assessments, and delivery systems of trans health care, and an unwillingness to confront and challenge the flaws of these systems to advocate for appropriate, accessible trans care must be addressed in current social work practice.

In disrupting the process of delegitimizing gender-variant narratives, social work practitioners must reflect upon and challenge their own notions, learning, and ideals of gender. Practitioners must work to set the tone for a low-barrier, trusting relationship that will not replicate impersonal service models of professionalism that imbue practitioners with the power of knower and cast the service user as helpless recipient. A model of self-reflexivity, critical awareness building, and radical affirmation and acceptance of the circumstances of each individual community member should be strived for. Trans and gender-variant folks, particularly those who are racialized, under-housed, or psychiatric or prison industrial complex survivors, experience a high degree of pathologization, exclusion, invisibility, and abuse resulting from pervasive systemic and interpersonal traumas (Grant et al., 2011). It is important that practitioners expand their awareness of the many possibilities for trans existence in terms of individual narratives, histories, and meaning-making, so that the process of erasure and supplanting of medicalized trans narratives is replaced with one of supportive self-determination.

In examining existing systems of restricted access, protocols, and guidelines vis-à-vis practitioners' potential regulatory, gatekeeping function in their work, I would like to propose the following tasks:

- Any social workers or counsellors working with people must do extensive work to understand the social construction of their own gender identity as part of systems and laws maintaining gender normativity.
- These social workers and counsellors must become familiar with the variety and diversity of trans experiences as they relate to differences in experiences of oppression with regard to ability, racialization, indigeneity, class, sexuality, trans-misogyny, and gender identity and expression.
- Social workers and counsellors must understand the effects of the psychiatrization of trans experience and the promotion of suffering on the mental health and functioning of trans people.

- Social workers and counsellors must challenge and advocate for appropriate, self-determined health care within a primary-care model based in informed consent.
- Social workers and counsellors must challenge workplace settings and colleagues to examine the systemic or institutional barriers that specifically impact trans people in a particular service setting (e.g. separated dorms, gender-segregated washrooms, open shower facilities/change rooms, language used in brochures/websites and amongst staff, responsiveness to transphobia experienced from staff or other community members, and understandings of trans experience).
- Social workers and counsellors must help individuals understand their narrative within the context of systems of gender-based oppression, and imposed legal and psychiatric definitions.

Social workers and others implicated in trans health care play a crucial role in how trans and genderqueer folks experience systems restricting access to diverse narratives and self-directed means of transition (Bockting, Knudson, & Goldberg, 2006). We especially have an ethical obligation to use resistance strategies from within the structures we are a part of to reduce and remove barriers affecting the marginalization and oppression of anyone identifying outside of the gender binary (Ida, 2007).

In order to provide relational space that promotes physical and emotional wellness, practitioners must consider how current practices may re-invoke and replicate systemic and interpersonal traumas that folks may experience, particularly across intersections of racialization, class, mental health status, sex work, housing status, and disability. This can be accomplished by developing a critical awareness of one's role in the (de)legitimization of acceptable trans narratives and embodiment, and by cultivating an ability to practise within the context of *radical affirmation* (Nuttbrock et al., 2002). Radical affirmation simply means accepting a person-centred approach that locates and roots out shameful messaging, while promoting unconditional acceptance of diverse experiences. An essential part of affirmation is developing clients' own ability to feel compassion for their circumstances, and an understanding of the impacts of systemic and institutional processes affecting meaning-making of their identity. In doing so, practitioners must practise reflexively to provide a radically non-judgmental, positive, and supportive space that encourages exploration and re-storying as directed by the client.

For example, as a frontline mental health practitioner I carry the power to affirm or deny individual experience, help people make sense and meaning of their trauma histories, and help them externalize and shed shame, guilt, and stigma collected in the spirit, body, and soul over a lifetime. I can help clients deconstruct their experiences with transphobic, racist, trans-misogynist, binary-based service systems, broader social norms, and dominant culture, to help them name experiences of emotional violence, erasure, and exclusion while seeking out services I know to be trans-positive. I can help individuals steer clear of those services that have been known to be obtrusive, insensitive, and erasing. I can write letters and make phone calls that will gain access to medical means of transition or trans health care when individuals would not otherwise have access based on their authentic understanding of their identities, histories, and goals. I may help individuals interpret their own lived experience and historical narrative in order to make sense of where they are at in terms of self-identification, and affirm and create space for alternative interpretations, meaning, and language around gender and identities that do not conform to medical guidelines and psychiatric diagnoses.

Additionally, when directly involved in the assessment and screening process for accessing trans-specific health care, practitioners can take active roles in supporting folks to understand what their social, medical, and legal options are for gender expression, as well as taking specific actions to increase the realm of possible expressions. Individuals may enter into a counselling relationship having not decided on any identity term that fits their experience of their body, spirit, sex, or gender. In this case, it is possible to help the individual understand how existing identity terms may represent useful shorthand for certain types of identity categories, while helping the client assess whether aspects of their own experience more or less fit with their understanding of those terms.

Information or knowledge regarding the use of particular identity terms amongst those who self-identify with those terms can be shared with clients in order to provide examples of some of the ways folks recognize a fit for themselves within such terms. It is important to hold conversational space for individuals to question their own understanding of trans identity, especially given community norms and pressure to be seen as a particular *type* of trans person who conforms to dominant narratives within a specific trans or queer community. As well, practitioners must familiarize themselves with the diversity of experiences, understandings, and language used within clients' own particular cultural contexts so as not to replicate norms of whiteness. Affirming individuals' desire to use and explore language, dress, imagined embodiment, and various degrees of disclosure in different settings, as well as co-creating strategies for navigating others' reactions to their presentation and understandings of self, will greatly facilitate the growth, healing, and authentic expression of identities so desperately needed by gender-diverse people and so absent in current social service settings.

Conclusion

A commitment to unlearning biases related to understandings of biology, sex, sexuality, and gender is crucial in critically engaging with systemic processes that perpetuate normative gender expressions and possibilities for embodiment. Developing an interest and awareness of issues faced by trans people with regard to systemic discrimination and processes of erasure is key to becoming a therapeutic ally or advocate, no matter the setting one works in. Cultivating a relational and structural environment that supports autonomy and informed decision-making lies at the foundation of dismantling pathologizing systems. The role of the social worker is not simply to be supportive, but to thoroughly and actively root out harmful processes that negatively impact the capacity for self-determination. This role requires moving deeply into a reflexive space that considers, provides safety for, and listens carefully to the experiences and knowledge of trans people. Helping clients challenge the legitimacy of medical and psychiatric processes that control trans identities becomes central to restoring the health, wellness, and wholeness of those we serve.

Notes

1. I would like to extend a sincere thank-you to Nael Bhanji and Rupaleem Bhuyan for their valuable time, energy, and feedback on this chapter.
2. *Gender-variant* refers to anyone who identifies outside of traditional binary gender norms, including genderqueer, genderfluid, agendered, androgynous, and trans.
3. *Trans* is used to replace the medicalized or academic use of *transgender* with what is more commonly used by trans people to describe our identities.
4. Transphobia is the reaction individuals, systems, and institutions exhibit when they impose notions of normalcy on gender-variant and trans people. It is a physically, spiritually, and emotionally violent action designed to erase trans people and enforce gender norms.
5. *Cisgender* has been used to describe the alignment of one's internal sense of gendered self with that assigned at birth (i.e. non-trans people). I would like to shift the use of *cis* to emphasize socially approved gender expressions and identities perceived to match with assigned sex at birth. This definition allows more space for non-trans, non-cis people (e.g. butches, queens, intersex individuals, straight masculine women, and straight effeminate men).
6. *Folks* is a gender-neutral word trans people use to describe ourselves.
7. Transition is the process of attaining congruence and affirmation of the gender identity and presentation one feels most comfortable with.

Transition most often refers to a medical process of hormone replacement therapy (HRT) and/or surgeries, in order to induce sex characteristics that society largely constructs as "opposite" to the gender assigned to a person at birth. Distinctions have been made between "social" and "medical" transition, but each trans person determines for themselves what a transition looks like. Changes can involve choice of dress, physical embodiment, gender role, social perceptions/pronoun use, and name change, for example.
8. Sherbourne Health Centre in Toronto, Vancouver Coastal Health, the Mazzoni Center in Philadelphia, Callen-Lorde Community Health Centre in New York City, Lyon-Martin Health Services in San Francisco.
9. Cisnormative or cis-sexist actions, thinking, or words carry the assumption that there can be only two biologically valid and provable sexes or genders that organize our social worlds.

References

Bauer, G. R., Hammond, R., Travers, R., Kaay, M., Hohenadel, K. M., & Boyce, M. (2009). "I don't think this is theoretical; this is our lives": How erasure impacts health care for transgender people. *Journal of the Association of Nurses in AIDS Care, 20*(5), 348–361.

Bockting, W. O., Knudson, G., & Goldberg, J. M. (2006). Counseling and mental health care for transgender adults and loved ones. *International Journal of Transgenderism, 9*(3/4), 35–82.

Brotman, S., Ryan, B., Jalbert, Y., & Rowe, B. (2002). Reclaiming space-regaining health: The health care experiences of Two-Spirit people in Canada. *Journal of Gay & Lesbian Social Services, 14*(1), 1–22.

charismatics are dangerous. (2012). Working together to break down normative trans narratives. Retrieved from charismaticsaredangerous.com/2012/04/29/working-together-to-break-down-normative-trans-narratives

Coleman, E., Bockting, W., Botzer, M., Cohen-Kettenis, P., DeCuypere, G., Feldman, J., ... Zucker, K. (2012). Standards of care for the health of transsexual, transgender, and gender-nonconforming people, version 7. *International Journal of Transgenderism, 13*(4), 165–232.

Feldman, J. L., & Goldberg, J. (2006). Transgender primary medical care: Suggested guidelines for clinicians in British Columbia. Transgender Health

Program, Vancouver Coastal Health, 1-58. Retrieved from citeseerx.ist.psu.edu/viewdoc/download?doi=10.1.1.212.5537&rep=rep1&type=pdf

Gehi, P. S., & Arkles, G. (2007). Unraveling injustice: Race and class impact of Medicaid exclusions of transition-related health care for transgender people. *Sexuality, Research, and Social Policy: Journal of NSRC, 4*(4), 7-35.

Grant, J. M., Mottet, L. A., & Tanis, J. (2011). Injustice at every turn: A report of the national transgender discrimination survey. *National Centre for Transgender Equality, National Gay & Lesbian Task Force*. 1-228.

Hage, J. J., & Karim, R. B. (2000). Ought GIDNOS get naught? Treatment options for non-transsexual gender dysphoria. *Plastic and Reconstructive Surgery, 105*(3), 1222-1227.

HBGDA. (1979). Standards of care for gender identity disorders. Harry Benjamin International Gender Dysphoria Association. Retrieved from web.ebscohost.com.myaccess.library.utoronto.ca/ehost/detail?vid=20&hid=21&sid=818c44b0-262a-497b-920f3719238329de%40sessionmgr14&bdata=JnNpdGU9ZWhvc3QtbGl2ZQ%3d%3d#db=qth&AN=16142647

Ida, D. J. (2007). Cultural competency and recovery within diverse populations. *Psychiatric Rehabilitation Journal, 31*(1), 49-53.

(in)visible. (2012). I used to be a boy: Challenging trans narratives. Retrieved from invisiblyqueer.blogspot.ca/2012/03/i-used-to-be-boy-challenging-trans.html

Nuttbrock, L., Hwahng, S., Bockting, W., Rosenblum, A., Mason, M., Macri, M., & Becker, J. (2010). Psychiatric impact of gender-related abuse across the life course of male-to-female transgender persons. *Journal of Sex Research, 47*(1), 12-23.

Nuttbrock, L., Rosenblum, A., & Blumenstein, R. (2002). Transgender identity affirmation and mental health. *International Journal of Transgenderism, 6*(4). Retrieved from www.iiav.nl/ezines/web/IJT/97-03/numbers/symposion/ijt-vo06no04_03.htm

Raj, R., & Schwartz, C. (2013). "Collaborative preparedness and informed consent model: Guidelines to assess trans candidates for readiness for hormone therapy and supportive counselling throughout the gender transitioning process." Manuscript submitted for publication.

Rotondi, N. K., Bauer, G. R., Travers, R., Travers, A., Scanlon, K., & Kaay, M. (2011). Depression in male-to-female transgender Ontarians: Results from the Trans PULSE Project. *Canadian Journal of Community Mental Health, 30*(2), 113–133.

Sanchez, N. F., Sanchez, J. P., & Danoff, A. (2009). Health care utilization, barriers to care, and hormone usage among male-to-female transgender persons in New York City. *American Journal of Public Health, 99*(4), 1–8.

Serano, J. (2007). Whipping girl: A transsexual woman on sexism and the scapegoating of femininity. Emeryville, CA: Seal Press.

Sherbourne Health Centre. (2009). Guidelines and protocols for comprehensive primary health care for trans clients. Toronto, ON: Sherbourne Health Centre. Retrieved from www.sherbourne.on.ca/wp-content/uploads/2014/02/Guidelines-and-protocols-for-comprehensive-primary-care-for-trans-clients.pdf

Valentine, D. (2007). Imagining transgender: An ethnography of a category. Durham, NC: Duke University Press.

Walters, K. L., Evans-Campbell, T., Simoni, J. M., Ronquillo, T., & Bhuyan, R. (2006). "My spirit in my heart": Identity experiences and challenges among American Indian Two-Spirit women. *Journal of Lesbian Studies, 10*(1), 125–149.

PART III
Social Work Education and Pedagogy

CHAPTER 14

Christian Fundamentalism and Anti-Oppressive Practice Social Work Pedagogy: Rethinking the Inclusion of Fundamentalist Beliefs within the Queer-Positive Classroom

Sarah Todd and Diana Coholic[1]

This chapter reconsiders an article that we wrote in 2007, entitled "Christian Fundamentalism and Anti-Oppressive Social Work Pedagogy" (Todd & Coholic, 2007). We are thankful for the opportunity to rethink this earlier work regarding how to negotiate Christian fundamentalist beliefs in queer-positive social work classrooms. In this chapter we first offer a brief summary of the original paper, outlining the key themes and arguments we made, then we move to unpack a number of theoretical concepts and pedagogical experiences. We use these experiences to consider the possibilities that exist for social work educators who are negotiating between anti-oppressive practice (AOP) approaches to sexuality and Christian fundamentalist beliefs. We also revisit our original arguments, with the intent to deepen some of the theoretical terrain upon which we try to "teach through" spaces where LGBTQ students and teachers learn alongside educators and students who believe in a fundamentalist Christianity. In particular, we explore what intersectionality (Garry, 2011) and queer theory (Hicks, 2008) might offer to our work in this area. We also explore the classroom dynamic again, paying attention to new literature on what silence might mean (see Reda, 2009).

Nearly a decade later, there remain no tidy solutions to the concerns that we raised in 2007. In fact, queer theory opens up larger, often more troubling, questions, and our questions have shifted, becoming more textured as we attempted to continue with our vision of pedagogical spaces that help shape compassionate, progressive social work practitioners.

Incorporating Spirituality in the AOP Classroom

Our original work emerged from discussions that we had had about how we were interested in challenging the exclusion of spirituality from the classroom, but that in taking this position, we also opened up space for those with fundamentalist religious views to share these perspectives in the classroom. Our own experiences were that this presented significant challenges, particularly when teaching in the areas of feminism, sexuality, and HIV/AIDS. In many ways, it seemed to us that the views of fundamentalist Christians in particular often caused hurt or harm when shared in classrooms where people claimed a variety of gender identities/performances and sexual orientations. We struggled with the possibilities of creating an inclusive classroom for both queer students and fundamentalist Christians. For us, the challenge was to include people whose belief systems we did not necessarily share, but whom we felt did have something to offer the profession.

In 2007 we outlined the ways in which discussions of fundamentalism and its intersections with social work were appearing in American social work journals and in books that were considering spirituality in social work (Canda & Furman, 2009; Dinerman, 2003; Hodge, 2003 Reamer, 2003). We also discussed existing literature that explored the need for social work education to address the realities of heteronormativity and cisnormativity (Appleby & Anastas, 1998; Morrow, 2006; van Wormer, Wells, & Boes, 2000). We observed that, in the United States, these positions had resulted in a rather problematic compromise, wherein "CSWE [Council on Social Work Education] exempts religious institutions from the nondiscrimination standard related to sexual orientation and, as a result, some schools of social work are not required to provide affirmative knowledge about gay and lesbian persons" (Hunter & Hickerson, 2003, p. 2). While such exemptions do not exist within the Canadian regulations of schools of social work, the tension between fundamentalist religious beliefs and secular attempts to provide gender and sexual equality remains ever present. We used the term *fundamentalism* to describe those movements that understand themselves as upholding an orthodoxy or right practice and regard members of their group as "instrumental in preserving tradition from erosion ... they tend toward self-separation or exclusivity.... Their practices also claim, by tacit or explicit decree, a masculine hegemony" (Schick, Jaffe, & Watkinson, 2004, p. 3). The reader should note that this definition is not used pejoratively but denotes a strong commitment to beliefs that are considered true and correct. We limited our original discussion to Christian fundamentalism[2] in order to provide some clarity, and we continue to do so in this current chapter despite its Eurocentric focus. While a variety of fundamentalist religious faiths could be analyzed and interrogated by way of intersectionality and queer theory, fundamentalist beliefs and faiths that are also linked with cultures originating in the developing world, experiences of migration and oppression, and so forth, pose layers of complexity that are beyond the scope of this current chapter.

The context in which we reflected on the tension between sexual and gender diversity and fundamentalism was that of an anti-oppressive classroom grounded in critical theory. Using this frame, we argued that while the silencing and/or marginalization of students with Christian fundamentalist beliefs required a rethinking of our imagined inclusive anti-oppressive classrooms, we did not suggest that these students' negative experiences were equivalent to the oppressive experiences of those in our classrooms who endure sexism, heterosexism, racism, and/or colonialism. Christian fundamentalists are not systematically oppressed through economic, social, and political institutions. However, they can be discriminated against within social work and secular organizations (Ressler & Hodge, 2000), which challenges us to establish clear limits of exclusion or to broaden our pedagogy to make room for those with competing worldviews.

Our paper concluded with a reflection on our experiences in the classroom. We discussed the dilemma of marking papers in which students draw upon fundamentalist values; accommodating fundamentalist students in classrooms that we assert to be explicitly queer-positive; and the challenge of working with male students with fundamentalist beliefs in predominantly female groups of students. We reflected on the harm that these situations left us having to deal with. We suggested it was important that our truths remain open for discussion. We need to remain open to the possibility that those students who hold personal values and beliefs that do not converge with social work values may, given space for critical reflection, shift those beliefs or become reflexive practitioners and find ways to manage their beliefs within a professional practice committed to social work values. We hoped that our analysis would encourage further reflection on how secularity, justice, heterosexism, fundamentalism, and spirituality shape and are shaped by experiences in the social work classroom.

Other Theoretical Possibilities: Intersectionality and Queer Theory

As we returned to this work five years later, we wanted to further reflect on our classrooms and the social context in which we teach. While some students have asserted that today's young people are more open to diverse sexual and gender identities, recent news reports and academic studies about bullying and teenage suicide suggested that, in fact, many queer students entering our classrooms have not experienced the educational system as a safe space (Burke, 2011; Community Team, 2011; Duggan, 2012; Mishna, Newman, Daley, & Solomon, 2009). Writers also noted that, at least for some students, social work is experienced as a spiritual "calling" or as a way in which they can put their Christian beliefs and responsibilities into practice (Canda & Furman, 2009). While we still teach in a heterosexist society, and one in which religion plays a significant role in many students' lives, we would like to posit that the opposition we established—of fundamentalist versus queer students—is messier than we had previously conceptualized. There are people who find a way to bring together fundamentalist interpretations of Christianity and a queer identity (Lee, 2007). In the next sections, we consider two distinct theoretical underpinnings for imagining a pedagogical space in which we respond to queer students and students who identify as fundamentalist. Each takes on the tensions we explored from different perspectives that could shift the way we work with queer and fundamentalist students.

Intersectionality

In our original paper, we were concerned about the creation of harm within the classroom. We now think that a framework of intersectionality may offer a strategy to help all students think deeply about and discuss their interlocking oppressions and privileges across various contexts, theorizing these as fluid and dynamic (Samuels & Ross-Sheriff, 2008). Intersectionality is a complex construct that emerged from the writings of women of colour during the 1960s and 1970s (e.g. Combahee River Collective, 1977; Lorde, 2007). While there are certainly strong convergences between AOP and intersectionality, intersectionality operates at a more theoretical level, while concepts such as social location (which social workers are well versed with) indicate the results of the interaction of identity categories, which shift over time and place (Hulko, 2009). Minimally, intersectionality is the idea that various forms of oppression interact with one another in multiple complex ways (Garry, 2011). It is a paradigm with which we can explore the complexities of individual and group identities, making visible the ways in which diversity within a group is often ignored or essentialized, and helping students to consider the impacts of interlocking oppressions in more complicated ways

(Mehrotra, 2010). Also, as Garry (2011, p. 829) explains, the awareness of our social location that results from intersectional thinking helps to improve our scholarship and allows us to face up to dominant group members' unacknowledged privileges. It can help us to understand how people might have different interests at stake in a particular issue: for example, a lesbian's interest in marriage. So an analysis of one's interlocking oppressions and privileges moves us beyond the identification of one's social locations to a more nuanced understanding of one's identity categories, which are "complex, messy, and fluid" (Garry, 2011, p. 830).

Challenging ourselves and our students to delve more deeply into analyses of how various social locations intersect is a difficult but important endeavour. Theorizing intersectionality is complex, as some students face their complicity in oppression for the first time (Chapman, 2011). Chapman (2011) used research-based narratives with students to help them reflect on how the stories resonated in their own lives, which helped them reflexively evaluate legacies of oppression in social work and their own participation in these, without this signifying that they were "bad." We can relate to the issue of some students becoming defensive when faced with their own membership in a group or identity that has oppressed others. For instance, in our original paper we discussed an example of a mature male student with Christian fundamentalist beliefs who challenged the use of the word *oppression* and expressed beliefs that the professor was trying to indoctrinate the other students into feminism. He also had conflict with another professor over her use of a case example involving a lesbian. Although we cannot know for certain, we suspect that his anger was caused in part by his inability to analyze and accept (without feeling personally blamed) that his social location represented several groups/categories that had been, and were, oppressive to marginalized groups including women, in some contexts, and LGBTQ people. We are contemplating how intersectional thinking could help us to identify convergences and areas of mutual interest that might help navigate these sometimes painful realizations. Mehrotra (2010) suggests using narratives from film and literature to develop understandings of intersectionality in lived lives. Accordingly, we have found Andi Simcha Dubowski's (2007) film *Trembling Before G-D* particularly helpful in exploring the intersections between fundamentalist religious faith and queer identities. As Mehrotra (2010) states, and this film highlights, we need to understand how intersectionality plays out at the level of individual identities, structural inequalities, and discursive constructions because ultimately we are concerned with promoting social justice and change.

We imagine that by using a paradigm of intersectionality, students with fundamentalist affiliations and queer students might be able to identify areas of interest and mutual focus, and that the diversities within these categories might be further interrogated. We need to be careful not to essentialize students with fundamentalist beliefs and students who identify as queer (Hankivsky, Reid, Cormier, Varcoe, Clark, Benoit, & Brotman, 2010). Obviously, not all of these students are going to experience their fundamentalism or queerness in the same way. For one example, it is possible that a student who believes homosexuality is sinful would not support homophobic campaigns, keeping their religious beliefs somehow separate from some of their lived experiences as a social worker. On the other hand, some queer students might also have affiliations with Christian sects that do not support same-sex relationships (O'Brien, 2004; Walton, 2006). Contradictions abound in people's identities that are also always in process, which is an important concept to emphasize with students.

For another example, in an undergraduate sexuality course that the first author taught several times, the first assignment was one in which students interviewed each other about an experience with sexuality or gender. Increasingly, students articulated a strong desire to not have sexual intercourse until after marriage in order to be congruent with their religious beliefs. As an educator, these types of disclosures gave me pause and I found myself bracing for discussions on queer sexuality and gender bending. However, these same students who drew upon fundamentalist religious commitments to regulate their own sexual behaviours tended to be quite critical of religious discrimination against queer persons. I was often surprised by their frustration with the response the Catholic school system has toward their LGBTQ peers. Their discourse was rarely one of love the sinner, but not the sin. Instead it seemed to be frustration in response to inequality. The tensions in the classroom were generally subtler than I anticipated. Instead of the bigger social justice questions, I ended up trying to unpack moral hierarchies around sexuality and gender: we were questioning our deep anxiety about sex as pleasure, and wondering, if we understand ourselves as "good" or "normal" in terms of sexuality and gender, what does that mean when we are working with someone whose behaviours and desires are viewed as "bad" and "abnormal"? How does good practice happen when the relationship is between someone who understands himself or herself as "well behaved" sexually and someone who is perceived as, and may perceive himself or herself as, "bad" sexually? Kinsman's (2003) work on the creation of sexual problems is vital here to helping us understand how deeply society is invested in creating certain desires and sexual practices as social problems. The process of intersectionality challenges us all to see how we are implicated in complex networks of oppression that religious and political institutions are deeply invested in, and that create spaces in which some of us can understand ourselves as "good and normal," while others are never offered such opportunities.

In the process of applying the lens of intersectionality to our lives, it is also important to identify areas of resilience and resistance to domination and oppression so that we do not over-emphasize only aspects of our victimization (Hankivsky et al., 2010). Change in attitudes and the development of critical thought often occurs when people feel supported and valued, and this is more likely to occur if we do not become bogged down in problem-saturated narratives. By focusing on the complexities in students' identities, including the ways they resist oppression, we are more likely to create a space for fruitful discourse. Perhaps then it is possible, sometimes, to have conversations in a classroom between students with fundamentalist beliefs and students who identify as queer, without the creation of harm. Megan Boler (2005) suggested that

> the obligation of educators is not to guarantee a space free from hostility—an impossible and sanitizing task—but rather, to challenge oneself and one's students to crucially analyze *any* statement made in a classroom, especially statements that are rooted in dominant ideological values that subordinate on the basis of race, gender, class or sexual orientation. (p. 4)

This suggests that our obligation is to view discursive spaces as those that provide material for work. If we use ourselves as an example to begin these analyses, stressing that we all have some privileges and some discriminations or oppressions in our lives, as well as being part of oppressive systems, we might be better able to create a context wherein students would be willing to engage in this reflexive process with an open mind. In this analysis, we could stress the authority we have as professors in determining grades and professionalizing students, to name just two examples, understanding that talking about our own identities may shape some students' desires to share their narratives; a student with fundamentalist beliefs could feel anxious about juxtaposing her identity and beliefs against a professor's divergent values. Also, encouraging students to conduct intersectional analyses privately, by way of individual assignments, may be a less threatening beginning.

However, while we have moved from our previous position that identification of fundamentalist beliefs should occur primarily outside of the classroom, there will still be times when it is more prudent to converse with some students outside of the group context. We are thinking here about students who, for whatever reason, are highly resistant to examining their attitudes and beliefs, and the impact of these on others (such as the male student in the example mentioned earlier). Also, another perspective to consider is the expectation that everyone will share details of their lives is a disciplinary strategy.

> From a Foucauldian perspective, the silent teachers, like priests or psychotherapists, are able to exercise institutional power over the students because they are in the position of judging students' self-disclosure. At the same time, students can employ silence as a device for resisting knowledge transmission. (Li, 2005, p. 71)

It is a complex endeavour to professionalize students; indeed, many students resist professionalization, which entails challenging them to examine their identities while remaining cognizant of how we are implicated in these disciplinary techniques. It is also difficult to create spaces where the voices of those who engage in diverse gender and/or sexual performances and those who hold fundamentalist beliefs are equally welcome. In general we are often amazed at students' determination not to say anything, which is disabling to a pedagogy of dialogue, as much social work education is. However, we have begun a more thorough questioning of the role that silence plays in our classroom. First, in considering the connections between pedagogy and social justice, we engage with those questions that explore how the speaking of some students silences others, and what is happening when an educator asks people to participate and they choose not to (Burbules, 2005). This leaves us to wonder what our responsibility is in terms of determining the tone of the classroom and what the dangers are of doing too much or too little in terms of this responsibility.

In recent years, more work has emerged to make sense of silence in the classroom. In particular Mary Reda's (2009) book asks us to consider what we as educators see with silent students. Do, in fact, some students need to be protected from the speech of others? In our experience teaching, especially in the area of sexuality in social work, it is the fundamentalist students who remain silent, while many queer students feel that the pedagogical space is one where they can freely participate. The second line of questioning wonders, as Reda does, what silence means for students. For instance, what do queer students and fundamentalist students hear when they come up against silent students? What does it mean when they, themselves, are silent? How do these perceptions of silence shape the pedagogy of the classroom? Can we understand them as useful? Do we want to consider leaving them intact or do they need to be troubled? Is it possible, as Reda asked, to celebrate the silent student as receptive to new knowledge or is it imperative that we continue to see student-initiated silence in dialogic education as a sign that something is not working? By definition, dialogue requires the silence of listeners in addition to the voice of the speakers (Reda, 2009, p. 23). In this framework, we understand silence and speech as functionally equivalent (Li, 2005). When we, as educators, worry as much as we did in 2007 about silence in the classroom, we might overlook students' relationship to their own voices and silences (Reda, 2009, p. 24).

Some of the ways we have tried to address silence in the classroom include developing relationships with our students through individual conferencing, having students introduce each other and ourselves, having more small-group work where students report back to the larger group, encouraging shared activities in the classroom, and talking about the silence. Often, these interventions challenge the silence we find worrisome, while respecting space for more contemplative silence. The challenge is, of course, the contemporary context, with larger class sizes that shape our abilities to achieve what we have discussed so far in this chapter. We are discouraged that, almost a decade after we wrote the original paper, dealing with personal and professional values/beliefs seems more difficult today because we are now teaching larger classes with more students. This situation makes it easier for some students to remain silent and disengaged, and more difficult for us to engage with every student. With smaller classes one can utilize methods such as individual student conferences, exercises to promote familiarity, role-plays, and small-group discussion, which may be more effective in facilitating in-depth discussion and analyses. We have also noticed a change in the students that we are teaching, as a shift in their expectations seems to have taken place. Perhaps as students juggle multiple demands, it has become harder for them to prepare for classes, and we notice it is often more challenging to engage them with material that is not "entertaining." In addition, the common notions of how we respect one another as a learning community are no longer shared and need to be restated and regulated. This particular problem not only impacts the cognitive parts of learning but limits the emotional components of learning wherein we often need to become uncomfortable in order to learn to see our world differently. We turn our attention now to another theory that might offer possibilities for interrogating identities in the classroom: queer theory.

Queer Theory

Queer theorists ask three fundamental questions: (1) How do we take up our sexualities and genders? (2) How do those categories come to have specific meanings? and (3) What institutional practices give meaning to these categories and how do these meanings both enable and constrain us? (Jagose, 1996). What queer theorists have come to show is that the categories of gay, lesbian, and bisexual are under-determined and that while categories may be useful for understanding ourselves and others, no category is itself necessary and all categories are subject to revision (Marinucci, 2010; see also Chapter 1). Stephen Hicks (2008) draws on this theory to raise a number of concerns that anti-oppressive approaches to social work have the effect of fixing and limiting the possibilities for lesbians, gay men, and bisexuals. Even a positive identity in AOP discourses tends to be fixed and stable and, as a result, is limiting. Within this approach there is "an inherent assumption that social descriptors, such as lesbian and gay, just *are*" (Willis, 2007, p. 191). This also extends to heterosexuality, which is assumed to exist as unquestionable. In contrast to this, Hicks (2008) draws on queer theory to ask how sexual identities are produced in social work and what the significance is within the profession of perceiving sexuality as disclosing a "truth" about identities. This offers an alternative framework in which all aspects of social life are re-examined for how heterosexuality is privileged and institutionalized (Willis, 2007).

How might this type of analysis be useful in considering the pedagogical space that we are interrogating? Do we, in our establishment of the AOP context for discussing sexuality, inadvertently fall into the trap that is similar to those created through fundamentalism, that is, a new rigid orthodoxy? Of course, grappling with these questions is always challenging because the students with whom we are working tend not to be working from within queer theory, and the importance of identity is never as important as it is in a social work classroom where an individual asserts a belief that threatens the value of LGBTQ persons.

Queer theory offers a framework within which we can ask ourselves how our thinking about sexuality and gender within the social work classroom produces sexuality and gender in particular ways. For example, when we only interrogate the problematic ways in which religious institutions produce a marginalized or shameful version of sexual and gender diversity, we do not interrogate the ways in which social work has a tendency to construct sexual and gender identities in problem-saturated ways that require social work intervention and support. As Hicks (2008) and Willis (2007) suggest, such constructions, while well intentioned, can be restrictive and even oppressive. In addition, as we reflect on how identities are produced in our classroom, we tend to invert hierarchies so that queer identities are valued as requiring more attention and focus than more traditional practices of sexuality and gender. In so doing, we fear that we create a pedagogical space in which those who hold fundamentalist beliefs might feel excluded, and thus possibly increase their resistance to the knowledge we are trying to share. Increasingly, this has felt like it might be a stumbling block in creating transformative pedagogical spaces. What would it mean to challenge the AOP notion that one must always ally on the side of the oppressed and pause, just momentarily, to have a discussion about what it means to live in a society where one's attraction to someone is perceived as a marker of identity. Might we also reflect upon how identities that are outside of heterosexist norms have been historically, and continue to be, both formally and informally excluded? At the same time, how do we make sense of this in a society where many people measure the value and worthiness of themselves and their lives within religious discourses that understand sexual and gender diversity as sinful? It seems this might lead us down a path where we have to understand sexuality as Foucault did, as a system of knowledge that creates moral hierarchies, not much different in "type" than those within fundamentalist belief systems. In this way, we reconsider sexuality as a system of knowing that we are inviting students to unpack and not as something someone possesses or is a truth about them. Would this conversation produce something different from the "safe spaces" we were earlier struggling to produce? How can we respond to students' and faculty's fears of erasing and negating queer experiences when using such an approach? What happens when we unpack and challenge, as Hicks (2008, p. 77) suggests, social work's "inquiry and classification of" sexuality, in terms of how this can happen both progressively and regressively? What does it look like in our classrooms to do as Hicks suggests and "develop an account of sexuality that is reflexive and accountable, that makes the intellectual *process* of arriving at a version visible?" (Hicks, 2008, p. 77).

Our efforts to deploy this type of analysis in our classrooms has had limited effect. It is a challenge because most students do tend to want knowledge about sexuality but find the questioning and unsettling that is required by queer theory to work against their desire for truth and certainty. Our pedagogy has been most successful when we have used various descriptions of queer persons and asked small groups to discuss what they felt these descriptions told them about a person and the work that they should do with them. We then looked at how these interpretations can limit practice. So, when we talked about sexuality and risky behaviour, many small groups suggested that they needed to work on self-esteem with the client. Instead we encouraged students to rethink how notions of risk are constructed in our society and in whose interests they are constructed. This enabled us to shift into discussions of the regulation of sexuality when it is solely associated with pleasure and the reasons why state, religious, and educational institutions are uncomfortable with such activities. We began to identify how behaviours rather than identities are dealt with, and why it is dangerous to reduce someone to their sexual or gendered behaviours.

Also, what would it mean for students engaging in various sexual and gender performances, and students with a range of secular and fundamentalist beliefs, to contemplate the end of sexuality? Hicks posits that there is

> no "sexuality" to be understood or liberated because it is deployed in that very understanding. That is, trying to understand "sexuality" as such is a process of producing and using it in particular forms. Therefore, it may well be that moving away from the idea of an identity-based set of sexual categories will help social work to contemplate other models and to ask about the versions of sexuality that it is implicated in. (2008, p. 77)

We think that this might provide an opening for deconstructing the moralistic narratives that fundamentalist students sometimes silently harbour while, at the same time, challenging secular students to see themselves as implicated in creating moral hierarchies of sexuality.

Conclusion

As Garry (2011) argues, it is hard work to dig into "the details of the ways that the full range of oppressions and privileges interact in our societies, lives, and theories" (p. 844). Intersectional thinking requires solid critical thinking skills, and good critical thinkers are creative thinkers.

Critical thinking, writing, and communicating skills are also absolutely essential for effective social work practice. This is even more important when thinking through issues of gender and sexuality that tend to evoke reactive, emotional responses that are deeply engrained and, as such, are taken for granted. We cannot expect students to engage in an in-depth level of intersectional analyses without first teaching them how to think, and supporting them in developing their self-awareness so that they can be reflexive. This is a fairly obvious statement, as developing critical thinking is a component of the Canadian Association for Social Work Education's Standards for Accreditation (CASWE, 2013). The challenge is that for students for whom faith is centrally important, critical thinking can be quite a threatening approach. If one's faith or beliefs around sexuality and gender are threatened when interrogated with reason, there can be a strong defence against, or resistance to, intellectual work. This demands that along with critical analysis, we must always attend to the emotional and psychological work of education such as argued by Boler (1999) and Britzman (2009). Over the past several years, we have made the teaching of critical thinking more overt in our courses, teaching the components of critical thought, such as universal intellectual standards, and emphasizing that critical thinking is a skill that needs to be practised in order to develop and improve. To this end, we have found the material developed by the Critical Thinking Community useful (see www.criticalthinking.org). Other social work educators have written papers on teaching critical thinking and these are also helpful for students to consider (Gibbons & Gray, 2004; Horton & Diaz, 2011).

In drawing upon interesectionality and queer theory in our classrooms, we are still negotiating the tensions we explored in 2007. While these theories have not brought us resolution, they have encouraged us to create engaging pedagogical spaces for queer and fundamentalist students with more care and caution, pushing us into places where we have felt our own discomfort. Intersectionality has asked us to view the identities in the classroom as more complex and fluid. This is something we have learned from theory and from our classroom practices where students' lived experiences are often complex and surprising. Even those who seem to hold rather rigid belief systems show themselves to have spaces of contradiction that suggest they have something to contribute to how we, as a society, move to embrace and celebrate queer persons. When drawing on queer theory, we have begun to explore how all institutions, including religion and social work, use sexuality as a system of knowledge, a way of defining and regulating people. In this way, we are drawn together to interrogate discursive productions of identities, rather than engage in the ongoing battle between those of various identities and political perspectives. These approaches have their challenges, particularly given the contemporary context of social work education, where the relationships we used to build, in order to help us through difficult learning, are less possible. It is, however, a path we make by walking with as wide a range of people as possible.

Notes

1. Correspondence concerning this chapter should be addressed to Sarah Todd, School of Social Work, 509 Dunton Tower, 1125 Colonel By Drive, Carleton University, Ottawa, Ontario, Canada K1S 5B6. Email: sarah_todd@carleton.ca
2. We use this term to encompass a range of ways in which religious texts and teaching are brought into the classroom when sexuality is discussed. Students who bring up such perspectives do not always identify in any particular way, but instead draw upon biblical texts and/or religious teachings about same-sex relations as the basis of their struggles with embracing queer sexuality or beliefs that such relationships are immoral.

References

Appleby, G., & Anastas, J. (1998). *Not just a passing phase: Social work with gay, lesbian, and bisexual people*. New York, NY: Columbia University Press.

Boler, M. (1999). *Feeling power: Emotions and education*. New York, NY: Routledge.

Boler, M. (2005). All speech is not free: The ethics of "affirmative action pedagogy". In M. Boler (Ed.), *Democratic dialogue in education: Troubling speech, disturbing silence* (pp. 3–14). New York, NY: Peter Lang.

Britzman, D. (2009). *After education*. New York, NY: SUNY.

Burbules, N. (2005). Introduction. In M. Boler (Ed.), *Democratic dialogue in education: Troubling speech, disturbing silence* (pp. xiii–xxxii). New York, NY: Peter Lang.

Burke, A. (2011, October 18). Gay Ottawa teen who killed himself was bullied. *CBC*. Retrieved from www.cbc.ca/news/canada/ottawa/story/2011/10/18/ottawa-teen-suicide-father.html

Canda, E., & Furman, L. D. (2009). *Spiritual diversity in social work practice*. New York, NY: Oxford University Press.

Canadian Association for Social Work Education (CASWE). (2013). Standards for Accreditation (June 2013). Ottawa, ON. Retrieved from caswe-acfts.ca/commission-on-accreditation/coa-standards

Chapman, C. (2011). Resonance, intersectionality, and reflexivity in critical pedagogy (and research methodology). *Social Work Education: The International Journal, 30*, 723–744.

Combahee River Collective. (1977). The Combahee River Collective statement. Retrieved from zinelibrary.info/files/Combahee3.pdf

Community Team. (2011, December 4). Bullied gay teen's emotional online testimonial. *CBC*. Retrieved from www.cbc.ca/newsblogs/yourcommunity/2011/12/bullied-teens-emotional-online-testimonial.html

Dinerman, M. (2003). Editorial: Fundamentalism and social work. *Affilia, 18*(3), 249–253.

Dubowski, S. D. (Producer) (2007). *Trembling before G-D*. New York, NY: Mongrel Media.

Duggan, E. (2012, February 29). Bullying gay teen attempted suicide. *Vancouver Sun*. Retrieved from www.richmond-news.com/news/bullying-led-gay-teen-to-attempt-suicide-1.497424

Garry, K. (2011). Intersectionality, metaphors and the multiplicity of gender. *Hypatia, 26*, 826–850.

Gibbons, J., & Gray, M. (2004). Critical thinking as integral to social work practice. *Journal of Teaching in Social Work, 24*, 19–38.

Hankivsky, O., Reid, C., Cormier, R., Varcoe, C., Clark, N., Benoit, C., & Brotman, S. (2010). Exploring the promises of intersectionality for advancing women's health research. *International Journal for Equity in Health, 9*, 1–15.

Hicks, S. (2008). Thinking through sexuality. *Journal of Sexuality, 8*, 65–82.

Hodge, D. R. (2003). Hodge Responds. *Social Work, 48*(3), 431–432.

Horton, E. G., & Diaz, N. (2011). Learning to write and writing to learn social work concepts: Application of writing across the curriculum strategies and techniques to a course for undergraduate social work students. *Journal of Teaching in Social Work, 31*, 53–64.

Hulko, W. (2009). The time- and context-contingent nature of intersectionality and interlocking oppressions. *Affilia, 24*, 44–55.

Hunter, S., & Hickerson, J. (2003). *Affirmative practice: Understanding and working with lesbian, gay, bisexual, and transgender persons*. Washington, DC: NASW Press.

Jagose, A. (1996). *Queer theory: An introduction*. New York, NY: New York University Press.

Kinsman, G. (2003). Constructing sexual problems: These things may lead to the tragedy of our species. In L. Samuelson & W. Antony (Eds.), *Power and resistance* (pp. 85–119). Black Point, NS: Fernwood Press.

Lee, D. (Producer) (2007). *In God's House: Asian American Lesbian and Gay Families in the Church*. (DVD). Berkeley, CA: PANA Institute.

Li, H. L. (2005). Rethinking silencing. In M. Boler (Ed.), *Democratic dialogue in education: Troubling speech, disturbing silence* (pp. 69–86). New York, NY: Peter Lang.

Lorde, A. (2007). Age, race, class and sex: Women redefining difference. In A. Lorde, *Sister outsider: Essays and speeches by Audre Lorde* (pp. 114–123). Berkeley, CA: Crossing Press. (Original work published 1984.)

Marinucci, M. (2010). *Feminism is queer: The intimate connection between queer and feminist theory*. London, England: Zed Books.

Mehrotra, G. (2010). Toward a continuum of intersectionality theorizing for feminist social work scholarship. *Affilia, 25*, 417–430.

Mishna, F., Newman, P., Daley, A., & Solomon, S. (2009). Bullying of lesbian and gay youth: A qualitative investigation. *British Journal of Social Work, 39,* 1598–1614.

Morrow, D. (2006). Gay, lesbian, bisexual, and transgender adolescents. In D. Morrow & L. Messinger (Eds.), *Sexual orientation and gender expression in social work practice: Working with gay, lesbian, bisexual, and transgender people* (pp. 177–195). New York, NY: Columbia University Press.

O'Brien, J. (2004). Wrestling the angel of contradiction: Queer Christian identities. *Culture and Religion, 5*(2), 179–202.

Reamer, F. G. (2003). Social Work, evangelical Christians, and values. *Social Work, 48*(3), 428–430.

Reda, M. (2009). *Between speaking and silence: A study of quiet students.* New York, NY: SUNY.

Ressler, L. E., & Hodge, D. R. (2000). Religious discrimination in social work: An international survey of Christian social workers. *Social Work and Christianity, 27,* 49–70.

Samuels, G., & Ross-Sheriff, F. (2008). Editorial, identity, oppression, and power: Feminisms and intersectionality theory. *Affilia, 23,* 5–9.

Schick, C., Jaffe, J., & Watkinson, A. M. (2004). *Contesting Fundamentalisms.* Black Point, NS: Fernwood.

Todd, S., & Coholic, D. (2007). Christian fundamentalism and anti-oppressive social work pedagogy. *Journal of Teaching in Social Work, 27,* 5–25.

van Wormer, K., Wells, J., & Boes, M. (2000). *Social work with lesbians, gays, and bisexuals: A strengths perspective.* Needham Heights, MA: Allyn and Bacon.

Walton, G. (2006). "Fag church": Men who integrate gay and Christian identities. *Journal of Homosexuality, 51*(2), 1–17.

Willis, P. (2007). "Queer eye" for social work: Rethinking pedagogy and practice with same-sex attracted young people. *Australian Social Work, 60,* 181–196.

CHAPTER 15
Somewhere over the Rainbow: Reflections on Teaching a LGBT-S Bachelor of Social Work Course

Norma Jean Profitt

When I began teaching in the Saint Thomas University Department of Social Work (now a school) in 1999, I noted the paucity of material on sexual and gender diversity in the Bachelor of Social Work (BSW) curriculum. As a feminist troubled by heteronormativity and heterosexism in social work education and practice, I developed a course called Social Work and Lesbian, Gay, Bisexual and Two-Spirited Peoples (LGBT-S) and offered it as an elective in 2001, 2003, 2005, and 2007. When the school dismantled the four-year BSW in 2007, the LGBT-S course remained on the list of electives in the post-degree BSW. However, given that decisions about electives were based on student majority wishes, the LGBT-S course was not offered again during my tenure (I departed in 2011). Unfortunately, the Women and Social Work course that I taught met the same fate. Since these courses occupy a marginal status reflecting social oppression, it is unlikely they will be chosen as the "top choices" by students, as these are increasingly driven by employment considerations in the current neoliberal environment. The loss of these offerings in the curriculum is concerning because attitudes of sexism and heterosexism are closely interrelated with negativity expressed toward those individuals who are perceived as transgressing sex and gender norms (Black, Oles, & Moore, 1996; Martinez, Barsky, & Singleton,

2011; Stark, 1991). Although courses on "oppressed social groups" have been criticized for inadvertently reinforcing subordinate social status and the very categories constructed to oppress, they do provide focused opportunities for students to understand the material history of systemic domination and oppression. Students also examine their self-implication in oppressive social arrangements and deepen their knowledge and skills for practice.

Given the pervasive ideology and practice of heteronormativity in society, many students come to social work education with dominant assumptions about heterosexuality (Berkman & Zinberg, 1997; Brownlee, Sprakes, Saini, O'Hare, Kortes-Miller, & Graham, 2005; Chinell, 2011; Hylton, 2005; Martinez et al., 2011; Messinger, 2004; Newman, Dannenfeiser, & Benishek, 2002; Renn, 2000). The Standards for Accreditation of the Canadian Association for Social Work Education (CASWE, 2012) affirm "diversity," including gender and gender and sexual identities, in a human rights and social justice framework. Nevertheless, how this affirmation translates into social work curricula and field education and what theoretical and ethical-political approaches to teaching about gender and sexual diversity exist in schools of social work are impossible to discern from this document. Within the core learning objectives for students, outlined in the standards, there is certainly ample room for gender and sexual diversity to be addressed structurally, materially, and discursively in substantive ways. My experience with the LGBT-S elective, which I analyze in this chapter, underscores the need to educate all students on gender and sexual diversity in the context of social justice and ethics.

Course Overview

Content of the LGBT-S course included the history of the gay liberation and lesbian activist movements (Warner, 2002); community and culture; heteronormativity and heterosexism as a dominant form of social organization; youth, family life, health, violence and hate crimes; and affirmative practice. A key objective was to identify ways that we, as citizens and social workers, can challenge heteronormativity, heterosexism, and homo-ignorance in our professional practice and social world. To help translate positive attitudes into competence in the helping process (Green, Kiernan-Stern, Balley, Chambers, Claridge, Jones, Kitson, Leek, Leisey, Vadas, & Walker, 2005), I asked students to create a personal manifesto for practice (Foreman & Quinlan, 2008).

Conscious of the representation of gender and sexual diversity, I sought to reduce the objectification of queer people. Where possible, I used material authored by queers and reflective of the intersectionality of experience. Highlighting positive aspects of our lives, I tried to disrupt the notion of queer people as miserable and isolated, especially important when master narratives present non-heterosexuality as a "challenge" (Willis, 2007, p. 189). Unfortunately, homophobia in social work literature has been discussed in terms of its effects on queer psychological well-being, leaving unexplored "the logic and practice of heterosexual people's homophobia" (Jeyasingham, 2008, p. 144). I also emphasized diversity within LGBT-S communities to contest the notion that "there is something inherently biological about being gay, bisexual, or lesbian"; heterosexual populations are not perceived as a separate species (Willis, 2007, p. 191).

On the four occasions I taught this course, students were predominantly white and female and first-generation university goers from Atlantic Canada. At the outset, I let all students know that self-identification was not a course expectation. At the same time, I acknowledged that self-disclosure, critical in the struggle for gay and lesbian rights, can enhance personal and collective dignity and reduce feelings of alienation and isolation (Cain, 1996).

Political Objectives of the Course

As a feminist with a clear ethical-political project, I had political objectives for the course. First, I have always believed that as social workers we have an ethical responsibility to understand social structures and the operation of power in order to practise in socially just ways with individuals and communities. "Diversity" of sex, gender, gender expression, and sexuality is imperative to understand and embrace, yet in our conservative climate, "diversity" is easily individualized and viewed as if it were purely an individual characteristic, stripped of its context, and disconnected from structural roots and material conditions, thus obscuring the necessity of deep cultural and structural change.

Second, I wanted students to examine the ways in which heteronormativity and heterosexism construct heterosexuality "as the 'natural' and 'normal' sexuality, by which all 'Other' sexualities are measured and subordinated" (Ferfolja, 2007, p. 148). As an axis of power in everyday social relations that intersects with other axes, heteronormativity affects everyone, even those without conscious knowledge of it (Sedgwick, 1990). I hoped course material would open up spaces for rethinking gender and sexuality beyond the dominant heterosexist frame. In other words, I wanted to "broaden perception, to complexify cognition, and to amplify the imagination of learners" (Sumara & Davis, 1999, p. 191).

A related political objective was to examine the politics of heteronormativity, a strategy that goes beyond a liberal humanist inclusion-based approach that assumes that attitudinal change can be accomplished by uncovering "true images" of queer people (Ford, 2004). Making queers known through visibility by providing "true images" and "information" simply reproduces the hetero/homosexual binary in which heterosexuality remains privileged (O'Brien, 1999; Willis, 2007). "Images, whether positive or not, are one way in which we are turned into objects examined by those who do not themselves need to be defined in terms of difference" (Jeyasingham, 2008, p. 141). In this logic, whiteness and heterosexuality remain invisible and unexamined.

To counter liberal humanist systems of knowledge that privilege "ways of *not knowing*" (Jeyasingham, 2008, p. 141), I drew on queer theory to foster critical thinking about socially constructed binary systems of knowledge and categories assumed to be based on "nature" rather than historically, socially, and politically constructed (Cashore & Tuason, 2009; LaSala, Jenkins, Wheeler, & Fredriksen-Goldsen, 2008; McPhail, 2004; Willis, 2007). The intent was to take apart assumed linkages between sex, gender, psychological gender, and desire (Butler, 1999; McPhail, 2004; Willis, 2007) since the sex/gender system reifies sex "as a biological base from which the social world of gender is built" (Drabinski, 2011, p. 13). Sexuality is understood as a social relation (Sumara & Davis, 1999) with attention paid to analyzing "the operations and consequences of homophobia and heteronormativity" rather than on identifying who is sexually different (Jeyasingham, 2008, p. 149).

To critically explore heteronormativity and heterosexism, I presented queer theory and the sex/gender system and then asked students to participate in an in-class guided journey.[1] This exercise implicitly prompts students to locate themselves in social practices of gender and sexuality (Sumara & Davis, 1999) rather than position themselves as innocent bystanders to the oppression experienced by non-normative sexual and gender identities (Ford, 2004). For heterosexually identified students, this process of locating themselves helps disrupt their preoccupation with knowing the "other" (Fox, 2007), especially prevalent in current neoliberal and social work discourse with its gaze on the "disadvantaged," the "marginalized," and the "vulnerable."

Inside/Outside the Classroom: Challenging Heteronormativity and Heterosexism

The guided journey asked students to trace key influences, experiences, and formative moments in the development of their gender, sex, sexuality, and identities as they intersected with social markers such as class, ability, culture, "race," and so forth.[2] Students individually drew images of what arose for them on a large piece of paper, and in the process of sharing their representations, we collectively reflected on connections between lived experiences and normative expectations of gender and sexuality. As Drabinski (2011) queries, "What is the connection between personal experience/selfhood and the social structures that delimit even as they enable the personal in the first place?" (p. 13).

In class discussion and reflection papers, I identified student learning in four areas, illustrating the benefits of using the guided journey and queer theory ideas.[3] First, students gained a new appreciation of the overtly oppressive as well as subtle insidious power of heteronormativity. For example, they reflected on their ubiquitous exposure to devaluations of those outside the confines of "compulsory heterosexuality" (Rich, 1980), spoke of pressures to define themselves as "something," and made links between heterosexism, sexism, and racism in lived experience. Second, they consciously recognized and appreciated the richness and multifaceted nature of their lived experience, which contained aspects of pleasure as well as policing. This led to insights and questioning about what categories of gender and sexual identity tell us about our attitudes, desires, and behaviours over time and our experiences that exist outside of categories themselves.

Third, they achieved greater freedom and understanding for self and others. For example, a heterosexually identified white man shared that he was able to accept himself. He had been judged by others throughout his life for being "effeminate" and had often been perceived as gay and, by implication, not a "real" man according to notions of heterosexualized masculinity. Lesbian students confronted myths and stereotypes about bisexuality and came to understand their experience and that of others in a more satisfying and politically significant way. Fourth, some students, who self-identified as members of fundamentalist churches, spoke of a renewed commitment to discerning whether they believed in the teachings of their family and church, and to learning more about affirmative social work practice, human rights, and ethical social work. They wanted to offer the best possible service to all service users (see also Todd & Coholic, this volume).

My experience teaching this elective was the richest of my teaching career. Touched by the diversity and complexity of student experience obscured by heteronormative discourse and practice, I witnessed students' desires to express themselves more fully in terms of gender(s) and sexualities. Interestingly, most students reflected that they had not thought much about their own gender and sexual formation. I believe that the value of this course for many was in opening up spaces of freedom and possibility for living for self and others.

However, some gay and lesbian students were dismayed with queer theory deconstruction. Out and proud through political struggle, they refused the idea that their sexual orientation wasn't fixed or stable. Although gender, sexuality, and "race" may be continua or social constructs, sexism, heterosexism, and racism are very real, with material effects (Hill Collins, 2000; Pérez, 1998). As a feminist, queer, and activist, I realize the personal significance of gender and sexual identity, whether or not they are socially constructed (Willis, 2007), and my own critique of post-modernism and queer theory includes concern about the ramifications of deconstruction for collective identities and political activism (Butler, 1993; McPhail, 2004; Willis, 2007). Yet politically, I hold onto the hope that opening up the space between political identity for social struggle (what queers require) and identity in terms of gender and sexual diversity (what queers are or could be) (Rose, 1986) will generate ground for identifying common values and goals across differences in the political struggle for gender and sexual freedom and expression.

For some heterosexually identified students in the course, the distance they had to travel in terms of de-othering queer people was substantial. After viewing *The Matthew Sheppard Story*, some commented they had come to see queers as people who had feelings and lives: in other words, as human beings. Indeed, a feature of heteronormativity is that the gender and sexual identities of queers are perceived as standing in for the whole person, while the same does not apply to heterosexuals. Although emotional shifts away from being "consumers" and "voyeurs" (Bryson & de Castell, 1993), fostered through films, may signal movement toward de-othering, how do we simultaneously stimulate movement toward examining identities of naturalness and unquestioned privilege vis-à-vis others?

Although I tried to identify heterosexism as the operation of power and dominance (Cain, 1996) in philosophical, intellectually curious, and non-dichotomous ways, queer and heterosexually identified students commented that those who made obvious heterosexist comments appeared oblivious to my efforts. In his discussion of anti-racist education, Pon (2007) analyzes how teachers can feel responsible for correcting students and posits that corrective intervention is rooted in rationalist assumptions that proper thinking or perspective can be instilled in recalcitrant students. He suggests that such education "be understood as a chaotic, interminable, indeterminate journey in which we are always just beginning to labour a response to difficult knowledge" (p. 151). In this way, teachers and students find themselves in moments where they are immersed in the "self-implicating predicament of struggling to respond to histories of striking hatred and to our shocking human capacity for social violence" (p. 151). While this strategy may ease my sense of responsibility, I am not convinced it necessarily self-implicates all students in struggling to labour a response to systems of knowledge that produce hatred or in thinking about "how often and casually vehemence is unleashed by the ignorant" (personal communication with former BSW student, April 13, 2012). As educators, we need to continue to foreground social ethics and justice and diligently raise questions of privilege and penalty, the objectification of queers, and heteronormativity in multifaceted ways.

While teaching this course I constantly wrestled with the notion of "safer classrooms." How fair is it that students who have deep personal knowledge of sexual and gender diversity are again exposed to the "insidious traumatization" (Root, 1992) involved in living every day in a systemically oppressive world, even when those making heterosexist comments are trying to learn something about social arrangements and the lives of queers? Is it important that queer students can take a course that values and affirms them and promotes affirmative self-naming, critical analysis of social issues, and the building of spaces of solidarity that facilitate their survival, flourishing, and resistance? (Fox,

2007; Pérez, 1998). Is it realistic to presume we can meet the learning needs of those students who expect the course to reflect them back to themselves? (Drabinski, 2011). Are we assuming a deficit identity or being condescending when we assume that queer people require affirmation? Although queer students in my course did refuse "a version of middle-class liberal whiteness ... in which minority peoples perform their pain for us" (Kelly & Srivastava, 2003, p. 75), as learners we existed in an "always already heterosexualized classroom" (Bryson & de Castell, 1993, p. 296), even as we tried to imagine another kind of world. "How to problematize heterosexuality without invoking an Other?" (Bryson & de Castell, 1993, p. 298) remains a salient question.

In sum, I believe the LGBT-S course provided a valuable opportunity for deeper critical self/social exploration and acquisition of practice knowledge, something that may be less likely to happen in courses where there are one or two classes on gender and sexual diversity. However, since the course was an elective, the majority of students were released from this self and social examination.

Outside/Inside the Classroom: Challenging Heteronormativity and Heterosexism

Queer students in schools and universities across the globe face multiple forms and degrees of overt and covert heterosexism—psychic violence, physical and sexualized violence, harassment, and marginalization (Dragowski, Halkitis, Grossman, & D'Augelli, 2011; Ferfolja, 2007; Fox, 2007; Hillier & Harrison, 2004; Taylor, 2008; Willis, 2007). During the course and long afterward, I heard from students (some of whom did not take the course) who were concerned about the heterosexism of fellow students.[4] Their questions included, for example, why was there a need for a LGBT-S course in the first place? Was the assumption that gay, lesbian, bisexual, Two-Spirit, transgender, transsexual, intersex, queer, and/or questioning peoples are never recipients of social work services or was it that they would immediately identify themselves for referral to someone else more knowledgeable and ethically capable? Statements suggesting that gender and sexual diversity only has to do with those objectified others indicate room for integration of personal, professional, and political aspects of the self (Profitt, 2008). Such integration is critical since practice stems from social workers' own "matrix of identities, values and beliefs" (Ford, 2004, p. 3).

Speaking about me as the professor, a student purportedly said she did not wish to take a course from a lesbian (assumed) pushing "a political agenda," while faculty with more heteronormative agendas appeared to be acceptable. In exploring "personal biases" in a field preparatory course that I taught, another student remarked she would be open to working with gay and lesbian clients "as long as they didn't come on to her." What are the implications of such attitudes and practices for clients in field placements? Will they be shared by field supervisors and co-workers, and the status quo reproduced, or will students be challenged in the field to "reflect the values of the relevant Social Work Codes of Ethics"? (CASWE, 2012, p. 13).

Newman, Bogo, and Daley (2008) state that agency and organizational environments are critical in influencing student comfort levels about disclosure of sexual orientation. In their research, field instructors recommended self-disclosure by all students in the service of facilitating learning such as "working toward developing a professional identity that merges with their personal and social identities" (p. 232). Although self-disclosure may facilitate learning, not all students feel safe to disclose their gender and sexual identities, especially in the neoliberal environment of some field placements. Have these instructors considered the consequences for queer students of disclosing to field instructors or co-workers who may be unable to respond affirmatively or even humanely (see Chapter 17, this volume)? Unfortunately, students with critical perspectives who question white heteronormativity can quickly be marginalized in the classroom and field practicum, possibly threatening future employment. These students might benefit from joining with like-minded colleagues and others to practise critical, collective self-care (Profitt, 2008).

Yet another student, three years after graduation from the program, shared his concern that a professor had allowed a student to miss a compulsory workshop on working with gay youth because as a Christian, homosexuality was against her beliefs. Certainly, the freedom of conscience and religion is a right enshrined in the Canadian Charter of Rights and Freedoms (1982) but in terms of ethical social work, where does this leave clients and co-workers in field placements and places of future employment? For example, a student who took my course supported a transgender person in her practicum when co-workers in the agency were uncomfortable with doing so. Taylor (2008) clarifies that the limits of freedom of religious expression, as affirmed by the Supreme Court of Canada and in reference to Section 15 of the Canadian Charter of Rights and Freedoms, include the right to hold specific beliefs but not to discriminate. In other words, an individual can hold her or his own beliefs about homosexuality (and presumably about other aspects of sexual and gender diversity), but not act on them through discrimination. In addition, freedom of religious expression can be interpreted by others as inciteful speech when proclaiming the immorality of homosexuals (Dessel, Bolen, & Shepardson, 2011). How do schools work with religious beliefs and sexual and gender diversity in ways that foster discernment about the fit between personal values and professional values, and support diversity as a social justice issue? Particularly applicable is a core student learning objective of the CASWE Standards for Accreditation (2012), which states students should "acquire skills to monitor and evaluate their own behaviours in relation to the relevant codes of ethics" (p. 9).

The student comments presented above simply reflect the dominant liberal humanist environment of the university institution of St. Thomas University. The normalcy of white heteronormativity and heterosexism seems to be difficult to recognize and name in such a framework. The social, political, and economic climate in Canada, particularly over the last decade and more recently under the Harper regime, has inevitably shaped schools of social work and social work education in ways that remain imperceptible to some. An atmosphere of conservatism, the shrinking of democratic spaces in which to discuss issues of substance and depth, the narrowing of what is permissible for some to say in everyday discourse, and the constant exhortation to be positive are all palpable in the everyday life of university institutions.

The more I taught the LGBT-S course and supported queer and questioning students, the more I viscerally experienced the pervasiveness and tenacity of heteronormativity in the school and university institution. Is it so difficult to grasp the tedious weight of "systemic heterosexism and heteronormativity" (Kopelson, 2002, p. 20) that falls on those who don't fit heterosexual sexual and gender moulds?

A whole field of social relations becomes intelligible as heterosexuality, and this privatized sexual culture bestows on its sexual practices a tacit sense of rightness and normalcy. This sense of rightness—embedded in things and not just in sex—is what we call heteronormativity (Berlant & Warner, 1998, p. 551).

Jeyasingham (2008) states that "heterosexual culture" ascribes meaning to heterosexuality in a myriad of everyday ways that have little to do with sex. Therefore, to create meaningful change, Fox (2007) exhorts us to trouble the white heteronormative order of our schools and "the ways in which we organize them around the heteronormative family and kinship structures that connote our most meaningful interactions and lived experiences through reproduction and generational succession" (p. 504). We must move "beyond a gesture of 'including' queers and queer relationships within a heteronormative frame of reference" (p. 505). Furthermore, she clarifies that in white heteronormativity, the public, not private, issue of sexuality is "constantly under regulation and intricately connected with nation- and race-making" (p. 505). In my experience teaching the LGBT-S course, elective courses on sexual and gender diversity taken by a handful of interested students will do little to change social work education with its "continuous and inescapable backdrop of white heterosexual dominance" (Bryson & de Castell, 1993, p. 285), and much less when they are not offered at all. Sexual and gender diversity taught in a social justice framework that challenges heteronormativity can broaden our understanding of ethics as concerned with social justice, power, privilege, and penalty (Weinberg, 2010).

During the curriculum review of the BSW program in the mid-2000s, faculty developed an integrated curriculum that contained critical content on gender, "race," class, sexual orientation, disability, and other axes of oppression in all courses. While such content complemented and reinforced the LGBT-S course, does a class here and there of content integrated into courses such as Theory or Family significantly deconstruct heteronormativity and shift heterosexism?[5] For students who hold highly heterosexist views, even minimal content may be too much (Brownlee et al., 2005). How are linkages of intersectionality made in courses and reinforced among them? As a critique of my course, the title I chose communicated a focus on the identities of LGBT-S peoples rather than the practices and acts that step outside the boundaries of gender and sexual normativity (Drabinski, 2011). Although an evaluation of the integrated curriculum in relation to sexual and gender diversity is overdue, a constructive question for all schools of social work to ask is this: what is a school's ethical-political agenda in relation to teaching about gender and sexual diversity? What are the theoretical, conceptual, and political frameworks and pedagogical approaches used to teach about gender and sexual diversity? Does "diversity" include heterosexually identified people for whom identity can be experienced as restrictive and confined (Sumara & Davis, 1999)? What are our liberatory and ethical goals of teaching about gender and sexual diversity for faculty, future social workers, and our communities?

Directions for Increasing Learning about Gender and Sexual Diversity

- Engage school faculty in exploring gender and sexual diversity theoretically, conceptually, ethically, and pedagogically and

clarify an ethical-political agenda for teaching about it with the goal of preparing students for ethical and competent practice.
- Collectively commit to gender and sexual diversity as an issue of social justice and deepen analyses of the intersectionality of gender and sexual diversity with other social markers.
- Collectively identify heteronormative and heterosexist discourse and behaviour in all facets of the culture of schools of social work and plan to strategically address them in order to build a more non-heteronormative culture. As the women's movement has taught us, naming is a critical step in designing strategies to tackle systemic oppression.
- Be attentive to how social work education produces certain ways of knowing in which "ignorances are as much a part of the structure of heteronormativity as are privileged knowledges" (Jeyasingham, 2008, p. 149). Teaching about heteronormativity should examine relations, processes, practices, and behaviours that implicate everyone in the production of difference rather than focus only on queers.
- Strive to continually build the necessary conditions for reflection and dialogue about what might constitute "safer" environments for marginalized peoples (Fox, 2007).
- Educate field instructors, through a developmental process, about heteronormativity, heterosexism, and sexual and gender diversity. Field instructors must have opportunities to develop a framework for understanding and examining their values, feelings, and beliefs about their own and others' gender and sexual diversity.
- Nurture relationships with community and activist groups that are working with sexual and gender diversity and partner with them in course delivery, specific events, and activism for social change.
- Increase messaging around sexual and gender diversity in schools of social work. Obviously, this will only be fruitful

in a context where faculty, the overall teaching and learning environment, and curriculum (overt and hidden) disrupt and change the culture of heteronormativity and heterosexism.
- Elevate knowledge, among students, of harassment policies that address multiple forms of harassment, including those of gender, sex, sexuality, and gender expression, within an understanding of power relations and human rights.

Conclusion

Reflecting on my experience with the LGBT-S course, I am more conscious of how much openness and effort it takes to comprehend the reality of another. Wagner (2009) writes that if we were to read how social work describes itself in its literature, we would think that social workers were the "superheroes of the world, fighting for social justice, social change" and "at the same time (incongruously) also [fighting for] community equanimity and spirituality" (p. 104). He observes that "most of the time social workers seem to define *liberalism* (or the ever-present *progressivism*) as meaning radical, rather than referring to any sort of revolutionary transformation" (p. 104). It strikes me that the profession and social work education are still labouring a response (Pon, 2007) to the reality that tackling structural, material, and discursive injustice necessarily involves politics and struggle. Resistance and uncomfortable truths about the self, others, and our cultural arrangements do arise from engaging with the contradictions among our professed social work values, demands for justice, and investments in our identities and positions. To really make a difference for queer students, and indeed for all students, a social work course on LGBT-S peoples is better than nothing, dangerously far from good enough, and sadly, still labouring to live social work values and ethics.

Notes

1. I adapted my exercise from the guided journey designed by Marc Gunning, GAYNET. A revised copy of his original guided journey was retrieved May 28, 2014, from www.residential-life.unh.edu/diversity/guidedjourney.pdf
2. For a detailed analysis of this exercise and its fruits, see Profitt (2004).
3. Students gave signed permission to share their learning from reflection papers, without any identifying information, for use in presentations and articles.
4. Students who spoke with me did not identify the speaker(s) in these instances.
5. For example, a colleague who teaches theory emphasized how processes of normalization work in heteronormativity.

References

Berkman, C. S., & Zinberg, G. (1997). Homophobia and heterosexism in social workers. *Social Work, 42*(4), 319–332.

Berlant, L., & Warner, M. (1998). Sex in public. Intimacy. *Critical Inquiry, 24*(2), 547–566.

Black, B., Oles, T. P., & Moore, L. (1996). The relationship between attitudes: Homophobia among students in social work programs. *Journal of Baccalaureate Social Work, 2*(1), 23–41.

Brownlee, K., Sprakes, A., Saini, M., O'Hare, R., Kortes-Miller, K., & Graham, J. (2005). Heterosexism among social work students. *Social Work Education, 24*(5), 485–494.

Bryson, M., & de Castell, S. (1993). Queer pedagogy: Praxis make im/perfect. *Canadian Journal of Education, 18*(3), 285–305.

Butler, J. (1993). *Bodies that matter: On the discursive limits of sex*. London, England: Routledge.

Butler, J. (1999). *Gender trouble* (2nd ed.). New York, NY: Routledge.

Cain, R. (1996). Heterosexism and self-disclosure in the social work classroom. *Journal of Social Work Education, 32*(1), 65–76.

Canadian Association for Social Work Education (CASWE). (2012). CASWE Standards for Accreditation. Ottawa, ON: CASWE.

Canadian Charter of Rights and Freedoms (1982). Retrieved from laws-lois.justice.gc.ca/eng/Const/Const_index.html

Cashore, C., & Tuason, M. T. G. (2009). Negotiating the binary: Identity and social justice for bisexual and transgender individuals. *Journal of Gay and Lesbian Social Services, 21*(4), 374–401.

Chinell, J. (2011). Three voices: Reflections on homophobia and heterosexism in social work education. *Social Work Education, 30*(7), 759–773.

Dessel, A., Bolen, R., & Shepardson, C. (2011). Can religious expression and sexual orientation affirmation coexist in social work? A critique of Hodge's theoretical, theological, and conceptual frameworks. *Journal of Social Work Education, 47*(2), 213–234.

Drabinski, K. (2011). Identity matters: Teaching transgender in the women's studies classroom. *Radical Teacher, 92*, 10–20.

Dragowski, E. A., Halkitis, P. N., Grossman, A. H., & D'Augelli, A. R. (2011). Sexual orientation victimization and posttraumatic stress symptoms among lesbian, gay, and bisexual youth. *Journal of Gay and Lesbian Social Services, 23*(2), 226–249.

Ferfolja, T. (2007). Schooling cultures: Institutionalizing heteronormativity and heterosexism. *International Journal of Inclusive Education, 11*(2), 147–162.

Ford, T. (2004). Queering education from the ground up: Challenges and opportunities for educators. *Canadian Online Journal of Queer Studies in Education, 1*(1). Retrieved from jqstudies.oise.utoronto.ca/journal/viewarticle.php?id=5

Foreman, M., & Quinlan, M. (2008). Increasing social work students' awareness of heterosexism and homophobia—A partnership between a community gay health project and a school of social work. *Social Work Education, 27*(2), 152–158.

Fox, C. (2007). From transaction to transformation: (En)countering white heteronormativity in "Safe Spaces". *College English, 69*(5), 496–511.

Green, R. G., Kiernan-Stern, M., Balley, K., Chambers, K., Claridge, R., Jones, G., Kitson, G., Leek, S., Leisey, M., Vadas, K., & Walker, K. (2005). The Multicultural Counseling Inventory: A measure for evaluating social work student and practitioner self-perceptions of their multicultural competence. *Journal of Social Work Education, 41*(2), 191–208.

Hill Collins, P. (2000). *Black feminist thought* (2nd ed.). New York, NY: Routledge.

Hillier, L., & Harrison, L. (2004). Homophobia and the production of shame: Young people and same sex attraction. *Culture, Health & Sexuality, 6*(1), 79–84.

Hylton, M. E. (2005). Heteronormativity and the experience of lesbian and bisexual women as social work students. *Journal of Social Work Education, 4*(1), 67–82.

Jeyasingham, D. (2008). Knowledge/ignorance and the construction of sexuality in social work education. *Social Work Education, 27*(2), 138–151.

Kelly, J., & Srivastava, A. (2003). Dancing on the lines: Mothering, daughtering, masking, and mentoring in the academy. In D. Keahey & D. Schnitzer (Eds.), *The madwoman in the academy: 43 women boldly take on the ivory tower* (pp. 58–76). Calgary, AB: University of Calgary Press.

Kopelson, K. (2002). Dis/Integrating the gay/queer binary: "Reconstructed identity politics" for a performative pedagogy. *College English, 65*(1), 17–35.

LaSala, M. C., Jenkins, D. A., Wheeler, D. P., & Fredriksen-Goldsen, K. I. (2008). LGBT faculty, research, and researchers: Risks and rewards. *Journal of Gay and Lesbian Social Services, 20*(3), 253–267.

Martinez, P., Barsky, A., & Singleton, S. (2011). Exploring queer consciousness among social workers. *Journal of Gay and Lesbian Social Services, 23*(2), 296–315.

McPhail, B. A. (2004). Questioning gender and sexuality binaries: What queer theorists, transgendered individuals, and sex researchers can teach social work. *Journal of Gay and Lesbian Social Services, 17*(1), 3–21.

Messinger, L. (2004). Out in the field: Gay and lesbian social work students' experiences in the field placement. *Journal of Social Work Education, 40*(2), 187–204.

Newman, B. S., Dannenfeiser, P. L., & Benishek, L. (2002). Assessing beginning social work and counselling students' acceptance of lesbians and gay men. *Journal of Social Work Education, 38*(2), 273–288.

Newman, P. A., Bogo, M., & Daley, A. (2008). Self-disclosure of sexual orientation in social work field education: Field instructor and lesbian and gay student perspectives. *The Clinical Supervisor, 27*(2), 215–237.

O'Brien, C. (1999). Contested territory: Sexualities and social work. In A. S. Chambon, A. Irving, & L. Epstein (Eds.), *Reading Foucault for social work* (pp. 131-155). New York, NY: Columbia University Press.

Pérez, E. (1998). Irigaray's female symbolic in the making of Chicana lesbian *Sitios y Lenguas* (Sites and Discourses). In C. M. Trujillo (Ed.), *Living Chicana theory* (pp. 87-101). Berkeley, CA: Third Woman Press.

Pon, G. (2007). A labour of love or of response? Anti-racism education and responsibility. *Canadian Social Work Review, 24*(2), 141-153.

Profitt, N. J. (2004). Mapping the personal in contested terrain: Educating students about heterosexism and affirmative social work practice. In S. LeMay Sheffield, C. O'Neil, K. L. Taylor, & D. Nevo, (Eds.), *Atlantic Universities' Teaching Showcase 2004 – Proceedings IX* (pp. 111-119). Halifax, NS: Dalhousie University.

Profitt, N. J. (2008). Who cares for us? Opening paths toward a critical, collective notion of self-care. *Canadian Social Work Review, 25*(2), 147-168.

Renn, K. A. (2000). Including all voices in the classroom: Teaching lesbian, gay, and bisexual students. *College Teaching, 48*(4), 129-135.

Rich, A. (1980). Compulsory heterosexuality and lesbian existence. *Signs, 5*(4), 631-660.

Root, M. (1992). Restructuring the impact of trauma on the personality. In L. Brown & M. Ballour (Eds.), *Personality and psychopathology* (pp. 108-118). New York, NY: Guilford Press.

Rose, J. (1986). *Sexuality in the field of vision*. London, England: Verso.

Sedgwick, E. (1990). *Epistemology of the closet*. Berkeley, CA: University of California Press.

Stark, L. P. (1991). Traditional gender role beliefs and individual outcomes: An exploratory analysis. *Sex Roles, 24*(9/10), 639-650.

Sumara, D., & Davis, B. (1999). Interrupting heteronormativity: Toward a queer curriculum theory. *Curriculum Inquiry, 29*(2), 191-208.

Taylor, C. (2008). A human rights approach to stopping homophobic bullying in schools. *Journal of Gay and Lesbian Social Services, 19*(3/4), 157-172.

Wagner, D. (2009). Radical social work as conceit. *Journal of Progressive Human Services, 20*(2), 104-106.

Warner, T. (2002). *Never going back: A history of queer activism in Canada*. Toronto, ON: University of Toronto Press.

Weinberg, M. (2010). The social construction of social work ethics: Politicizing and broadening the lens. *Journal of Progressive Human Services, 21*(1), 32–44.

Willis, P. (2007). "Queer eye" for social work: Rethinking pedagogy and practice with same-sex attracted young people. *Australian Social Work, 60*(2), 181–196.

CHAPTER 16
Qualitative Arts-Based Inquiry into Transgender Subjectivities in Social Work Education

Arkell Wiley

Individuals in Canada who exist outside of Western society's dominant understanding of gender are markedly vulnerable to discrimination and often face many material, social, and psychological consequences (Trans PULSE, 2010). As the social work profession endeavours to mitigate the effects of oppression on marginalized peoples and promote social justice, the situation of trans issues are poignantly relevant. Drawing from the interview data collected in my graduate research, this chapter illustrates the perspectives of five social work students who identify as transgender and studied social work at Canadian universities (Wiley, 2012). By exploring the subjective experiences of the five participants in their respective social work programs, this chapter demonstrates how participants experienced different aspects of their social work education in relation to their chosen identities and strives to provide insights into the current state of the discipline in regard to the inclusion and knowledge of trans issues. This chapter will introduce the concept of transgender and intersectionality, outline the research process, present findings, discuss implications for social work education, and conclude with recommended changes.

Conceptualizing Transgender

Gender is a fundamental social organizing principle within the current Western paradigm that impacts almost every aspect of one's life. The dominant discourse in our society, as expressed through various social, cultural, and political fields, promotes the belief that it is "natural" for one's gender to be either man or woman, and to be consistent with the sex assigned at birth. In this context, the term *sex* refers to the status of either male or female, which is assigned based on current interpretations of biology, while the term *gender* refers to the social role one lives (Stryker, 2008a). From the time one's sex is assigned, one's location within the gender binary is perpetually constructed both socially and structurally. The gender binary is so dominant that even children who are born without clear sexual traits are reassigned to one of only two categories. Burdge (2007) explains, "even in cases in which the genitalia are ambiguous, medical professionals and families generally pursue surgical modifications to make one gender fit... very literally, our bodies must fit our words" (p. 245).

In spite of the popular perception an individual's gender is "natural" and consistent with the sex assigned at birth, the diversity of transgender communities demonstrates neither sex nor gender constitutes a fixed binary. Rather, there is a wide range of human expression regarding sex and gender. Both Lev (2004) and Mallon (2009) define *transgender* as an umbrella term relevant to a diversity of individuals who express their gender in non-dominant ways. *Transgender* has commonly come to refer to people who find their internal sense of self as female, male, or other to be dissonant with the gender role assigned to them at birth. Some identities within trans communities consist of those who self-identify as genderqueers, cross-dressers, bigenders, Two-Spirits, gender fucks, gender b(l)enders, transsexuals, female to male, and male to female. Individuals in transgender communities make different choices about how to negotiate being trans, from sex reassignment surgery to transgressing gender norms through dress and performance. Recognizing this diversity as well as the unique circumstances and needs that various different trans individuals experience, those who identify as trans share many common social and structural inequities. Accordingly, within this chapter I will treat transgender and trans as a single field of study.

Unlike having gender assigned at birth, transgender is a category of *self-identification* adopted by individuals who move away from the original imposed designation (Stryker, 2008a). Transgender theorists have thus emphasized the importance of framing *transgender* as a social and political term rather than as a medical one. According to Scott-Dixon (2006), this reframing allows for the subjective experiences of transgender individuals and communities to take preeminence over medical perspectives that claim objectivity. Stryker (2008a) proposes that one of the main goals of transgender activism is to "break apart the forced unity of sex and gender, while increasing the scope of livable lives" (p. 12). While transgender identity is an authentic expression of gender that is inherent to one's internal understanding of self and not a choice, the adoption of a transgender identity is a conscious act of becoming. Through movement between and settlement within gender categories, and by challenging the discourse that reinforces the gender binary as biologically determined categories, transgender communities expose how gender is an act of becoming for everyone.

Recognizing that the category of transgender represents a diverse group of people, many of whom lead healthy, productive lives, the literature reveals that the transgender population has been marginalized in a number of different ways. Kaufman (2008), for example, indicates transgender individuals lack access to basic mental and physical health care and are at a high risk for unemployment or underemployment, homelessness, involuntary sex work, and violent hate crimes. As a population at risk, transgender communities should be a significant concern for social work. However, the literature indicates transgender-appropriate medical, mental health, and social services are limited, and there are significant barriers for gender-variant individuals who are trying to access existing services (Goldberg, Ashbee, Bradd, Lindenberg, & Simpson, 2006).

Conceptualizing Intersectionality

Intersectionality is a complex concept that has been applied within feminist theory, research, and practice in different ways over the past 20 years. Mehrotra (2010) argues that because intersectionalty has been used in many diverse and ambiguous ways it has a fluidity that allows it to be applied to many contexts. Due to this plurality of meanings, she suggests we must approach intersectionality not as a single framework, but as "a continuum of different intersectional theories with potentially varying epistemological bases that social work scholars can draw upon, depending on the goals and needs of a particular community, practice setting, or project" (Mehrotra, 2010, p. 418).

Intersectionality challenges the notion that gender inequality affects all people in the same way and acknowledges the limitation of gender as a single category of analysis. Shields (2008) indicates that "the facts of our lives reveal that there is no single identity category that satisfactorily describes how we respond to our social environment or are responded to by others" (p. 304). As such, different aspects of social identities are experienced simultaneously and "intersect with each other to produce a complex pattern with specific effects influenced by a changing historical, political, and social context" (Lundy, 2004, p. 72). Further, as Scott-Dixon (2006) points out, how we perceive our gender and how others perceive us is "racialized, classed and shaped by other elements of social location, such as age, ability and sexuality" (p. 18). In the context of transgender communities, multiple forms of gender oppression may intersect with each other, as well as with other forms of oppression related to diverse identities. Not taking into consideration other social locations, transgender politics have the potential of contributing to other oppressive forces.

Research Process

Drawn to this inquiry by my own position as a trans social work student, the objectives of this research were to make visible trans identities in social work, to destabilize the dominant discourses that can oppress transgender individuals, and to initiate a dialogue about how to increase awareness and acceptance of gender diversity within the discipline. This research also aimed to give participants the opportunity to reflect on what their experiences in social work education meant to them and to promote a critical consciousness.

As a queer person seeking to elicit transgender perspectives on social work education, my research was informed by queer methodologies. Queer methodologies strategically employ research methods as a means of understanding and producing resistance to structures of domination concerning sexual and gender normalization (Denzin & Lincoln, 2008). Queer theoretical perspectives have been critiqued for being focused on theory and disengaged with the material realities and lived experiences of transgender individuals (Monro, 2007). This research attempted to bridge this gap by concurrently embracing a queer fluidity that disrupts the dominant discourse while attending to the material realities of the participants. This was addressed by employing arts-based research methods that accounted for partial, situated knowledge coupled with semi-structured interviews that focused on specific experiences within social work education.

After gaining a letter of approval from the UNBC Ethics Review Board, I advertised the project electronically by sending a letter and poster to schools of social work and pride organizations. Five participants were selected from across Canada based on their self-identification as transgender and their attendance at a school of social work. To maintain anonymity, the participants were given the pseudonyms Jordan, Carter, Elijah, Zoe, and Corey. Participants represented both graduate and undergraduate perspectives and contained both current and recently graduated students. Each participant came from a different school across Canada, thus the sample also represented some diversity of geographical location.

Both visual arts–based practice methods and semi-structured interviews were employed to elicit response from participants. Visual arts–based practice methods were chosen because they provide an effective way for participants to explore subjectivity, connect with, represent, and give meaning to inner experiences (Jongeward, 2009). Additionally, visual inquiry is apt for addressing individuals' experiences of gender variance. Rollings (2009) proposes that constructed narratives dictate what is "socially visible" and that meaning and experience are embedded in a visual context. Through this process, certain bodies are masked from normativity and made invisible. Eliciting visually descriptive data can give participants the opportunity to respond with their own transgressive materials to a constructed visual context in which they are either not present or misrepresented.

In order to use visual arts–based practices as a means of data collection, I constructed an activity book that directed participants through creative work (Wiley, 2012). In the activity book, participants were invited to share any challenges they faced while studying social work, the ways in which they were supported in social work schools, how their gender informed their experiences studying social work, and what they hoped social work education would look like in the future.

Once participants had completed creating their art, semi-structured interviews were conducted via Skype. As Leavy (2009) suggested, doing a verbal follow-up after the creative process can be an "empowering experience for the research participants where they retain control, share their experience, and have their feelings and perspectives taken seriously (which is a form of validation)" (p. 229). In addition, through the process of reflecting on their art, respondents contributed to the analysis of their own visual data.

Given my relationship to the inquiry, I also participated as a subject in the research and incorporated autoethnography. Autoethnography is the process by which researchers search for understanding about culture and society through focusing on the self (Chang, 2008). It was my hope that the telling of my own story would function not only as a piece of data, but also as a means of further accounting for my subjectivity as an inquirer.

After the interviews, the data was analyzed using thematic analysis in which patterns were identified, selected, and reported (Braun & Clarke,

2006). It is important to note that the themes and codes developed were actively constructed from the data. This is not meant to downplay the contribution of the participants and the influence of their perspectives, but rather to highlight the role that I played in choosing, editing, and employing specific pieces of evidence to contribute to the goals of my research (Braun & Clarke, 2006).

Findings and Analysis

A diversity of identities under the trans umbrella was represented by the participants and reflects how they have chosen to self-identify. Jordan, Elijah, and Carter all conveyed a masculine gender identity. Jordan mentioned that he identifies as a "trans-masculine creature," while Elijah said that, although he identifies as a female to male transgender person, in the "outside world" he simply identifies as male. Similarly, Carter mentioned that to most people he is male and that, although being trans is important to him and not something that he keeps secret, in some environments he does not advertise it. Zoe expressed her gender identity as female and female transsexual but mentioned that she liked the term *trans* best. Corey expressed her gender identity as something that is constantly evolving and mentioned having a "trans experience that's not within the male or female form." Personally, although my relationship with my gender is complex, I principally identify as a trans man.

The findings include visual data, autoethnographic writing, and narrative information from the semi-structured interviews that captured the respondents' reflections on their art-based material. The different types of data will be presented together, based on the themes that were constructed during data analysis.

Others' Perceptions and Sense of Belonging

Others' perceptions of trans people in general as well as others' specific perceptions of participants greatly impacted participants' experiences in schools of social work. In some cases, others' perceptions contributed to the creation of an environment that was not affirming of trans identities and had a negative impact on participants' sense of self. For example, two participants shared experiences in which fellow social work students expressed transphobic attitudes by making fun of trans people in their presence. Some participants also experienced having their personal gender identity discredited in the schools of social work they attended.

Being persistently misgendered was a particular struggle for many participants. Zoe reported, "when people would misgender me and would use my old name and pronouns while I was transitioning at school, it was very challenging for me." The narrative that I wrote reflected my personal perceptions and feelings about being misgendered:

> It kills me when someone perpetually refers to me as "she" after I've explicitly made a point of telling them about my identity and pronoun preference. Not making an effort to refer to me in the way that I have requested to be addressed makes me feel like I'm a failure at conveying my gender; it invalidates my struggle and is disregarding, not only of me personally but of transgender identities at large.

When sharing the meaning of their art, two participants spoke to the impact of others' perception on them. I invite you to take a minute to look at the images before reading my (re)presentation of the participants' thoughts.

Corey described a box she drew and indicated it represented the box she felt she was placed in with regard to her gender. Speaking to the image of the curly haired person in the picture, she stated the person is trying to push the box off the cliff so it will open. However, the character is struggling against the people chained to the box; people who want to stop her from opening it. Corey indicated the image represents the

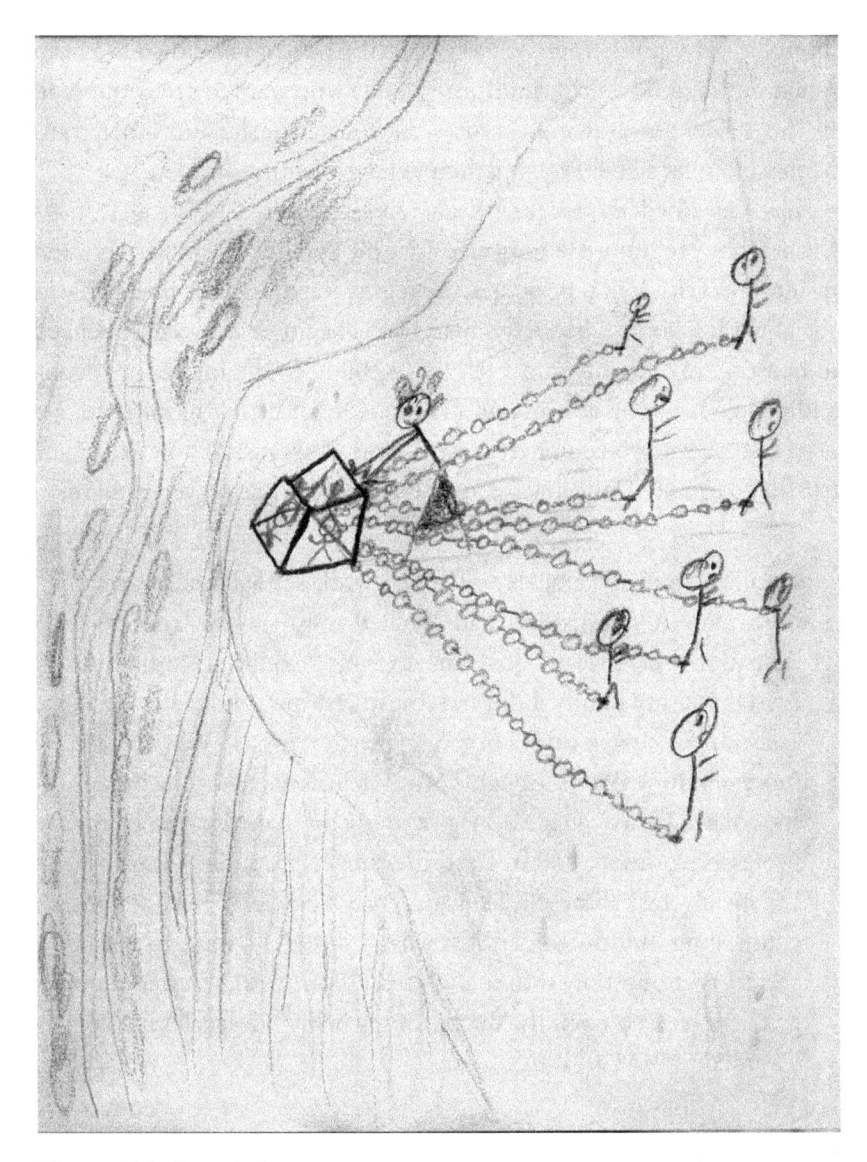

Figure 16.1: Corey's Image

Source: Photo taken by author and reproduced with the consent of the study participant.

interplay between the people who want the box to remain so they can retain power and control, and those people who want to break out of it. In this sense, her drawing captures the resistance she and other trans people often face in expressing their gender identity.

Elijah described his piece as a visual representation of his struggle in his social work program. He indicated that the symbol of smaller children inside larger children represented the regression he experienced while in social work school. "I had to go back to the beginning. I was challenged to question my identity and I felt like a child." In the image, he identified people laughing at him and mentioned that he felt humiliated. He used an emaciated person to represent himself because of how extremely frustrated he felt. Alongside his art, Elijah wrote these powerful words:

> I walked into my first day of social work school feeling every bit a man. My transition had enabled me to move from self-destructive behaviours [to] an attempt to build a future for myself and my family. I did not know that my gender would be questioned at every turn. I began to question myself. Was my face more feminine than I thought? Was I delusional? Was my binder too loose? I was called "a bright young woman" by one of my professors. Almost no one used the proper pronoun. I was lost. Frantically, inside myself, I began to break down. When I sought counselling, my trans identity (what I did NOT want to speak about) was questioned and analyzed. "I am mad," I cried, and grief bubbled up from the depths of my belly. "Please, let me be." I wanted to WALK AWAY.

Elijah's narrative deeply communicates how others' perceptions can impact one's sense of self and one's ability to succeed in the social work school environment.

While Zoe found being misgendered challenging, her experience contrasts with the previous two participants. Rather than creating distress,

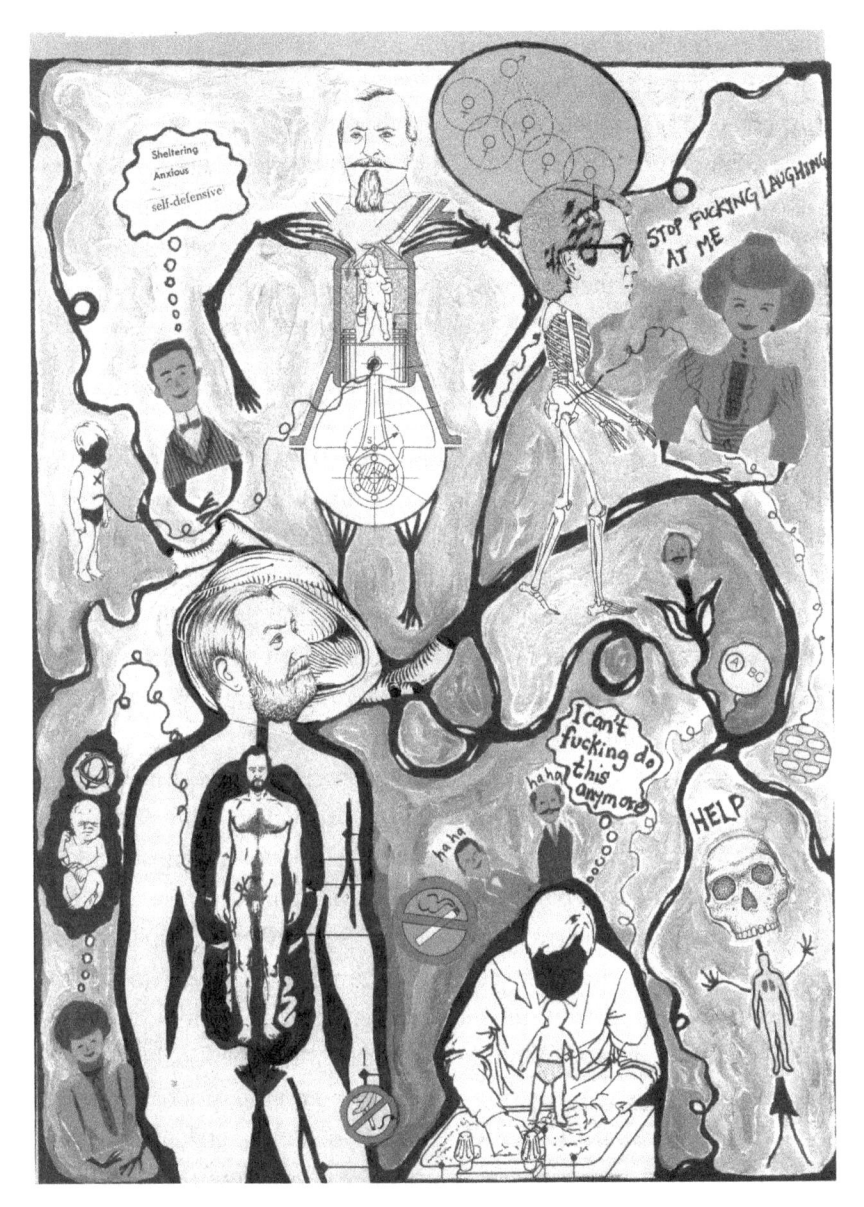

Figure 16.2: Elijah's Image
Source: Photo taken by author and reproduced with the consent of the study participant.

others' perceptions had a positive impact. Zoe talked about her fears that surrounded transitioning and suggested her concern about others' perceptions stopped her from moving forward with her transition sooner. When she did come out, however, she encountered many supportive responses from her peers at school. Zoe emphasized the fact that these positive responses were very important to her and pointed out that others' affirmations had helped her become more confident and gain the agency to become the person she wanted to be.

Token Trans Student

All of the participants, save one, indicated they were the only trans-identified person in their program, and this contributed to a sense of rejection and/or fears of rejection. Three participants noted that being the only trans-identified person in the school made them feel "alone" and "isolated." Elijah specifically suggested that being the only one impacted the ways in which the school dealt with trans-related issues. He explained his school was reluctant to address trans issues because they considered him to be the only person affected.

A lack of knowledge about trans issues in classes was something all participants had experienced at some point in their education. They found trans experiences, if discussed at all in the classroom, were often relegated to a couple of pages in a textbook or a single lecture by a "person from the local queer resource centre." All of the participants indicated they often found themselves in circumstances where, to varying degrees, they had to educate fellow students, faculty, and administration about trans issues. While in some cases, they willingly took the initiative to do this, at other times they felt put on the spot or pressured by faculty to take on this responsibility. Generally, respondents were ambivalent about being in a position where they were the "teachers." For example, Elijah stated "being open to dialogue with people about my gender identity has been a bit of a dichotomy for me because on the one hand, I don't want to talk about it and on the other hand, I have to." Although another participant acknowledged he shouldn't always have to assume the responsibility of educating, he felt there was no other than him to do it. Zoe similarly professed, "I felt like I had a voice to share and I had to share it, otherwise my voice would be swallowed up by the cisgender[1] population."

Programs' Approaches to Trans Issues

Participants shared the perception that schools of social work did not adequately address trans issues. Corey noted trans issues are "still at the background of our program" and that "it is very much a closed conversation." Similarly, Zoe maintained trans issues are "ignored in academia." More than one participant suggested that the lack of meaningful trans content and discussion in social work education had implications for practice because most social workers would, at some point, encounter a trans client. Zoe stated, "clinicians would benefit from the expertise that our community has to offer" because if a social worker "does not know what they're talking about, then that's one more person that a trans person isn't going to be helped by." Furthermore, the lack of exposure to trans issues in social work education contributed to the unsupportive environment that trans students encountered. Speaking to his struggles around the lack of relevant trans content, Elijah indicated other students often made excuses for this situation and made comments like "I've never dealt with a trans person before"—comments that from his perspective did not justify treating someone with "less respect and cultural competence."

Trans Erasure

Beyond a lack of educational trans content, some participants believed their trans voices were silenced. Carter commented there was a "don't ask, don't tell" understanding in his program and "[people's attitudes] were like, 'can you please stop talking about that, we don't really want to hear about that' (Sigh). What I noticed, is that if you're quiet then it's not a problem." He remarked, "you don't want to be the circus freak, but, on the other hand, you do want someone to see that this could be a valuable perspective."

16.3: Arkell's Image
Source: Photo taken by author.

My own experiences of being silenced were conveyed in a piece of art I did prior to communicating with the participants. My work is a self-portrait representing me in my desired gender identity. The portrait is covered by a grey layer that effectively muted the image and represented how I felt while in my social work program. Although my trans identity was not denied or completely absent, I felt it was muted or not fully recognized. Although the image represents me personally, it was also meant to communicate the general silencing of trans people's voices in social work education.

Intersectionality

Participants found that gender did not operate in isolation, but that their experiences were significantly impacted by aspects of the other identities they occupied. Participants identified that their gender identity intersected with such things as poverty, sexual orientation, race, (dis)ability, parenthood, spirituality, and history of addiction. These intersections resulted in generating a complex web of unique meanings for each participant.

Participants' experiences highlighted the fact that intersectionality must be conceptualized in a way that acknowledges not only the intersections between distinct social categories, but also the intersections that occur within different aspects of a single category, such as gender. All participants described how multiple aspects of gender impacted them in complicated ways. Carter, for example, indicated that his behaviour and analysis has been influenced by his previous experiences as a queer woman. Jordan, reflecting on the male privilege he gained after transitioning, indicated he now has to put energy and intention into being clear about the ways he does anti-misogynist or feminist work. Zoe commented, "I feel I didn't really get feminism until I transitioned. I always thought everyone was equal." She indicated that, outside of being trans, she is also impacted by sexism and misogyny.

Some participants reported that their own experiences of being oppressed opened their eyes to other elements of oppression. Corey commented that being trans "influences my understanding of oppression, of what it's like when a group is not acknowledged as being as legitimate as other groups." Several of the participants recognized the struggles they were having in social work education weren't necessarily separate from those of other marginalized groups, and two participants spoke about supportive alliances they were able to form with members of other marginalized groups. Based on their personal experiences, participants acknowledged the need for an intersectional approach to studying social work. Jordan, in particular, felt strongly about the importance of an intersectional approach. He commented, "what I hope and dream for social work is that it develops an intersectional analysis around oppression. I don't actually think that more trans content alone is where I would want to steer social work education." Carter gave an example that illustrates why an intersectional approach is so important when discussing trans issues in social work. He suggested that without taking race and gender into consideration when talking about violence against trans people, we won't see that the reality is that most people who are experiencing violence are trans women of colour. If we don't take other factors, such as race, into consideration when thinking about trans issues, then we could be missing a significant part of the picture.

Discussion

The words of the participants highlighted how schools of social work were failing them by falling dramatically short of providing education around trans issues. They indicated both a lack of information and misinformation regarding trans communities in their programs. One way in which trans identities were seen to be erased and misrepresented was through social work's tendency to collapse trans issues with those of sexual identity, and present them as one all-encompassing LGBT category. Stryker (2008b) argues that because of the reliance on the dominant gender constructions, lesbian, gay, and bisexual individuals often have more in common with the straight world than they do with trans communities. Though there are important community connections between the two causes, defining gender variance in relation to and in terms of sexuality disregards many of the unique issues of the transgender population, including how gender identity impacts every aspect of a person's daily life.

Several of the participants encountered transphobic attitudes by students and faculty, specifically within schools of social work. Negative attitudes, misinformation, and discrimination toward trans people in social work not only creates challenges for trans students who enter the discipline, but also has the potential of discouraging trans people from entering the field and/or results in trans individuals' concealing their identity when they do. One participant explicitly mentioned they did not divulge their trans status in social work classes because they did not feel safe. When trans people within the discipline are driven to conceal their identity because of the perception of a hostile, non-affirming environment, the discipline loses the gift of the trans individuals' knowledge and experience on the subject, and further distances itself from achieving the competence to practise with trans communities.

It is important to understand that even when gender is not the presenting issue when seeking services, being trans will still affect a person's experience. Hansbury (2005) reported that when accessing counselling services "many trans people will have fears about sharing their trans identities and stories with someone who is not trans and who may not only misunderstand trans clients, but also mistreat them" (p. 262). Seeking help from ill-informed clinicians may not just be unhelpful, but harmful for trans clients. For example, Bauer, Hammond, Travers, Kaay, Hohenadel, and Boyce (2009) indicated that mental health providers may conflate unrelated mental health issues with a trans person's gender identity, which can result in inadequate or inappropriate care. Having negative experiences can lead to a variety of barriers in accessing health and social services that are readily available to the general population (Erich, Bouttè-Queen, Donnelly, & Tittsworth, 2007).

Participants consistently indicated that having a foundation of progressive social work values is imperative to understanding trans issues. Participants' reflections indicate an inconsistency among different schools with regard to the existence of this theoretical framework, as well as to whether or not this framework impacted how schools addressed trans issues. The focus on social justice is both an expectation in social work education (CASWE, 2012) and an important aspect of the Canadian Association of Social Workers' Code of Ethics (2005). Harris (2006) states, "a social justice framework requires the willingness to challenge the status quo, and to address the hegemony that predominates" (p. 254). In relation to trans issues, this entails breaking down assumptions that everyone's gender naturally matches what they were assigned (cisnormativity), as well as challenging and understanding the privilege and legitimacy given to those who are perceived as "normal" men and women. Serano (2007) argues that this assumption is an active process that makes trans experiences and people invisible. Schools of social work must be conscious of the ways in which they promote cisnormativity in both a passive and active capacity. For example, a failure to identify trans participants in social work research can contribute to cisnormativity. Bauer and colleagues (2009) note that because health research doesn't commonly identify trans participants or consider questions relevant to trans communities, "trans people have been systematically erased, and by extension, trans experiences and subjectivity have been similarly rendered invisible" (p. 352).

Recommendations

Schools of social work must be accountable for providing students with the knowledge, values, and skills to work with diverse populations. In order to achieve this, all schools must educate students about trans issues and work toward creating an affirming environment. Erich and colleagues (2007) found exposure to educational content regarding trans communities not only increased social workers' knowledge but also their comfort level in working with trans people. Several of the participants directly called for those within social work to become aware of their feelings about gender identity and attitudes toward transgender individuals so that any negative attitudes or prejudices could be exposed and worked through. Corey noted that, because of the prevalence of "biases and mythologies" toward trans people, it is important for students in schools of social work to engage in self-reflexive activities. Elijah expressed a hope that social work education would provide a conversation about discrimination toward trans people and outline basic trans etiquette at the very beginning of their programs. He declared, "due to the very personal nature of some of the material you're dealing with in social work classes, [for the safety of trans students], it's really important to get it out of the way quickly."

Schools of social work must strive to create a culture and learning environment where trans perspectives are valued, not simply tolerated. Social work can actively indicate that it values trans voices by incorporating materials that have been created by trans people. Establishing an environment where trans identities are affirmed and materials by trans academics are highlighted may also take some of the pressure off trans students to persistently have to be the educators. Furthermore, if trans voices were valued and a basic knowledge about trans identities established, then trans students, faculty, and professionals might be more comfortable sharing their insights.

Reflecting on their involvement in the arts-based components of the research, the participants stressed the importance of schools of social work developing alternative pedagogical and practice approaches that include opportunities to engage in artistic practices. For example, Jordan found that the imaginative element of the creative process was empowering for him. He commented, "it was awesome because I just had so many ideas; it was so easy to dream. I just had so many ideas of what I wish for and that felt really powerful." Gray and Webb (2008) propose that "the art's work does not only 'open up' in disclosing a radical alterity, or making visible that which has been previously closed down or excluded, but it also endures as a new narrative" (p. 193). By making space for creative expression and critical imagination, students are given the chance to explore their unique perspective on issues and imagine solutions to complex and intersectional challenges.

Conclusion

In highlighting some of the experiences of transgender individuals in social work education, we can see that schools of social work have considerable work to do before they meaningfully address trans issues and approximate social work values that emphasize social justice. Although the Canadian Association for Social Work Education (CASWE, 2011) aims to ensure that social work education offers "equitable educational opportunities and participation of all member groups and individuals" (Mission Statement section, para. 1), the participants' experiences illustrate the fact that schools of social work can be exclusionary. For the healthy development of transgender individuals and communities, social workers must fundamentally familiarize themselves with transgender identities and struggles in order to create transgender-affirming environments.

Notes

1. *Cisgender* is a term used to describe someone who is not trans, a person whose gender identity is congruent with what he or she was assigned at birth.

References

Bauer, G. R., Hammond, R., Travers, R., Kaay, M., Hohenadel, M. M., & Boyce, M. (2009). I don't think this is theoretical; this is our lives: How erasure impacts health care for transgender people. *Journal of the Association of Nurses in AIDS Care, 20*(5), 348–361.

Braun, V., & Clarke, V. (2006). Using thematic analysis in psychology. *Qualitative Research in Psychology, I, 3*(2), 77–101.

Burdge, B. (2007). Bending gender, ending gender: Theoretical foundations for social work practice with the transgender community. *Social Work, 52*(3), 243–252.

Canadian Association of Social Workers (CASWE). (2005). *Code of ethics.* Ottawa, ON: Canadian Association of Social Workers.

Canadian Association for Social Work Education (CASWE). (2011, April 11). Mission statement. Retrieved from www.caswe-acfts.ca/en/Mission_Statement_24.html

Canadian Association for Social Work Education (CASWE). (2012). *Standards for accreditation.* Ottawa, ON: Canadian Association for Social Work Education.

Chang, H. (2008). *Autoethnography as method.* Walnut Creek, CA: Left Coast Press.

Denzin, N. K., & Lincoln, Y. S. (2008). Introduction: Critical methodologies and indigenous inquiry. In N. K. Denzin, Y. S. Lincoln, & L. T. Smith (Eds.), *Handbook of critical and indigenous methodologies* (pp. 1–20). Los Angeles, CA: Sage.

Erich, S., Bouttè-Queen, N., Donnelly, S., & Tittsworth, J. (2007). Social work education: Implications for working with the transgender community. *Journal of Baccalaureate Social Work, 12*(2), 42–52.

Goldberg, J., Ashbee, O., Bradd, S., Lindenberg, D., & Simpson, A. J. (2006). *Recommended framework for training in transgender primary medical care.* Vancouver, BC: Vancouver Coastal Health Authority.

Gray, M, & Webb, S. A. (2008). Social work as art revisited. *International Journal of Social Welfare, 17*(2), 182–193.

Hansbury, G. (2005). The middle men. *Studies in Gender & Sexuality, 6*(3), 241–264.

Harris, B. (2006). A First Nations' perspective on social justice in social work education: Are we there yet? (A post-colonial debate). *The Canadian Journal of Native Studies, 26*(2), 229–263.

Jongeward, C. (2009). Visual portraits: Integrating artistic process into qualitative research. In P. Leavy (Ed.), *Method meets art: Arts-based research practices* (pp. 239–251). New York, NY: Guilford Press.

Kaufman, R. (2008). Introduction to transgender identity and health. In H. Makadon, K. Mayer, J. Potter, & H. Goldhammer (Eds.), *The Fenway guide to lesbian, gay, bisexual, and transgender health* (pp. 331–364). Philadelphia, PA: American College of Physicians.

Leavy, P. (2009). *Method meets art: Arts-based research practice*. New York, NY: Guilford Press.

Lev, A. (2004) *Transgender emergence: Therapeutic guidelines for working with gender-variant people and their families*. New York, NY: Haworth Press.

Lundy, C. (2004). *Social work and social justice*. Peterborough, ON: Broadview Press.

Mallon, G. P. (2009). Knowledge for practice with transgender and gender variant youth. In G. P. Mallon (Ed.), *Social work practice with transgender youth* (pp. 22–37). New York, NY: Routledge.

Mehrotra, G. (2010). Toward a continuum of intersectionality: Theorizing for feminist social work scholarship. *Journal of Women and Social Work, 25*(4), 417–430.

Monro, S. (2007). Transmuting gender binaries: The theoretical challenge. *Sociological Research Online, 12*(1). Retrieved from www.socresonline.org.uk/12/1/monro.html

Rollings, J. H., Jr. (2009). Invisibility and in/di/visuality: The relevance of art education in curriculum theorizing. *Power and Education, 1*(1), 94–110. dx.doi.org/10.2304/power.2009.1.1.94

Scott-Dixon, K. (2006). *Trans/forming feminisms: Transfeminist voices speak out*. Toronto, ON: Sumach Press.

Serano, J. (2007) *Whipping girl: A transsexual woman on sexism and the scapegoating of femininity*. Emeryville, CA: Seal Press.

Shields, S. (2008). Gender: An intersectionality perspective. *Sex Roles, 59*(5/6), 301–311.

Stryker, S. (2008a). *Transgender history*. Berkeley, CA: Seal Press.

Stryker, S. (2008b). Transgender history, homonormativity, and disciplinary. *Radical History Review, 100*, 144–157.

Trans PULSE. (2010). Ontario's trans communities and suicide: Transphobia is bad for our health. *TransPULSE E-Bulletin, 1*(2). Retrieved from www.transpulseproject.ca/documents/E2English.pdf

Wiley, A. (2012). *Qualitative arts based inquiry into transgender experiences in social work education*. Unpublished master's thesis, Prince George, BC: University of Northern British Columbia.

CHAPTER 17
Transformative Engagement in LGBTQ Student/Field Instructor Relationships

Tracy A. Swan and Sheri M. McConnell

Field placements are a significant element in the preparation of social work students for professional practice (Bogo, 2005; Bogo & Vayda, 2004; Rogers, 1995). Placements provide opportunities to apply theory, hone practice skills, employ new methods, and integrate a professional identity. Preparedness for professional practice is dependent on the commitment of the school of social work and the field agency to field education, and the partnership among the field education coordinator, field liaison, and field instructor. The organizational culture and the ideological, theoretical, and practice orientation of the agency and school also impact student learning (Bogo, 2005; Bogo & Vayda, 2004; Rogers, 1995). However, the key contributor is the field instructor. It is within the context of a positive and productive student/instructor relationship that power, privilege, and trust are navigated and negotiated.

Depending on their intersecting identities, students vary greatly in their experiences of power, privilege, and oppression. Recognizing this, critical academics have explicitly addressed students' field experiences and relationships with field instructors. Early writings focused on racialized and LGBTQ students (Messinger, 2002, 2004, 2007; Razack, 2001, 2002). More recent publications have addressed students' intersecting identities. With few exceptions (e.g. Bogo, 2010, 2012; Clark et al., 2013; Drolet, Clark, & Allen, 2012; Newman, Bogo, & Daley, 2008,

2009), field instructors' intersecting identities have not been considered. Nor has there been a focus on how intersections of disadvantage, power, and privilege influence the construction of students' and field instructors' respective worldviews and subjectivity (Bogo, 2012; Clark, 2012; McConnell & Swan, 2013). Few authors consider how intersecting identities and subjective perspectives dynamically influence student learning and student/instructor relationships.

Informed by post-modern and post-structural feminist pedagogical and social work approaches to supervision and practice (hooks, 1994; Kaiser, 1997; Falendar, 2010; Parsons & Swan, 2013), this chapter emphasizes the value of adopting an intersectional framework to guide field instruction with LGBTQ students. To demonstrate this, we employ an exemplar involving a middle-class, heterosexual child welfare field instructor and a student who is a working-class lesbian mother. By applying an intersectional framework, potential issues and differing meanings impacting student/instructor relationships become visible, making it possible to navigate emerging tensions. To contextualize this, we outline the field instructor role and traditional conceptualizations of power, then provide an overview of LGBTQ students' field experiences and how their identities have been addressed.

Field Instructors' Role and Conceptualizations of Power

Ideal field instructors are envisioned as seasoned practitioners with experience in and knowledge of their agency and the people they serve. They are well grounded in their agency's theoretical and practice orientation, and are familiar with the school's orientation and expectations. Through modelling, regularly scheduled field instruction, and ongoing evaluation, field instructors help students integrate theory and practice. They are instrumental in facilitating students' personal and professional growth (Bogo, 2010; Bogo & Vayda, 2004), and fostering learning-centred partnerships based on trust, mutual respect, and accountability (Bogo, 2010, 2012).

Literature dating back to the 1990s focuses on field instructors' expertise and professional/positional power. While appreciative of their knowledge and expertise, students have been presented as aware, even fearful, of field instructors' power to pass or fail them. Although more attention has been directed at the power and oppression associated with specific student identities, few have focused on students' power in the student/field instructor relationship or on the power associated with students' and field instructors' intersecting identities. Power in their relationship has been conceptualized as a commodity, creating an oppositional binary relationship between all-powerful field instructors and powerless students (Fook, 2012; Mullaly, 2010).

LGBTQ Students, Agency Policies, and Field Instructors' Power

It is impossible to comprehensively describe the diverse experiences of LGBTQ, racialized, Aboriginal, or other marginalized students. Thus we highlight only a few dominant themes salient to student/instructor relationships.

With the ongoing acquisition of human rights in Canada, LGBTQ people's lives have generally improved. Although great strides have been made in achieving equity around sexual orientation, only now are gender expression and identity beginning to receive the attention they deserve. While significant gains have been achieved, sexual and gender oppression persist and placements are fraught with challenges. Students also experience classism and poverty (hooks, 1994; Parsons, 2008), physical and mental health challenges (Dunn, Hanes, Hardie, & MacDonald, 2006), racialization (Jeffery, 2009; Razack, 2002), and colonization (Baskin, 2011; Clark et al., 2013) in schools and in the field. Heteronormative, transphobic, racist, ableist, and classist attitudes permeate agency and academic cultures such that oppressive comments and behaviours typically go unchallenged. Many policies reflect the neoliberal discourse, failing to recognize and address the unique challenges facing marginalized people (Baines, 2011; Pollack & Rossiter, 2010).

Although field instructors are aware of similarities and differences in cultural, ethnic, gender, class, age, sexual orientation, and gender expression and identity between themselves and students, they rarely discuss the relevance of student identities to social work practice or to the student/field instructor relationship (Newman et al., 2008). Failure to do so compromises student learning and contributes to students' anxiety and confusion about their acceptance by field instructors and agency personnel (Bogo, 2010, 2012; Dooley, 2007; Newman et al., 2008). Even when blatant forms of oppression are not evident, silence about identities contributes to students' anxiety and isolation (Bogo, 2010; Swan, McConnell, Sinnott, & Brothers, 2010).

Regardless of their awareness, many field instructors are unable to meaningfully navigate the differences and power differentials between themselves and students (Bogo, 2012; Drolet et al., 2012; Newman et al., 2008, 2009; Razack, 2002; Swan, et al, 2010). Although the rhetoric of anti-discriminatory and anti-oppressive practice is embedded in the discourse of most schools and agencies, alternative perspectives on the meaning and role of power and difference are rarely explored (Cosis Brown & Cocker, 2011, as cited in Fairtlough, Bernard, Fletcher, & Ahmet, 2013). Accordingly, students' experiences of oppression within agencies and student/instructor relationships exacerbate students' marginalization. This significantly impacts any meaningful learning, the integration of students' professional identity, and compromises future relationships with colleagues and supervisors.

The Conundrum of Visibility/Invisibility

Despite these concerns, some LGBTQ students are open about their sexual orientation and gender expression. However, when students do disclose, they are often stereotyped or made hyper-visible. Agency personnel often rely on stereotypes grounded in non-traditional gender expression to determine sexual orientation. They may be confused by LGBTQ students whose gender expression is congruent with their sex, and assume they are heterosexual. In contrast, students, regardless of sexual orientation, whose gender expression is not congruent (i.e. butch/masculine women, femme/feminine men) may be assumed to be lesbian or gay (Newman et al., 2008). Students who identify as bisexual, polysexual, pansexual, or asexual typically are mislabelled as lesbian or gay if they fit stereotypes. Those who do not fit stereotypes remain invisible unless they disclose their identities.

For those who do not disclose, fear of being found out leads to invisibility and isolation, and perpetuates the invisibility of their intersecting identities (Fairtlough et al., 2013). Presenting only one identity privileges one form of inequality and contributes to a matrix of multiple and interlocking oppressions (Daley, Solomon, Newman, & Mishna, 2007). This is particularly complex for students from different cultures whose worldviews differ from those of their field instructors, and whose identities are both visible and invisible (e.g. LGBTQ students who are racialized, newcomers to Canada, or Two-Spirit).

As noted, few authors propose an intersectional framework to address the complex challenges of student/instructor relationships. Opportunities to think inclusively and to adequately address the broad range of experiences and concerns are missed (Fairtlough et al., 2013). Field instructors need to create safer spaces and provide multiple opportunities for students to explicitly discuss the significance of differences and intersecting identities. If not, associated conflicts will remain unresolved and impede students in integrating their personal, social, and professional identities (Clark, 2012; Newman et al., 2008; Pfohl, 2004). This failure demands new understandings of diversity, identity, and oppression, entailing meaningful critical reflexivity and the integration of intersectionality into the discourse and practice of field education.

Intersectionality and Critical Reflexivity

Conceptual Components of Intersectionality

While never losing sight of structural influences, intersectionality captures the multiple complex ways identities, oppression, and privilege mutually reinforce and interact with one another (Fook, 2012; Garry, 2011; Hulko, 2009). Intersectionality disputes hierarchies of oppressions and notions of essential identities that possess "natural, intrinsic, unchanging qualities that determine what a person can be in the world" (Brown, 2011, p. 98). One form of oppression or identity is never considered more significant than another. Binaries of power are disputed and individuals are not viewed as either all-powerful or totally powerless. Rather, people are recognized as possessing multiple sources of power and privilege, and experiencing different forms of oppression associated with their intersecting identities and worldviews (Fook, 2012; Hulko, 2009).

An intersectional lens captures the influence of various contexts contributing to the construction of each person's worldview and situated subjectivity (Fook, 2012; Hulko, 2009). By highlighting the influence of historical, cultural, and social contexts, intersectionality captures the impact of multiple structural influences on experiences and interpretations (Hulko, 2009; Mehrotra, 2010; Shields, 2008; Spitzer, 2011). Thus, identities may shift, appearing congruent, in contrast, or oppositional and contradictory to each other. The identity privileged at any given moment can vary by context and relationship (Fook, 2012; Spitzer, 2011), and identities can be highly visible or invisible, "chosen or imposed, stable or unstable" (Enns & Sinacore, 2005, p. 179, as cited in Anastas, 2010). The subjective sense of self constitutes "a resource, a strategy for everyday life that is constantly in a state of creation, maintenance, and reconfirmation" (Spitzer, 2011, pp. 15–16). However, there also are moments of relative stability, allowing people to navigate their worlds more easily (Dei, Karumanchery, & Karmunchery-Luik, 2004; Garry, 2011; Jeffery, 2005).

Intersectionality provides a more nuanced understanding of the person in context and the complex sources of potential misunderstanding and conflict embedded in every relationship and interaction. Accordingly, what is credited and emphasized by individual field instructors and students may differ considerably depending on their respective intersecting identities, subjectivities, histories, and current contextual influences (Garry, 2011; Mullaly, 2010). Although complex, an intersectional lens captures multiple influences contributing to conflicts within student/instructor relationships and is a significant tool for unravelling potential tangles.

What can field instructors, who are responsible for creating a productive learning context for diverse LGBTQ students, actually do? Norma Jean Profitt, who contributed her very thoughtful Chapter 15, maintains, "certain necessary conditions must exist for revealing aspects of our selves such as sexuality and gender identity, which may be assumed or interpreted by others regardless of self-identification" (personal communication, August 20, 2013). This holds true for other intersecting identities. Given that students and field instructors bring their unique worldviews to their relationship and make assumptions about each other, critical reflexivity is essential to an intersectional approach.

Critical Reflection and Reflexivity

Reflection-in-action, which highlights the importance of student opportunities to reflect on and make new meaning from their experiences, has influenced field education for decades (Anastas, 2010; Bogo, 2010; Schon, 1987). Although reflective practice has been critiqued for being too individually focused and for emphasizing objectivity (Baines, 2011; Pollack & Rossiter, 2010), critical reflection and critical reflexivity are both critical components of anti-oppressive practice. A reflexive stance explores how feelings and beliefs, "backgrounds, embodiments, personalities and perspectives [all] intermingle in a holistic context" (Fook, 2012, p. 47). Critical reflexivity and reflection focus on how structures of oppression are created and perpetuated, and unmask power relations on personal and subjective levels (Fook, 2012). Engaging in critical reflexivity enhances understanding of how knowledge is actively created, and provides insight into how people experience multiple forms of oppression based on intersecting identities, and how they contribute to the oppression of others (Fook, 2012; Hulko, 2009). Critical reflexivity demands self-interrogation of power, privilege, and subjective meanings (Fraser & McMaster, 2009). It compels people to grapple with the multiple meanings in all relationships and consider how feelings contribute to constructing others and situations (Fook, 2012).

Deconstructing worldviews is an ongoing process that builds understanding of the complex and nuanced influences of the inter- and intra-subjective meanings "underlying [all] lived experience" (Clark, 2003, pp. 257–258). Recognizing that critical reflexivity is a foundational step that informs all relationships and actions, Chapman (2011) encourages movement beyond an abstract understanding of the insights gained, and challenges us to engage with others within the context of their worlds. Failure to do so risks the imposition of experiences and meanings on others, further denying the veracity of their feelings, experiences, and voice. Critical empathy, which predisposes people to listen for meanings (Clark, 2003), is an excellent way to minimize these risks. As the understanding of people's meanings is deepened, the capacity for empathy is enhanced. Deeper empathy and insight into different meanings allows individuals to further engage with others within the context of their worlds. Through these processes, people recognize the limitations of their own interpretations, knowledge, and practices, setting the stage to enter relationships with others from a tentative, not-knowing stance. Entering their world as a learner who values their knowledge and insights provides opportunities to mutually define shared meanings and understandings, a foundation of trusting and mutually respectful relationships (Clark, 2003; Fook, 2012).

A critically reflexive intersectional framework provides a comprehensive anti-oppressive approach to field education. Field instructors are called to engage students and field education as learners. Accordingly, they need to actively model reflexivity and transparency, demonstrate humility, listen for meanings, engage in open dialogue, and share power. They need to risk sharing examples of the personal and professional challenges they have encountered when navigating differences of power, privilege, and oppression in their practice, agency, and society (Clark, 2012; McConnell & Swan, 2013; Riggs & das Nair, 2012). Doing so contributes to student learning and the development of an integrated professional identity rooted in critical empathy and social justice.

Employing an Intersectional Framework
What Gerrie and Myrna Bring to the Student/Instructor Relationship

Gerrie is a 32-year-old BSW student beginning her first placement in a child protection agency. She identifies as a white female butch lesbian mother. As a butch, her gender expression fits the stereotypes. Most people, at first glance, assume that she is either a man or a lesbian. Gerrie is the lone parent of a six-year-old son beginning grade one. Since the recent break-up with her female partner of five years over parenting differences, Gerrie and her son are barely getting by on social assistance and have moved into a basement apartment. Gerrie is ambivalent about her placement. An outspoken lesbian and activist from a homophobic family, she worries about her son being apprehended. This fear has increased considerably as her embittered ex-partner, knowing Gerrie's fear, has threatened to call child welfare.

Her field instructor, Myrna, is 50 years old, middle-class, white, and heterosexual. She has been married for 25 years to an electrical engineer, and is the mother of a 19-year-old daughter in university and 25-year-old son working in the North. Myrna, an MSW social worker who has been employed in child protection since her BSW graduation, has excelled in her field and is a manager and team leader. Consistently providing field instruction for more than 25 years, Myrna is well liked and respected by students. She actively promotes anti-oppressive and intersectional approaches with service users and colleagues, and advocates for more inclusive agency policies and programs. Myrna views herself as very aware of and sensitive to all types of difference, and works collaboratively for social justice in the broader community.

Discussion Points

How can Myrna create a collaborative, dialogical relationship with Gerrie based on trust and mutual respect and address the significance of their respective intersecting identities and unique worldviews? How can she begin to co-create this relationship while also focusing on orienting Gerrie to her agency and to child protection?

Field instructors must recognize the many sources of their power and privilege and own how they exercise it. How students perceive and relate to field instructors is influenced by their unique experiences and understandings of others who have exercised power in their lives. Given the power dynamics inherent in the agency and the student/instructor relationship, field instructors need to make field instruction dialogical and collaborative. Building on critical reflexivity, they must help students recognize the intersecting sources of their power and privilege, and facilitate students in exercising their power.

Students need to have a genuine voice in their relationship and their placement. Field instructors must recognize that students have knowledge to share, actively reach for students' input, and, wherever possible, share power and decision-making. They must remain sensitive to the historical, cultural, and social contexts that contribute to students feeling vulnerable. They need to provide support and mentor students in navigating the challenges they face, and their accompanying feelings. Field instructors need to acknowledge and honour students' strengths, wisdom, and unique contributions. They must actively listen to students and strive to understand how daily stresses and experiences of intersecting oppressions impact students on all levels. Field instructors then can communicate genuine empathy, openly and transparently taking risks and sharing their real selves.

The First Day of Placement

In preparation for their first meeting, during which she will orient Gerrie to the placement and the agency, Myrna has been reflecting critically on potential hurdles they might encounter in establishing their relationship. She has considered how Gerrie might perceive and construct her, and how she might perceive and construct Gerrie, given their respective intersecting identities, power, privilege, and oppression.

When she meets Gerrie, Myrna welcomes her warmly and invites her to her office. Myrna notices that Gerrie fits a number of stereotypes. Recognizing the intersection of gender expression and sexuality, Myrna wonders if Gerrie might be a lesbian. As they walk down the hall, Myrna reflects on the curious looks Gerrie is getting from her coworkers. She hopes that Gerrie perceives these looks as curiosity about her as a new student, not about her sexuality or gender expression. Aware of the importance of explicitly and sensitively addressing identities, Myrna makes a mental note to check out Gerrie's interpretation once they have established a beginning level of trust.

Conscious of the importance of signage and visible cues, the hallway is decorated with posters addressing a range of social identities. The bookshelves and pictures in Myrna's office reflect her anti-oppressive approach and her knowledge of and support for various identities, including LGBTQ people. She wonders if Gerrie has picked up on these cues and hopes they help her to feel more comfortable.

Sitting around a small table, rather than across from each other at her desk, Myrna begins to lay the foundation for co-creating their relationship and co-constructing a safer learning environment. Myrna introduces herself on a professional and personal level, telling Gerrie about who she is in the world and discussing some of her professional passions. She invites Gerrie to share whatever she is comfortable telling her. Thus, Myrna sets the stage for open discussion and dialogue, while recognizing Gerrie may not feel ready to share this early in their relationship.

Myrna then describes her hopes for their relationship, grounded in a vision based on critical feedback from previous students, whose knowledge and insights she values. Myrna commits to ensuring that Gerrie will have a voice and a role in co-creating a mutually beneficial, honest, open, respectful, and transparent relationship, and in co-constructing productive, meaningful learning experiences. She stresses the importance of collaboration and honouring each other's knowledge and experiences, as well as respecting their individual, yet different, experiences of power, privilege, and oppression. Further, Myrna encourages Gerrie to speak from her own perspective about their differences and similarities, and to express her ideas about how best to work together.

Myrna explicitly discusses power, privilege, and oppression within the agency and child protection practice, highlighting some of her own challenges in working anti-oppressively, using an intersectional approach, within this context. Having addressed issues of power within their relationship associated with their different identities, Myrna outlines her evaluation and grading role. Recognizing that there will be times when she is obligated to exercise her positional power, she promises to do so transparently and respectfully, remaining cognizant of her impact.

Myrna commits to weekly field instruction and apologizes in advance for times that agency or client obligations may interfere with regularly scheduled sessions. Myrna reassures Gerrie that she and her learning are a priority and that they will reschedule if either needs to change times. She recognizes that life presents a variety of challenges and that students often have multiple competing academic and personal demands. Myrna will be as flexible as possible should Gerrie encounter any scheduling conflicts. She commits to planning together to address Gerrie's concerns, balancing her personal and professional responsibilities to service users and the agency.

Myrna discusses how people perceive her, and how colleagues and service users have made assumptions about who she is and what to expect from her. She suggests the same may be true for Gerrie, and welcomes discussion of her experiences. Myrna wonders out loud about how Gerrie might have interpreted initially being checked out by agency personnel when she arrived, communicating her awareness and creating an opportunity for Gerrie to respond.

Myrna suggests that she and Gerrie may have divergent perspectives and may approach situations differently. She invites Gerrie to join her in respecting their common ground and divergent perspectives as they learn and work together. Myrna acknowledges that she will not always be the person she aspires to be, and that she will make assumptions about Gerrie based on her own worldview and expects Gerrie may do the same. She hopes these challenges will become teachable moments for both of them. Myrna also hopes that together they can build sufficient trust and respect that Gerrie can share her concerns with her. She trusts they each will take responsibility for their respective roles in any difficulties, and work together to resolve any misunderstandings.

Discussion Points

How will Myrna and Gerrie manage conflicts? How can they care for themselves and support each other? What can they teach each other about navigating intersecting differences, advocacy, and anti-oppressive practice?

When conflicts arise, field instructors need to listen for meanings and respond with understanding and empathy. They then can share their rationales for decisions and explore opportunities for compromise. If compromise is not possible, they must strive to make decisions that leave students empowered. When students are overwhelmed or discouraged, field instructors need to listen actively, respond empathically, and share their experiences of feeling discouraged. They need to use challenging times as teaching moments about the nature of structural and intersecting oppressions, speak to the importance of allies, and assist students to celebrate their accomplishments.

Field instructors need to actively model working anti-oppressively and advocating for social change within and beyond their agencies. They need to support students in advocating for service users and in promoting change. Further, they need to commit time to work with students to deconstruct hurdles to change, and to provide opportunities to explore different approaches. It is crucial that field instructors are honest with themselves and students about what they know and do not know, modelling the significance of a similar stance for practice with diverse service users with different intersecting identities and subjectivities.

Future Field Instruction

While Gerrie may or may not disclose her identities or discuss her expectations openly or in depth during their first or subsequent meetings, Myrna continues to provide a foundation for future work. She recognizes the importance of Gerrie hearing these messages, and that establishing trust and openness takes time.

Myrna will build on and strengthen their relationship by connecting with Gerrie about their common experiences. She will encourage discussion around their common role as mothers, recognizing how Gerrie's experiences will be different, as a lone parent living in poverty and as a butch lesbian. While recognizing the boundaries between field instruction and therapy, Myrna will address Gerrie's fears about her son being apprehended, by consciously modelling how she would share with clients what she has learned from other lone mothers. She will explain that most mothers within the purview of child protection experience similar fears and that many situations do not result in the apprehension of children. Myrna has learned that many mothers have an abiding commitment to and love for their children, but are constrained by socially constructed circumstances beyond their control. This may lead to discussion about how Gerrie could take a similar approach with other mothers during her placement. Myrna will mentor Gerrie in providing mothers with opportunities for a meaningful voice in planning to create a safe, caring, nurturing environment for themselves and their children. She will actively reach for Gerrie's ideas about approaches to navigate differences and establish trusting relationships with mothers who have a variety of intersecting identities and cultural origins. In doing so, Myrna will acknowledge when Gerrie inspires her and contributes to her growth, knowledge, and insight.

Myrna will revisit these messages and encourage deeper learning through further mindful conversations and modelling. She will expand on early discussions, facilitating Gerrie's critical reflection on the impact and the influence of her intersecting identities and subjectivity on relationships with diverse service users and colleagues, and on practice issues and professional identity. Myrna will focus on the importance of advocacy and promoting social change and justice, within and beyond the agency. She will explicitly support Gerrie's efforts to influence change by brainstorming alternatives based on the principle of least contest. Myrna will address the importance of working collaboratively when promoting social change, and of self-care and self-preservation. Myrna will share her own experiences of feeling discouraged. She will speak to the significance of taking time to celebrate small steps and victories, and of borrowing hope and inspiration from colleagues who share a commitment to dismantling oppression and contributing to social justice.

Final Discussion Points

What are the key points that Myrna must keep in mind as a field instructor? How can she model an intersectional/anti-oppressive approach to field education and social work practice? Field instructors must be cognizant that their knowledge is only partial. They can never fully understand students' circumstances, and misunderstandings are inevitable. It is crucial that they be gentle with themselves and students. They must strive to be honest and genuine, recognizing that students and field instructors are both learners, possessing differing knowledge, worldviews, power, and privilege. Field instructors need to humbly accept that all learning and understanding about themselves, students, and the nature of intersectionality and oppression is continuous, emergent, and perpetually evolving and deepening.

Conclusion

Understandably, the construction of the exemplar and the description of what could transpire between Myrna and Gerrie is informed by the authors' own understanding of field education; respective intersecting identities and subjectivities; reflection on our histories; experiences of power, privilege, and oppression; and the social, cultural, and organizational contexts of our lives. Our subjectivities predispose us to emphasize different aspects of Myrna and Gerrie, what they bring to their relationship, and how Myrna implements an intersectional approach to field education. Others might construct the exemplar quite differently, privileging different aspects of identity, and conceptualizing the student/instructor relationship from equally valid perspectives.

We recognize that the exemplar has limitations and when constructing it, grappled with a number of questions. Which intersecting identities/subjectivities would we include? Would Gerrie and Myrna engage in dialogue and conflict? Given limited space, we chose to highlight how a field instructor could draw on different intersectional concepts and anti-oppressive principles, make visible some complex issues that impact student/instructor relationships, and model a similar approach to practice for students. The exemplar also provides opportunities for further reflection on how multiple intersecting identities and subjectivities might be navigated in different contexts as the placement unfolds.

We place particular emphasis on critical reflexivity, as *"curiosity and openness to alternative worldviews* [must be] central to approaching diversity and oppression issues" (Anastas, 2010, p. 91) for all engaged learners. Because critical reflexivity, navigating multiple differences, and applying an intersectional anti-oppressive approach is not for the faint of heart, "field supervision must be a space where difficult and courageous conversations can occur" (Clark, 2012, p. 91). Reflexive practice renders the invisible visible, allowing field instructors and students to become comfortable with the uncomfortable. By grappling with tensions arising in their relationship, both are challenged intellectually, and their beliefs and values disrupted and altered. By embracing these challenges, each will grow personally, professionally, and spiritually (Dudziak, 2010). This all evolves from field instructors' capacity to listen empathically and meaningfully engage in dialogical partnerships, essential elements of field education informed by an intersectional/ anti-oppressive approach. Together they can journey through the sadness, confusion, and hopelessness often evoked by reflexive practice and experience genuine human connectedness, whereby they discover a source of hope within each other.

References

Anastas, J. W. (2010). *Teaching in social work: An educator's guide to theory and practice*. New York, NY: Columbia University Press.

Baines, D. (2011). *Doing anti-oppressive practice: Social justice social work* (2nd ed.). Halifax, NS: Fernwood Publishing.

Baskin, C. (2011). *Strong helper's teachings: The value of indigenous knowledges in the helping professions*. Toronto, ON: Canadian Scholars' Press.

Bogo, M. (2005). Field instruction in social work: A review of the research literature. In L. Shulman & A. Safyer (Eds.), *Supervision in counseling: Interdisciplinary issues and research* (pp. 163–193). New York, NY: The Haworth Press.

Bogo, M. (2010). *Achieving competence in social work through field education*. Toronto, ON: University of Toronto Press.

Bogo, M. (2012). Importance of field education: Current trends and historical context. In N. Drolet, N. Clark, & H. Allen (Eds.), *Shifting sites of practice: Field education in Canada* (pp. 1–17). Toronto, ON: Pearson Canada.

Bogo M., & Vayda, E. (2004). *The practice of field instruction in social work theory and process* (2nd ed). Toronto, ON: University of Toronto Press.

Brown, C. (2011). Reconceptualizing feminist therapy: Violence, problem drinking, and re-storying women's lives. In D. Baines (Ed.), *Doing anti-oppressive practice: Social justice social work* (pp. 98–115). Halifax, NS: Fernwood Publishing.

Chapman, C. (2011). Resonance, intersectionality, and reflexivity in critical pedagogy (and research methodology). *Social Work Education: The International Journal, 30*(7), 723–744. dxdoi.org/10.1080/02615479.2010.520120

Clark, J. (2003). Reconceptualizing empathy for anti-oppressive, culturally competent practice. In W. Shera (Ed.), *Emerging perspectives on anti-oppressive practice* (pp. 247–263). Toronto, ON: Canadian Scholars' Press.

Clark, N. (2012). Beyond the reflective practitioner. In J. Drolet, N. Clark, & H. Allen (Eds.), *Shifting sites of practice: Field education in Canada* (pp. 79–96). Toronto, ON: Pearson Canada.

Clark, N., Reid, M., Drolet, J., Waltoln, P., Peirce, J., Charles, G., ... Arnouse, M. (2013). Indigenous social work field education: "Melqílwiye" coming together towards reconciliation. *Native Social Work Journal, 8*, 105–127.

Daley, A., Solomon, S., Newman, P., & Mishna, F. (2007). Traversing the margins: Intersectionalities in the bullying of lesbian, gay, bisexual and transgender youth. *Journal of Gay & Lesbian Social Services, 19*(3), 9–29.

Dei, G. J., Karumanchery, L. L., & Karumanchery-Luik, N. (2004). *Playing the race card: Exposing white power and privilege.* New York, NY: Peter Lang Publishing.

Dooley, J. (2007). Coming out in field internship: Some considerations for LGBT students. *The New Social Worker, 14*(4), 10–12. Retrieved from www.socialworker.com/feature-articles/field-placement/Coming_Out_in_Field_Placement%3A_Some_Considerations_for_LGBT_Students

Drolet, J., Clark, N., & Allen, H. (Eds.) (2012). *Shifting sites of practice: Field education in Canada.* Toronto, ON: Pearson Canada.

Dudziak, S. (2010). Lifelines. *Canadian Social Work Review, 27*(1), 147–149.

Dunn, P. A., Hanes, R., Hardie, S., & MacDonald, J. (2006). Creating disability inclusion within Canadian schools of social work. *Journal of Social Work in Disability & Rehabilitation, 5*(1), 1–15. Retrieved from www.researchgate.net/journal/15367118_Journal_of_Social_Work_in_Disability_Rehabilitation

Fairtlough, A., Bernard, C., Fletcher, J. & Ahmet, A. (2013). Experiences of lesbian, gay and bisexual students on social work programmes: Developing a framework for educational practice. *British Journal of Social Work, 43*, 467–485.

Falendar, C. A. (2010). Relationships and accountability: Tensions in feminist supervision. *Women & Therapy, 33*(1), 22–41.

Fook, J. (2012). *Social work: Critical theory and practice* (2nd ed.). Washington, DC: Sage.

Fraser, H., & McMaster, K. (2009). Gender, sexuality and power. In M. Connolly & L. Harms (Eds.), *Social work: Contexts and practice* (2nd ed., pp. 81–93). South Melbourne, Australia: Oxford University Press.

Garry, A. (2011). Intersectionality, metaphors, and the multiplicity of gender. *Hypatia, 26*(4), 826–850. Retrieved from onlinelibrary.wiley.com/doi/10.1111/j.1527-2001.2011.01194.x/abstract

hooks, b. (1994). *Teaching to transgress: Education as the practice of freedom.* New York, NY: Routledge.

Hulko, W. (2009). The time- and context- contingent nature of intersectionality and interlocking oppressions. *Affilia, 24*(1), 44–55.

Jeffery, D. (2005). "What good is anti-racist social work if you can't master it?": Exploring a paradox in anti-racist social work education. *Race, Ethnicity & Education, 8*(4), 409–425. Retrieved from www.tandfonline.com/doi/abs/10.1080/13613320500324011#.UiH_HyqF-_A

Jeffery, D. (2009). Meeting here and now: Reflections on racial and cultural differences in social work encounters. In J. Carriere & S. Stega (Eds.), *Walking this path together: Anti-racist and anti-oppressive child welfare practice* (pp. 45–61). Black Point, NS: Fernwood.

Kaiser, T. L. (1997). *Supervisory relationships: Exploring the human element.* Pacific Grove, CA: Brooks/Cole.

McConnell, S. & Swan, T. (2013, June). *Intersectionality: Transformative engagement in the LGB student / field instructor relationship.* Paper presented at the Canadian Association for Social Work Education Conference, Victoria, BC, Canada.

Mehrotra, G. (2010). Toward a continuum of intersectionality theorizing for feminist social work scholarship. *Affilia, 25*(4), 417–430.

Messinger, L. (2002). Policy and practice: A holistic approach to addressing homophobia and heteronormativity among social work students. *Journal of Lesbian Studies, 6*(3/4), 121–132. Retrieved from link.springer.com/article/10.1007%2Fs10734-008-9172-y

Messinger, L. (2004). Out in the field: Gay and lesbian social work students' experiences in field internship. *Journal of Social Work Education, 40*(2), 187–204.

Messinger, L. (2007). Supervision of lesbian, gay, and bisexual social work students by heterosexual field instructors: A qualitative dyad analysis. *The Clinical Field Instructor, 26*(1/2), 195–222. Retrieved from www.tandfonline.com/doi/abs/10.1300/J001v26n01_13

Mullaly, B. (2010). *Challenging oppression and confronting privilege* (2nd ed.). Toronto, ON: Oxford University Press.

Newman, P. A., Bogo, M., & Daley, A. (2008). Self-disclosure of sexual orientation in social work field education: Field instructor and lesbian and gay student perspectives. *The Clinical Supervisor, 27*(2), 215-237. Retrieved from www.tandfonline.com/doi/pdf/10.1080/07325220802487881

Newman, P. A., Bogo, M., & Daley, A. (2009). Breaking the silence: Sexual orientation in social work field education. *Journal of Social Work Education, 45*(1), 7-27.

Parsons, J. E. (2008). Life chances, choices and identity: Single mothers in postsecondary education. *Atlantis, 32*(2), 136-146. Retrieved from journals.msvu.ca/index.php/atlantis/article/view/585/575

Parsons, J. E., & Swan, T. A. (2013). SW6012 Social Work Leadership for Social Justice (MSW course). Unpublished lecture notes, Memorial University of Newfoundland, St. John's, NL.

Pfohl, A. H. (2004). The intersection of personal and professional identity: The heterosexual field instructor's role in fostering the development of sexual minority supervisees. *The Clinical Supervisor, 23*(1), 139-163. Retrieved from www.tandfonline.com/doi/abs/10.1300/J001v23n01_09

Pollack, S. & Rossiter, A. (2010). Neoliberalism and the entrepreneurial subject: Implications for feminism and social work. *Canadian Social Work Review, 27*(2), 155-169.

Razack, N. (2001). Diversity and difference in the field education encounter: Racial minority students in the internship. *Social Work Education: The International Journal, 20*(2), 219-232. Retrieved from www.tandfonline.com/doi/abs/10.1080/02615470120044310

Razack, N. (2002). *Transforming the field: Critical anti-racist and anti-oppressive perspectives for the human services practicum.* Black Point, NS: Fernwood.

Riggs, D. W., & das Nair, R. (2012). Intersecting Identities. In R. das Nair & C. Butler (Eds.). *Intersectionality, sexuality and psychological therapies: Working with lesbian, gay and bisexual diversity* (pp. 38-73). Chichester, England: John Wiley & Sons.

Rogers, G. (1995). *Social work field education: Views & visions.* Dubuque, IA: Kendall/Hunt Publishing.

Schon, D. (1987). *Educating the reflective practitioner.* San Francisco, CA: Jossey-Bass.

Shields, S. A. (2008). Gender: An intersectionality perspective. *Sex Roles, 59,* 301–311.

Sinacore, A. L., & Enns, C. Z. (2005). Diversity feminisms: Postmodern, women of color, anti-racist, lesbian, third wave and global feminism. In C. Z. Enns, & A. L. Sinacore (Eds.), *Teaching and social justice: Integrating multicultural and feminist theories in the classroom* (pp. 41–68). Washington, DC: American Psychological Association Press.

Spitzer, D. L. (Ed.) (2011). *Engendering migrant health: Canadian perspectives.* Toronto, ON: University of Toronto Press.

Swan, T., McConnell, S. M., Sinnott, R., & Brothers, D. (Queer Consultation Group) (2010). *Creating visibility and belonging: Reflections on being queer in the School of Social Work.* St. John's, NL: Memorial University of Newfoundland School of Social Work.

CHAPTER 18

Shaking the Foundations: Moving Gender and Sexual Diversity Education to the Centre of the Child and Youth Development Classroom

Andrea Ridgley, Marilyn McLean, Mandy Bonisteel, and Soni Dasmohapatra

How do we as educators provide professional education to diverse student populations in ways that challenge conventional teaching about child and youth identity development, while also understanding that learners and educators are products of the very systems we seek to challenge? How do we teach and learn in ways that enable exploration of the richness of a full-spectrum awareness of gender and sexual diversity rather than reinforce the rigid binary thinking that limits the consciousness raising necessary for social transformation. In this chapter, four educators collaborate to explore the challenges involved in designing and delivering gender and sexual diversity curriculum in child and youth development courses, identify delivery strategies, and pose questions emerging from our experiences. We begin by presenting the theoretical and pedagogical roots and social action goals of our work. Next we discuss the challenges we face in teaching lifespan development from a perspective that views both gender and sex as spectral rather than binary, and classroom strategies we undertake to address those challenges. In conclusion, we query the future of our work, anticipating that our teaching of this material will evolve in tandem with the further expansion of our own understandings of gender and sexual identity.

Who We Are

We are four members of a team of about 20 educators who provide critical social work education to a diverse student group. The female and genderqueer-identified learners in our program, the Assaulted Women's and Children's Counsellor/Advocate Program (AWCCA) at George Brown College in Toronto, are training to be anti-violence counsellors, advocates, and activists. Students' and educators' demographics reflect those of Toronto in relation to race, nationality and status, language, ethnicity, ability, and sexual identity. Students' field work takes place in a range of anti-violence and community organizations including shelters and rape crisis centres, programs supporting parents and children in the aftermath of violence, literacy and anti-poverty organizations, organizations supporting youth, and policy and advocacy groups and coalitions.

Our teaching team embraces an approach rooted in a feminist epistemological view of knowledge acquisition (Crabtree, Sapp, & Licona, 2009) that employs both queer and constructivist pedagogies. What does this mean for us as educators? First, our use of feminist epistemology—particularly a Black feminist epistemology (Narayan, 1989) emphasizes the importance of lived experience, promotes dialogue rather than debate, and requests personal accountability in knowledge acquisition (Hill Collins, 1990; Lather, 1991). This requires that we construct transformative learning environments in which the experiences students bring to the classroom are both valued and critically explored as sources of knowledge.

Second, a queer pedagogy demands that our materials represent, and our curriculum employs, what Malinowitz (1995) describes as "thinking about the ways margins produce not only abject outsiderhood, but also profoundly unique ways of self-defining, knowing and acting" (p. 252). This queer pedagogy values the "sharp vision that comes from living with friction and contradiction" (p. 252) and creates space for learners to insert themselves into layered and nuanced conversations about the tensions that arise in modern critical social work practice. It demands they reflexively examine discourses concerning race, poverty, disability, childhood, gender, and sexual identity that surround them. This pedagogy inspires learners to explore and value difference (Lorde, 1984) rather than—as diversity education is so often at risk of doing—erasing or flattening it (Alexander, 2008).

Finally, constructivist methodologies blended with feminist epistemology create opportunities for learners and instructors with multiple identities and ways of knowing to work collaboratively to create meaning, and evaluate and validate learning. They do this by encouraging an ongoing exploration of power dynamics within the classroom (Crabtree et al., 2009); requiring instructors to model and students to question received knowledge and beliefs; and empowering instructors and students to vocalize and test their emerging theories about themselves and the world (Gezinski, 2009). Students in our program explore issues related to violence and the effects of trauma. This deconstruction of popular narratives about violence and social inequality lays the foundation for the reconstruction of vibrant new narratives that mirror back to students the grit, complexity, and beauty of their lives.

Some of the most important reconstruction activities, which are also among the first students explore in the course of our program, focus on teaching and learning about gender and sexual identity. While gender and sexual identity studies are woven throughout the two-year curriculum, they are a central focus of exploration in the child and youth oriented courses taught over the two years, starting in the first semester.

What We Do

In the AWCCA program's child and youth themed courses, students examine a range of topics: child and youth development, children who witness and/or experience violence, psychology of women, and adult survivors of child sexual abuse. These courses integrate theory with the applied skills needed to advocate and work with individuals, families, and communities. The foundational course is Child and Youth Development: Gender Identity. The outcomes of this Ontario college-level course include demonstrating knowledge of widely accepted child development and milestone theories that meet both college and work sector requirements (Bandura, 1977; Bronfenbrenner & Morris, 2006; Erikson, 1950; Freud, 1923; Gillian, 1982; Piaget, 1971; Thelen & Smith, 2006; Vygotsky, 1992). However, it is apparent in the classroom that these theories and milestones do not describe the lived reality of most of the students in our classes. Therefore, it is imperative that we centralize the role of learner identities related to culture and community, social exclusion based on gender and sexual diversity, and the experience of violence, in the critical analysis of the dominant theories and ideas within the course.

Child and youth development courses in colleges and universities are most often grounded in developmental psychology, the "branch of psychology concerned with interaction between physical and psychological processes and with stages of growth from conception throughout the entire life span" (American Psychological Association, 2012). A survey of textbooks widely available for use in such courses reveals a commonality of theories developed in Europe from the mid-twentieth century onward, describing the ages and stages of child development based on certain physical, cognitive, language, and emotional/social milestones (Berk, 2012; Boyd, Johnson, & Bee, 2012; Shaffer, Kipp, Wood, & Willoughby, 2012).[1] Derived from observational studies of children from the dominant European/North American culture, such theories imply that they are historically rooted, universal, and scientifically sound, while they ignore the rich knowledge that exists in non-colonial and non-dominant cultures (Almeida, Woods, & Messineo, 1998; Anderson, 2011; Matlin, 2012; Simard & Blight, 2011).[2]

The descriptions of sex, gender, and sexuality development in texts we surveyed are consistently brief. The theories in which sex is only "male" and "female" are binary, essentialist, universalizing, colonizing, medicalized, and exclusionary—neither thoroughly explored nor critically analyzed. Some more recent texts include "transsexual" and "intersex," but in ways that pathologize and medicalize and deny the personhood of people who identify as transsexual (Serano, 2007) and people who identify as intersex (Koyama, 2003).

Theories of gender development are most often limited to psychoanalytic theory, behavioural learning theory, cognitive learning theory, social learning theory, evolutionary theory, gender schema theory, and social cognitive theory. Some texts now include ecological and systems theory (Berk, 2012; Boyd et al., 2012; Shaffer et al., 2012). These theories are often presented in historical order, implying an evolution in thought and an increase in validity over time. Occasionally, "cross-cultural"/anthropological approaches describe those who do not "fit in" to colonial definitions of gender, such as Calabai, Calalai (Davies, 2010; Rupp, 2009), Two-Spirit (Jacobs, Thomas, & Lang, 1997; Swanson, 2012), Fa'afafine (Vanessa, 2009; Taulapapa, 2011), and Hijra (Galliano, 2002; Reddy, 2005). Whether self-identified or identified by the observer, this exoticizing intensifies the already privileged patriarchal, Western dominant culture notion of gender and ensures silencing of the very voices that bring lived experience into the classroom.

In regard to sexuality, the texts we surveyed only provide definitions of "sexual orientation": gay, lesbian and bisexual (Berk, 2012). The enormous range of human sexual diversity is absent or erased. Missing is a discussion of the ever changing, ever nuanced complexities of attraction, sexuality, the erotic, and the politics of identity (Driskill, Justice, Miranda, & Tatonetti, 2011). Erased are the multiple ways that racialization, ethnicity, class, and ability join with sexuality to defy the constraints of the ideological box (Bilodeau & Renn, 2005). That "sexuality," as the dominant culture has labelled it, is a social and historical construct is not considered (Foucault, 1990), nor is the colonial practice of labelling and pathologizing a variety of behaviours and identities (Cannon, 2012). If theories of homosexuality are present, they are limited to hereditary/genetic and possible environmental influences (Berk, 2012). The texts do not critique the research or pose questions about the arbiters of knowledge, who, in keeping with scientific methodology, are not themselves situated in the discourse.

It is evident from this brief analysis that dominant discourse and theory on gender and sexuality are deficient, failing to recognize that intersections such as racialization, gender, class, and culture are central pillars that structure development (Almeida et al., 1998). They also fail to recognize the impact that violence has on an individual or a culture. This includes all forms of violence against women and children (including, but not limited to, assault, emotional assault, sexual assault, female genital mutilation, sexual harassment, criminalization, control of women's reproductive rights, control of women's sexuality, and the pathologizing of women's experience). These theories do not acknowledge the interconnectedness of overt and systemic forms of violence in all forms of oppression (including, but not limited to, colonialization, sexism, racism, anti-Semitism, classism, heterosexism, ableism, ageism, ethnocentrism, lookism, and fat prejudice) (Davis, 1990; Smith, 2006; Whalen, 1996).

We attempt to bring the narratives, worldviews, models, and practices that have been silenced in mainstream approaches to the study of gender and sexual development into the course and the classroom. Students are asked to consider how they, their families, their communities, and their nations view child and youth development. How and where do gender and sexuality fit in to these understandings of development? The objective here is to explore, challenge, interrogate, create, and celebrate diverse ways of being and knowing. Starting by identifying the personal connections the students make to the course topics and then adding a variety of secondary sources results in lively discussion.

How We Do It

Most of the learners and educators in our programs have been raised and educated in societies that have either produced, or had forced upon them, the discourses about child and youth development discussed above. The legacies of colonizing governments include the criminalization of consensual sex acts and the pathologizing of gender expressions that transgress the constructed gender binaries (Cannon, 2012). One of the consequences of this legacy is the suppression of multiple ways of expressing, experiencing, or conceptualizing gender and sexuality (Bilodeau & Renn, 2005; Morgensen, 2011; Wilchins, 2002). It is not surprising that the terrain of gender and sexuality studies as it relates to child and youth development can seem harsh and dangerous. Our experience tells us that traversing this terrain can also be transformative and promote healing of the wounds inflicted when complex identities are forced into tight spaces marked by razor-sharp edges. Experience also tells us that careful planning, collaboration with colleagues, and support from both the college and the external communities in which we are rooted are vital to our work.

When designing and delivering curriculum, we have found that course content and the environment in which we deliver it are inextricably linked. The work we do to establish an open and supportive learning environment is key to our ability to deliver challenging content and rests upon four foundational strategies: using a children's human rights perspective as a starting point to frame discussion; situating our classrooms within the college's rights-based policies and practices (George Brown College, 2012); requiring that students apply the interpersonal communication and group-process skills they are acquiring in concurrent classes; and mapping gender and sexual identity studies across the two-year curriculum on an ongoing basis.

The first strategy, setting the stage for complex discussions about gender and sexual identity within a children's human rights framework, has been incredibly successful. It allows us to begin discussions from a starting point that bypasses conventional debates. Students enter our program with a desire to support children's growth and safeguard children's rights, so they are curious about arguments based on children's rights, even as their learning challenges closely held values and beliefs rooted in their own upbringings. For example, using a graphically illustrated photo essay (UNICEF, n.d.) that explores the United Nations Convention on the Rights of the Child (United Nations General Assembly, 1989 [signed by 149 member nations]), students learn about various articles of the convention by creating group-generated examples and writing scenarios illustrating rights protection or violation.

The diagram below (Figure 18.1) illustrates the five key articles in the convention that intersect to inform a rights-based analysis that strengthens children's interpretations of their own identities. While the articles do not explicitly codify the right to sexual and gender identity and expression, they certainly lend themselves to this interpretation (United Nations, 2012). They also provide instructors with an internationally authored focus for discussion that displaces the religious and moral objections that often arise.

Figure 18.1 identifies the articles that form the foundation for applying a human rights framework to child and youth development and decision-making. Article 8, the right to identity, is layered with other core rights—right to participation, freedom from discrimination, survival and development, and primary consideration of best interests of the child—to create openings for advocates, states parties, and children themselves to begin discussion of how the right to identity can be understood and applied to children's lives. A social justice interpretation of Article 8 includes the opportunity for a child or youth to explore, express, and be informed about gender as they see fit, and should be considered and applied to all children, regardless of social location.

The strategy of situating the classroom within the college's human rights policies and positive space practices requires instructors to read aloud the student code of conduct and the equity statement posted on the front page of all course outlines. Many instructors have worried that such readings are gratuitous. However, when one of us conducted informal research with racialized, Indigenous, and queer students within our program, several commented on the importance of this very act: "We already know about the Code and the statement; you reading it to us is your way of showing us that you know about it and are open to

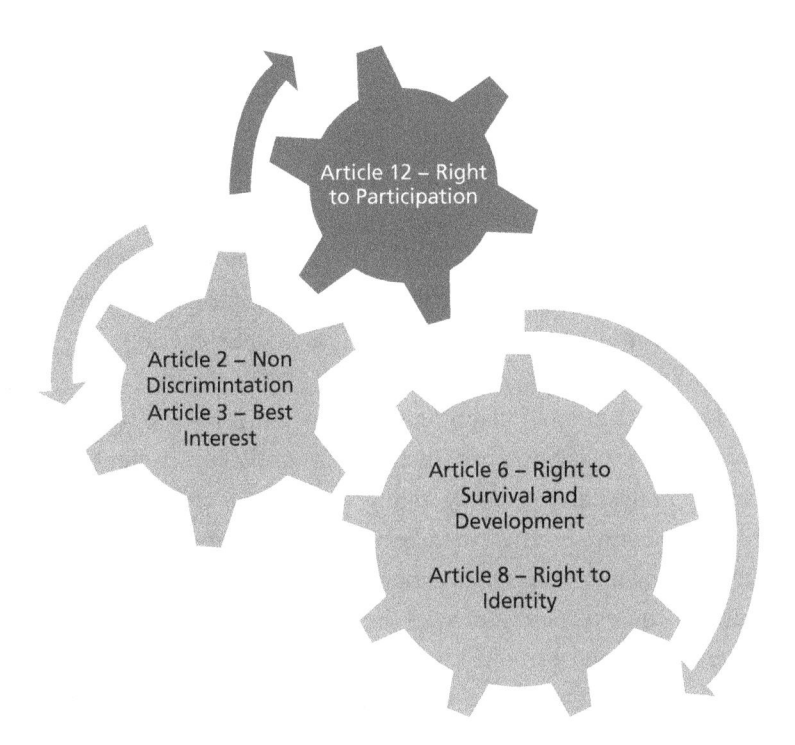

Figure 18.1 Articles from the United Nations Convention on the Rights of the Child that work in combination to support rights to sexual and gender identity and expression.

Source: Dasmohapatra, 2012.

discussing it when something goes wrong" (McLean, 2007). Students also indicated they look in faculty offices for the rainbow ribbon that signifies an individual has completed the Positive Space training; one instructor who brings the ribbon to class has elicited overwhelmingly positive responses.

Students in our program develop interpersonal communication and group process skills throughout their studies. They learn and practise skills by collaborating to create group guidelines for classrooms that support learning and dialogue across difference; using active listening skills to navigate difficult conversations; providing respectful and concrete feedback to others; being open to being challenged, challenging, and listening to challenges to one another's thinking; and working constructively and creatively with conflict. The more that instructors in child and youth classes are able to demonstrate a commitment to drawing on students' use of these skills, the greater the possibility of stepping outside conventional discourses on child and youth development and moving beyond rights-based conversation to deeper investigations of development and identity as they relate to constructions of gender and sexuality.

Finally, the strategy of mapping sexuality and gender studies subject matter across the curriculum ensures that both key content and the development of skills necessary to fully explore this content are embedded in curriculum, rather than relying on individual instructors to include it. Working across the curriculum ensures learning is reinforced in multiple contexts, and increases the likelihood that students' diverse learning styles and needs will be met. It also demonstrates to learners that the content is critical to their learning, and illustrates that while faculty may differ in approach and perspective, we agree that these are topics worthy of serious study.

Using Constructivist Methods to Invite Engagement and Analysis

A constructivist approach to teaching about sexual and gender diversity requires curriculum that invites the participation of all learners while also engaging their critical analytical skills in the process of collaboratively constructing meaning. Even though we use a rights-based framework as an entry point into child and youth development studies, and students are aware that they are expected to behave in ways consistent with the student code of conduct and contribute to the creation of a positive learning environment, our queer pedagogy and constructivist methods require more from students than simple compliance with a human rights framework. Ford (2004) notes that a queer pedagogy avoids ready-made understandings, requiring students to "adopt a self-conscious, investigative stance toward the course content in order to regain their equilibrium and understanding" (p. 6). Learning activities that encourage reflexivity, collaboration, and shared construction of meaning are crucial. While a human rights framework provides a clear articulation of the rights to which all human beings, children included, are entitled, such a framework is not intended to assist in deeper-level exploration of difference and marginalized identities. Alexander (2008) cautions about teaching that leaves learners with flattened everyone-is-the-same understanding. We strive to prevent the kinds of erasure of difference that can occur when curriculum focuses on singular narratives of oppression, essentialized identities, and/or imposes homogenous views on vibrant, dynamic, and diverse movements of resistance.

While constructivist strategies lend themselves to noisy and sometimes chaotic classrooms, they also result in explorations that bring forward suppressed knowledge about gender and sexuality. While it is easier to rely on predetermined narratives, the rewards for trusting in learners' capacity to contribute to the construction of knowledge are immense. Learners in our classes are excited and even relieved at times to share stories, make observations, and convey bits of family history that have been irritating or disrupting their understandings of gender or sexuality for years, often since childhood. Their contributions include teachings received from Indigenous Elders about practices and ceremony that support children in creating gender identity as they grow; information about Hijra identities passed on by parents with varying perspectives on colonial governments' impositions of sodomy laws and restrictive gender practices; and tales of maiden aunts and bachelor uncles that challenge normative discourse on family structures in North America.

In addition to our responsibility to invite learners' lived experience and analysis into the centre of the classroom, we have an obligation as curriculum designers to ensure that multiple narratives of difference are woven through our course materials. Attempting to centralize the lived experience of people who may not be present in the room is a challenge, but it is critical to explorations of gender and sexual identity that challenge mainstream paradigms. While knowledge rooted in learners' lived experience is at the heart of a constructivist classroom, it is, at the same time, never acceptable to place learners whose voices are marginalized by the very theories we are critically investigating in the position of bearing the responsibility for educating the class. Incorporating methods that invite lived experience to the centre of the classroom is not the same thing as an instructor expecting marginalized learners to speak not only for themselves but for the complex and diverse communities they may (or may not) choose to identify with. It is also worth noting that we have learned to not make assumptions about who is in the room when it comes to student identities and histories.

When choosing materials to include in our curricula, we have learned to interrogate the academic training that has taught us to privilege text-based demonstrations of knowledge over other ways of knowing. We strive to centre the voices of children and youth as much as possible, looking far beyond textbooks for narratives that, when brought together for the brief period of time that our courses exist, have the capacity to illustrate spectra of gender and sexual diversity that vibrate with contradiction and concordance, that resound with voices emerging from multiple marginalized positionalities. These narratives can and do take the form of print, video, or digital media, and they can be introduced by instructors and by learners; for example, we have had success with creating assignments where small groups of learners collect and curate resources in small groups using social bookmarking programs. These materials do not need to be located in the classroom or cyberspace; learners have participated in Sisters in Spirit vigils, the annual rally and march for missing and murdered Indigenous women, Take Back the Night, and SlutWalk; attended Jules Koostachin's exhibit *Alive with Breath* (2014), which celebrates the lives of Mushkegowuk (Cree) Elders; the *Envisioning* exhibit (The Envisioning Project, 2010–2012) in which women with disabilities and physical differences present themselves using photography and digital media; and productions of Waawaate Fobister's *Agokwe* and Trey Anthony's *'da Kink in My Hair*.

It is not our intention in this chapter to allow our passion for our work to obscure the challenges of embracing constructivist methods rooted in queer pedagogy. The reality is that these methods produce, in both learners and educators, a range of emotions including discomfort, anxiety, guilt, frustration, and grief. Paying attention to the physical circumstances in which we work is beneficial: it helps to take breaks, to encourage students to move their bodies physically, to celebrate hard work with sensory treats such as sweets or essential oils for hand massage, and to provide aesthetically pleasing and stimulating visuals. We have been amazed at learners' capacity to be vulnerable with each other and with their capacity to create strategies for mutual care and support.

Challenges and Future Directions

In closing, we will elaborate on some ongoing challenges we face in facilitating shared learning on sexual and gender diversity in child and youth development classrooms. We will then conclude with a brief description of a paradigm shift currently underway in our program.

As educators, we understand that challenges are an inevitable consequence of our methods. The strategies and practices we employ are not always welcomed by students who have, for the most part, been schooled in a world of textbooks and multiple-choice quizzes. Some students will resist constructivist classroom activities, taking the position that their desire is not to deconstruct anything, but rather to study prescribed knowledge from assigned texts, and to reproduce it in conventional tests in order to acquire practical skills deemed essential for employment in the field. This position reflects the desires of a number of students, particularly at the time of entry, and is due, at least in part, to the huge costs of post-secondary education. Consequently, we walk a fine line between designing activities that encourage participation and respecting that for some learners classroom engagement will be minimal.

In addition to working with learners who do not anticipate benefitting from constructivist methods, our classes include students whose gender and/or sexual identities are systemically marginalized, and who may not wish to collaborate with learners whose self-definitions place them more comfortably into systemically constructed gender and sexual binaries. In our experience, some learners find working across such differences empowering, while others are irritated, frustrated, or silent. Other factors that affect their experience are the skills and knowledge of the other learners in their group, the design of the activity itself, and the instructor's ability to facilitate it. Given all of these variables, it is important learners have the choice to opt out of certain activities and to make up for any lost marks. In some instances learners will be in different places of understanding in relation to the deconstruction of marginalized knowledge. Queer and/or gender-independent learners may find they are held back from holding particular conversations in the larger group, and may want opportunities to work together on subject matter that engages them. On occasions when the instructor frames the conversation supportively, members from all social locations can benefit from witnessing discussions among queer and/or transgender learners about topics in their communities. We have found that maintaining a balance between supporting constructive learning through dialogue across difference, ensuring safer spaces for learners with marginalized identities, and maximizing each student's potential for learning is exciting and requires constant vigilance (Crabtree et al., 2009; Ayers, Quinn, & Stovall, 2009).

An ongoing challenge of a different nature is ensuring that the students in our program are reflective of the communities they will be working with. The rising financial cost of post-secondary education, coupled with the increasing reliance on degrees and professional accreditation in community and social service agencies and institutions (Willats, Bonisteel, & McLean, 2005) can have the effect of keeping students from marginalized populations shut out of the classroom and field placement opportunities. The subsequent homogenizing of identities in classrooms makes the kinds of dialogue and deconstruction we are advocating significantly more difficult.

As educators who choose to use constructivist methods and queer pedagogy, we expect to face disequilibrium and disruption in our thinking and practice. One profound consequence of adopting a constructivist methodology is the requirement that we continue to engage in the act of creating meaning alongside our students and in partnership with allied field organizations. This curriculum and partnership development is time- and resource-consuming. The inherent nature of academic institutions does not allow for the efforts required to collaboratively produce vibrant and flexible curricula.

Queer pedagogy requires reflexivity, demanding that we, as educators, look inward as well as outward (Bryson & de Castell, 1993). An inward gaze leads us to reflect on the uncomfortable reality that we are products of the same systems that have produced the rigid binaries we are engaged in deconstructing (Grace & Hill, 2001). The authors are FAAB (female assigned at birth), white and brown, straight and queer, able-bodied, and with layered, complex socio-economic class backgrounds and gender identities. We work in a staff team whose membership is diverse in racial, ethnic, and linguistic identities, and spans several sexual and gender identities, many socio-economic class positionalities, and a variety of abilities and disabilities. Therefore, we strive to check ourselves and each other to ensure that we do not replicate the same silencing and exclusionary tactics of the dominant culture.

It is not coincidental that while the authors of this chapter have participated in shaking the foundations of gender and sexuality studies in our program, the program has been undergoing a profound shift away from Eurocentric knowledge and methods, and toward Indigenous ways of knowing and worldviews. This paradigm shift began seven years ago (Bryson & de Castell, 1993), with the first formal work being the mapping of our curriculum for Indigenous content. The authors of this chapter, who claim non-Indigenous and settler identities, are engaged in the ongoing process of decolonizing our thinking, worldviews, and actions at the same time that we continue the life-long process of revising our understandings of gender and sexuality.

The project of decolonizing Eurocentric constructions of gender and sexual identity requires moving Indigenous worldviews of children's development, roles, and responsibilities to the centre of the child and youth development classroom. Looking to queer Indigenous movements and studies produces interesting results: Morgensen's (2010) assertion that the "sexual colonization of Native peoples produces modern sexuality as a function of settlement" (p. 105) turns on its head the Eurocentric notion that categories of sexual identity exist apart from history or politics. As we develop our understandings of Indigenous knowledge and culturally restorative practices in relation to children and youth (Simard & Blight, 2011), some of the questions making their way into our classes include the following: What does it look like to talk about the development of gender and sexuality when Indigenous ways of knowing frame the discussion? Would centring Indigenous teachings on lifespan development and the roles and responsibilities of children require us to shift our queer understandings of sex, sexuality, and gender? How does the colonization of Indigenous sexuality relate to theories of gender and sexual identity development? While we do not have fully formed responses to these questions, the learning we are doing in pursuit of answers inspires hope and excitement about possibilities for change and restorative practice. We look forward to future learning and dialogue with our colleagues and our students.

Notes

1. Our statements about lifespan development textbooks are not based on any rigorous hermeneutics/philology/linguistics research study. They are based on years of instructors in our program attempting to find a textbook to use. We have examined best-selling textbooks, textbooks publishers have sent us, and textbooks used in academic programs across Canada. In the process of writing this chapter, we revisited eight textbooks found in the George Brown College Library and in our program collection.

2. One creation of an Aboriginal worldview on development states, "Applying non-Aboriginal developmental theories with Aboriginal youth exclusively will not provide a complete or exact description nor will it show positive outcomes" (Simard & Blight, 2011, p. 32). In Anishinaabe culture(s) there is an honouring of a child's development that is non-linear, holistic, and flexible. Children are not measured against one another (Anderson, 2011; Simard & Blight, 2011).

References

Alexander, J. (2008, September). Queer pedagogy: Critical multiculturalism must avoid "the flattening effect." *College composition and communication.* Retrieved from cccc-blog.blogspot.ca/2008/09/queer-pedagogy-multiculturalism-must.html

Alive with Breath exhibit at Nippising University. (2014, January 22). Retrieved from www.nipissingu.ca/departments/external-relations/nunews/Jan-22-2014/Pages/-Alive-with-Breath-exhibit-at-NU.aspx

Almeida, R. V., Woods, R., & Messineo, T. (1998). Child development: Intersectionality of race, gender, class, and culture. *Journal of Feminist Family Therapy, 10*(1), 23–47.

American Psychological Association. (2012). Glossary of psychological terms. Retrieved from www.apa.org/research/action/glossary.aspx#d

Anderson, K. (2011). *Life stages and native women: Memories, teachings, and story medicine.* Winnipeg, MB: University of Manitoba Press.

Ayers, W., Quinn, T., Stovall, D. (Eds.) (2009). *Handbook of social justice in education.* New York, NY: Routledge.

Bandura, A. (1977). *Social learning theory.* Englewood Cliffs, NJ: Prentice-Hall.

Berk, L. E. (2012). Infants, children, and adolescents. Boston, MA: Pearson Educational.

Bilodeau, B. L., & Renn, K. A. (2005) Analysis of LGBT identity development models and implications for practice. In R. L. Sanlo (Ed.), *Sexual orientation and gender identity: Research, policy and personal perspectives: New directions for student services 111* (pp. 25–39). San Francisco, CA: Wiley.

Boyd, D., Johnson, P., & Bee, H. (2012). *Lifespan development.* Toronto, ON: Pearson Education Canada.

Bronfenbrenner, U., & Morris, P. A. (2006). The bioecological model of human development. In W. Damon & R. M. Lerner (Series Eds.) & R. M. Lerner (Volume Ed.), *Handbook of child psychology: Vol. 1, Theoretical models of human development* (6th ed., pp. 793–828). Hoboken, NJ: Wiley.

Bryson, M., & de Castell, S. (1993). Queer pedagogy: Praxis makes im/perfect. *Canadian Journal of Education*, 18(2), 285–305.

Cannon, M. (2012). The regulation of First Nations sexuality. In M. FitzGerald & S. Rayter (Eds.), *Queerly Canadian: An introductory reader in sexuality studies* (pp. 51–64). Toronto, ON: Canadian Scholars' Press.

Crabtree, R. D., Sapp, D. A., & Licona, A. C. (2009). *Feminist pedagogy: Looking back to move forward*. Baltimore, MD: Johns Hopkins University Press.

Davis, A. (1990). *Women, culture and politics*. New York, NY: Random House.

Davies, S. (2010). *Gender diversity in Indonesia: Sexuality, Islam and queer selves* (ASAA Women in Asia Series). New York, NY: Routledge.

Driskill, Q., Justice, D. H., Miranda, D., & Tatonetti, L. (Eds.) (2011). *Sovereign erotics: A collection of two-spirit literature*. Tucson, AZ: University of Arizona Press.

Erikson, E. (1950). *Childhood and society*. New York, NY: Norton.

Ford, T. (2004). Queering education from the ground up: Challenges and opportunities for educators. *Canadian Online Journal of Queer Studies in Education*, 1(1). Retrieved from jqstudies.library.utoronto.ca/index.php/jqstudies/article/view/3273

Foucault, M. (1990). *The history of sexuality. Volume one: An introduction*. New York, NY: Vintage Books.

Freud, S. (1923). *The ego and the id*. London, England: Hogarth.

Galliano, G. (2002). *Gender: Crossing boundaries*. Belmont, CA: Wadsworth.

George Brown College. (2012). Code of conduct and discipline policy. Retrieved from tinyurl.com/brvazfj

Gezinski, L. (2009). Addressing sexual minority issues in social work education: a curriculum framework. *Advances in Social Work*, 10(1), 103–113.

Gillian, C. E. (1982). *In a different voice*. Cambridge, MA: Harvard University Press.

Grace, A. P., & Hill, R. J. (2001). Using queer knowledges to build inclusionary pedagogy in adult education. Paper presented at the Annual Meeting of the Adult Education Research Conference, Lansing, MI. Retrieved from www.eric.ed.gov/PDFS/ED481587.pdf

Hill Collins, P. (1990). *Black feminist thought: Knowledge, consciousness and the politics of empowerment*. Boston, MA: Unwin Hyman.

Jacobs, S. E., Thomas, W., & Lang, S. (Eds.) (1997). *Two-Spirit, Two-spirit People: Native American Gender Identity, Sexuality, and Spirituality*. Champaign, IL: University of Illinois Press.

Koyama, E. (2003). Teaching intersex issues: A guide for teachers in women's, gender and queer studies. Intersex Initiative Portland. Retrieved from eminism.org/store/pdf-zn/ipdx-teacher.pdf

Lather, P. (1991). *Getting smart: Feminist research and pedagogy with/in the postmodern*. New York, NY: Routledge.

Lorde, A. (1984). "The Master's tools will never dismantle the master's house." In A. Lorde, *Sister outsider* (pp. 110–113). Freedom, CA: Crossing Press.

Malinowitz, H. (1995). *Textual orientations: Lesbian and gay students and the making of discourse communities*. Portsmouth, NH: Heinemann.

Matlin, M. W. (2012). *The psychology of women*. Belmont, CA: Wadsworth.

McLean, M. (2007). Weaving a knowledge web: Students document the impact of violence of their learning. Unpublished raw data. Toronto, ON.

Morgensen, S. (2010). Settler homonationalism: Theorizing settler colonialism within queer modernities. *GLQ: A Journal of lesbian and gay studies, 16*(1/2), 105–131.

Morgensen, S. (2011). *Queer settler colonialism and Indigenous decolonization*. Minneapolis, MN: University of Minnesota Press.

Narayan, U. (1989). The project of feminist epistemology: Perspectives from a nonwestern feminist. In A. M. Jaggar & S. R. Bordo (Eds.), *Gender/Body/Knowledge: Feminist reconstructions of being and knowing* (pp. 256–269). New Brunswick, NJ: Rutgers University Press.

Piaget, J. (1971). *Biology and knowledge*. Chicago, IL: University of Chicago Press.

Reddy, G. (2005), *With respect to sex: Negotiating Hijra identity in South India*. Chicago, IL: University of Chicago.

Rupp, L. (2009). *Sapphistries: A global history of love between women*. New York, NY: New York University Press.

Serano, J. (2007). *Whipping girl: A Transsexual woman on sexism and the scapegoating of femininity*. Emoryville, CA: Seals Press.

Shaffer, D. R., Kipp, K., Wood, E., & Willoughby, T. (2012). *Developmental psychology: Childhood and adolescence* (4th ed.). Toronto, ON: Nelson College Indigenous.

Simard, E., & Blight, S. (2011). Developing a culturally restorative approach to Aboriginal child and youth development: Transitions to adulthood. *First Peoples Child and Family Review, 6*(1), 28–55.

Smith, A. (2006). *Color of violence: The INCITE! anthology*. Cambridge, MA: South End Press.

Swanson, K. (2012). The noble savage was a drag queen: Hybridity and transformation in Kent Monkman's performance and visual art interventions. In M. FitzGerald & S. Rayter (Eds.) *Queerly Canadian: An introductory reader in sexuality studies* (pp. 565–576). Toronto, ON: Canadian Scholars' Press.

Taulapapa, D. (2011). Fa'afafine notes: On Tagaloa, Jesus, and Nafanua. In Q. Driskill, C. Finley, B. J. Gilley, & S. L. Morgensen (Eds.), *Queer Indigenous studies: Critical interventions in theory, politics, and literature* (pp. 81–94). Tucson, AZ: University of Arizona Press.

The Envisioning Project. (2010–2012). Envisioning new meanings of disability and difference. Retrieved from www.envisioningnewmeanings.ca/?page_id=2.

Thelen, E., & Smith, L. B. (2006). Dynamic systems theories. In W. Damon & R. M. Lerner (Series Eds.) & R. M. Lerner (Volume Ed.), *Handbook of child psychology: Vol. 1. Theoretical models of human development* (6th ed., pp. 258–312). Hoboken, NJ: Wiley.

UNICEF. (n.d.) Photo essay: The rights of the child. Retrieved from www.unicef.org/photoessays/30048.html

United Nations General Assembly. (1989, November 20). Convention on the Rights of the Child. Retrieved from www.icrc.org/ihl/INTRO/540?OpenDocument

United Nations. (2012). Born free and equal: Sexual orientation and gender identity in international human rights law. Human Rights Office of the High Commissioner. Retrieved from www.ohchr.org/Documents/Publications/BornFreeAndEqualLowRes.pdf

Vanessa. (2009). *Memoirs of a Samoan, Catholic, and Fa'afafine*. Baltimore, MD: Publish America.

Vygotsky, L. S. (1992). *Educational psychology*. Boca Raton, FL: St. Lucie Press. (Original work published 1926.)

Whalen, M. (1996). *Counseling to end violence against women: A model for working with battered women*. Thousand Oaks, CA: Sage.

Wilchins, R.A. (2002). Queerer bodies. In J. Nestle, C. Howell, & R. A. Wilchins (Eds.), *Genderqueer: Voices from beyond the sexual binary* (pp. 33–47). Los Angeles, CA: Allyson.

Willats A., Bonisteel, M., & McLean, M. (2005). The struggle to maintain grassroots feminist responses to male violence. *New Socialist, 53*, 16–18.

CONTRIBUTOR BIOGRAPHIES

Mandy Bonisteel, RN, is the coordinator of the Assaulted Women's and Children's Counsellor/Advocate Program at George Brown College and is the director of Program Development at Respect-At-Work. Throughout her career, she has focused primarily on anti-violence work. Mandy also founded the Sexual Assault Centre for Quinte and District in Ontario and has been involved in numerous local and international social justice training and education initiatives. She is a recipient of the Colleges Ontario Premier's Award and the Ontario Medal for Good Citizenship. Mandy is a lesbian parent of two grown children and a grandparent of one.

Mirna E. Carranza, RSW, MTS, PhD, is an associate professor in the School of Social Work at McMaster University. Her primary research interest is individual and collective trauma in immigrant and refugee groups and the effects of trauma on acculturation processes, family dynamics, and community organizing. Her research also explores forced migration for the purpose of commercial sexual exploitation of children (CSEC) in Central American countries and the Caribbean basin. Her research methodology includes participatory community-based and grounded theory approaches and is informed by human rights, social justice, and anti-colonial perspectives. Mirna has worked as a family therapist with immigrant and refugee families for more than 20 years and is also an advocate and community organizer.

Diana Coholic, MSW, PhD, is a clinical social worker and director and associate professor in the School of Social Work at Laurentian University in Sudbury. Since 2007 she and her research team have been studying the benefits and effectiveness of arts-based mindfulness group methods for the improvement of resilience and self-concept in vulnerable children. This applied research has been conducted in collaboration with the local child protection and children's mental health agencies. Diana is an experienced qualitative researcher interested in utilizing creative methodologies. More information about her research (including publications and links to films) can be found at www.dianacoholic.com.

Soni Dasmohapatra, BA, is a longtime advocate for human rights and the advancement of women, children, youth, and minority communities. Her 20-year career path has focused on immigration, social determinants of health, mental health, early childhood development, youth engagement/participation/employment, gender equity, social justice, advocacy, human rights, child welfare, poverty reduction, and Indigenous communities. From government to non-profit agencies, from policy think tanks to the classroom, Soni has been an educator, community developer, strategic planner, and researcher. She currently lives in Toronto with her husband and two children.

Ron Goodine, MEd, is a licensed counsellor and has been working with clients in the Vancouver area for over 15 years. He has been active in the LGBT community and recently facilitated a bisexual support group. His interests include queer theory and the creation of a more inclusive and fluid narrative to explore and understand sexuality and gender.

Wendy Hulko, MSW, PhD, is an associate professor in the School of Social Work and Human Service at Thompson Rivers University. She is also affiliated with the Institute for Intersectionality Research and Policy at Simon Fraser University and with two interdisciplinary research units at the University of British Columbia. Her teaching includes social work courses on theory and ideology, research, aging, and sexual orientation and gender expression, as well as a graduate-level education course on diversity and equity. Wendy also leads a field school in Cuba and conducts research on aging and health in collaboration with equity-seeking groups, including queer youth and older adults.

Hossein Kia, MSW, has close to five years of social work experience, both in clinical and academic roles. Currently, he is pursuing doctoral studies at the University of Toronto's Dalla Lana School of Public Health. His research interests centre on applying a framework of intersectionality to examine the health and social service needs of lesbian, gay, bisexual, and transgender adults.

Andrea Lagios, MSW, was a research assistant at Ryerson University at the time of contributing to this chapter. Andrea is a social work practitioner in Toronto and currently works in the community health sector with marginalized women and their children. She has worked in various settings, both in Toronto and overseas, in the fields of health, mental health, human trafficking, child protection, and settlement, and has also completed research around the topic of forced migration.

Bill Lee, DASW, EdD, is an associate professor (retired) in the School of Social Work at McMaster University and is the author or co-author of three books and a number of articles on community organization and development. His teaching, practice, and research have focused on community organization in a range of populations in Canada and internationally. He has worked with various Indigenous groups in Canada, including community development training with Anishnawbe Health Toronto; he has also worked with environmental groups in El Salvador, and women's groups in Uganda.

David Lewis-Peart, HSC, MES, is a graduate of George Brown College and York University, where his research focused on community interventions, qualitative research methods, and sexual minority Black youth. Trained in human services counselling with a specialization in mental health, David has worked in frontline social service delivery for nearly a decade. David was previously the Research and Prevention Program coordinator with the Black Coalition for AIDS Prevention and is the principal investigator on Toronto's first evidence-based community-level HIV prevention intervention for gay Black males, entitled Many Men, Many Voices. This initiative is supported by the Ontario HIV

Treatment Network and the Canadian Institute for Health Research Social Research Centre in HIV Prevention Student/Trainee Award.

Sheri M. McConnell, MSW, PhD, is a field education coordinator at the Memorial University School of Social Work, where she teaches courses in social work practice and provides field instruction in community agencies. Her research interests include child sexual abuse, disclosure, field education, and all things LGBTQ. She has worked with women in conflict with the law, individuals affected by substance abuse, the LGBTQ community, and women who were sexually abused as children. Each summer, Sheri, an out butch lesbian, brings her experience in group work, psychodrama, and sociometry to Camp Eclipse: Out in the Woods, a leadership retreat for LGBTQ youth and their allies.

Susan McGrath, CM, PhD, is a professor in the School of Social Work at York University. Her areas of research include community organizing and refugee studies. For over 15 years she has been working with a network of researchers on issues of marginalization and community development with refugee, Aboriginal, and LGBT populations. Susan has extensive experience in social work practice in direct service and in the management of agencies. She leads a global Refugee Research Network that seeks to create knowledge to benefit people who have been forcibly displaced. In recognition of her contributions to social work and refugee studies, McGrath was made a member of the Order of Canada in 2015.

Marilyn McLean, MA, is a faculty member in the Assaulted Women's and Children's Counsellor/Advocate Program at George Brown College. She teaches courses on gender studies, critical resistance, and the impact of interpersonal and systemic violence on children and youth. Her research has explored the relationship between learning and violence, the desires and concerns of queer youth in academic settings, and the use of collaborative and collective approaches in the creation of liberationist movements. Her work has been rooted in an ongoing process of deconstructing her own white privilege and settler identity. She is a recipient of the Province of Ontario Leadership in Faculty Teaching Award.

Jeffrey J. McNeil-Seymour, MSW, recently completed his degree in the Social Justice and Equity specialization at the Factor-Inwentash Faculty of Social Work at the University of Toronto. Jeffrey is currently working for Aboriginal Legal Services of Toronto as a Gladue Caseworker, writing reports at the request of defence counsel, the Crown Attorney, or the judge, on the life circumstances of Aboriginal offenders. Jeffrey also sits as a board member at Two-Spirited People of the First Nations, Toronto.

Ken Moffatt, MSW, PhD, is a professor in the School of Social Work at Ryerson University and in the Communication and Culture Program, a joint program between Ryerson University and York University. He is the editor of *Troubled Masculinities: Re-imagining Urban Men* (University of Toronto Press, 2011). His research interests include gender and queer studies, cultural studies and social work, and the influence of the new managerialism on social work education.

Nick J. Mulé, MSW, PhD, is an associate professor at the York University School of Social Work, where he teaches policy, theory, and practice. His research interests include the social inclusion/exclusion of LGBTQ populations in social policy and service provision and the degree of their recognition as distinct communities in cultural, systemic, and structural contexts. He also engages in critical analysis of the LGBTQ movement and the development of queer liberation theory. A queer activist for many years, Nick is also a psychotherapist in private practice, serving LGBTQ populations in Toronto.

D. Margo Nelson, MSW, PhD, is an instructor at Langara College in the Department of Health Sciences and in the Social Service Worker Program. Her teaching, practice, and research have employed a developmental and human rights approach to children's well-being and social service practice with children and families. Her areas of research and practice include Aboriginal child welfare, diversity and equity in sexual health education, and adolescent/parent transitions to secondary school.

Brian J. O'Neill, MSW, PhD, is an associate professor at the University of British Columbia School of Social Work. His teaching and research have focused on intersecting forms of structural oppression, particularly heterosexism in the delivery of social services. He has explored settlement services in relation to LGB newcomers, evaluated methods in inter-professional education regarding practice with people living with HIV, and looked at social work education from the standpoint of gay men. He also provides counselling to gay and bisexual men regarding a range of mental health and relationship issues.

Norma Jean Profitt, MSW, PhD, presently serves as the Women's Services Coordinator, Mental Health and Addiction Services in Yarmouth, Nova Scotia. She has a long history of involvement in women's issues and feminist movements in Nova Scotia and Costa Rica, particularly regarding forms of violence against women. From 1999 to 2011 she was an associate professor in the School of Social Work at St. Thomas University, where she taught the Women and Social Work course and developed the first course on social work and gay, lesbian, bisexual, and Two-Spirit peoples. Her current research interests include women, substance use, and gender violence as well as the intersection of institutional, socio-political, and relational trauma.

Jake Pyne, MSW, is a PhD student in Social Work and Gender Studies at McMaster University, where he also holds a Trudeau Scholarship and a Vanier Scholarship. For the past 14 years, his community work has focused on trans communities' access to homeless and anti-violence services, health care, and family law justice. Most recently, he has led a number of initiatives to build resources and supports for families with gender non-conforming children. Jake's research interests focus on how different knowledge systems, including biomedical and psychiatric knowledge and queer and feminist theory, both foreclose and create opportunities for gender non-conforming people.

Andrea Ridgley, MSW, is currently a professor and online course developer in the Assaulted Women's and Children's Counsellor/Advocate Program at George Brown College in Toronto. She is an advocate, activist, resource developer, community researcher, and counsellor. Her fields of interest include neighbourhood health, LGBT and Two-Spirit communities, HIV, youth engagement, and community-based participatory action research. Andrea is also an event producer and back-up dancer for several of her talented friends.

Marie-Jolie Rwigema, MSW, is a doctoral student in the Faculty of Social Work at the University of Toronto and holds a Bachelor of Arts (honours) in African Studies and International Development Studies from York University. She is a community- and arts-based educator, a social work course instructor, and a documentary filmmaker. Marie-Jolie's doctoral research examines the racialized politics of knowledge production about the 1994 Rwandan genocide and resistant knowledge traditions within survivor communities. She is also active in a number of local and global LGBTTQQI research projects, including research examining the sexual health of queer women in Toronto and queer youth experiences of bullying.

X. Sly Sarkisova, MSW, is a Toronto-based queer and trans-identified psychotherapist who has been working in the field of mental health and addictions counselling for the past 14 years, first in occupied Musqueam, Tsleil-Waututh, and Squamish territories (Downtown Eastside, Vancouver) and now in Mississauga and Anishinaabe territories (Regent Park, Toronto). He works to create a safe space for folks who are managing inadequate systemic responses to trauma, mental health, and substance use, and who experience structural poverty and oppression related to race, class, ability, sexuality, gender diversity, and indigeneity. He brings a deeply structural, pro-survivor lens to his work.

Lawrence Shapiro, MA, is a disability rights activist and author whose writing on sexual diversity and disability has appeared in a number of academic journals, including *Disability Studies Quarterly* in the United States as well as European publications. Lawrence studied at Ryerson University's School of Disability Studies and has taught at many different universities in the developing world. From 2009 to 2010 he served as a visiting researcher on disability at the School of Oriental and African

Studies at the University of London, and in 2014 he was selected to speak on the issue of homo-ableism at the World Pride Human Rights Conference. Lawrence is a proud member of the Sexual Health and Disability Alliance and is passionately committed to the sexual liberation of people with disabilities.

Louise Stern, MSW, PhD, is a professor in the Faculty of Health and Human Services at Vancouver Island University where she teaches in the Social Service Diploma Program and the BSW program. Prior to this, she worked for 20 years as a practising social worker in the field of aging. This experience has informed her research and teaching interests, which focus on aging and diversity issues, inter-professional education and practice within gerontology and health care, inter-cultural practice, and mental health issues related to an aging demographic.

Tracy Swan, MSW, PhD, was an associate professor in the School of Social Work at Memorial University until her retirement on August 31, 2014, near the completion of this book. She has extensive experience teaching critical and anti-oppressive approaches to social work practice and critical analysis of theory in undergraduate and graduate programs. Her research has focused on foster caregivers' experiences of caring for sexually abused girls, the well-being of caregivers' own children, and lone mothers who struggle with poverty. Tracy employs feminist participatory methods that involve collaboration with research participants in creative approaches to disseminate findings, like popular theatre. She is an active agent of change in the academy and the community regarding intersecting LGBT issues, and has been involved in field education throughout her professional career.

Sarah Todd, MSW, EdD, is an associate professor in the School of Social Work at Carleton University. Her teaching and research has focused around the areas of community, sexuality, and pedagogy. Recently she was engaged in a project with colleagues from Ryerson University exploring how new managerialism is reshaping progressive social work education. She also writes in the areas of post-structural theory and its use in social work education and practice.

Onyinyechukwu Udegbe is the founder of the Disabled Young People's Project, where she works with disabled youth of colour. Her work in community development sectors includes policy, evaluation, and direct service provision in and with diverse marginalized populations including youth and folks with disabilities, as well as race, immigration, and gender-based violence. Onyinyechukwu took on issues of disability, race, sexuality, and representation in her video short *Everyday Monsters*, which was screened at the 2009 Inside Out Festival in Toronto.

Arkell Aislinn Wiley, MSW, is a Youth Clinician at the Northern Health Authority in Prince George, BC. His research focuses on the effectiveness of meditation and visualization for mental health and well-being, as well as the use of arts-based research methods in highlighting subjective experiences. Since settling in northern BC, he has been involved in the grassroots development of LGBTQ support services in his community.

Index

Page numbers followed by n refer to notes

ableism
    and homo-ableism, 57–58, 64
    hostile ableism, 59
    prejudice in minority groups, 61
    and sexuality, 158, 160–161, 164
Aboriginal peoples
    and collective trauma, 214
    "coming in," 96
    cross-dancing, 90–92, 96, 101–102
    cultural remembrance, 91–92
    diversity of Two-Spirit identity interpretations, 88
    heteropatriarchy, 91, 95
    imposition of colonial identities, 6–7, 88, 92
    nationhood empowerment, 102–103
    pow-wows, 89–90
    racism, 256
    residential school experience, 95–96
    Ske'lep, trickster figure, 92–93
    Two-Spirit identity study, 93–96
    worldview on child and youth development, 364–365, 377n2
    youth, role models for, 98–99
    See also Two-Spirit identity
acceptance, by assimilation, 17, 26
accessibility issues, and disability, 57–58
advocacy
    of critical social worker, 31, 32
    for LGBTQ youth, 181, 186
    and neoliberal governance of non-profits and charities, 24–25, 32n1
    for older LGBTQ adults, 80–81
    politicization of LGBTTTSQ community, 217–218
    and social justice, 353
    See also politicized queers

Africa, history of queerness, 45–46
Afrocentric spirituality, 46, 49–50
age
    and informal caregiving, 8, 156–157, 163–164
    as social location, 19
ageism
    and homophobia, 75–78
    and informal caregiving, 166
    invisibility of sexuality, 67–69, 75–78
    resistance to, 80–82
    and sexuality, stigmatization of, 77–78
    against youth, 181
agency (personal)
    development of in service recipients, 29
    of queer Black youth, 41
    queer liberation perspective, 30, 32
    of trans women, 140
agency policy(ies). *See* policy making
agendered, 271n2
aging, 67–86
    Baby Boomer cohort, 72
    CARP (Canadian Association of Retired Persons), 81
    categorization of LGBT adults, 72–75, 80, 82
    as cultural construct, 75–76
    experiential differences between lesbians and gay men, 78–79
    gerontological research, 73–75, 81–82
    intersectionality, and intra-category diversity, 69–70
    invisibility of LGBTQ seniors, 6, 67–69, 73–75
    non-heterosexual experiences of, 6

SAGE (Services and Advocacy for GLBT Elders), 80–81
senior pride networks, 81
sexuality, invisibility of, 67–69, 76–77
socio-historical context of invisibility, 70–72
Agokwe (Fobister), 373
AIDS. *See* HIV/AIDS
AIDS Action Now, 218
AIDS Committee of Toronto, 219
alcohol use, 120
Alexander, J., 371
AmericaBlog.com, 117
androgynous, 271n2
androgyny, 134
Anthony, Trey, *'da Kink in My Hair*, 373
anti-categorical approach to sexuality, 111
anti-homophobia workshops, 45–46
anti-oppressive practice (AOP)
    Christian fundamentalism, and sexuality, 277
    critical reflection, 345–347
    critical reflexivity, 343–347
    in field instruction, 345–347, 351–352, 354
    and queer theory, 288–291
    spirituality in classroom dynamic, 278–280
anxiety, 40, 120, 262
appropriation, of Two-Spirit concept, 99–100
Aravois, John, 117
Archie, Carl, 92
artistic expression in disabled community, 61–63
arts-based inquiry, 317–338
    activity book, 322
    Arkell's image, 330–331
    Corey's image, 324–326
    Elijah's image, 326–327
    findings and analysis, 323–332
    intersectionality of gender identity, 331–332

invisibility of transgender issues, 11
    recommendations, 334–336
    research method, 320–323
Asian Community AIDS Service, 219
Assaulted Women's and Children's Counsellor/Advocate Program (AWCCA), 362
    Child and Youth Development: Gender Identity course, 364
    textbook survey, 364–365, 376n1
    topics, 363
assimilation
    as acceptance seeking, 17
    impact of media on, 97
    resistance to, 61–62
    same-sex disability relationships, 60
attachment theory, 90–91, 102
autoethnography, 322
Axtell, Sara, 60

Baby Boomers, aging experience, 72
Bailey, J. M., 118–119
Baldwin, James, 56
Bauer, G. R., 333, 334
BC Adolescent Health Survey, 195
Beauvoir, Simone de, *The Second Sex*, 137
Berube, Allan, 100
bigenders, 318
biphobia, 19, 119, 123n5, 196
bisexuality, 37, 107–126
    acceptance of, 119
    and AIDS crisis, 108–109
    axes of definition, 109
    binegativity, 119, 123n5
    and coming out, 108–110
    and disabled community, 54–55
    in dominant culture research, 117–119
    erasure of, 7, 107, 111–114, 121–122
    gerontological research, 75
    health care impact, 120–121
    invalidation of by psychology, 108
    invisibility of, 115–116
    marginalization stressors, 120–121
    and monosexuality, 112–114

population studies, conflation of, 119–120
theoretical considerations, 111–112
bisexual women
  in geographic location scholarship, 193–194, 209n3
  invisibility, and geographic location, 8–9
  safety in educational settings, 199–200
Black Coalition for Aids Prevention (Black CAP), 218, 219
body image
  preoccupation with in gay culture, 54–57
  youth-centric nature of LGBTQ community, 77–78
Bogo, M., 306
Boler, Megan, 285, 292
Bonisteel, Mandy, 12, 361–381
Boyce, M., 333, 334
bridging, 47–49
British Columbia, immigrant settlement experiences, 233–253
  research design, and participant selection, 236–238
Britzman, D., 292
bullying, 176, 186, 199, 280
Burdge, B., 318
Burstow, B., 215, 226

Calabai identity, 365
Calalai identity, 365
Campaign for Equal Families, 218
Canada
  bureaucratization of non-profit sector, 22
  Canadian Human Rights Act, 178, 179
  Charter of Rights and Freedoms, 1, 178, 179, 233, 235, 307
  immigration policy, 236
  Multiculturalism Act (1985), 233
  provincial human rights legislation, 179–181

refugee determination system, 236
trans activism, history of, 134
Canada Council for the Arts, 62
Canadian Association for Social Work Education
  Mission Statement, 336
  Standards for Accreditation, 292, 298, 307
Canadian Association of Social Workers
  Code of Ethics, 185–187, 334
caregiving, informal, 8, 151–171
  ableism, and sexuality, 158, 160–161, 164
  caregivers as decision-makers, 167
  caregiver support, 80, 159–160, 161, 162
  choice, perceptions of, 161–162
  commitment considerations, 155–157
  by family members, 76, 152, 167
  and geographic location, 158–159, 164–165
  homophobia, experiences of, 153, 156–158, 162, 164, 166
  instrumental support, 159
  intersectionality of structural factors, 165–166
  literature gaps, 152–153
  spousal priority, and families of choice, 76–77
  stress and burden theory, 8, 152–153, 158, 162–163
  in Western welfare states, 151–152
  See also caregiving study (Kia)
caregiving study (Kia)
  chronic illness, and informal caregiving, 156–161
  constructivist epistemological position, 154–168
  experiences of homophobia, 156–158, 162, 164
  factors affecting caregivers, 162
  findings, 161–166
  implications for social work practice, 166–168

intersectionality in analysis of
findings, 163–165
narrative analysis model, 155–156
research participants, 154–156
Carey, Benedict, "Straight, Gay or Lying?
Bisexuality Revisited," 118
caring professions, "business model" vs.
"community-based model," 22–23
CARP (Canadian Association of Retired
Persons), Pink Chapter, 81
Carranza, Mirna, 9, 213–232
Case, P., 120
categorization
of LGBTQ seniors, 72–75, 82
resistance to, 80
Centre for Addiction and Mental Health
(CAMH), 264
Chapman, C., 282, 346
charities, neoliberal funding regulations,
24–25, 32n1
Charter of Rights and Freedoms, 1, 178,
179, 235, 307
child and youth development courses, 12,
361–381
Aboriginal worldview of, 364–365,
376n2
anti-violence counselling education,
362
curriculum materials, choosing,
372–373
decolonizing perspectives in, 375–376
design and delivery challenges, 361
employment considerations in
course choice, 373
field work, 362
foundational strategies, 367–370
future directions, 373–376
gender, in sexual diversity
curriculum, 361
homogenizing of identities in
classrooms, 374–375
opt out option, 374
textbook survey, 364–365, 376n1
Child and Youth Development: Gender
Identity course, 364

Children's Aid Society of Toronto
(CAST)
service provision policy framework,
186–187
child welfare practice, 173–192
and attachment theory, 90–91
developmental needs of child,
183–184
ethical practice, 185–187
ethic of care, principles of, 182–183
feminist ethic of care, 8
foster home placements, 176
gender identity formation,
183–184
heteronormative assumptions, 186
minority-related stress, 176
out-of-home care, 188
provincial human rights legislation,
179–181
recognition of LGBTQ youth, 184
risk profiles, factors affecting, 173,
175–177
youth/family support, 187
Chivers, M. L., 118
Christian fundamentalism
discrimination, and religious
freedom, 307
discrimination against in social
work, 279–280
fundamentalism, described, 279,
293n2
intersection with queer identities,
283–284
as masculine hegemony, 279
non-discrimination standard,
exemptions from, 278–279
and sexuality, 277
silence, and student engagement,
286–288
social work as spiritual "calling,"
280–281
spirituality in classroom dynamic,
277–280
chronic illness, and informal caregiving,
156–161

cisgenderism, 19, 101, 175
    cisgender, defined, 13n2, 122n2
    and gender binary, 257, 271n5
    and trans health care, 263–266, 272n9
    and trans women, 129
class, and classism, 341
    and culture of whiteness, 19
    and feminization of social work profession, 22
    and gender identity, 109–110
    against Two-Spirit people, 93, 94
classroom dynamic
    anti-oppressive practice (AOP) approaches, 278–280
    compromise in inclusiveness, 278–279
    constructivist methodologies, 363
    fundamentalist vs. queer students, tension between, 280, 281
    group-process skills, 367, 369–370
    human rights-based policies, and positive space practices, 367, 368–369
    interpersonal communication, 367, 369–370
    intersectionality, and queer theory, 292–293
    intersectionality of interlocking oppressions, 281–284
    safety of, 304–305
    of self-disclosure, 306
    silence, and student engagement, 277, 286–288
    small-group work, 287–288
    spirituality in, 278–280
    students participation in acceptance of oppression, 282–283
    students self-implication in oppression, 298
Code of Ethics (CASW), 334
Coholic, Diana, 10, 277–293
collaborative community practice, 9
collective trauma, 9, 213–232
    effects of, 215–216
    and group solidarity, 216, 224–225, 226, 227–228
    and HIV/AIDS, 221, 222–223
    implications for social work practice, 227–228
    as political phenomenon, 226
    public awareness, 227–228
    and recovery, 216, 225
    research method, 219–220
    and resilience, 225–226
    retraumatization risk, 227
    as shared experience, 213–216, 220–226
    social relations of dominance, 228
    sources of, 221, 223–224
    transnational impacts of, 221–222
Colligan, Sumi Elaine, 54–55
colonialism
    as creation of separations, 46–47
    decolonizing perspectives, in settler discourse, 101
    imposition of colonial identities, 6–7
    residential school experience, 95–96
    sexuality as function of settlement, 376
    in suppression of gender and sexuality, 367
    and white supremacy, 46–47, 50
coming out
    Aboriginal experience, 94
    as act of bravery, 108
    age of disclosure, 184
    and bisexuality, 108–110
    and "coming in," 96
    conflict with invisibility, 342–343
    and family rejection, 173, 176, 188–189, 201, 239, 243
    Out and Proud program, 186–187
    and queer youth, 38
    and resilience, 79
    self-identification, 109, 122n2, 184, 239
    support services, 23
commercialization of media-created popular gay culture, 19–20

communities of affinity
    and collective trauma, 9
    role models, and mentors, 207–208
    as support for queer youth, 200–205
    See also families of choice
community, impact on queer youth, 196, 197
community-based alliances, 207
community spaces, racial segregation in, 45–47
Compton Cafeteria Riot, 134
conservatism, role in shaping schools of social work, 307–308
constructivism
    approach to teaching, 370–373
    and informal caregiving, 162–163
    of sexuality and gender identity, 112
    student resistance to, 373
Convention on the Rights of Persons with Disabilities, 53
coping mechanisms, 40–41
    and resilience, 79–80
Council on Social Work Education (CSWE)
    non-discrimination standard exemptions, 278–279
counselling psychology, 2
counselling services, 23
Cox, Laverne, 138
Craigslist, 203
critical empathy, 12, 346, 347, 354
critical reflexivity
    in field instruction, 348
    and intersectionality, 343–347
critical social work approach
    advocacy in, 31, 32
    responsibilities of informed practice, 28–31
critical thinking
    and intersectionality, 291–292
    and queer theory, 300–301
Critical Thinking Community, 292
cross-dance, 89
    as culturally restorative practice, 90–92, 96, 101–102

cross-dressers, 318
cross-gender affiliation, 262
culturally restorative practice, 7
    cross-dancing, 90–92, 101–102
    and cultural safety, 102

'da Kink in My Hair (Anthony), 373
Daley, A., 306
Daly, Mary, 135
Dasmohapatra, Soni, 12, 361–381
David, S., 74
Day of Silence, 204–205
DeLamater, J. D., 111–112
delegitimization, 113
depression, 38, 40, 120, 262
developmental psychology, and lifespan development, 364
deviantart, 203
Dickey, G., 75
disability, 53–65
    accessibility issues, 5, 57–58, 64
    artistic expression in disabled community, 61–63
    definitions of, 53–54
    and gay culture, 54
    and homo-ableism, 55–56, 64
    identity, and social function, 54–55
    learned political correctness, 58–59
    Queer Disability Conference (2002), 53, 54
    queer youth with disabilities, 37, 189
    same-sex relationships, 60
    and sexual functioning, 60–61
    and sexuality, 5–6, 54–55
    sexual violence against, 58
    Sins Invalid, 62–63
    and social integration, 58
    as social location, 19
    unemployment rate, 58
disability rights movement, 53, 54
Disability Studies Quarterly, 54
discrimination
    heterosexism, 174–175
    against LGB immigrants/refugees, 240–241

in LGBT communities, 19
sexuality- and gender-based, 235
Drabinski, K., 301–302
Driskill, Qwo-Li, 91, 92
DSM-III
  homosexuality as psychiatric diagnosis, 23, 71
Dubowski, Andi Simcha, *Trembling Before G-D*, 283
Dworkin, Andrea, 135

educational settings (high schools, universities)
  anti-bullying policies, 208
  citizenship development of queer youth, 38
  Day of Silence, 204–205
  GSAs (gay/straight alliances), 196, 197
  heteronormativity in, 307–309
  heterosexism of students, 305–306
  learned political correctness, 58–59
  on-campus queer student club, 198
  pride clubs, 200
  queer-positive teacher mentors, 208
  safety and acceptance in, 199–200, 280, 304–305
  Social Justice (SJ), 12, 197–198, 206, 208
  as support for queer youth, 204–205
Egale Canada, 208
elitism, of gay white men, 55, 56–57
Elliott, Beth, 135
Elliot, P., 136
El Salvadorian refugee community, 214
Envisioning exhibit, 372–373
Equity Studies, 3
Erich, S., 334
essentialism, categories of sexuality and gender identity, 111–112, 118
ethics
  ethic of care principles, 182–183
  in social work education and pedagogy, 11

ethnicity
  homophobia of dominant-group communities, 9–10
  non-Western ethnicity, and sexuality, 238–239, 246, 247
  and sexual orientation, 243
  as social location, 19
  variations in same-sex expressions, 238–239
ethnocentrism, 240–241
exposure, fear of, 205, 238–239, 242, 243
Eyerman, R., 215, 226

Fa'afafine identity, 365
Facebook, 203
familial violence, 40
families of choice, 38, 41
  aging experience of, 72
  in caregiving literature, 152–153
  constructions of in caregiving, 162
  and spousal priority policies, 76–77
family
  as barrier in citizenship development of queer youth, 38
  rejection of LGBTQ youth, 173, 176, 188–189, 201
  support of queer youth, 196
feminist ideology
  on biology, 137
  ethic of care, 182
  and gender transition, 139–140
  inclusion of trans women in feminist research, 143–144
  and informal caregiving, 8, 152, 162
  and intersectionality, 69
  and knowledge acquisition, 362, 363
  second wave feminism, 132, 133, 137–138
  and transfeminism, 132–133, 136–142
  and trans women, 7–8, 130–131
  waves of, 132
feminization of social work profession, 22
field instruction, 339–359
  anti-oppressive practice (AOP), 345–347, 351–352, 354

boundaries with therapy, 352–353
collaboration, importance of,
　348–350
conflict management, 351–352
critical reflection, 345–347
critical reflexivity, 12, 343–347,
　354–355
education of field instructors, 310
example of intersectional framework,
　347–353
instructors' professional/positional
　power, 341–342, 348, 350
instructors' role, 340–341
instructor-student relationships,
　11–12, 339–340, 347–353
and LGBTQ students, 341–342
mentorship, 349, 352–353, 354
organizational commitment to, 339
self-disclosure, conflict with
　invisibility, 342–343
trust, establishment of, 349, 352
findlay, b., 142
Fine, M., 80
First Nations. *See* Aboriginal peoples
Fish, J., 76
519 Church Street Community Centre,
　The, 145n2
Fobister, Waawaate, *Agokwe*, 373
Ford, T., 370–371
foster-care system, 40
Fotopoulou, A., 107, 111
Foucault, Michel, 290
Fox, C., 308
Francis, Daniel, *The Imaginary Indian*, 97

Garry, K., 282, 291
gay, as Western construction, 238, 239
Gay.com, 203
gay community
　ableism within, 61
　AIDS, and bisexuality, 108–109
　body image, attitudes towards,
　　54–57, 64
　and disability, 5–6, 54–57
　exclusion of older adults, 74

immutable defence argument,
　116–117
media portrayal, 56
white gay culture, 38, 99–100
youth-centric nature of, 77–78
gay/lesbian associations, 201–202
gay liberation movement, 18–19, 71, 218
gay men
　experiential differences of
　　oppression, 78–79
　gerontological research, 74, 75
gay rights, politicization of, 114
gay/straight alliances (GSAs). *See* GSAs
　(gay/straight alliances)
gender
　and binegativity, 119, 123n5
　colonial definitions of, 365
　directions for increasing learning,
　　309–311
　fluidity of, 19, 318
　hybridity of, 107
　imposition of Western
　　understandings, 101
　and intersectionality, 69–70
　limitations of as single category, 320
　moral hierarchies with sexuality, 284
　and sex, nature of, 136–137
　in sexual diversity curriculum, 361
　and sexual identity, 13n1
　and sexuality, 91, 92
　Ske'lep, trickster figure, 92–93
　social and biological constructs of,
　　257–258
　as social location, 19, 109, 122n2,
　　137, 318
　in social work education and
　　pedagogy, 11
Gender and Women's Studies, 3
gender b(l)enders, 318
gender binary
　and affirmative trans health care,
　　255–274
　categorization within, 318
　and cisnormative thinking, 10,
　　256–257, 271n5

INDEX

in lifespan development textbooks, 364–365
gender development, theories of, 365
gender dysphoria, 23, 261
gender expression, 1, 23
   stereotypes of, 347, 349
genderfluid, 271n2
gender fucks, 318
gender identity, 1, 23
   age of awareness, 184
   and arts-based inquiry, 321–322
   bodies, and bodily sovereignty, 138–140
   decolonizing Eurocentric constructions of, 376
   essentialist perspective, 111–112
   fluidity of, 74, 112
   international human rights legislation, 178–179
   Internet as source of information, 203–204
   intersectionality of, 331–332
   intersection with class, 109–110
   invisibility, and geographic location, 8–9
   language and terminology, development of, 131–133
   mental health assessments in diagnosis of difference, 265
   and mental health issues, 333
   provincial human rights legislation, 179–181
   role of choice, 112
   self-understanding of, 200–201
   social constructivist perspective, 112
   terminology usage, 174–175
   and Two-Spirit expression, 88
gender identity disorder, 261
gender minority role models, 173, 189, 205, 206, 207
gender-neutral language, 251, 271n6
gender oppression, 9, 74
gender policing, 110
   transsexual/transgender health care as, 263–266, 272n9

genderqueer, 18, 131, 132, 174, 261, 268, 271n2, 318
Gender-Specific Binegativity Scale, 119, 123n5
gender-variant people, 271n2
   psychiatrization of, 255–256
geographic location
   age/gender identity in qualitative research literature, 195–197
   and aging, 75
   impact on lived experience, 8–9
   and informal caregiving, 8, 158–159, 164–165
   safety issues, 250
   scholarship on, 193–194
   small cities vs. rural/urban areas, 193–194, 206–209
   small city context, 197–198
   support services, rural/urban differences, 195–206
George Brown College, 362
gerontological research, 73–75, 81–82
globalization, and corporate impact on social order, 25–26
Goldberg, J., 133, 142
Goodine, Ron, 7, 107–126
   as bisexual man, 108–110, 122n1
government(s)
   and conservatism, 307–308
   funding reductions, 22
   and neoliberalism, 25–26, 50
   relationship with NPIC, 21
Gray, M., 335
Greer, Germaine, 135, 140
GSAs (gay/straight alliances), 196, 202–203, 204–205, 206, 208, 228
guided journey exercise, 301–303, 312n1
"Guidelines and Protocols for Comprehensive Primary Health Care for Trans Clients," 261

Hall, R. L., 80
Hammond, R., 333, 334
Hankivsky, O.
   ethic of care principles, 182–183

intersectionality-based policy
   analysis (IBPA) framework, 30–31
Hansbury, G., 333
harassment, 38
Harris, B., 334
Harrison, J., 77
Harry Benjamin Standards, 260, 264–265
Hassle Free Clinic, 219
hate crimes, 235, 319
Hausman, B., 139
health care services
   caregivers as decision-makers, 167
   heterosexist assumptions of, 161
   homophobia, and non-heterosexual
      caregiving, 153, 156–158
   and institutional racism, 40
health care system
   ageism, shift in, 81
   and bisexuality, 121
   and cis-sexist gender norms,
      263–266, 272n9
   homosexuality as psychiatric
      diagnosis, 23, 71
   and normative conceptualizations of
      gender, 10
   person-centred approach to
      transition, 261
   resource inaccessibility, 243
   and Standards of Care (SOC7),
      260–263, 265
   transgender health care, 255–256,
      264, 319
   See also long-term care facilities
Hellen, M., 184
Hemmings, C., 112
Herman, J. L., 216
heteronormative social structures
   and bisexuality, 7
   in care facilities, 75–78
   and marginalization of politicized
      queers, 4–5
heteronormativity
   in educational settings, 307–309
   and LGBTQ identity, 303
   politics of, 300

power of, 302
heteropatriarchy, 103
   in Aboriginal reserve communities,
      91, 95
heterosexism
   and ageism, 75–78
   and caregiving, 153, 166
   and collective trauma, 221
   as form of oppression, 37, 174–175
   immigrant/refugee experiences of,
      9–10, 247
   intersection with racism, 5
   and LGB immigrants/refugees,
      240–241
   in long-term care facilities, 76–77
   power dynamics of, 304
   privileging of "straightness," 235
   in racialized communities, 19
   and racism, 42
   youth experiences of, 9, 37
heterosexuality
   invisibility of, 300
   social privileging of, 289
   students assumptions of, 298
heterosexual social structures
   emulation of by mainstream LGBTQ
      members, 4–5, 17
   and erasure of bisexuality, 107
   investment of straight-identifying
      people, 113
   questioning of by politicized queers,
      26–27
Hicks, Stephen, 288–289, 291
Hijra identity, 365, 371
HIV/AIDS
   and bisexuality, 108–109
   and collective trauma, 222–223
   community supports, 219
   as disability, 61
   as form of marginalization, 219
   HIV-related discrimination, 40, 157,
      159, 165
   informal caregiving, 156–157,
      158–159
   as source of trauma, 221

Hohenadel, K. M., 333, 334
holistic community healing, 42, 47–49
homelessness, 173, 176, 181, 262, 319
homo-ableism, 55–56, 64
homo-negativity, 74
homophobia, 9, 235
    in Aboriginal reserve communities, 95–96
    and ageism, 75–78
    anti-homophobia workshops, 45–46
    and bullying, 176, 186
    and caregiving, 153, 156–158, 162, 164, 166
    and collective trauma, 221, 223
    education and training on, 186
    hate crimes, 235
    homophobic violence, 38, 40
    institutional homophobia, 76–77
    and political correctness, 58–59
    in racialized communities, 19
    and racialized queer youth, 38, 39
    in social work literature, 299
    against Two-Spirit people, 93, 94
    in white queer theory, 47–48, 50
    youth experiences of, 9, 38, 39, 176, 186, 196
homosexuality
    in lifespan development textbooks, 365–366
    as psychiatric diagnosis, 23, 71
hooks, bell, 90
Hornick, J. P., 138
housing, precarious, 40
Hughes, D. L., 74
Hulko, Wendy, 8–9, 193–212
    oppression, and resilience, 79
human rights
    barriers to securing rights, 181–182
    Charter of Rights and Freedoms, 1, 178, 179, 233
    of children, 367–368, 369
    and child welfare, 178–182
    Code of Ethics (CASW), 185–187, 334

International Covenant on Civil and Political Rights, 178, 179
    protections under, 1, 8
    provincial legislation, 179–181, 233
    and sexual orientation, 235
    United Nations Convention on the Rights of the Child (UNCRC), 178–179
Hyde, J. S., 111–112

identity development, 12
identity disclosure. *See* coming out; self-disclosure
identity politics, 19
    and disability, 54–55
    and queer theory, 111
Imaginary Indian, The (Francis), 97
immigrants and refugees, 233–253
    challenges of racialized queer youth, 38
    cross-service collaboration, 244–245
    differing perceptions of need, 245–246, 248
    fear of exposure, 205, 238–239, 242, 243
    identity issues, non-Western variations in, 238–239, 247
    LGB-friendly settlement support, 241–243
    marginalization experiences, 247, 248–249
    as newcomers, 234
    refugee determination system, 236
    research design, and participant selection, 236–238
    safety issues, 242, 247–248
    settlement experiences, 9–10, 233–234, 240–243
    settlement needs, 233, 240–243
    summary of study findings, 247–251
immutable defence argument, 114, 116–117
Indigenous peoples. *See* Aboriginal peoples

informal caregiving. *See* caregiving, informal
institutional racism, 40
instructor–student relationships. *See* field instruction
interdependence, in same-sex disability relationships, 61
interdisciplinary studies, 2–3
International Covenant on Civil and Political Rights, 178, 179
International Day Against Homophobia (IDAH), 204–205
International Two-Spirit Gathering, 96
Internet, 199, 203–204
intersectionality
    age/gender identity and geographic location, 194–196
    in analysis of caregiving, 163–165
    applications of, 1–2
    as continuum of theories, 320
    and critical thinking, 291–292
    of ethics and social justice, 11
    of geographic location, 193–212
    interaction of subordination/domination, 153
    of interlocking oppressions, 281–284
    negative intersectionality of NPIC, 21–25, 32
    of oppression, 37
    and organizations of oppression, 70
    in social work education and pedagogy, 10
    theoretical lens of, 69–70
intersectionality-based policy analysis (IBPA) framework, 30–31
intersex people, 193–194
invisibility
    of bisexual identities, 115–116
    of caring labour, 152
    conflict with self-disclosure, 342–343
    erasure of bisexuality, 111–114
    and heterosexism, 185
    of heterosexuality, 300
    intersection with geographic location, 8–9
    lesbians, 8–9, 240–241
    of LGBTQ seniors, 6, 67–69, 73–75
    of LGBTQ youth, 185, 189
    of LGBTTTSQ community, 218
    as protective device, 72
    in service delivery, 41
    of sexuality in long-term care facilities, 67–69, 75–77
    socio-historical context of, 70–72
    of trans content in education and pedagogy, 11
    of trans people, 334
    whiteness, culture of, 300

Jeffreys, S., 139
Jeyasingham, D., 308
Jorgensen, Christine, 133
Journal of Gay, Lesbian and Bisexual Identity, 55

Kaay, M., 333, 334
Kaufman, R., 319
Kennedy, N., 184
Kia, Hossein, 8, 9–10, 151–171, 233–253
Kimberley Nixon vs. Vancouver Rape Relief, 135–136, 139, 140, 142
Kinsman, G. W., 216, 284
Knight, B. G., 74
knowledge acquisition, feminist epistemological view, 362, 363
Koostachin, Jules, *Alive with Breath*, 372
Kovach, Margaret, 101
Koyama, E., 138, 140

labels, and labelling, 74, 238. 365
Lagios, Andrea, 9, 213–232
Lakeman, Lee, 136–137
Lamm, Nomy, 54
Lansberg, M., 140
Leavy, P., 322
Lee, Bill, 9, 213–232
lesbians/lesbianism, 37
    aging, and self-esteem, 78–79

butch stereotype, 347, 349
and disability, 5–6
disabled, sexual surrogates for, 54
exclusion of by feminist ideology, 7–8, 74
experiential differences of oppression, 78–79
fear of exposure, 205
in geographic location scholarship, 193–194, 209n3
gerontological research, 73
hostility towards trans women, 134–135
inter-generational support, 207
invisibility of, 8–9, 240–241
role models, 207
Lev, A., 318
Lewis-Peart, David, 5, 37–51
LGBT Diversity Steering Committee and Toolkit, 81
LGBTQ
  as marginalization, reinforcement of, 97
  terminology usage, 1, 13n1, 174–175
LGBTQ community
  ageism, resistance to, 80–82
  ageist attitudes of, 77–78
  as consumer market, 19–20
  discrimination against, 19, 174–175, 235
  diversity within, 1, 3, 72–73
  legal protections of, 235
  marginalization of politicized queers, 4–5, 17–18
  neoliberalism, and social oppression, 25–26
  as non-monolithic, 18
  oppression by, 3
  racism within, 9–10
LGBT-S course
  in Bachelor of Social Work (BSW) curriculum, 297–298
  course overview, 298–299
  employment considerations in course choice, 297

heterosexism/heteronormativity, challenges to, 301–305
  political objectives, 299–301
LGBTTSIQ, 193
LGBTTTSQ community
  and collective trauma, 214
  marginalization of, 216–217
  moral regulation of, 216–217, 218
  politicization of, 217–218
  rejection of by family, 217
liberalism, 311
liberationist politics, 217–218
lifespan development. *See* child and youth development courses
long-term care facilities
  heterosexism, and aging, 75–78
  institutional homophobia, 76–77
  and institutionalization, 80
  LGBT Diversity Steering Committee and Toolkit, 81
  sexuality of older adults, 67–69, 75–77
  staff training, 76–77, 81

Malinowitz, H., 362
Mallon, G. P., 175, 181, 318
Many Men, Many Voices (3MV), 37
  Afrocentric spirituality, 46, 49–50
  experiences of YBMSM, 40–41, 42
Manywounds, Beric, 98–99
marginalization
  changing social contexts of, 228
  classification as means of exclusion, 263–266
  and collective trauma, 9, 214, 220
  in erasure of bisexuality, 7, 120–121
  as form of oppression, 214–215
  of LGB immigrants, 240–241, 247, 248–249
  of LGBTQ seniors, 6, 75–78
  of LGBTQ youth, 173–174, 305–306
  of LGBTTTSQ community, 216–217
  of minorities, 2, 3
  mitigation of, 243–246
  and outsiderhood, 362–363

of politicized queers, 4–5, 17–18
positive marginalization, 80
of racialized populations, 22–23
resistance to identification, 74–75
of same-sex caregiving, 166
training development, 167–168
of trans people, 7–8, 319
Two-Spiritedness, 6–7
marital status, as social location, 19
masculinities
working-class masculinities, 109–110
Matthews, A. K., 74
Matthew Sheppard Story, The, 303
Maynard, S., 109–110
McCall, L., 69, 111
McConnell, Sheri, 11–12, 339–359
McGrath, Susan, 9, 213–232
McLean, Marilyn, 12, 361–381
McNeil-Seymour, Jeffrey, 6–7, 87–105
media
as colonial technology, 97–101
commercialization of popular gay culture, 19–20, 97
erasure of bisexuality, 113
politic of homonormativity, 97–98
portrayal of gay culture, 56
social media, 97, 98
Mehrotra, G., 282–283, 320
mental health
and bisexuality, 120–121
and gender identity, 333
impact of discrimination on, 240
medical interventions, psychiatric diagnosis for, 23, 140, 261–262
and queer youth, 38, 40
support services, rural/urban differences, 195–196
mentorship
community education of Two-Spirit roles, 96
and dominant modes of being, 43
in field instruction, 349, 352–353, 354
Many Men, Many Voices (3MV), 46
of Two-Spirit people, 103

Milk, Harvey, 56
minority-related stress, 176
Moffatt, Ken, 9, 213–232
monosexuality, 111, 112–114, 122n3
Morgan, Robin, 135
Morgensen, S., 376
Mulé, Nick J., 1–13
marginalization of politicized queers, 4–5, 17–36
Multiculturalism Act (1985), 233

Namaste, V., 141
Nelson, D. Margo, 8, 173–192
neoliberalism, 25–26, 50
Newman, P. A., 306
New York Times
bisexuality in mainstream media, 118, 123n4
Nexopia, 203
Nixon, Cynthia, 116–117
Nixon, Kimberley, 135–136, 139, 140, 142
non-profit industrial complex (NPIC)
"business model" vs. "community-based model," 22–23
feminization of social work profession, 22
in mixed welfare economy, 22
negative intersectionality of, 21–25, 32
neocolonial aspects of, 24–25
neoliberal funding regulations, 24–25, 32n1
role of as low-income support system, 20
social accountability of, 22
social workers as actors in, 5, 17
social work principles of, 20–21
and societal narcissism, 27
systemic relationships of, 21–22
NPIC. *See* non-profit industrial complex (NPIC)
nursing, 2

occupational therapy, 2
O'Connor, D., 79

INDEX

O'Neill, Brian J., 9–10, 233–253
Ontario
    trans health care, and government funding, 264
oppression
    ageism, 166
    of agency/academic cultures, 341–342
    anti-categorical approach, 111
    and bridging, 49
    bullying, 176, 186, 199
    elimination of through social change, 2
    experiences of racialized queer youth, 39–41
    experiential differences between lesbians and gay men, 78–79
    and heterosexism, 174–175, 185
    heterosexism in long-term care facilities, 75–78
    homo-ableism, 55–56
    identity-related, 240–241
    immigration status-based, 38, 39
    intersectional analysis, 331–332
    intersectionality of, 37, 70, 144, 248–249
    by LGBTQ community, 3
    of LGBTQ youth, 8
    liberation from as social justice, 47–48
    and marginalization, 214–215
    by minority groups, 59
    of neoliberal systemic structures, 20–21
    and public remembering practices, 141–142
    and resilience, 79–80
    and resistance to domination, 284–285
    self-education by service providers, 256
    students participation in acceptance of, 282–283
    and violence, 366
organizational change, 1–2

"other"/"otherness"
    fear of by white social workers, 48
    and gender stereotypes, 110
    and heterosexuality, 305
    of LGB immigrants, 249
    stigma of labelling, 74
Out and Proud program, 186–187
out-of-home care, 188

pansexuality, 123n3
Parks, C. A., 74
"passing" strategies
    and gender binary, 263
    and gender policing, 110
    and standards of professionalism, 42–44
Paul, J. P., 108
pedophilia, 95
personal agency. *See* agency (personal)
personhood, sense of, 62
Phinney, A., 79
Pink Sofa, 203
policy making
    discriminatory impacts of, 3–4
    impact of invisibility on, 70
    inclusive policies, development of, 4, 142
    mezzo level social work, 29–30
    oppression in agency culture, 341
    transfeminist activism, impact on, 142–143
political correctness, learned, 58–59
politicized queers, 17–36
    advocacy of, 23–24
    disordering of social order, 25–27
    marginalization of, 4–5, 17–18, 31–32
    NPIC's co-optation of social justice issues, 24–25
    re-ordering of social order, 27–31
Pon, G., 304
Poon, C. S., 195
positionality, and self-reflexivity, 42–44
positive marginalization, 80
Positive Space training, 369

post traumatic stress disorder (PTSD), 61
poverty, 341
    and aging, 75
    role of NPICs as support system, 20
    and the trans community, 129
power dynamics, 101
    binaries of, and situated subjectivity, 344–345
    and critical reflexivity, 345–346, 348
    of critical social work approach, 28–31
    in fear of the "other," 48
    of gender identity, 113
    harassment, and human rights, 311
    instructors' professional/positional power, 341–342, 348, 350
    instructor–student relationships, 339–340
    of male privilege, 258, 259
    paternalism in social work practice, 43
power sharing, in field instruction, 12
pow-wows, as culturally restorative practice, 89–90
prejudice, and trauma, 213
pride celebrations
    corporatization of, 26
    homo-ableism, 57–58
    International Two-Spirit Gathering, 96
    racial segregation in, 45
Profitt, Norma Jean, 11, 297–316, 345
progressivism, 311
psychosis, 262
public remembering practices, 141–142
Pyne, Jake, 7–8, 129–149

qualitative research
    age/gender identity and geographic location, 195–197
    use of experience and story, 155–156
queer, terminology usage, 18, 174
queer Black youth, 5, 40
Queer Disability Conference (2002), 53, 54, 63

queer liberation perspective, 5
    and personal agency, 30, 32
    vs. queer theory, 18–19
Queer Nation, 18, 218
queer pedagogy, 362–363, 370–371, 375
queer social work practitioners, 37–51
    de-centring whiteness, 44–47
    invisibility of as queer "youth," 41
    mentorship of, 43
    "passing" strategies, 42–44
    self-reflexivity, and positionality, 42–44
    themes of practice, 42
    See also queer youth of colour; youth
queer theory
    conceptualization of emotional states, 213–214
    and critical thinking, 300–301
    deconstruction of, 303
    guided journey exercise, 302–303
    and identity politics, 111
    as post-modernist, 19
    vs. queer liberation, 18–19
    in social work education and pedagogy, 10, 288–291, 292
queer (LBQ) women, 37
queer youth of colour, 5, 37–51
    challenges of racialized queer youth, 38–39
    coping mechanisms, 40–41
    drop-in programs, 41–42
    intersecting oppressions of, 39–41
    Many Men, Many Voices (3MV), 37, 42
    "outsider role identities," 40–41
    "relationships of convenience," 39
    social workers connection with, 49
    social workers fear of the "other," 48
    See also queer social work practitioners; youth

race
    and culture of whiteness, 19, 22–23
    as ideological construct, 44–45

and informal caregiving, 8, 156–157
  intersection with age, 156–157,
    163–164
racial superiority
  as ideological construct, 44–45
  of white queer theory, 47–48, 50
racism
  anti-racism training, 244–245, 304
  and culture of whiteness, 19
  as form of oppression, 37
  and heterosexism, 42
  and informal caregiving, 166
  institutional racism, 40
  intersection with heterosexism, 5
  against LGB immigrants/refugees,
    9–10, 240–241
  in LGBT communities, 74
  in queer community spaces, 45–47
  and racialized queer youth, 38, 39
  in trans inclusion debate, 137–138
  and trans people, 256
  and transphobia, 141–142
  against Two-Spirit people, 93, 94
Ranzijn, R., 75
rape crisis centres, 133
Raymond, Janice G., *The Transsexual Empire*, 135, 136, 140
Reda, Mary, 286, 287
reflective practice, 185–186
reflexive practice
  and critical reflection, 345–347
  in field instruction, 12, 343–347,
    354–355
  in queer pedagogy, 370–371
  in trans-related care, 10, 256–257,
    335
refugees. *See* immigrants and refugees
Rehaag, S., 236
rejection, fears of, 328
"relationships of convenience," 39
religion
  as barrier in citizenship development of queer youth, 38
  discrimination, and religious freedom, 307

as risk factor for LGBTQ youth, 177,
  188–189
as social location, 19
and spirituality in social work,
  278–280
See also Christian fundamentalism
research, qualitative
  age/gender identity and geographic location, 195–197
  use of experience and story,
    155–156
resilience, 41
  and collective trauma, 225–226
  factors associated with, 177
  and oppression, 79–80
  and resistance to domination,
    284–285
  and stigmatization, 82
restorative practice, as reconnection and cultural safety, 101–102
Rich, Adrienne, 135
Ridgely, Andrea, 12, 361–381
Rieger, G., 118
risk construction, and regulation of sexuality, 290–291
Robinson, T. L., 91, 92
Rodriguez, D., 21, 24–25
Rollings, J. H., Jr., 322
Rosenthal, A. M., 118–119
Ross, M., 134
runaways, 176
rural locations
  and aging, 75
  rural/urban differences in support services, 195–206
Rwigema, Marie-Jolie, 5, 37–51
Ryerson University
  School of Disability Studies, 54

Saewyc, E. M., 184, 195
safety, 94, 206
  in classroom dynamic, 304–305
  cultural safety, 102
  educational settings, 199–200, 280
  in educational settings, 333

immigrant settlement experiences, 242, 247–248
public vs. private spaces, 199–200
in queer youth groups, 200–201
settlement services, universalizing access to, 243–244, 249–250
safety plan development, 187
Safron, A., 118–119
SAGE (Services and Advocacy for GLBT Elders), 80–81
Saint Thomas University, 297
same-sex marriage
    California Proposition 8, 114
    as emulation of heterosexual social structure, 17, 26
    and heterosexual marriage status, 77
    and the Imaginary Indian, 99–100
    rights of in Canada, 235
same-sex relationships
    Canadian immigration policy, 236
    and collective trauma, 221–222
    and disability, 60
    homophobia, and non-heterosexual caregiving, 153
    and spousal priority policies, 76–77
    See also caregiving, informal
Sarkisova, X. Sly, 10, 255–274
Savage, Dan, 118, 123n4
Schope, R. D., 78
Scott, K., 215, 226
Scott-Dixon, K., 131, 319, 320
second wave feminism, 132, 133
Second Sex, The (Beauvoir), 137
self-awareness, development of, 292
self-disclosure
    conflict with invisibility, 342–343
    factors influencing, 306
self-identification, 109, 122n2, 184, 239
self-reflexivity, and positionality, 42–44
seniors
    categorization of LGBT adults, 72–75, 80
    gerontological research, 73–75, 81–82
    pride networks, 81
    SAGE (Services and Advocacy for GLBT Elders), 80–81
    sexuality, invisibility of, 67–69, 75–77
    youth-centric nature of LGBTQ community, 77–78
    See also long-term care facilities
sensitization, 184
Serano, J., 137, 139, 140, 141, 259, 334
Services and Advocacy for GLBT Elders (SAGE), 81
settlement services
    about, 234
    "best practices," amendment of, 249
    confidentiality, 251
    cross-service collaboration, 244–245, 250
    differing perceptions of need, 245–246, 248
    gender-neutral language, 251
    LGB-friendly settlement support, 241–243
    needs of LGB immigrants/refugees, 9–10, 233, 240–243
    program planning, factors affecting, 238
    research design, and participant selection, 236–238
    settlement, defined, 234
    summary of study findings, 247–251
    universalizing of, 243–244, 247–248
settler imaginary
    decolonizing Eurocentric constructions of gender identity, 376
    decolonizing perspectives in, 101
    heterocentricity of, 92, 97
    and identity formation, 98
sex, as biologic status, 318
sex reassignment surgery, 318
sexual abuse, 176
sexual assault, 40, 58, 221
sexual colonization, 90
sexual diversity, 13n1
    directions for increasing learning, 309–311

as issue of social justice, 310
in social work education and
  pedagogy, 11
sexual education, rural/urban differences, 195-196
sexual exploitation, 176
sexual identity confusion, 93-94, 184
sexual identity formation theory, 184
sexuality
  anti-categorical approach to, 111
  as choice, 116-117
  and Christian fundamentalism, 277
  concealment of, 40, 70-71, 333
  construction of in social work
    education, 308-309
  and disability, 5-6
  essentialist perspective, 111-112
  fluidity of, 19
  and homo-ableism, 55-56
  imposition of Western
    understandings, 101
  invisibility of in care facilities, 67-69, 75-77
  in lifespan development textbooks, 365-366
  moral hierarchies with gender, 284
  perception of as "truth" of identities, 288-289
  raceless/white construction of queer sexuality, 38
  regulation of, and risk, 290-291
  same-sex disability relationships, 60
  sexual practices as social problems, 283-284
  social constructivist perspective, 112
sexually transmitted diseases, 38
sexual orientation
  and Charter of Rights and Freedoms, 1, 178, 179
  concealment of, 40, 70-71, 333
  decolonizing Eurocentric
    constructions of, 376
  fluidity of, 74
  homosexuality as psychiatric
    diagnosis, 23, 71
  immutable defence argument, 114, 116-117
  in intersectionality research, 194-196
  in lifespan development textbooks, 365-366
  and marital status, 77
  non-discrimination standard
    (CSWE), 278-279
  non-normative orientations, 18
  prejudice against, 233
  in refugee determination system, 236
  rural/urban differences, 195-196
  self-disclosure, 306
  and self-identification, 109, 122n2, 184, 239
  and Two-Spirit identity, 90
sexual surrogates, 54
sex work, involuntary, 319
sex workers
  sex and disability symposium, 62
  social action by, 134
  as surrogates for disabled, 54
  violence against trans women, 141
shame, 213, 228
Shapiro, Lawrence, 5-6, 53-65
shelter services
  abuse in, 40
  anti-violence counselling, 362
  exclusion of trans women, 129-131, 132, 135-136
  intake process, and trans women, 143
  Kimberley Nixon vs. Vancouver Rape Relief, 135-136
  transfeminist activism, impact on, 142-144
  woman-specific services, 133
Sherbourne Health Centre, 261
Shields, S., 320
silence
  in classroom dynamic, 277, 286-288
  cultural expectations of, 74-75
  in social work education and
    pedagogy, 10

of trans voices in social work
    education, 329–331
Simard, Estelle, 90–91, 102
Sins Invalid performance project, 62–63
Sisters in Spirit vigils, 372
SlutWalk, 372
small cities vs. rural/urban areas,
    193–212
  attitudes towards same-sex
    orientation, 237
  community-based alliances, 207
  queer role models, 206
  research participants, 198
  safety and acceptance, 199–200
  sources of support, 200–205
  support services, 197–198
  youth programs, 207–208
Snively, C. A., 207
social constructivism. *See* constructivism
social conventions, disruption of, 213
social integration, 58, 63
social isolation, of LGBTQ youth,
    173–174
social justice
  approaches to, 89–90
  barriers to securing rights, 181–182
  ethical-political agenda in teaching
    diversity, 309–311
  ethic of care, principles of, 182–183
  human rights, and child welfare, 8,
    178–182
  and intersectionality, 1–2
  liberation from oppression, 47–48
  and neoliberal governance of non-
    profits and charities, 24–25, 32n1
  and right to identity, 368
  in social work education and
    pedagogy, 11, 334
  visibility, and restorative practice, 102
Social Justice (SJ), 12, 197–198,
    206, 208
social locations
  intersectionality of interlocking
    oppressions, 281–284
  multiplicity of, 19

social media, 97, 98, 194
  community-based alliances, 207
  memes on same-sex marriage, 99–100
  virtual communities of peer support,
    196, 203–204
social networks, 213
social order
  disordering of, 25–27
  impact of globalization on, 25–26
  intersectionality-based policy
    analysis (IBPA) framework, 30–31
  questioning of by politicized queers,
    26–27
  re-ordering of, 27–31
social reform movements
  disability rights movement, 53, 54
  gay liberation movement, 18–19
  transgender activism, 319
  See also transfeminism, and
    transfeminist theory
social services, and institutional racism,
    40
Social Work and Lesbian, Gay, Bisexual
    and Two-Spirited Peoples (LGBT-S)
    course. *See* LGBT-S course
social work education and pedagogy
  accountability of, 334–335
  affirming environment, creation of,
    334–335
  analytic approaches to, 289–291
  anti-oppressive practice (AOP)
    approaches, 277–280
  arts-based inquiry, 317–338
  BSW curriculum review, 309
  child and youth development
    courses, 12, 361–381
  child welfare policy framework,
    186–187
  conservatism, role in shaping schools
    of social work, 307–308
  constructivist approach to teaching,
    370–373
  corrective intervention, 304
  critical thinking, and
    intersectionality, 291–292

cross-service collaboration, 244–245, 250
as culture of domination, 90
directions for increasing learning, 309–311
diversity, imperative of understanding, 300
educators, role and obligations of, 285, 304
employment considerations in course choice, 297, 373
equity statement, 368
ethical-political agenda, 309–310, 311
exclusionary experiences of trans students, 336
field instruction, 11–12, 339–359
flattened understanding, caution about, 371
fundamentalist beliefs in queer-positive classrooms, 277–293
future directions, 373–376
gender, in sexual diversity curriculum, 361
group-process skills, 367, 369–370
guided journey exercise, 301–303, 312n1
hierarchical inversion of identities, 289–290
homogenizing of identities in classrooms, 374–375
human rights-based policies, and positive space practices, 367, 368–369
identity development, 12
Indigenous epistemology, 101
interpersonal communication, 367, 369–370
intersectionality in, 10, 194–195
knowledge acquisition, feminist epistomological view, 362, 363
limitations of, 4
mapping of gender and sexual identity studies, 367, 370
marginalization issues, training in, 167–168

nondiscrimination standard (CSWE), 278–279
oppression in academic culture, 341
opt out option, 374
Positive Space training, 369
professionalization, student resistance to, 285–286
queer pedagogy, 362–363, 370–371, 375
queer theory, 10, 129, 288–291
reflexivity, student engagement with, 285
silence, in classroom dynamic, 277, 286–288
small-group work, 287–288
and social justice, 334, 336
Standards for Accreditation, 292, 298
stereotyping of LGBTQ students, 342–343
student code of conduct, 368, 370
student contributions to teaching diversity, 371–372
student identities, relevance of, 342
trans erasure, 329–331
trans etiquette, instruction on, 335
transfeminist activism, implications for, 142–143
transfeminist content, inclusion of, 144
transgender perspectives on, 320–323
and transgender theory, 129
trans issues, addressing of, 329
social workers
as agents of change/control, 20–21, 27, 31
and change from within, 17–18, 268–269, 299
critical social work approach, 27–31
fear of the "other," 48
gender expression, support of, 266–270
heteronormative assumptions of, 76, 175
impact on trans individuals, 266–267

marginalization issues, training in, 167–168
in non-profit industrial complex (NPIC), 5, 17
reflexive practice in trans-related care, 10, 256–257, 267
responsibilities of informed practice, 28–31
understandings of gender identity, 262–263, 266–270
unlearning of gender biases, 267–268, 270
varied roles of, 266, 270–271
social work practice
attitudes towards transgender individuals, awareness of, 335
"best practices," amendment of, 249
bridging of separations, 47–49
case management approaches, 49–50
and Christian fundamentalism, 279–280
client/worker barriers, 46–47
Code of Ethics (CASW), 185–187, 334
collaborative community practice, 9
and collective trauma, 227–228
culturally restorative practice, 7
de-centring whiteness, 44–47
differing perceptions of need, 245–246, 248
discriminatory impacts of, 3–4
erasure of trans identities, 332–333
ethic of care principles, 182–183
exclusion of trans women, 129–131
feminization of by NPIC, 22
and fundamentalist religious views, 277–280
and human rights, 175, 178–182
inclusive policies, development of, 4
informal caregiving, 166–168
marginalization of politicized queers, 4–5, 17–18, 31–32
mezzo level, 29–30
micro level, 29
organizational policy development, and transfeminism, 143–144

power dynamics, 31, 43, 48, 101
reflective practice, 185–186
service delivery systems of trans health care, 255–256
sexual identities, perception of, 288–289
sexuality of older adults, 67–69
Standards of Care (SOC7), 260–263
and subjugation of Turtle Island, 89–90
trans-access training, 129–131, 145n2
transfeminist activism, implications for, 142–143
whiteness, manifestations of in practice, 42, 44, 46–47
Society of Medicine (England) sex and disability symposium, 62
socio-cultural capital, development of, 42–43
spousal priority policies, 76–77
Standards for Accreditation (CASWE), 292, 298, 307
Standards of Care (SOC7), 260–263, 265
state discipline, as source of trauma, 221
Stern, Louise, 6, 67–86
stigmatization
ageism, and sexuality, 77–78
of bisexuals, 121–122
within cultural communities, 74–75
of labelling, 74, 82
of LGBTQ youth, 174–175
Stone, S., 139
Stonewall Inn Riot, 134
stress and burden theory, 8, 152–153, 158, 162–163
Stryker, S., 135, 138, 319, 332
subjective sense of self, 344–345
substance use, 40, 262
among bisexuals, 120
and queer youth, 38
support services, 23, 195–196
suicidal ideation, 38, 40, 120, 176
suicide/suicide prevention, support services, 23

support services, 23
    cross-service collaboration, 244–245, 250
    GSAs (gay/straight alliances), 196, 202–203, 204–205, 206, 208, 228
    informal help networks, 195–196
    inter-generational support, 207
    for LGBTQ youth, 187, 194
    local gay/lesbian associations, 201–202
    peer support, 196, 200
    pride clubs, 200
    queer youth groups, 200–201
    small city context, 197–198
    virtual communities, 196
survival strategies
    of gender-diverse youth, 173
    and resilience, 177, 188
Swan, Tracy A., 11–12, 339–359
Sweeney, B., 139
switch-dance, 89
Sylva, D., 118–119

Tafoya, T., 91, 92
Take Back the Night, 372
Talbot, M., 114
Taylor, C., 307
Thomas, G., 119
    Gender-Specific Binegativity Scale, 123n5
3MV. *See* Many Men, Many Voices (3MV)
Todd, Sarah, 10, 277–293
Tolley, C., 75
Toronto Rape Crisis Centre/Multicultural Women Against Rape, 142
Trans Access Project, 130, 145n2
trans-access training, 129–130, 145n2
Trans Alliance Society, 142
transfeminism, and transfeminist theory, 7–8, 129–149
    action strategies, 132–133
    activism, impact on women's service provision, 142–144
    development of, 132–133
    and feminism, 132–133, 136–142
    on nature of sex and gender, 136–137
    public remembering practices, 141–142
    as resource for social workers, 144
    and "women's experience," 137–138
transgender
    as category of self-identification, 318–319
    conceptualizing, 318–319
    defined, 122n2, 271n3
    as Eurocentric terminology, 257
    language and terminology, development of, 131–133
transgender activism, 319
"Transgender Primary Medical Care," 261
transgender seniors, 73, 75
transgender youth
    communities of affinity, 200–205
    fear of exposure, 205
    in geographic location scholarship, 193–194
    queer youth groups, 200–201
    safety in educational settings, 199–200
    See also youth
trans health care
    delivery systems, 255–256
    and government funding, 264
trans identity
    arts-based inquiry, findings and analysis, 323–332
    arts-based inquiry, research method, 320–323
    and "crossing over" of experience, 258
    misgendered perceptions, 324, 326
    others' perceptions, and sense of belonging, 323–328
transitioning, fears surrounding, 328
trans men, 132
    and masculine privilege, 258–259
trans-misogyny, 132, 256

trans people, 255–274
    age of awareness, 184
    centrality of self-identification,
        257–260
    classification as means of exclusion,
        263–266
    concealment of identity, 333
    criteria of assessment, 261–263
    education of cisgender population,
        329
    female to male, 318
    gender identity formula, 262
    gender-neutral language, 251, 271n6
    health care guidelines, 260–263
    hormone therapy, 261, 272n7
    hostility towards, 134–136
    male to female, 318
    marginalization of, 319
    medical interventions, psychiatric
        diagnosis for, 23, 140, 261–262
    modes of transition, 257, 271n7
    and normative conceptualizations of
        gender, 10
    police harassment of, 134
    psychiatrization of, 255–256,
        264–265
    psychosocial risks of assessment
        criteria, 264–265
    racism, 256
    sex reassignment surgery, 318
    silencing of in social work education,
        329–331
    and Standards of Care (SOC7),
        260–263, 265
    supportive counselling, 265–266
    trans health care, and government
        funding, 264
    transition, person-centred approach
        to, 261
    trans-misogyny, 256
    vulnerability to violence, 226, 265
    See also trans women
transphobia, 19, 271n4, 324
    within feminism, 134–136
    and racialized queer youth, 39
    and racism, 141–142, 256, 271n4
    residential school experience, 95
    responses to, 143
    within schools of social work, 333
    youth experiences of, 196
trans rights movement, 133–134
Transsexual Empire, The (Raymond), 135,
    136, 140
transsexualism, 131, 318
    criteria of assessment, 261–263
trans social work students, arts-based
    inquiry, 317–338
trans subjectivity, 131
trans women
    bodies, and bodily sovereignty,
        138–140
    as danger to cisgender women,
        135–136, 140–142
    exclusion from women's shelters,
        129–131
    exclusion of by feminist ideology,
        7–8, 74, 134–136
    gender transition, 138–140, 259
    in geographic location scholarship,
        193–194, 209n3
    hostility towards, 134–136
    impact of systemic exclusions,
        259–260
    invisibility, and geographic location,
        8–9
    *Kimberley Nixon vs. Vancouver Rape
        Relief* case, 135–136
    male privilege of, 138
    and poverty, 129
    pressure to conform, 259–260
    "realness" of, and "women's
        experience," 137–138, 259
    sex and gender, nature of, 136–137
    social supports, 194
    stereotypes of, 139, 260
    trans-misogyny, 132, 256
    violence against, 129, 132, 140–142,
        332
    See also transfeminism, and
        transfeminist theory

trauma, 262
  described, 215
  effects of, 215–216
  and recovery, 216
  See also collective trauma
Travers, R., 177, 333, 334
Trembling Before G-D (Dubowski), 283
Truth, Sojourner, 138
Tuller, David, "No Surprise for Bisexual Men," 118–119
Two-Spirit identity, 131, 174, 318, 365
  within Aboriginal communities, 6–7
  colonization of, 6–7, 88, 92
  community acceptance, 95–96
  and cross-dancing, 90–92, 96, 101–102
  diversity of in Aboriginal interpretations, 88
  exclusion of on- and off-reserve, 93–94
  fluidity of, 100
  and geographic location, 193–194
  International Two-Spirit Gathering, 96
  as located in LGBTQTS acronym, 87–88
  pow-wows as culturally restorative practice, 89–90
  rejection of terminology, 97
  responsibilities of as yucamin'min, 92, 100
  as sexual colonization, 90
  See also Aboriginal peoples
Two-Spirit study
  experiences related to identity, 93–94
  offensiveness of Two-Spirit term, 94–95
  participants' recommendations, 96
  recurring themes, 93

Udegbe, Onyinyechukwu, 5, 37–51
unemployment/underemployment, 319
United Nations Convention on the Rights of the Child (UNCRC), 178–179, 367–368, 369

United States
  bureaucratization of non-profit sector, 22
  California Proposition 8, 114
  senate hearings on gays in US military, 100
  trans rights movement, 133–134

Vachon, W., 129
Vancouver Coastal Health, 261
Vancouver Rape Relief, 140
  trans women, access to women's services, 136–137
Vancouver Rape Relief, Kimberley Nixon vs., 135–136, 139, 140, 142
victimization, and collective trauma, 215–216
violence
  anti-violence counselling education, 362, 372–373
  and collective trauma, 217, 221, 223, 226
  domestic violence against bisexual women, 120
  familial violence, 40
  as form of moral regulation, 218
  hate crimes, 319
  homophobic violence, 38, 40
  and oppression, 366
  physical assault, 176
  in queer communities, 40
  sexual assault, 40, 58, 221
  survivors' trauma, 141
  trans-misogyny, 132
  against trans women, 129, 132, 140–142, 332
visibility
  of Aboriginal LGBT people, 96, 98–99, 101–102

Wagner, D., 311
Walker, M., 109–110
Ward, N., 76
Watt, S. K., 91, 92
Webb, S. A., 335

West Coast Lesbian Feminist Conference (1973), 135
White, C., 133, 134, 142
white heteronormativity, 306, 308–309
whiteness, culture of, 19
    de-centring of in social work practice, 42, 44, 49
    invisibility of, 300
    as manifested in social work practice, 46–47
    and marginalization of racialized populations, 22–23, 270
    and queer sexuality, 38, 305
    in second wave feminism, 133, 137–138
    white gay culture, 38, 99–100
    white heteronormativity, 306, 308–309
white queer theory, 47
Whitman, Ezra Redeagle, 97
Whittle, S., 131
Wiley, Arkell, 11, 317–338
Willis, P., 76, 289
Wilson, Alex, 96
World Pride 2014, and homo-ableism, 57
Woronoff, R., 181

YBMSM (young Black men who have sex with men). *See* queer youth of colour
Yoshino, K., 112–114
Yost, M., 119
    Gender-Specific Binegativity Scale, 123n5
youth
    Aboriginal role models, 98–99
    academic difficulties, 176
    age/gender identity and geographic location, 195–197
    barriers to securing rights, 181–182
    bullying, 176, 186, 199
    challenges of racialized queer youth, 38–39, 40
    and child welfare, 8
    coping mechanisms, 40–41
    with disabilities, 37
    emergence of LGBTQ identity, 183–184
    experiences of homophobia, 9, 38, 39, 176, 186, 196
    fear of exposure, 205
    foster home placements, 176, 188
    gender identity formation, 183–184
    homelessness, and street youth, 173, 176, 181
    human rights, and child welfare, 8, 178–182
    immigrants and refugees, 37
    institutional racism, 40
    inter-generational support, 207
    invisibility of LGBTQ youth, 185, 189
    out-of-home care, 188
    peer support, 196, 200
    recognition of as LGBTQ, 184
    reflective practice, 185–186
    rejection of by family, 173, 176
    resilience, 177, 188
    risk profiles, factors affecting, 173, 175–177
    role models, 173, 189, 205, 206, 207
    safety plan development, 187
    social isolation, 173–174
    and social media, 196, 203–204
    sources of support, 187, 200–204
    suicidal ideation, 176
    survival sex, 173
    survival strategies, 173
    teenage suicide, 280
    terminology usage, 174–175
    virtual communities, 196
    See also educational settings (high schools, universities); queer youth of colour; transgender youth
YouTube, 203